The Modernization of the Western World

The Modernization of the Western World presents an overview of the history of Western civilization and provides readers with the intellectual tools they need to comprehend how societies function and change. Covering Western history from ancient history to the current era of globalization, it draws on the tradition of historical sociology to describe the forces of social change and what they have meant to the lives of the people caught in the midst of them.

This second edition is revised throughout to bring the content up to date with recent developments and discusses key themes such as terrorism, refugees, the European Union, and multinational corporations. It also includes a new chapter on the Ancient World, covering this era from the advent of urbanization and agriculture in the Middle East to the fall of Rome and emergence of Christianity, providing valuable historical context.

Clear and concise, this book succinctly illustrates the essential turning points in the history of Western society and identifies the economic, social, political, and cultural forces that are transforming the wider world to this day. Illustrated with maps and images, and containing a glossary and new boxed features explaining key concepts, this is the perfect introductory book for students of the development of Western civilization.

John McGrath is Associate Professor of Social Sciences at Boston University, USA. His publications include *The French in Early Florida: In the Eye of the Hurricane* (2000).

Kathleen Callanan Martin is Senior Lecturer of Social Sciences at Boston University, USA. Her publications include *Hard and Unreal Advice: Mothers, Social Science and the Victorian Poverty Experts* (2008).

The Modernization
of the Western World

A Society Transformed

Second Edition

**John McGrath and
Kathleen Callanan Martin**

with Jay P. Corrin, Michael G. Kort,
Susan Hagood Lee, John W. Mackey,
and Benjamin E. Varat

Routledge
Taylor & Francis Group

NEW YORK AND LONDON

Second edition published 2018
by Routledge
711 Third Avenue, New York, NY 10017

and by Routledge
2 Park Square, Milton Park, Abingdon, Oxon, OX14 4RN

Routledge is an imprint of the Taylor & Francis Group, an informa business

First edition published by M. E. Sharpe in 2012

British Library Cataloguing-in-Publication Data
A catalogue record for this book is available from the British Library

Library of Congress Cataloging-in-Publication Data
A catalogue record for this book has been requested

ISBN: 978-1-138-06854-4 (hbk)
ISBN: 978-1-138-06856-8 (pbk)
ISBN: 978-1-315-15779-5 (ebk)

Typeset in Galliard
by Keystroke, Neville Lodge, Tettenhall, Wolverhampton

Contents

Illustrations

Maps

Figures

Contributors

Kathleen Callanan Martin is Senior Lecturer of Social Sciences at Boston University, USA. Her publications include *Hard and Unreal Advice: Mothers, Social Science and the Victorian Poverty Experts* (2008).

Jay P. Corrin is Professor of Social Science and Chair of the Division of the Social Sciences at the College of General Studies, Boston University, USA. His graduate degrees are from the University of Hawaii (MA, Asian History) and a PhD from Boston University in Modern European and British History. He is an intellectual historian and has written books and articles on the Catholic religion and politics, the most recent of which is a study of the English Catholic New Left. He is also a co-author of *Modernization and Revolution in China* (2009).

Professor **Susan Hagood Lee** is a sociologist whose work focuses on women in the developing world. She is the author of *"Rice Plus": Widows and Economic Survival in Rural Cambodia* (2006) and is a non-governmental observer at the United Nations. She is also the Rector of St. Luke's Church in Fall River, Massachusetts, USA.

Michael G. Kort is Professor of Social Science at the College of General Studies, Boston, USA. He is the author of *The Soviet Colossus: History and Aftermath (2014); The Columbia Guide to the Cold War (2001); The Columbia Guide to Hiroshima and the Bomb (2012);* and *A Brief History of Russia (2008);* and a co-author of *Modernization and Revolution in China* (2009). He has also written more than a dozen books on a variety of topics for young adult readers.

John W. Mackey is Senior Lecturer and Chair of the Division of Social Sciences at the College of General Studies, Boston University, USA. He holds an MA and PhD in History from Boston College, and a BA from Dickinson College. His work has appeared in *Salon, BU Today,* and *We're History.* He is on Twitter at @ProfMackey.

John McGrath is Associate Professor of Social Sciences at Boston University, USA. His publications include *The French in Early Florida: In the Eye of the Hurricane* (2000).

Benjamin Varat is Senior Lecturer of Social Sciences and History at the College of General Studies, Boston University, USA. He received his BA from Trinity College of Hartford, Connecticut in 1993 and completed his PhD in History at Boston University in August 2005. He currently is turning his dissertation, an analysis of French-American relations between 1958 and 1963, into a manuscript for publication.

Preface

Over the centuries, practically every society has thought it important to know something about the past. Even before the development of writing, people have meticulously memorialized the reigns of leaders, kept records of births or harvests, or commemorated great events like wars, catastrophes, and migrations. With the passing of years, such information, even as it was often blended with religion or folkways, created a cultural context that helped to explain the eternal questions of "Who are we? And where did we come from?" Frequently the history of a given society can attain a sacred quality that provides essential guidance and knowledge for the individuals who belong to it.

The contributors to this volume believe that knowledge of the past is equally essential for people in the modern world, to help us make informed choices that will serve both ourselves and the larger society. But it is not enough for students to learn simply *what* happened. It is at least equally important for people to need to know *why*. Especially in today's information-rich global society, there is a far greater need for people who understand how the world works than there is for successful *Jeopardy!* contestants. The questions of "Who are we?" and "Where did we come from?" remain critically important ones to consider if we are to untangle the challenges presented by an ever more complex global society.

We have developed this book over the course of many years teaching in an undergraduate liberal arts program, the College of General Studies at Boston University. As professors in the Social Science Division, we have been charged with the task of developing a two-semester curriculum suitable for incoming freshman students who arrive with a spectrum of backgrounds, academic skills, and interests. As the student body has changed, our course has evolved to meet their needs, and so too has the material that we ask them to study. This book is largely the product of our course.

In both the course and the book, we draw on the tradition of historical sociology, which is today far less in evidence on university campuses in the United States than in Europe. In reaction to grand schemes of historical evolution and societal convergence that were fashionable within living memory, many American historians are understandably wary of attempts to force the messy and complex details of history into preordained pigeonholes. Our course makes no such attempt. What we do is to explore the basic questions about an individual's relationship to his society and to history: How does society shape us? How do the institutions and ideas we inherit from previous generations influence—and even constrain—our choices in making history of our own? How is social change possible, and what effect does it have on the people who experience it? How did the world we inhabit come into being, and what are the implications of its present organization for our future?

Our course begins with an introduction to social science methodology, primarily sociology, to give our students some basic intellectual tools to comprehend how societies function and change. Rather than presenting a smorgasbord of concepts and terminology, we have had great success using a social-theory approach that relies on ideas of the early pioneers of social science, especially Émile Durkheim, Karl Marx, and Max Weber. Once our students have armed themselves with a basic understanding of social dynamics, we then turn our attention to the study of Western society as it emerged from the world of antiquity and became "modern." Over the rest of the year we bring our students into the present, helping them learn how the West developed a way of life that was fundamentally different from any that had appeared before. In doing so, Western society unleashed powerful economic, social, political, and cultural forces that are transforming the wider world.

The approach we use here focuses on these forces of social change, and what they have meant to the lives of the people caught in the middle of them. As opposed to more traditional courses, we are selective with the choice of the material we ask our students to learn. Our experience with more conventional history textbooks, such as the expensive Western Civilization texts we had periodically used, taught us that today's students can be overwhelmed with "facts" that induce boredom (or worse) if they lack a meaningful context. In our course and in this book, we cannot omit entirely names, dates, and so on, but we use them only when they help illustrate essential turning points, problems and accomplishments in the history of Western society. In other words, facts are employed as a means to the greater end of understanding how the modern world came to be. Over the years, our students have resoundingly confirmed that this approach is far more interesting, meaningful, and intellectually enriching than the typical historical surveys they have previously encountered.

We anticipate that this book will be used as a course text, often together with other readings, both secondary and primary. To facilitate the integration of primary sources into a course framework, we have consciously devoted significant attention to certain historical figures and their ideas (such as Machiavelli, Voltaire, and J. S. Mill). Throughout the text we have also highlighted, in boldface type, certain key terms and concepts that we want our students to take note of as they are employed in the text.

Acknowledgments

The Modernization of the Western World has evolved as a collaborative effort by editors, writers, colleagues, and other associates. We'd like to take the opportunity here to express our thanks and appreciation. First and foremost, we'd like to stress that, to a significant degree, this book is the product of thousands of classroom hours, and thus we must credit our students for providing us with both ideas and energy.

We would also like to acknowledge the support and encouragement of many others in the College of General Studies (CGS) who, over the years, have helped us put this course together. These include Barbara Storella, Natalie McKnight, Tracey Dimant, Bob Oresick, Stacy Godnick, Danielle Vinciguerra, Matt Dursin, Matt Hallgren, and Naomi Lomba-Gomes. Other CGS faculty, whose names do not appear as authors but who have helped in various important ways, include June Grasso, Ed Rafferty, Bill Tilchin, Leslie Kriebel, Shawn Lynch, Sam Deese, Tom Whalen, Scott Marr, Polly Rizova, Jean Dunlavy, Cheryl Boots, and Robert Wexelblatt. Without the contributions of all of these individuals, this project would have been far more difficult and might never have been undertaken and completed at all. Our editors at Routledge, Eve Setch and Amy Welmers, offered intelligent suggestions and made the production process about as problem-free as book production can be.

Finally, we'd like to express our appreciation for the folks on the home front who have had to put up with, for years, our frequently incomprehensible ravings and mutterings about bureaucracies, *gemeinschafts*, *anomie*, neomercantilism, the Invisible Hand, and the like. We hope that this book will demonstrate that this stuff actually does make sense.

J.M. and K.C.M.
Boston, MA

1 The Modernization of the Western World

John McGrath and Jay P. Corrin

Key Terms

anomie, collective conscience, conflict theory, empiricism, modernization, social norms, socialization, *verstehen*, *wertfrei*

Any understanding of how societies function and change requires some basic understanding of the way that human beings interact. The fact that different societies encourage different sorts of behavior is one of the things that makes studying history and social science interesting. Yet beneath the obvious differences, there are also certain behavioral constants and commonalities shared by all societies. Appreciating these aspects of social life provides an important key to meaningful analysis.

To begin at the beginning, so to speak, we need to recognize that humans have evolved over time to meet certain challenges to their survival. The first anatomically modern humans survived on the savannas of Africa, tens of thousands of years ago, because natural selection, operating over several million years, had given them certain characteristics that made them successful as a species. These included both physical attributes and intellectual qualities that allowed them to meet their needs. Humans began to communicate, learn, and plan in ways that were far superior to any previous creature.

Certain behavioral tendencies also helped people to survive. Like many other species, humans fared best in groups that made it possible for them to act cooperatively to meet the challenges of existence. Though there have been many sizes and types of human groups, or "societies," the survival of solitary individuals has been immeasurably more difficult from earliest times right up until the present. This is because collective action facilitated certain key activities, such as food gathering, learning culture, child raising, and defense against human and animal predators. Group living made this possible. The result is that humans have long recognized the need to be "social animals," and they have adjusted their emotions and behavior accordingly.

This need for group living has only increased as societies have become more "modern." Over the history of humanity, our ancestors have nurtured their unparalleled intellectual abilities to enable the creation of such complex entities as languages, philosophical systems, and technologies. Such developments have raised our standard of living by quantum leaps and transformed our world in both literal and figurative senses. Doing so, however, has not lessened our reliance on each other, but in fact has only increased it, and as our societies have become more complicated, we as individuals have lost much of our self-sufficiency. In the modern age, we still depend on social living for material and emotional survival, and we possess a powerful urge to feel a sense of belonging to a larger group, or what we call a "society."

It is perhaps stating the obvious that this aspect of human behavior, the need to belong, has been a central factor in the history of humanity, perhaps as much as the need for food and protection, to which it is related. It has been a powerful influence on the way that societies have evolved and changed, and the student of history must keep this in mind. To put it another way, it is impossible to understand history in any meaningful way without understanding the centrality of society in the lives of individuals. Our study concentrates upon the social forces that have created history and that continue to shape our destinies.

The Individual and Society

Social scientists analyze how social forces affect actions, ideas, and values. A process known as **socialization** is a starting point in understanding the behaviors of both individuals and groups, and it is an essential concept in the social sciences. During socialization, an individual learns how a society works and the normal behaviors expected from its members, or **social norms**. Understanding and conforming to social norms is how a person gains acceptance in a given society, and during socialization people constantly adapt their behavior in response to the reactions of others and their perceptions of these reactions. While much of this learning may take place unconsciously during social interaction, socialization is usually accomplished willingly and even eagerly, because it allows a person to feel like a member of their society, imparting to them this precious sense of belonging.

Understanding the impact of socialization on both individual and collective behavior is critical for understanding the workings of human societies. This basic concept—the symbiotic relationship between individuals and society—underlies much of the contribution made by the pioneers of sociology who emerged during the industrial age more than a century ago. Living in societies that were confronting rapid and complex social change, social scientists including Karl Marx, Émile Durkheim, and Max Weber analyzed the impacts of such transformations. Their studies focused upon how societies functioned and changed, and what this meant for the relationship between the individual and the larger society. These three social theorists, as well as others, contributed valuable principles of social behavior that are highly relevant today, and which provide the foundation of this study.

Karl Marx (1818–1883) is best known to some people as the originator of "Marxist" revolutionary doctrines, yet to reduce his ideas to these alone is to undervalue his larger contributions to social theory. Much of his work, such as his magisterial study *Capital*, provided an analysis of the operation and impact of capitalist economic systems.[1] As an observer of a rapidly industrializing Europe that was fraught with social and political instability, Marx attributed many of the problems of his age to what he considered the fatal flaws of industrial capitalism: its promotion of inequality between social classes, its tendency toward monopoly, and what he believed to be its inherent instability. Though Marx's predictions of inevitable revolution have proven to be mistaken, his critiques of capitalism and its problems have proven to be prophetic. Moreover, social scientists and historians who have employed the sociological perspective he originated, known as **conflict theory**, where change is seen as the result of class conflict, have contributed many insights that are useful for understanding the processes of social change.

The French social scientist Émile Durkheim (1858–1917) applied a rigorous methodology based on **empiricism**—the systematic analysis of past experience—to the study of how societies functioned and evolved. Regarding any given society as an entity in its own right, he examined the interplay of the subgroups and individuals who comprised its parts.[2] What held the parts together, and allowed them to work together for the benefit of all, were common cultural elements that not only provided direction but also gave a society's members a sense of belonging. Chief among these were what he called a "**collective conscience**," a shared sense of values often expressed as ethical and religious beliefs. It is from the collective conscience that we derive our guidelines, or social norms, for proper social behavior; these not only provide order and social cohesion, but also allow each individual to develop the critically important sense that he or she belongs to a larger whole. In the late nineteenth and early twentieth centuries, Durkheim first explained how the process of social change could undermine traditional values and social structures, which promoted the deadly social malaise he called "*anomie*," where individuals have a difficult time understanding changing roles and social norms. He argued that anomie, or normlessness, was a particular danger in rapidly modernizing societies, where the members had difficulties adjusting to changing social expectations and consequently suffered from widespread despair. The phenomenon of *anomie*, in turn, made it difficult for the larger society to function in a healthy way, and anomic societies became vulnerable to a host of social problems.

Durkheim's German contemporary Max Weber (1864–1920) developed many of the central principles of modern sociological analysis, including many now-standard sociological concepts and terms. Like Marx and Durkheim, he was concerned about the impact of **modernization**, especially its tendency to make individuals feel helpless in the midst of large social forces over which they had little control. He had a particular interest in the development of new sorts of power and authority in modern life, and he examined how the increasing dominance of rational and formal social structures transformed individuals' values and outlooks.[3] He urged social scientists to always employ *verstehen* (a deeper understanding based on an appreciation of the cultural views of the society itself) while maintaining strict objectivity by taking a *wertfrei* ("value-free") approach. Both of these have become fundamental principles of modern social science.

These three social theorists collectively laid a lasting foundation for analytical, empirical, and logical social analysis. They were concerned with identifying and explaining the cause and effect behind social change, and understanding how traditional societies could evolve into more complex entities that would continue to evolve, often at accelerating rates. The problem of the individual's relationship to the larger society was a central issue in all of their work, and each believed that understanding this was absolutely necessary for understanding historical processes. Their theories and concepts, as well as contributions from other notable social scientists, provide the foundation for our study of the modernization of the Western world.

Modernization

Modernization, as a historical process, has had many different definitions and interpretations. It is a relative term, and a modernizing society is one that moves in a direction where certain aspects are becoming increasingly important. These characteristic aspects are generally mutually reinforcing, and it is often difficult to draw distinct borders between them. If one tried hard enough, a person could probably identify dozens of social character-istics that are found exclusively, or almost exclusively, in what we might consider "modern" societies, but that many characteristics probably makes a definition that is unwieldy and not especially useful.

For our purposes in this book, we use the term modernization to refer to a process that has eight identifiable elements. In no particular order, these are:

Rationalism
Specialization of Labor
Political Centralization
Bureaucracy
Urbanization
Faustian Ethos
Secularism
Individualism

Any society where these eight features—or even most of them—are prominent can be considered to be "modern" to a significant degree. As we will see, they are often interconnected. The precise nature of these characteristics may differ considerably from one society to another, or change over time; in fact, different people may even define them differently. Yet as a template that is useful for understanding the nature of this particular sort of social change, we have found that these characteri-stics collectively give a reasonably thorough and useful definition of modernization.

Modernization as a Process

Europe had a unique and globally transforming historical experience in that it gave birth to what is recognized as **modernization**, a process of institutional and individual change that produced revolutionary alterations in social structures and human consciousness. Modernization defies facile definition, but for our purposes we can consider it to be the transformation of a society from rural and agrarian conditions to urban and industrial modes of living. This transformation brings about certain predictable, mutually reinforcing elements. (See Box).

Modernization represents the most powerful engine in history for transforming social institutions and human consciousness. It is a process that necessarily affects all aspects of society. Historically, traditional patterns of social ordering have arisen as solutions to challenges presented by the environment and by other societies, and tradition allows a society to function, and even prosper, as a collective whole. As we have seen, especially during the last 1,000 years, traditional societies have been vulnerable to the transformative power of modernization, as it is expressed through cultural, economic, and political forces. The rapid social change produced by modernization can be both liberating and psychologically discombobulating, depending on the cultural conditions in which the experience takes place. Durkheim recognized this and sought to help the society around him adjust successfully to the inevitable reality of modernization. Although he understood that it could be destructive under many circumstances, he also recognized the potential benefits of this process to increase prosperity, social tolerance, and individual freedom. In today's world, as in the past, there are efforts to utilize traditional elements, such as religion, to thwart the onslaught of modernization, but historical evidence suggests that it is a process that cannot be reversed. We must, instead, understand how this process operates, and how it has operated in the past, so that we can take advantage of the opportunities it presents to us.

What are the factors that produce modernization? There are a variety of theoretical explanations, but the most pioneering and ultimately seminal were provided by Marx and Weber. Marx believed social change was essentially the product of economic forces. "It is not the consciousness of men that determines their existence," wrote Marx, "but, on the contrary, their social existence determines their consciousness."[4] These "conditions," Marx insisted, were the product of the ways in which societies meet their material needs. The expansion of wealth, made possible by innovations in the productive process, enabled some groups to control social institutions for their own benefit. This inequality would ultimately lead to social conflict thereby bringing on social and economic change. For Marx, the engine of history that led to modernization was fueled by conflict in the material realm of society.

Weber, on the other hand, had a more nuanced view of modernization. Although he appreciated the role of economic forces, he thought other factors were also important, especially the commonly held views of a society. Social change in Weber's view was often the result of powerful, conflicting ideas and values that arose out of a variety of cultural experiences. Putting it another way, for Weber, consciousness could be the cause of social change not simply the effect of other material factors.

The Modernization of the West

The thematic structure of this book draws on such perspectives to illustrate how alterations in social structures and consciousness propelled Europe toward conditions of modernity, giving birth to a set of dynamic economic and ideological forces that literally transformed the world. The past presents us with many difficult problems involving human behavior, and a social theory approach enables us to gain valuable insights into many otherwise puzzling questions. These include, for example: Why did the Reformation era unleash such savagery upon a society that was becoming prosperous, literate, and intellectually sophisticated? What did the constructive, rational ideas of the Enlightenment have to do with the arrival of revolution and war, on an unprecedented scale, during the late eighteenth and early nineteenth centuries? How could a society that appeared to have achieved such material progress over the course of the Industrial Revolution have seemed so hell-bent on destroying itself in the first half of the twentieth century, apparently fulfilling the direst warnings of observers like Marx, Durkheim, and Weber? Examining these sorts of questions helps make sense of the past and helps us to understand today's world by explaining how we got here.

The issue of modernization also raises a host of essential questions relating to the future: Can Europe's *sui generis* experience as a "first-comer" to modernization serve as a model for others? Is modernization the same as Westernization? Does modernization mean that there will be a convergence of societal types? How much of modernity is controlled and directed by human agency? Is modernization the product of large, impersonal forces that are beyond the control of individual actors? Does the advancement of modernity require the destruction of traditional and local cultures? In what ways have modern ways of living benefited humankind? What is the impact of modernization on the natural environment? Does modernization promote human rights? Will modernization ultimately lead to democratic aspirations and free market capitalism?

As this book traces the first instance of modernization in world history, it examines these sorts of questions. They are ambitious ones, to be sure, and it may be that some, or even all, may never be answered definitively. However, they are important questions to ask if one wants to comprehend the modern world. We believe that the ideas of Marx, Durkheim, and Weber have never been more relevant than they are today. Their approaches to the study of historical change transform history from a collection of facts into a cohesive process that has brought about the phenomenon of modernity. For citizens of the twenty-first century to understand the world they live in, they must develop a sense of how this process has worked in the past, and how it is still working today.

Notes

1 Marx's best-known works are *The Communist Manifesto* (1848) cowritten with Friedrich Engels, and the three volume *Capital* (1867, 1885, 1894). His 1847 *Wage, Labour and Capital* is a valuable introduction to his economic ideas.
2 Durkheim's three major works are *The Division of Labor in Society* (1892), *Suicide* (1897) and *The Elementary Forms of Religious Life* (1912).
3 Weber's *The Protestant Ethic and the Spirit of Capitalism* (1905) and *Economy and Society* (1922) are among his most influential works, though he contributed numerous other studies of religion, power, and economics.
4 Karl Marx, "Preface," *A Contribution to the Critique of Political Economy*, www. marxists.org/archive/marx/works/1859/critique-pol-economy/preface.htm (1857), 1.

Suggested Readings

Durkheim, Émile. *The Division of Labor in Society*. Trans. W. D. Halls. New York: Free Press, [1893] 1997.
———. *The Elementary Forms of Religious Life*. New York: Oxford University Press, [1912] 2008.
———. *Suicide*. New York: Free Press, [1897] 1997.
Marx, Karl. *Preface, A Contribution to the Critique of Political Economy*. www.marxists. org/archive/marx/works/1859/critique-pol-economy/preface.htm
———. *Wage, Labour and Capital*. www.marxists.org/archive/marx/works/ [1857].
Marx, Karl, and Friedrich Engels. *The Communist Manifesto*. Ed. Samuel H. Beer. Wheeling, IL: Harlan Davidson, [1848] 1999.
Weber, Max. *Economy and Society*. Eds. Guenther Roth and Klaus Wittich. Berkeley: University of California Press, [1922] 1978.
———. *The Protestant Ethic and the Spirit of Capitalism*. Trans. Talcott Parsons. London: Scribner's, [1905] 1995.

2   Modernization and Social Change

Kathleen Callanan Martin

Key Terms

acculturation, *anomie*, cultural diffusion, culture, demographic transition, demography, division of labor, economic determinism, ideal type, *gemeinschaft/gesellschaft*, market economy, mechanical/organic solidarity, migration

Many forces promote social stability; among these are respect for tradition, ideological justifications for existing social institutions, and the effectiveness of socialization. And yet the social world does change, as even the most casual student of history realizes. The most profound sources of social change are changes that have a direct bearing on human lives: where people live, how many of them are born, and when they die. Changes of this kind are the subject of **demography**—the study of human populations. **Migration** has played an enormous role in the story of humanity from its earliest days, as the members of our species fanned out from their original home in Africa and populated five other continents. In the process, they had to adapt to new climates, resources, and circumstances. Since that time human groups and individuals have continued to migrate, driven by overcrowding, war, hunger, and persecution. The changes involved in modernization have greatly accelerated this process. The refugee crisis that has seized the world's attention in recent years is the latest in a long string of events that transported several million kidnapped Africans to the Western Hemisphere and filled the voter lists of American cities with names like O'Malley, Cohen, Martinez, Chen, and Khan.

Perhaps the most fundamental population change in the modernization process has been what we call the **demographic transition**. Demographers hotly contest both the details of the transition and what may happen in the future as more and more parts of the world join the group of industrialized nations. But there is little dispute as to what has happened already: in industrializing nations, patterns of births and death have shifted. Very high rates of birth and death (especially infant and child mortality) were characteristic of traditional societies. They are still characteristic of pre-industrial societies in the twenty-first century. But in the process of industrialization the pattern begins to shift. The usual sequence has been that as death rates begin to fall because of improvements in the standard of living and in available medical care, continued high birth rates cause the size of the population to increase dramatically. But as life expectancy increases, and more parents can expect their children to outlive them, many families begin to limit the number of children they produce. In fact, in the advanced industrial nations, it is widely true today that the annual number of births is lower than the number of deaths, causing the population actually to shrink unless immigration replenishes the numbers. And this produces a different kind of nuclear family: a family that is smaller and can succeed in raising most of its children to adulthood. It seems likely that relationships within such families differ somewhat from relationships in the families of the past.

Will this process continue into the future, throughout the world? It is always dangerous to assume that what has happened in the past will continue to happen in the future, as demographers are well aware. On the other hand, so far industrialization has brought about this change not only in the West but also in other societies that have traveled very far on the path of industrialization.

But not all social change is demographic in nature. When social scientists talk about social change, they are almost always discussing changes in both the **culture** and the institutions of a society—changes in values, ideas, patterns of social interaction, material culture, and economic processes. (Anthropologist Margaret Mead defined culture as "the systematic body of learned behavior which is transmitted from parents to children" in a society.[1]) These changes can be scarcely detectable or truly revolutionary, and their ultimate significance may not be immediately recognizable at the time of their occurrence. Change can originate within the society in question, or it can come from the outside.

New inventions, for example, can have a significant impact on daily life. Medical research has found new approaches to treating many forms of cancer, transforming what used to be terminal diseases into survivable health crises. Inexpensive, easily portable cell phones create new patterns of social interaction unimaginable only twenty years earlier, as well as problems like annoying interruptions to college lectures. Airplanes make the world a much smaller place, for better or for worse, facilitating both travel and war. The discovery of previously unknown natural resources can transform a barren wilderness into a very desirable piece of real estate. Just as the discovery of new resources can propel change, the loss of key resources can be disruptive; diminishing supplies of petroleum will undoubtedly cause profound changes in the near future for both consuming and exporting countries, unless new inventions intervene. Both invention and discovery can cause social change from within or from without a given society.

Another way in which change can come from the outside is the process of **cultural diffusion**, in which practices, customs, or other cultural elements are adopted from another society. Thus, many Americans now eat sushi, and baseball is a very popular sport in Japan. How significant are these changes? As far as we can tell, accepting baseball from the United States does not appear to have changed Japan very much. In contrast, accepting Buddhism from Korean and Chinese missionaries (nearly a millennium earlier) transformed Japanese society in many significant ways. It is difficult to imagine the cuisines of France and Italy without potatoes and tomatoes, both of which originated in the Western Hemisphere, or to picture the British without tea, which originated in East Asia. Foods, medicines, animals, games, artistic ideas, religious beliefs, and technology have traveled from society to society in this way for a very long time.

The type of adaptation involved in cultural diffusion is generally voluntary: people are introduced to new foods or artifacts or practices that they like and want to adopt. The same cannot be said for the process of **acculturation**, which is sometimes the result of coercion and is often unwelcome. Acculturation involves "major culture changes that people are forced to make as a consequence of intensive, first-hand contact between societies."[2] This occurs as a result of the military conquest and/or political and economic domination of one society by another. The dominant culture may use violence, the threat of violence, or economic penalties to force members of the subordinated culture to change their religion, language, institutions, or other cultural elements.[3] And acculturation can also occur as a result of migration to another country. Although immigrants have been known to take up the attitudes and customs of their new country not only voluntarily but even with great enthusiasm, shedding their old ones in the process, changes of this kind can be painful and disruptive if they involve core values, rather than superficial practices. (For the Eastern European Jews who sought refuge in the United States during the late nineteenth and early twentieth centuries, for example, it was much easier to learn to play American games like baseball than to deal with jobs that required work on Saturday, threatening their religious identity.) Immigrants and members of minority groups often have very little choice but to adapt their cultural practices to those of the majority in order to survive in their new circumstances. Slaves and colonial peoples may have even fewer choices. The process of acculturation has been a major factor in the history of the Western Hemisphere ever since Columbus. It was much in evidence in parts of Asia and Africa during the colonial era, and it can be seen at work today in cities like New York and Paris that attract many immigrants, in Guatemala and Tibet, and in Native American communities in the United States and Canada. The members of a minority culture may, if they feel their identity to be threatened, struggle to retain that identity, and conflict with the majority culture can result.

Theories of Social Change

The phenomenon of social change was central to the thinking of all of the founders of social science, for an obvious reason: the nineteenth-century Europe in which they lived was changing literally right before their eyes under the impact of industrialization and political revolution. How was society changing, and why? What were the implications of these changes for European life and culture? In what kind of world would their grandchildren live? No serious student of society could fail to ask these questions.

Social change was a central concern for the German social theorist Karl Marx (1818–1883). Marx believed that the most fundamental thing about any society is its economic arrangements; if the economy changes, then other aspects of that society will inevitably change accordingly. This is why we call Marx an **economic determinist**. Marx recognized as early as 1848 that European society was undergoing very rapid social change under the impact of industrialization. He saw this accelerated social change as a product of the rapid economic and technological developments dictated by the pressures of competition in a **market economy**, in which innovation is necessary for survival. (A market economy is one in which production, distribution, prices, and wages are determined by people's willingness to buy and sell, rather than by tradition or by a managing central authority.) Because of competition, Marx argued:

> Constant revolutionizing of production, uninterrupted disturbance of all social conditions, everlasting uncertainty and agitation distinguish the bourgeois epoch from all earlier ones. All fixed, fast-frozen relations, with their train of ancient and venerable prejudices and opinions, are swept away, all new-formed ones become antiquated before they can ossify. All that is solid melts into air, all that is holy is profaned.[4]

Thus in the modern era, according to Marx, rapid social change ceases to be exceptional; whether or not we like it, it has become the norm.

The great German sociologist Max Weber (1864–1920) was arguably the single most influential figure in the development of sociology as a discipline. Like Marx he was interested in the enormous changes that had taken place in European society during the process of modernization. Like Marx, he regarded economic change as a major factor in this process. But unlike Marx, he was also interested in the way ideas can retard or facilitate economic change. He was not the polar opposite of Marx with respect to the relationship between ideas and the economy; he never argued that all changes in the material world are caused by changes in ideas, although many people mistakenly believe that he did. Weber did, however, argue that ideas can play a major role in economic change. His best-known book, *The Protestant Ethic and the Spirit of Capitalism*, examines the role that changing European religious values in the sixteenth century and thereafter played in facilitating the rise of a capitalist, market economy to replace a medieval economy based on manorial agriculture. Protestant theology, unlike the Catholic view, saw faith alone as necessary to salvation; it did not encourage believers to give away their wealth as a way to merit God's grace, forbid the lending of money at interest, or disparage the wealthy as obvious sinners. The religious reformer John Calvin, in fact, suggested that the elect might be recognized in this life because of their success. In Weber's view, this change must at least have assisted the growth of capitalism, since it is far more compatible with the values of a capitalist market economy than was the Catholic, medieval view. Weber was committed to the idea that no single factor is likely to be, in itself, the cause of a major change in society. This is why an expert on Weber's sociology has said that it rests on "a principled and radical multicausality."[5] Economic change was, in Weber's view, extremely important, but it was not the whole story, nor was it unaffected by non-material elements of the society.

Max Weber on Bureaucracy

One change that Max Weber felt would become more and more important in the process of modernization was the increasing prevalence of bureaucracy: the use of formal structures, bound by rules and regulations, to govern large social groups in rational, formal ways. Each person in a bureaucracy is answerable to the officeholder above him or her for the performance of specific tasks in accordance with clearly defined rules. Bureaucracy is, of course, an ideal type, and real bureaucracies only approximate the model. But to a significant extent they operate impartially and impersonally; you are awarded a driver's license because you have fulfilled the requirements for obtaining one, filled out the required paperwork, and demonstrated your eligibility. In principle, it makes no difference who you are, whether or not the official behind the counter likes you, or whether you belong to an unpopular group. This impersonality seems like a very good thing when you have reason to doubt that you would be treated fairly otherwise; it seems less desirable when you feel that human compassion would dictate your being granted some leeway. Weber felt that the increasing prevalence of bureaucracy was inevitable with modernization, because despite their shortcomings bureaucracies are the only way to govern large, complex social organizations with any kind of efficiency. (Can you imagine the US Army, the Red Cross, or General Motors coordinating their internal and external affairs without a bureaucracy?) On the other hand, their very impersonality makes bureaucracies seem harsh and forbidding. For this reason, Weber feared that mankind was imprisoning itself inside an "iron cage" of rules and regulations from which no escape seemed likely as modernization progresses.

A key element in Weber's approach to historical sociology was his use of ideal types. An **ideal type** is an analytical model constructed from elements of reality that the theorist sees as important to the understanding of a social phenomenon. This model contains only the most essential features, not the vast number of individual details of each case. The ideal type can then be tested against the available empirical evidence to see whether or not it has any explanatory power. In real life, it may be impossible to find a perfect embodiment of the ideal type. We have yet, for example, to see a perfect democracy. Yet actual "democracies" do differ in systematic ways from monarchies and dictatorships, so the concept is an analytically useful one. Perfect or not, carefully designed and tested ideal types can be helpful in achieving a deeper understanding of human social interaction.[6]

Durkheim and Tönnies: Typologies of Social Change

Two influential pioneering social scientists, Durkheim and Tönnies, devised typologies that are also useful in understanding the social changes that have taken place in the modernization process. The French sociologist Émile Durkheim (1858–1917) was, like Marx and Weber, one of the giants of social science. Durkheim was particularly interested in the significance of the growing **division of labor** in society. In *The Wealth of Nations* (1776), Adam Smith had called the attention of economists to the importance of the **division of labor**—the allocation of various tasks to specialists, instead of having most members of society carry on the same processes from start to finish. Following the reasoning of social thinker Auguste Comte, Durkheim felt that increasing specialization over time had caused many significant changes whose impact went well beyond the economic sphere. To analyze these changes, Durkheim postulated a change over time from the "mechanical solidarity" of pre-modern European society to the "organic solidarity" that was emerging in the modern world.

What is the "glue" that holds a society together, that makes it possible for all of its institutions and groups and people to form a coherent system? Durkheim called this force that makes them able to work together as a functioning unit "solidarity." The **mechanical solidarity** that held a pre-modern society together was, according to Durkheim, a "solidarity by similarities."[7] Compared to modern Europe, pre-modern Europe had very little division of labor. Most people had precisely the same economic and social functions. In medieval Europe, for example, there were kings and priests and knights and a few craftsmen, but the vast majority of the population worked on the land. In such a society, according to Durkheim, there is an overwhelming uniformity not just in economic function but also in beliefs, customs, and values. People are more or less interchangeable, like iron particles or drill bits or ball bearings, and conformity is highly valued. Social solidarity is based on a kind of collective consensus, and punishments for violations of that consensus tend to be very severe—hence the terrible fates of heretics and criminals.[8]

In contrast, increasingly over time the social glue that holds the modern world together has come to be what Durkheim called **organic solidarity**, or "solidarity arising from the division of labor." Today's students often find this term confusing, because they associate the word "organic" with things that are completely natural, like additive-free yogurt. What Durkheim meant by this term, however, is that the high division of labor in modern society makes each member "only a part of the whole, the organ of an organism."[9] Your heart cannot exist without the rest of your body; nor can it be substituted for your lungs. Each is a specialized part of a functioning whole, dependent on the others for its survival. In the same way, each member of a society with a high division of labor depends on the other members. The plumber cannot remove his own appendix, and the surgeon cannot install her own furnace. In such a society, with specialized training, education, and functions, it is neither necessary nor desirable that everyone should be alike—in fact it is very unlikely that they will be. In order to function smoothly, therefore, a society of this type must learn to accommodate diversity. What holds it together is not conformity but mutual dependency.

The change is not absolute. The continued existence of public opinion, popular patriotism, and common codes of behavior demonstrates that to some extent mechanical solidarity still exists among us. (Indeed, it is difficult to imagine how any society could function *without* common sentiments of this kind.) But Durkheim felt that as the division of labor increases, organic solidarity must play a larger and larger role in maintaining social cohesion.

Durkheim had mixed feelings about this apparently irreversible tendency in the modernization process. On the one hand, lack of uniformity in customs and morals had led in many cases to **anomie**, the breakdown of a social consensus on behavior and values, which can result in a sense of meaninglessness and moral confusion. This, Durkheim felt, was a root cause of some suicides. On the other hand, growing diversity and lessened insistence on conformity made possible the greater freedom for individuals that seemed to him modernization's best gift. He concluded that "to be a person means to be an autonomous source of action. Thus, man only attains this state to the degree that there is something within him that is his and his alone, that makes him an individual."[10]

More pessimistic in his view of social change was the German sociologist Ferdinand Tönnies (1855–1936). Like Durkheim, he saw the growing division of labor as important, but Tönnies was primarily concerned with changes in the emotional relationships between people. His model of social change in modernization postulated a movement away from the *gemeinschaft* type of social organization toward the *gesellschaft* type. The word *gemeinschaft* in German means "community." Members of a group living together as a *gemeinschaft* enjoy a natural relationship that is "intimate" and "private."[11] They feel a strong natural connection to each other, and often a genuine affection. Relationships of this type are patterned on the family, and within them the idea of authority is based on the idea of fatherhood.[12] Tönnies saw this relationship as characteristic not just of families and groups of friends but also of kinship organizations like clans and tribes, and of rural villages and small towns as well. It is based on cooperation and mutual aid, reinforced by "easy and frequent meetings" as people go about their daily lives.[13] The commonly used phrase "one big happy family" would be a good description of a *gemeinschaft*.

For Tönnies, "*gemeinschaft* is old; *gesellschaft* is new as a name as well as a phenomenon."[14] A *gesellschaft*, or society, is an artificial, formally structured group of a type unknown to the pre-modern world but increasingly common with the growth of a market economy. A *gesellschaft* is neither an expression of natural ties nor patterned on the family. Its members need not know each other well and may not know each other at all. Relationships within it are not emotional; rather they are rationally organized, and based not on cooperation and mutuality but on self-interest. While *gemeinschaft* is characteristic of rural life, "wherever urban culture blossoms and bears fruits, *Gesellschaft* appears as its indispensable organ."[15] What holds a *gesellschaft* together is laws, contractual obligations, and the exchange of commodities—in other words, structured buying and selling. The state emerges as the ultimate arbiter and enforcer of rules and contractual obligations in this marketplace, issuing the paper money without which such commerce would be far more difficult.[16] The functions of individual members become more and more specialized as the ties between them become less and less intimate. This is nothing like a family. In fact, in modern German the word *gesellschaft* is identical in meaning to the English word "corporation," and is part of the formal name of incorporated German businesses.

As in Durkheim's typology, this change over time is not absolute. In the modern world there are still villages, clubs, monasteries and other small religious entities, friendships, and—last but not least—families. Probably there always will be. But as industrialization and urbanization advance in the modernization process, more and more people have lives primarily governed by organizations of the *gesellschaft* type.

Tönnies was not enthusiastic about the change that comes with modernization. He felt that the pursuit of financial gain was not a sound basis for a meaningful life, and that there is something inhuman about regarding another person as a means to an end. While the *gemeinschaft* social order "rests on harmony and is developed and ennobled by folkways, mores, and religion," the *gesellschaft* order is dependent on formal rules and political legislation.[17] Thus society is governed, not by a rich and imaginative tradition to which the common person feels connected, but by "new and arbitrary legal constructions" in whose formation he plays no role, and which therefore seem remote, alien, and coercive.[18] In the *gesellschaft* order, "only the upper strata, the rich and the cultured, are really active and alive. They set up the standards to which the lower strata have to conform."[19] To Tönnies, it seemed that much humanity was being lost in the process. This is probably why, late in his life, he favored the rise of the Nazis, who stressed the natural unity of the people and claimed that they would make Germany a *gemeinschaft* once again.

Social Theory and Modernization

When we look at the approaches of Marx, Weber, Durkheim, and Tönnies to the process of social change involved in modernization, some common themes emerge. All of them took note of the increasing division of labor. All of them saw the growth of a capitalist market economy as crucial to the changes they were analyzing. All of them saw changes in both public and private life and in both economic and emotional relationships. Marx stressed economic change as the key to *all* change, including the transformation of local markets into one great global market. Weber, Durkheim, and Tönnies all described both an increase in scale, with larger and larger social groups emerging, and a corresponding shift away from close personal relationships toward more formal, impersonal, structured relationships. Weber stressed the progress of a rational organization of life by means of bureaucracy, Durkheim the division of labor, and Tönnies the artificial nature of modern society. Despite their differences, all of them were quite evidently noting the same basic trends in nineteenth-century Europe. As the modernization process spread well beyond its original European context, each of these theorists has left us with concepts useful for understanding the changing social world around us.

Notes

1 Margaret Mead. "Preface," in Ruth Benedict, *Patterns of Culture* (Boston: Houghton Mifflin, 1989), xi.
2 William A. Haviland, *Cultural Anthropology* (Fort Worth, TX: Harcourt College Publishers, 2002), 487.
3 Ibid., 427.
4 Karl Marx and Friedrich Engels, *The Communist Manifesto,* ed. Samuel H. Beer (Wheeling, IL: Harlan Davidson, Inc., [1848] 1955), 13.
5 Stephen Kalberg, *Max Weber's Comparative Historical Sociology* (Chicago: University of Chicago Press, 1994), 10.
6 See Max Weber, "'Objectivity' in Social Science and Social Policy," in *Max Weber on the Methodology of the Social Sciences,* trans. and ed. Edward A. Shils and Henry A. Finch (Glencoe, IL: Free Press, 1949), 50–112.
7 Émile Durkheim, *The Division of Labor in Society,* trans. W. D. Halls (New York: The Free Press, [1893] 1997), 31.
8 Ibid., 68.
9 Ibid., 3.
10 Ibid., 335.
11 Ferdinand Tönnies, *Community and Society (Gemeinschaft und Gesellschaft)* (New Brunswick: Transaction Publishers, [1887] 1996), 33.
12 Ibid., 37–9. Like most European social theorists of his era, Tönnies could only picture natural authority as male.
13 Ibid., 43.
14 Ibid., 34.
15 Ibid., 35.
16 Ibid., 69–71. Tönnies was influenced in this view by Adam Smith and by Karl Marx, both of whom he acknowledges in his discussion.
17 Ibid., 223.
18 Ibid., 226.
19 Ibid., 227.

Suggested Readings

Chirot, Daniel. *How Societies Change.* Thousand Oaks, CA: Pine Forks Press, 1994.
Durkheim, Émile. *The Division of Labor in Society.* Translated by W. D. Halls. New York: The Free Press, [1893] 1997.
Kalberg, Stephen. *Max Weber's Comparative Historical Sociology.* Chicago: University of Chicago Press, 1994.
Marx, Karl and Friedrich Engels. *The Communist Manifesto.* Edited by Samuel H. Beer. Wheeling, IL: Harlan Davidson, Inc., [1848] 1955.
Nisbet, Robert A. *The Sociological Tradition.* New York: Basic Books, 1966.
Tönnies, Ferdinand. *Community and Society (Gemeinschaft und Gesellschaft).* New Brunswick: Transaction Publishers, [1887] 1996.
Weber, Max. *The Protestant Ethic and the Spirit of Capitalism.* Translated by Talcott Parsons. London: Scribner's, [1905] 1995.

3   The Ancient and Classical Inheritance

John McGrath

Key Terms

aristocracy, autocracy, bureaucracy, citizens, client states, democracy, division of labor, economic surplus, empire, money economy, oligarchy, rationalism, republic, social mobility, theology

The primates we call *homo sapiens* first appeared in northeast Africa around 200,000 years ago. Identifiably distinct from other advanced primates of the *homo* genus, these ancestors of ours were hunter-gatherers who roamed and foraged in small groups or clans. By 70,000 years ago, they had larger brains, better manual dexterity, and lighter bones than other *homo* species, used a variety of basic stone tools, and, critically, had developed languages, which represented a major advantage in their ability to learn, plan, and work together. It was at about this point—about 3,000 generations ago—that the first groups of humans migrated out of Africa to settle in a variety of physical settings.[1]

Around 15,000 years ago, if not earlier, humans inhabited every continent except Antarctica. By this point, different groups of humans had adapted their ways of living, including technologies and social organizations, to cope with a wide variety of physical environments, from temperate forest, to open savanna, tundra, to deserts, mountaintops, and seashores.[2] Their communication abilities gave them a tremendous advantage, and when they encountered other types of hominids, they were able to outcompete or displace them. For instance, in Europe and the present day Middle East, *homo sapiens* moved into areas already inhabited by larger and bulkier Neanderthals, whom they replaced through some combination of warfare and interbreeding, while it is believed that they similarly displaced other species of primates in Asia and Africa. Recent discoveries have found that traces of Neanderthal and other early varieties of hominids remain in the DNA of most of today's human beings, especially Europeans and Asians.[3]

Cities and Agriculture in Mesopotamia

Some of the earliest social changes that started the path to modernity took place in the area frequently referred to as the "Middle East," encompassing the regions of Anatolia, the Levant, and Mesopotamia; that is, more or less today's nations of

Turkey, Syria, Lebanon, Israel, Jordan, and Iraq.[4] It was in the last of these regions, Mesopotamia, that the first permanent settled societies, as opposed to groups who migrated on a regular basis, appeared sometime after 9000 BCE.[5] Whether the establishment of settlements encouraged agriculture, or agriculture encouraged settlements, is hard to determine, as they tended to reinforce each other.[6] What we do know is that, once established in a permanent location, these first settled peoples developed reliable varieties of wheat and barley as staple foods, and over the centuries added a variety of domesticated animals that both supplemented their diets and could be used for purposes such as transportation and plowing. For the first time, human societies could meet their basic needs with resources close at hand.

Around 4000 BCE the Sumerian city-state of Uruk, often considered to be "the first city in history," emerged in southern Mesopotamia, a region whose name means "between the rivers," in this case the Tigris and Euphrates and their tributaries.[7] With a population of about 10,000 persons, Uruk's food supply depended almost entirely upon the water from these rivers, since the region had little rainfall. This meant that irrigation projects that mobilized large numbers of people working together were needed for farming on any significant scale; this in turn required some sort of authority to plan and organize such projects.[8] The success of this new system allowed for an **economic surplus**, meaning that not every member of the community had to devote most of their labor to procuring food, enabling many workers to pursue other sorts of occupations in a **division of labor**. As a direct result, the economic and social organization became more complex.

In Sumer, dynasties of kings assumed responsibility for ensuring the order and security necessary to enable this new type of society to function. Religious tradition legitimized their power, while a **bureaucracy** employed the first real writing system and standard weights and measures to administer the system efficiently. Given stability and order, both internal and external social change took place in Mesopotamia and nearby areas. Early city-states made advances in construction, pottery, and tool making, which contributed to a higher standard of living. Even well before 3000 BCE, Sumerians traded regularly with increasingly distant neighbors, giving them access to new technology and cultural elements in addition to trade goods. This diffusion brought, among other things, bronze weapons and tools, horses, new crops, and the wheel. Not only did these contribute to an expanding regional economy, but they also contributed to warfare, which encouraged the development of even more centralized and concentrated forms of authority.

The relative prosperity of this town-based society also proved a magnet for newcomers, as over the next couple of millennia, new groups of peoples, especially from the north and east, migrated into Mesopotamia and surrounding areas. In the following centuries, peoples who included the Akkadians, Assyrians, Chaldeans, Babylonians, and Hittites succeeded the Sumerians in establishing, through conquest and settlement, a number of **empires**, incorporating varying societies under the formal authority of a single central power. Each of these groups dominated much or most of the entire Middle Eastern region for various periods of time prior to 1200 BCE.[9] Their societies relied increasingly on technology and writing, while developing even more economic specialization and social complexity.

In some cases, secular power, in the form of kings, competed with religious leaders for authority. The *Epic of Gilgamesh*, sometimes regarded as the first work of literature, probably evolved from historical events during the Akkadian Empire around 2500 BCE, attaining a written form by around 1200 BCE.[10] *Hammurabi's Code*, expressed in cuneiform symbolic writing, dated from the mid-1700s BCE, formally codified specific crimes and the punishments that authorities would impose for their commission.[11]

For about 2,000 years, these post-Sumerian societies experienced cycles of stability and instability, expansion and contraction, war and peace; much of Mesopotamia was even briefly dominated by the Egyptian state, discussed below. Meanwhile, during the first and second millennia BCE, relatively complex urban societies also emerged in outlying areas, such as Crete, Mycenae, Persia, and the Mediterranean coasts of North Africa and today's Israel, Lebanon, and Syria. Maritime trade links intensified cross-pollination of religious and social ideas, crops, domestic animals, and technology.

Egypt and the Nile Valley

While a variety of different peoples were gaining and losing power in the Tigris-Euphrates region, Egypt exhibited a stability that in ancient history is rivaled only by the Chinese. For three millennia starting prior to 3000 BCE, a succession of Egyptian royal dynasties maintained control of the Nile Valley with few interruptions from external powers. Even Egypt's conquest by Alexander the Great in the fourth century BCE represented only a minor change to their historical system, merely replacing one royal dynasty with another.

Geography had a great deal to do with this. The Nile Valley's fertility, due to the river's annual flooding, permitted an economic surplus that supported a large population and a division of labor. In contrast to the Mesopotamian societies that were overwhelmingly urban in nature, Egyptian peoples lived in various types of settlements ranging from rural to urban.[12] Irrigation systems, some of which have survived for 5,000 years, expanded the region's areas of cultivation and its agricultural yields, as Egyptians introduced new crops imported from the Middle East and elsewhere in the Eurasian continent.[13] Compared to virtually any other ancient society, average Egyptians not only enjoyed a varied diet, but seldom experienced famine.[14]

In addition, outside the green belt of the valley, inhospitable deserts to both the east and west made it quite difficult for hostile neighbors to invade in an age where horses and chariots were the most modern forms of transportation. While the Egyptians did engage in numerous wars over a period of thousands of years, few were conducted in their own settlement areas. These factors added up to a social, political, and cultural stability that enabled steady and gradual progress. Even though it was not until the mid-first century BCE that there was a standardized and widely recognized form of currency, or **money economy**, many Egyptians enjoyed not only a high standard of living compared to previous ancient societies, but also opportunities to improve their status and wealth, that is, **social mobility**.[15]

Social Stratification and Social Mobility

Every known human society, past and present, has had a system for ranking its members. (It may not be a coincidence that the social primates who are our closest relatives in the animal kingdom all display rankings, too, often referred to as a dominance hierarchy.) In the least complex societies, such as hunter-gatherer bands, there is very little wealth, but some members have more prestige and more authority than others. In societies of this kind the criteria of ranking are generally age, gender, and special abilities. In more complex societies the criteria tend to be more numerous, and there can be great disparities in wealth as a result of differences of status. These ranking systems are called systems of **social stratification**: the division of society into different and unequal layers. The ancient world created distinctions unknown to hunter-gatherer bands, such as the distinction between a slave and a free citizen, or between a hereditary king and his subjects. Caste systems, like the one that arose in Classical India, separated people into highly unequal groups on the basis of ancestry alone. The wealth, religious status, power and prestige of each caste was based on characteristics that could not be changed. Rankings based on race operate in very much the same way, even within the context of a comparatively open system, as do differentials in the relative power and prestige of men and women. Feudal societies were complex systems uniting the economic, social, and governmental orders in networks of allegiance and power, where status depended upon one's role in the collective, and for those at the bottom, it was extremely difficult to improve one's station in life.

Increasingly with modernization we see the kind of stratification system known as a class system. As the European economies became more and more oriented to the market over time, their systems of social stratification moved away from the feudal type and toward a more open, flexible system that allows for movement. According to sociologist Max Weber, the ranking in a class system takes into account the relative power, wealth, and prestige of individuals and families. (It also reinforces these differences.) Both in theory and in practice, class systems allow for more **social mobility**— movement from one level of the social hierarchy to another. (Keep in mind, of course, that mobility does not necessarily mean improvement; descending to a lower level also happens, and is also social mobility.) Certainly more upward social mobility has occurred under the class system than under any other. On the other hand, to the extent that distinctions based on race and gender, and likewise the advantages of inherited wealth, affect the life chances of individuals in a given system, the potential for social mobility is restricted.

As in other societies, Egyptian culture supported and reinforced its way of life. It was dominated by a polytheistic, nature-based religion that was obsessed with death and the afterlife.[16] Egyptians regarded their pharaohs as intermediaries between themselves and the divinities who protected them from the forces of chaos.[17] For literally thousands of years, Egyptian pharaohs exercised nearly unlimited power, relying on a class of literate officials who used a complex system of hieroglyphic writing. Egyptian culture made significant contributions to engineering, mathematics, astronomy, and medicine. The Egyptians' most lasting accomplishment (quite literally) was the construction of the pyramids of Giza more than four and a half thousand years ago. This enormous task demanded not only advanced engineering, but also required the pharaoh's officials to allocate and direct the labor of thousands of skilled and unskilled workers. Without constant warfare to engage the male population, and the advantage of not needing a year-round mobilization of the labor force to grow food, pharaohs could direct Egyptian resources toward the construction of monuments that had very little economic value in and of themselves.[18]

The Dark Age and the Iron Age

After the middle of the second millennium BCE, the Eastern Mediterranean region experienced an era of instability lasting several centuries, known as the "Dark Age."[19] One major cause was the arrival of foreign peoples, perhaps due to droughts in central Asia. The invasions of groups such as the Arameans and a somewhat mysterious society referred to as the "Sea Peoples" caused great instability and a decline in the size of urban settlements. The region's major states at this time, Egypt's New Kingdom and the Hittite Empire in Anatolia (modern-day Turkey), experienced political, social, and economic difficulties. Meanwhile, smaller independent states emerged, especially on the Mediterranean coast, such as Mycenae on the Greek peninsula. Additionally, the Phoenicians, a society built on maritime trade, unified several ancient cities on the coast of the Levant, and began establishing colonies along the North African coast, eventually colonizing the shores of the Atlantic Ocean more than 2,000 years ago.[20]

The instability of the Dark Age overlapped with the beginnings of what we call the Iron Age. Prior to 1200 BCE, the advanced societies in the Eastern Mediterranean region used bronze for tools and weapons, which required access to both copper and tin, which could not always be found domestically. After that date, Iron Age technology, particularly the ability to smelt iron ore with a charcoal process, diffused out of central Anatolia, reaching Egypt sometime after 1000 BCE and Greece a few centuries later. This allowed Eastern Mediterranean peoples to make use of the iron ore that was often more widely available than the ingredients needed for bronze, and the result was that they could craft superior tools more easily. The impact was widespread, contributing to improved agriculture, a higher standard of living, an even more complex social stratification system, and the expansion of centralized authority and bureaucracy.[21]

Two other notable achievements took place in this same era of social change. In the Levant kingdoms of Judea and Israel, the Jewish people developed the first lasting monotheistic religion, worshipping a single supreme god, unlike their polytheistic neighbors. In contrast to any previous faith in the region, Judaism relied upon a collection of sacred writings that were studied extensively by scholars to discover their single god's intention for his "chosen people." In addition to being the first Western religion based upon writing, Judaism was also important because it emphasized the importance of ethical behavior. Previous polytheistic religions had tended to accept that events were driven by the actions of fickle, flawed gods, and that puny humans had little impact on what they chose to do. Instead, the Judaism of late first century Israel and Judea stressed the importance of a conscience, where individuals tried to conform their behavior to moral standards illustrated in their holy scriptures, or Torah.[22]

It is also significant that the Jewish Torah was written and copied by hand using one of the first phonetic alphabets, that is, a writing system where symbols represented phonetic sounds that could be strung together to form printed words. Probably invented first by the Phoenicians, this way of writing proved far more adaptable and flexible than the earlier word symbols used by Sumerian cuneiform and Egyptian hieroglyphics, and in the next few centuries after 1000 BCE, other cultures in the region developed their own versions.

In these ways, the Dark Age and the recovery from it ushered in a new order in the Eastern Mediterranean region. Iron, monotheism, and the alphabet proved to be enormously significant developments that set the stage for what we refer to as "the Classical Age." Among the societies that achieved the most prominence during this time were the Greeks.

Greece: The Cradle of Western Civilization

As the Dark Age gradually subsided in the early first millennium BCE, a society we can identify as Greek emerged, one that had some cultural inheritance from the Minoans in Crete (ca. 3600 BCE–1400 BCE) and the militaristic Mycenaean society of southern mainland Greece (ca. 1600 BCE–1100 BCE). Here, too, geography played a major role. The mountainous mainland and numerous Aegean islands limited easy interactions among separate groups, which promoted the growth of largely independent city-states, usually composed of a walled city and its surrounding farmlands and villages. While they maintained formal independence from each other, the city-states were tied together by the bonds of culture and trade.

From 1000 BCE onwards, the Greeks, perhaps due to population pressure, expanded outward to establish both settler colonies and trading outposts, first in the Aegean islands and Anatolian coast, then elsewhere in the Mediterranean region, as far as the coasts of today's France and Spain. Maritime trade was an essential element of their economy, with well-established regular contact with Cyprus, the Levant, Egypt, Italy, Sicily, and elsewhere, which enabled much cultural exchange. Notably, the Greek city-states were not directly connected as parts of a political "empire," as had been the case with the previous major civilizations of the Mediterranean world. Yet they formed a distinctive type of society that contributed immensely to the development of what later would be called "Western Civilization."

By about 800 BCE, dozens of Greek city-states had emerged. All of them shared the Greek language and its alphabet, and shortly thereafter the Greeks adopted iron smelting techniques from the societies to their east.[23] Iron was particularly advantageous in this case, since the Greek peninsula contained accessible deposits of iron ore, but not tin and copper. Most of the city-states were societies where the elite social classes held a disproportionate amount of wealth and power. Some of them were **autocracies**, where a single individual, in this case a king, or "tyrant," held all formal power. Others were **aristocracies** ("rule by the best") and/or **oligarchies** ("rule by a few") where the elites appointed and/or elected officials responsible, for military jurisdiction, taxation, and the supervision of religious practices.[24]

Athens, the largest Greek city-state, developed a more egalitarian form of polity than most others, one that they called a **democracy**. There were other Greek city-states that also claimed "democratic" forms of government, but since the literature and historical evidence tells us far more about historical Athens than about other places, we know more about how democracy emerged and changed in Athens than we do about anywhere else.[25] And while earlier societies further east may have had political elements similar to those later seen in Athens, it is Athens that usually is considered the "birthplace of democracy."[26]

At the height of Athens' Classical Era, during the fifth century BCE (or 400s BCE), Athens had a population of perhaps 200,000 people, exceptionally large for the era in comparison to other Greek polities.[27] Prior to and during the Dark Age, Athens had been a comparatively prosperous society whose economy relied on the productive agriculture in the surrounding countryside of Attica. The term "democracy" refers to the *demos*, the approximately 40,000 collective native adult male Athenians who qualified as **citizens**, which gave them legally recognized status and rights. This did not mean that there was complete equality in Athens, since citizenship, and thus political influence, was denied to women, children, foreigners, and slaves, who together may have outnumbered the citizens four to one. Moreover, not every Athenian citizen had an equal amount of influence, since some organs of government were reserved for the wealthier classes. What was historically significant in Athens during the Classical Age was that everyone recognized as a citizen had some amount of political influence. This new civic concept was a major departure from usual practice in early settled societies, in that it did not put all authority in the hands of an autocratic ruler and/or an aristocracy. In Classical Athens, each citizen had a legal right to take part in debates over significant issues, and in many cases, to vote on new laws and for political representatives to hold authority on their behalf.

Over time, Athens and other early "democratic" polities experimented with different ways to do this. Democracy there, as elsewhere in history, was never a static, perfected form. From the seventh century BCE to the fourth century BCE, the city-state of Athens made numerous political adaptations and experiments, largely as a consequence of struggles for influence among different social factions. On three different occasions during this time, popular dissatisfaction with the government supported the rise of individuals (Solon, Cleisthenes, and Pericles) who acted autocratically to introduce more democratic elements, generally by increasing the political participation of the *demos* in different ways.[28] It is interesting that, in each case, a temporary suspension of democracy enabled the expansion of democracy. This would not be the last time in history that this paradox presented itself. It would also not be the last time that leaders justified autocratic power by claiming their devotion to democratic ideals.

Democracy was not the only product of a Greek culture that was increasingly based upon **rationalism**, that is, relying on reason instead of tradition or religion, as a guiding principle. While the Classical Era in Greece did not last as long as some other ancient civilizations, such as Egypt and Rome, it contributed to the development of a more modern way of life through the emergence of influential new ways of thinking. The relative freedom of thought and the relatively high level of literacy encouraged learned people to debate, discuss, and innovate. The list of Greek philosophers ("lovers of learning," in Greek) who significantly influenced the modernization of the Western world, directly and indirectly, is a long one.

During the Classical Age, Athens was the home of three of modern philosophy's foundational contributors: Socrates (469–399 BCE), Plato (429–347 BCE) and Aristotle (384–322 BCE). Plato had been Socrates's pupil, and Plato taught Aristotle, who was Alexander the Great's tutor. While the scarcity of original source material makes it difficult to untangle whose ideas were whose, all three of these Athenian philosophers established a skeptical, reason-based approach to understanding the world, one that had wide applications. They collectively pioneered an approach to argumentation known as rhetoric, which became an essential part of Greek education. Each of these individuals, as well as many others throughout the Greek-speaking world, believed that human reason could create a better society, as opposed to the passive, fatalistic ethos that generally ensured order in the ancient world. Well over a thousand years later, the rediscovery of this optimistic, positive rationalism became a driving force of the European Renaissance.

While Greek power and wealth varied after the Classical Age, Greek culture never collapsed and disappeared; in fact, it made a wide and deep impact on the entire region. Despite some remarkable military victories that kept the powerful kingdom of Persia at bay, subsequent strife among alliances of city-states (leagues) in the Peloponnesian War (431–404 BCE) weakened Greece. During the fourth century BCE, Philip of Macedon, king of the marginally Greek kingdom of Macedonia, forcefully incorporated most of the Greek city-states into his empire. His son, Alexander the Great, then expanded east and south, conquering not only the Persians but societies as distant as India and Egypt.

This empire stayed united for only a figurative blink of an eye. Almost immediately after Alexander's death, at the young age of about 33 in 323 BCE, it broke up into a number of smaller states controlled by Alexander's leading generals and allies, who struggled mightily to keep control. It is said that "the inheritance was so large that it destroyed everyone who reached to grasp it,"[29] yet war and instability did not prevent the continued spread of Greek learning and culture. New cities appeared, established by Greeks and others, and much cultural blending took place in terms of ideas, art, customs, religion, and language. Alexandria in Egypt, a new city founded by the conqueror himself, became the most learned and sophisticated city in the world, supporting an intellectual community that included Archimedes, Euclid, and Eratosthenes, among others. We call the 300-year era after 323 BCE the Hellenistic Age, which lasted until most of Alexander's former empire was swallowed up by the Romans.

Rome: Republic to Empire

As Classical Greece gave way to the Hellenistic Era, another powerful civilization was emerging further west on the Italian peninsula. Under a series of early kings, people we know as Romans established the city of Rome by the middle of the eighth century BCE. Even at that early date, certain identifiable social characteristics had appeared in their society. One was the emergence of an aristocratic class known as "patricians," in contrast to commoners were known as "plebeians."[30] While early Roman kings ruled autocratically, an institution known as the Senate, composed of leading patrician families, served as an advisory body, while a type of public assembly allowed plebeians to discuss public issues and formally confer authority upon the kings.[31]

Expanding gradually and steadily from the city of Rome, the Romans brought surrounding peoples into the kingdom through war and diplomacy. Around 500 BCE, the kingship gave way to a **republic** ("thing of the people," in Latin), dominated by the established senatorial families, who exerted control over legal, financial, and religious institutions. The Senate appointed individuals, at first only from the patrician class, to handle executive duties for fixed terms, while the military, whose leaders began to comprise another elite class, took a more visible role in politics and administration.[32]

By the time of Alexander the Great, around 325 BCE, the Romans had unified the entire Italian peninsula, and had even begun to expand beyond it. Successful wars against the Phoenicians in the Punic Wars (264–241 BCE, 218–201 BCE) allowed the Romans to seize many Phoenician colonies in the Mediterranean, which set the stage for more conquests. Soon the Romans added most of the former Hellenistic regions, including Greece itself in the late first century BCE. This gave Rome control of almost all of the Mediterranean coast, ruling some areas directly as provinces and others indirectly as **client states**, where local leaders pledged their allegiance to the Romans as a superior authority. The presence of Roman military forces and administrators reinforced this relationship. As Rome expanded through the Mediterranean, its republican government became a casualty of factional strife, and in its place the Roman Empire emerged.[33] This featured a more autocratic political system, controlled by a succession of emperors and their allies among the patrician classes. By the second century CE, additional conquests north and west of Italy and in the Middle East had brought Rome to its height in terms of geography, power, and wealth.

Urbanization was a critical feature of the evolution of the Roman state, as cities were centers of both the economy and political administration.[34] The population of Rome, which was probably the largest city in the world at the time, may have approached a million persons by the first century CE, increasing mostly through immigration from elsewhere in Italy and from the provincial areas.[35] The growth of such a large urban population was only made possible by government expenditure. The imperial government took an active role in importing grain for its urban populations, and probably 80 percent of the workers throughout the empire were directly involved in food production and transportation.[36] Public works projects, often financed by the senatorial class as a civic duty, created roads, aqueducts, sewer systems, assembly halls, and huge stadiums for public games. Both in the capital and elsewhere, the social stratification system continued to evolve, featuring expanding possibilities for social mobility through military and civil service, as well as opportunities for the ambitious to accumulate great wealth. Social mobility was even possible for the large slave population, composed of both prisoners of war and those bought through an extensive commercial slave trade; many were able to earn enough money, or accumulate enough favors, to buy their liberty and become "freemen."[37]

The development and administration of such an empire relied greatly upon advances in technology, especially in engineering, construction, and metalworking. Roman engineers constructed the famous Roman roads, while the growth of naval power and merchant shipping—in the long run, more important than overland transport—allowed for an imperial division of labor. In this complex system of exchange, Italy played a role much like that of later imperial systems in European history, importing food and raw materials from the empire's periphery, and exporting manufactured and luxury goods to the provinces. Established settlements in regions stretching from the Black Sea to the Baltic, and the Atlantic coasts to interior Africa, gave Romans access to a wide variety of resources, including a varied food supply, metals of all sorts, stone, timber, paper, textiles, spices, and even soldiers and slaves.[38]

As the Romans carried out this process of expansion, they consciously modeled their culture on Greece, which had a major influence on Roman science, literature, religion, education, and the arts. It has been argued that the Romans emphasized practical applications of knowledge more than the Greeks did.[39] Though their empire was largely the product of conquest, Roman emperors saw themselves as bringers of a higher form of civilization to the Mediterranean world. Under the empire, the various provinces and client states outside Italy included many different ethnicities, held together by a unified legal code that recognized rights for those who qualified as "Roman Citizens." In the western parts of the empire, the Latin language brought together varied peoples who spoke local languages, while the Greek language, already common in the eastern Mediterranean for hundreds of years, became the unifying tongue in Egypt and the Roman areas of the Middle East. These parts of the empire were administered by both local authorities and appointed governors supported by a significant military presence, all of which was paid for through local taxation. As it had been for the Egyptians, the priority of the political state was the preservation of order and stability, as epitomized by the Pax Romana, or "Roman Peace."

The Christian Era

Another critically important legacy of the ancient world was the spread of Christianity, which would become the most important unifying element in Europe for centuries. The figure later known as Jesus of Nazareth was probably a member of a Jewish sect. He lived in the kingdom of Judea, a client state of the Roman Empire, which had conquered most of the region in 63 BCE. In an era fraught with numerous conflicting interpretations of the Jewish Scriptures, Jesus preached a revolutionary message of love, nonviolence and the possibility of eternal salvation among his fellow Judeans. Sometime before 33 CE, he had gained a devoted following, and evidently posed a challenge to the Roman-appointed kings who held authority in the region. Evidently considering Jesus to be a threat to social order, the authorities executed him by crucifixion sometime around 33 CE.[40]

This did not end the challenge to authority, as Jesus's handpicked disciples, along with others who had been captivated by his message, spread his ideas not just in Judea, but throughout the eastern Mediterranean region, especially after the conquest of Jerusalem by the Romans in 70 CE.[41] Meanwhile, written accounts of Jesus's ministry were written, copied, and distributed through the region as testament to Jesus's message. Since this was an era before the printing press, each written copy of these works had to be copied by hand, which resulted in errors and changes in the texts.[42] Versions of four accounts presumably authored by Jesus's disciples Mark, Matthew, Luke, and John, known as Gospels, provided the foundation of the Scriptures that we call the New Testament. However, the originals—if indeed there ever were originals—were long lost even by 100 CE.

In an age of limited communication among the various regions of the Mediterranean world, early Christianity experienced the problem of consistency, as variants of the literature and conflicting interpretations of them led to different sects in different places. Under the Roman Empire, Christian communities had emerged in the Middle East, Egypt and North Africa, Anatolia, and Greece. Jesus's disciple Simon, later known as Peter (in Greek, "the Rock"), brought Jesus's ideas to Rome before the end of the first century CE. Early Christians in the Roman Empire faced intermittent but brutal persecutions, with hundreds and perhaps thousands dying as martyrs at the commands of both emperors and local authorities. Meanwhile, for more than two centuries, Christian scholars throughout the Mediterranean tried to arrive at some general agreement concerning what should be included, and what should not be included, in the New Testament.

The Roman oppression of Christians came to an end in 313 CE, during the reign of the Emperor Constantine (r. 306–337 CE). He himself converted to Christianity and proclaimed it henceforth the official religion in the empire, while transferring the capital of the empire to the eastern city of Byzantium, renamed Constantinople. In 325 CE, he called a council of church scholars at Nicaea, near his new capital, that made significant progress in unifying the religious beliefs and principles, or **theology**, of the Christian church. While this helped establish a more cohesive Christian message, it did not solve disagreements over religious practices. After Nicaea, church leaders were divided in their opinions as to whether the church should be based in the new capital, Constantinople, or in the city of Rome, where there was a significant concentration of Christian scholars. As it happened, church organizations evolved in both cities. In Constantinople, church leaders or "patriarchs" became part of the official state, sharing power with the emperors for more than a thousand years.

However, in the West, weak and later localized secular leaders were less able to contest the church's authority. In the city of Rome, early Christians created an institution known as the papacy, under the pope, or "father." The papacy directed what became known as the Catholic (meaning "universal") Church, establishing a hierarchy of authority radiating from Rome and steadily spreading from there, especially to the north and west, regions where the Roman Empire had recently been losing control. As secular power declined, spiritual power became more widespread. In the last half of the first millennium—that is, from about 500–1000 CE—political fragmentation in Europe was accompanied by a significant measure of religious unification under the Roman Church.

In the centuries that followed, attempts to unify the eastern and western branches had limited success. As the Roman Empire disintegrated in the early Middle Ages, church leaders in both capitals and elsewhere continued to disagree about both the contents and the meanings of the Old and New Testaments, and doctrinal unity for Christianity remained difficult to accomplish. As the Roman Empires, both west and east, faced challenges to their survivals, figures such as St. Augustine (354–430 CE) devoted much effort to unifying and interpreting the Christian message by studying the Gospels and other sacred writings. Meanwhile, those who relied on different testaments, different versions of testaments, and different interpretations of them, were branded as heretics and were often ruthlessly discouraged.

Nevertheless, in a Mediterranean world where there was little order and much insecurity, Christianity's message of redemption and salvation resonated with many people. In the early Middle Ages, in the recovering and developing societies of Western and central Europe, the Catholic Church of Rome would play an essential role, influencing not just the culture, but also political and social organization, for many centuries.

The Fall of Rome and the End of the Classical Era

The decline and breakup of the Western Roman Empire is a subject that has fascinated scholars for hundreds of years. While historians often use a few symbolic dates to mark its end, such as the sack of the city of Rome by invading Visigoths in 410 CE, the process took centuries. One can identify many reasons for the empire's decline. These include both internal and external developments, and involve economic, social, political, and cultural factors.

The empire reached its furthest territorial extent under the Emperor Trajan (r. 93–117 CE) and for the most part maintained its geographical integrity during

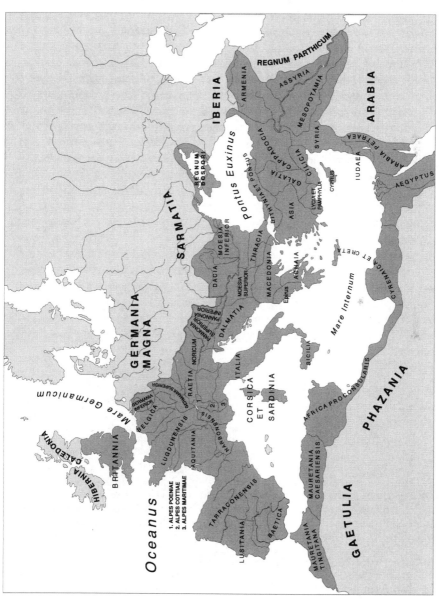

Map 3.1
The Roman Empire at its
furthest extent, 117 CE

the next century. Even before the accession of Constantine in the early fourth century, the empire had been administratively divided into a Latin-speaking West and a Greek speaking East, and after Constantine moved to Constantinople, the empire was effectively divided into halves. Meanwhile, the Roman military enga-ged in nearly continuous battles against peoples in the empire's borderlands, including northern Europe and the Middle East. Some of this conflict was due to population pressure created by migration of peoples such as the Huns from central Asia, which set in motion widespread movements of varied peoples who resisted assimilation into the empire. By the late fourth century CE, the Western part of the empire had begun to abandon some of its far-flung territories. In the next century, the "barbarians" were invading Italy itself.

By then, the political administration in the West was experiencing financial problems, while the gap in wealth between the aristocratic classes and the common population was widening. Taxes were insufficient to pay for a military that was by then largely composed of peoples from outside Italy. Disease, interruptions of Mediterranean commerce, and local revolts against Roman authority all disrupted the functioning of the imperial system.[43] By early in the sixth century, the last Western emperor was deposed, and the empire fractured into regions under varied local non-Roman authorities. However, some modern historians have argued that the situations in former imperial territories were not nearly as chaotic as historians in the Enlightenment had claimed, and that in Italy, in particular, manufacturing, economic specialization, and trade continued. In this view, even as power became decentralized in different parts of the empire after the sixth century, daily life for many Europeans was not dramatically different than it had been 500 years before.[44]

The Eastern Roman Empire, under Greek-speaking emperors in Constantinople, had enough problems keeping their own half of the empire intact, especially after the appearance of Islam during the seventh century. Constantly on the defensive from that point on, their rule survived until the mid-sixteenth century. By that time, a much different sort of society had arisen in Western Europe, one that we call medieval.

Notes

1 Luigi Luca Cavalli-Sforza and Francesco Cavalli-Sforza, *The Great Human Diasporas: The History of Diversity and Evolution*, (New York: Basic Books, 1995); Spencer Wells, *The Journey of Man* (New York: Random House, 2003)
2 Jared Diamond, *Guns, Germs, and Steel.* (New York: Norton, 1990), 35–51.
3 Benjamin Vernot, et al. "Resurrecting Surviving Neandertal Lineages from Modern Human Genomes," *Science* 343, no 6174 (February 28, 2014): 1017–1021.
4 For the purpose of simplicity, I will use the terms "Eastern Mediterranean" to refer to the larger region, including Greece and Egypt. The term "Middle East" is used here to refer to the mainland region from the east coast of the Mediterranean (today's Turkey, Syria, Lebanon, and Israel) to present-day Iran. "Mesopotamia" is more specific. Meaning "between the rivers" in Greek, it refers more or less to today's Iraq, the southern part of which was historically referred to as "Babylon."
5 For chronological references, "BCE" stands for "Before the Christian Era."

6 The conventional explanation that agriculture enabled settlement was first made by Ofer Bar-Yosef, "On the Nature of Transitions: The Middle to Upper Paleolithic and the Neolithic Revolution." *Cambridge Archaeological Journal*, 8, no. 2 (1998):141–63. For alternative views, see Yuval Noah Harari, *Sapiens: A Brief History of Humankind* (New York: Harper Collins, 2015), 77–88; Diamond, *Guns Germs and Steel*, 81–6; Nicholas Wade, *Before the Dawn: Recovering the Lost History of Our Ancestors* (New York: Penguin, 2006), 125–34. The last argues that sedentism preceded agriculture.

7 Marc Van de Mieroop, *A History of the Ancient Near East ca. 3000–323 BC*, 2nd ed. (London: Blackwell, 2007), 23.

8 Scholars are divided in their views about the connection between large irrigation projects and systems of authority. At the very least, however, centralized authority made it easier to organize labor for such projects. Brian Fagan, *Floods, Famines, and Emperors* (New York: Basic Books, 1999), 93–4; Diamond, *Guns, Germs, and Steel*, 272–73; Harari, *Sapiens*, 98–111. Elizabeth C. Stone "Mesopotamian Cities and Countryside," in Daniel Snell, *A Companion to the Ancient Near East*, (Oxford: Blackwell, 2005), 157–59.

9 L. de Blois and R.J. van der Spek, trans. Susan Mellor, *An Introduction to the Ancient World*, 2nd ed. (London: Routledge, 2008), 11–13.

10 On Gilgamesh, see Tawny Holm, "Ancient Near East Literature: Genres and Forms," in *A Companion to the Ancient Near East*, ed. Daniel Snell, (Oxford: Blackwell, 2005), 269–81.

11 Van de Mieroop, *Ancient Near East*, 211–15.

12 Douglas J. Brewer and Emily Teeter, *Egypt and the Egyptians*, 2nd ed. (Cambridge: Cambridge University Press, 2007), 74–5.

13 Diamond, *Guns Germs and Steel*, 173–75.

14 Fagan, *Floods, Famines, and Emperors*, 99–117.

15 Brewer and Teeter *Egypt and the Egyptians*, 39–40.

16 Ibid., 166.

17 Ibid., 102–04; de Blois, *Ancient World*, 14–16.

18 On the pyramids in their historical context, see Robert L. Tignor, *Egypt: A Short History* (Princeton: Princeton University Press, 2010), 35–44.

19 Van de Mieroop, 190–206; on the specific impacts on different societies, see de Blois, 33–45.

20 On the Phoenicians, a civilization frequently ignored by historians of the ancient world, see Maria Eugenia Aubet, *The Phoenicians and the West: Politics, Colonies and Trade*, 2nd ed., trans. Mary Turton. (London: Cambridge University Press, 2001).

21 The authoritative work on the development and impact of iron technology remains that of Theodore Wertime, ed. *The Coming of the Age of Iron* (Yale University Press, 1980).

22 David Fromkin, *The Way of the World: From the Dawn of Civilizations to the Eve of the Twenty-First Century* (New York: Vintage, 2000), 46–50.

23 Thomas R. Martin, *Ancient Greece* (New Haven: Yale University Press, 2013), 51–9.

24 de Blois, *Ancient World*, 68–9.

25 Martin, *Ancient Greece*.

26 John Keane, *The Life and Death of Democracy* (New York: Norton, 2009), ix–xiv; 1–10.

27 Martin, *Ancient Greece*, 69–70, 92.

28 Kurt A. Raaflaub, "Democracy," in Konrad H. Kinzl, ed. *A Companion to the Classical Greek World* (Oxford: Blackwell, 2010), 395–408.

29 Fromkin, *The Way of the World*, 74.

30 Kevin M. McGeough, *The Romans: An Introduction* (Oxford: Oxford University Press, 2004), 137–141; de Blois, *Ancient World,* 145–46.
31 McGeough, *The Romans,* 153–56.
32 Ibid., 151–62.
33 Ibid., 69–78.
34 David Kessler and Peter Temin, "The Organization of the Grain Trade in the early Roman Empire," *Economic History Review* 60, no. 2 (2007), 313–32; de Blois, 244.
35 McGeough, *The Romans,* 129–132; Walter Scheidel, "Roman Population Size: The Logic of the Debate," *Princeton/Stanford Working Papers in Classics* (Princeton: Princeton University Press, 2007), 3–15.
36 McGeough, *The Romans,* 97–109; M. I. Finley, *The Ancient Economy* (Berkeley: University of California Press, 1973), 128–29, 170–71.
37 de Blois, *Ancient World,* 232–36.
38 McGeough, *The Romans,* 105–18.
39 Ibid., 248.
40 On the historical Jesus, who is mostly known to us through the New Testament, there is still considerable speculation. See Karen Armstrong, *The Bible* (New York, Grove Press, 2007) 55–7. No serious academician would deny that the historical Jesus was a figure of considerable influence in the chaotic and often violent world of the Roman-dominated Levant two thousand years ago.
41 On the earliest written sources, see Bart D. Ehrman, *Misquoting Jesus: The Story Behind Who Changed the Bible and Why* (New York: HarperOne, 2005), 20–9; Armstrong, *The Bible,* 53–78.
42 Ehrman, *Misquoting Jesus,* 45–69.
43 Two recent studies presenting multicausal explanations are Peter Heather, *The Fall of the Roman Empire* (London: Oxford University Press, 2005) and Bryan Ward-Perkins, *The Fall of Rome and the End of Civilization* (London: Oxford University Press, 2006).
44 Most notably the Belgian scholar Henri Pirenne, and more recently argued by Peter Brown, *The World of Late Antiquity* (London: Thames & Hudson, 1971) and Robert-Henri Bautier, *The Economic Development of Medieval Europe* (New York: Harcourt Brace, 1971).

Suggested Readings

Armstrong, Karen. *The Bible: A Biography.* New York: Grove Press, 2007.

Aubet, Maria E. *The Phoenicians and the West: Politics, Colonies and Trade.* 2nd Ed. Translated by Mary Turton. London: Cambridge University Press, 2001.

De Blois, L, and R. J. van der Spek. *An Introduction to the Ancient World.* 2nd Ed. Trans. Susan Mellor. London: Routledge, 2008.

Diamond, Jared. *Guns, Germs, and Steel: The Fates of Human Societies.* New York: Norton, 1999.

Ehrman, Bart D. *Misquoting Jesus: The Story Behind Who Changed the Bible and Why.* New York: HarperOne, 2005.

Fagan, Brian. *Floods, Famines, and Emperors.* New York: Basic Books, 1999.

Fromkin, David. *The Way of the World: From the Dawn of Civilizations to the Eve of the Twenty-First Century.* New York: Vintage, 2000.

Harari, Yuval Noah. *Sapiens: A Brief History of Humankind.* New York: Harper Collins, 2015.

Kinzl, Konrad H., ed. *A Companion to the Classical Greek World.* Oxford: Blackwell, 2010.

McGeough, Kevin M. *The Romans: An Introduction*. New York: Oxford University Press, 2004.

Martin, Thomas R. *Ancient Greece*. New Haven: Yale University Press, 2013.

Snell, Daniel, ed. *A Companion to the Ancient Near East*. Oxford: Blackwell, 2005.

Tignor, Robert L. *Egypt: A Short History*. Princeton: Princeton University Press, 2010.

Van de Mieroop, Marc. *A History of the Ancient Near East ca. 3000–323 BC*. 2nd Ed. London: Blackwell, 2007.

Wade, Nicholas. *Before the Dawn: Recovering the Lost History of Our Ancestors*. New York: Penguin, 2006.

Wertime, Theodore, ed. *The Coming of the Age of Iron* (New Haven: Yale University Press, 1980.

4 Europe in the Middle Ages

Medieval Society

John McGrath

Key Terms

bourgeoisie, estate system, ethos, feudalism, fief, manorialism, national monarchies, nobility, peasants, regular clergy, secular clergy, serf, systemic social change, vassal

We generally define the medieval period of European history, or the "Middle Ages," as the era between the fall of the Roman Empire and the beginning of the early modern period. This covers a span of about a thousand years, between roughly 500 and 1500 CE. In past centuries, scholars considered this mostly as an era of decline between the civilizations of the classical era and the Renaissance, and the terms "Middle Ages" and "medieval" had somewhat negative connotations. In more recent years, however, we have come to appreciate that the Middle Ages was a unique period of time in its own right that provided the foundation of modern Western civilization.

When dealing with such a long period of time, it is often convenient to further divide the Middle Ages into three separate periods, each with a somewhat distinctive historical character. In a sense, the Middle Ages began after the gradual disintegration of Roman Empire's unifying influence, which led to a period of disorder and insecurity lasting several hundred years. This is often referred to as the early Middle Ages (ca. 500–1000 CE), and sometimes even as the "Dark Ages," due to the relative lack of written historical evidence that makes details hard to come by. The early Middle Ages featured large-scale movements of peoples, some entering Europe from the outside, and other groups migrating within Europe. Many of these migrations displaced other groups, who in turn displaced others as they established themselves in new lands. During this era, Roman, Celtic, Germanic, Slavic, and other peoples split apart, intermarried, and founded new settlements. Over hundreds of years, these coalesced to provide the foundations of modern European ethnic and linguistic groups.

Collectively, these movements left varying societies scattered through Europe's valleys, plains, peninsulas, and coasts. By the end of the early Middle Ages, although the peoples of Europe still differed significantly in terms of their origins, languages, customs, and economic systems, almost all of them had been brought into the unifying embrace of Christianity. The Western Christian Church, or Roman Catholic Church, thus provided the first effective unifying element to these disparate groups.

The years between around 1000–1300 CE, which saw a slowing of the movements of peoples, are known as the High Middle Ages, sometimes called the "Age of Faith." It was at the beginning of this period that two distinct societies began to take shape in different areas of Europe: the largely feudal and agrarian north, and the more urban and commercial society of Italy and the Mediterranean coast.[1] The former is what historians define as classic medieval society. Here, the emergence of the feudal system and the first large European kingships combined with Christianity to give this civilization a tenuous stability, which allowed Europeans during the High Middle Ages to enjoy steady population and economic growth. A recognizable medieval culture emerged during this time, one that contained the first stirrings of modernity.

In contrast, the late Middle Ages (1300–1500) was an era of more rapid, often violent and dramatic, change. Population growth suffered radical reversals due to famine, warfare, and—especially—the effects of the Black Death and other epidemic diseases. Not only did these traumas ravage the population, but they also destroyed or discredited many of the most important European outlooks and institutions, and, ultimately, accelerated the process that we define as "modernization."

It is possible to make some useful general observations concerning European civilization at the outset of the High Middle Ages, circa 1000 CE. At this point, we can see a reasonable conformity in the major European institutions, and we can also identify the very beginnings of a distinctive type of social change. By this time, feudalism had evolved to take on a characteristic form in many parts of the continent. The kingdoms of France and England, and the Holy Roman Empire that had emerged in Germany and Italy, contributed some political and cultural continuity. Furthermore, the papacy in Rome had achieved a powerful influence over various peoples who, despite certain differences, had come to represent an identifiably "medieval" culture.

It should be pointed out that the "typical" medieval society described here was characteristic of northern medieval Europe, especially England, France, Germany and the "Low Countries" of today's Belgium and the Netherlands. Elsewhere—such as in the Iberian Peninsula, Scandinavia, the mountainous regions of eastern Europe, and especially Italy—historical and social circumstances gave rise to significant variations, and the structure of society was considerably different in many respects from the model described here.

The Structure of Society

The stratification of medieval Europe can be described as an **estate system**, where the status of an individual depended upon one's function in the working of the overall society. Each of three estates had significantly different customs and expectations, and the three estates were ranked hierarchically. Moreover, each estate corresponds to one the three main institutions of medieval society: the

Roman Catholic Church, the political system of feudalism, and the economic institution of **manorialism**.

The First Estate was the clergy, whose responsibility was to provide the members of medieval society with the means to salvation through the church. This grouping had its own hierarchy and organization, headed by the papacy in Rome. This First Estate was divided into two branches. One was known as the **secular clergy**, because they lived in and interacted with the secular world. It included cardinals, bishops, and other officials, whose jurisdictions corresponded to geographic administrative units. At the bottom of this hierarchy were the priests who served as the face of the church for the vast majority of the medieval population.

The second group of clergy were known as the **regular clergy**, so called because they were sworn to follow the *regula*, or "rule," of a particular religious order. Starting in the early Middle Ages, such organizations had been created to allow their members to devote themselves to pious pursuits such as scholarship, education, and helping the poor. Most of the early orders were based in monasteries, and hence were known as monastic orders.

The Second Estate was comprised of the **nobility**. Noble status was generally inherited, and the function of the nobility was expected to be military service and secular political authority. The precise meanings of different noble titles varied from place to place and over time. Generally, dukes and princes were just below kings in the noble hierarchy, and were often their close relatives; other noble titles included marquises, barons, counts, viscounts, and other more localized titles. Though women had significant legal restrictions on their wealth and power, they also enjoyed ascribed status as nobles, and could often inherit feudal lands and privileges from fathers, husbands, and other relatives. As a group, the nobility of all ranks obeyed a common code of noble behavior, eventually known as *chivalry* in many places, which emphasized pious, honorable, and generous behavior.

Between them, these two highest estates comprised a small minority of the overall population; in England, for example, the nobility itself never exceeded 1 percent of the population, and the church was not much larger.[2] This meant that the vast majority of the population was consigned to the Third Estate of the common people, whose responsibility was to provide the work that met the society's material needs. Because this was essentially a rural, agrarian economy, most of the commoners were **peasants**, or relatively unskilled rural agricultural workers, who had various legal and customary restrictions on their freedom.

This estate system offered limited social mobility, but there was some. Those born into the Third Estate could, in return for extraordinary military or other service, be knighted and join the nobility.[3] By the beginning of the High Middle Ages, the clergy were required to take a vow of celibacy, and so their numbers needed to be replenished from the two lower orders, with high positions in the clergy reserved for those born into the nobility. In some cases, peasants could acquire more freedom, a practice that became more common as the High Middle Ages went on. One important aspect of social change that occurred after the eleventh century was that the Third Estate became more varied. Individuals who possessed specialized skills became more numerous, and in the towns, the number of people engaged in commerce and more dependent on a money economy rose significantly.[4] Still, medieval estates represented a largely closed stratification system, where birth circumstances determined a person's opportunities.

On the one hand, the members of each estate were expected to contribute to the collective welfare, and the sacred medieval ethos emphasized mutual responsibility. On the other hand, the differences between estates were quite significant and there was much inequality in terms of wealth, power, and prestige. In the words of one renowned historian, that this was "a highly stratified society,

---

Power and Authority

In the political thought of the Enlightenment era, an important concern was a clarification of the sources of the authority of government. Then as now, many people used the terms power and authority as if they were the same thing. Although they are clearly related, they are not identical, and confusing them obscures the ways in which governments operate, as well as how they sometimes fail.

The sociologist Max Weber (1864–1920) analyzed this difference in a way that is quite useful to our understanding of legitimate and illegitimate governments today. Authority, according to Weber, is a person's right to be believed and obeyed. In its origin, this authority can be traditional (like the authority of a father or tribal leader or medieval king); it can be charismatic (like the authority of a religious leader with extraordinary appeal to followers); it can be due to expertise (like the authority of a doctor over a patient or of an engineer over a builder); or it can be rational-legal (like the authority of the elected leader of a liberal democracy or the appointed leader of a government agency). Rational-legal authority is the newest kind, and it requires its possessor to act within the clearly defined boundaries set by law. This is a kind of authority that emerged with Enlightenment political thought.

Power, on the other hand, is merely "the ability to realize one's will, even against resistance." In other words, it is the ability to make other people do things even if they don't want to. A ruler or official whose authority to give orders is accepted by the recipients of those orders has no need to use coercion. If the authority of the leader is regarded as legitimate by most people, then they feel obligated to obey the rules; the use of power is required only against rule-breakers, and its use is widely seen as legitimate. (How many people complain when a convicted murderer is sent to prison?) But if most people in a society do not accept the authority of their government as legitimate, then that government must rely on power alone to force adherence to its rules. Such a government or ruler is regarded as illegitimate; people do not necessarily feel that they *ought* to obey the rules, but they know that the power of government will be used against them if they disobey.

in which power was vested in a small group of people who controlled from above the activities of the great mass of country folk."[5] It says a great deal about the priorities of this society that the functions of the two elite estates were salvation and warfare, respectively, while workers of all types were accorded the lowest status.

The Church

As with most traditional societies, religion had an enormous impact on the daily lives, culture, politics, and even the economic life of medieval European civilization. Perhaps most significantly, European life was characterized by a prevalent spiritual **ethos** or set of common values. Christians absorbed a set of cultural norms that gave them values consistent with church doctrine, teaching them to respect and abide by the traditional Christian virtues of obedience, humility, piety, and generosity.

Christianity had begun as a persecuted sect in pagan Rome, but by 395 CE it had become the one and only official state religion in the empire. After the division of the empire into East and West during the fifth century, the Bishop of Rome emerged as the pope, or head of the church, and by then his authority extended over the numerous Christian communities that had been established in the Western part of the empire. This branch of "Western" Christianity gradually diverged in doctrine and organization from its cousin, the "Eastern Orthodox" Church based in Constantinople. Especially in the years prior to 1000 CE, but occasionally afterwards, the Western Church overcame threats to its unity and authority from a number of "heretical" movements.

From Rome, the pope presided over almost all of Western and central Europe, which was subdivided geographically into a series of increasingly smaller units of the secular administration under a decentralized system of cardinals, archbishops, and bishops. Under their authority, priests reached the masses through uniform services in individual churches, giving the diverse populations of Europe a consistent and remarkably powerful cultural unity. The church also had considerable legal and economic power, as well as enjoying a near monopoly on literacy. The parish priest, at the bottom of the church hierarchy, was often the only regular contact that most people had with the world outside their village, which meant that news of the larger world only reached most people through the filter of the church. However, although smaller villages invariably had a church, they often had no regular priest, and many European peasants only saw priests or other church officials on an irregular basis.[6]

The regular clergy also played an important role in European life. Even during the early medieval period, many monasteries played major economic and social roles in their regions, and the monks who lived there grew food, produced cloth, and provided skilled services such as education and medical care. The monasteries were also chiefly responsible for the preservation of written texts, as monks frequently devoted themselves to copying manuscripts of church and later classical learning. The "monastic ideal," moreover, provided medieval Europeans with a model of pious behavior and faith to emulate.[7]

It is difficult to overestimate the influence that the church had over the popular imagination. Most people were not only illiterate but seldom traveled outside the village of their birth.[8] The church taught them to accept their station in life and that persevering though their mortal troubles as obedient Christians was the only way to achieve everlasting salvation in heaven. Like many other traditional peoples in history, medieval Europeans absorbed a moral code that was conformist and resistant to change, and discouraged them from innovation and questioning authority.

The Feudal System

The major secular institution of northern medieval Europe was **feudalism**, the means by which the nobility exercised both land ownership and political authority. Its historical origin lay in the frequent chaos and warfare of the early medieval period, as military leaders played important roles as protectors and providers for their followers. By the middle of the eleventh century, feudalism had attained a fairly regular form in most parts of Western and central Europe, and had incorporated elements from both the Roman and Germanic traditions.[9]

As this system developed, it became customary for military leaders, after seizing a territory, to reward their chief allies and supporters by granting them what became known as **fiefs**, which were hereditary rights to control certain portions of this territory. In this arrangement, the role assigned to that of the grantor was the lord and the recipient was called a **vassal**. In turn, these vassals were permitted to subdivide some of the granted territory among their own supporters, who could do the same, and in this way, a hierarchy of noble landowners was created. All nobles except for kings, who occupied the top of the feudal hierarchy, were sworn to serve higher lords as their vassals. All nobles except for knights, who were usually landless warriors at the base of the feudal hierarchy, also had vassals, that is, other nobles who were in their service.

The lord/vassal relationship was based upon personal mutual obligations and was consecrated by the church. In return for their fiefs, vassals were typically required to provide military service for their lords when asked, and/or the payment of goods or money on a regular basis. In this way, kings and the higher nobility were able to create powerful systems of military supporters that could be called upon when needed. The authority of each nobleman extended to most matters that involved the people who lived on these lands, for whom he served as the political and legal authority.

Though it seems fairly straightforward in principle, in reality feudalism became rather complicated over time, which created numerous problems. Marriages and inheritances often led to situations of multiple obligations and conflicts of loyalty when nobles acquired various fiefs. Disobedience by vassals, or even mere personal enmity between vassals and lords, could and did create warfare. Especially as the High Middle Ages progressed, feudal rights frequently conflicted with attempts by kings to create more centralized authority, while the involvement of high church officials, who often became vassals and lords, created further complications.

In general, since land was the basis of both wealth and power in the Middle Ages, both lords and vassals had a vested interest in pursuing warfare as a means of social mobility.[10] Thus, while feudalism provided Europeans with a recognized means of landholding and political authority, it was, by its very nature, an unstable system.

The Manor

Much of the economy of the Middle Ages was based upon **manorialism**, a term that usually refers to largely self-sufficient localized agricultural system that organized the labor of the village community.[11] Manorial villages varied in size from several hundred to several thousand acres, and could contain anywhere from a dozen to a hundred peasant families. The manorial system subjected these peasants to the authority of their lord, who was generally a nobleman but sometimes an official of the First Estate.

Such peasants enjoyed varying levels of freedom. Many were **serfs**, whose legal status fell somewhere between that of a slave and that of a free laborer. They, and their descendents, were bound by traditional obligations to remain on the manor and work for the lord, who served as their legal authority. Serfs on a manor were required to work the lord's fields, and to perform other services, in exchange for protection and the right to farm a part of the manorial land. Slavery in the Middle Ages was also common, and in some places, free peasants worked the land without restriction, and occasionally even owned land themselves.

The manor provided most of the necessities of life. In addition to fields for growing grain, a manor would typically also have a mill, storage facilities, at least one well, grazing land for sheep or cattle, and a blacksmith's shop. Agricultural practice and technology were primitive and largely determined by tradition, and there were few years where a manor could provide more food than was required by its inhabitants. Far more often, the yields were insufficient, and the serfs went hungry. Two or more years of low harvests in succession could, and frequently did, result in starvation. Yet people on a manor had little choice but to persevere, in the hope that through "God's will," they would get through the year with enough to eat, while also escaping the constant scourges of warfare and disease.

Systemic Social Change in the Middle Ages

The relative stability of the high medieval period allowed for some evolution of Europe's economy, system of authority, and social stratification. This era was marked by gradual and steady change, both through diffusion from within and outside Europe, as well as internally generated change.

Much of the change was stimulated by increased agricultural productivity. A surplus of food was essential to support a workforce engaged in non-agricultural pursuits such as commerce and manufacturing, and from the 1100s onwards, changes in agricultural practices allowed European agricultural yields to expand. It seems that there was no single factor that was most crucial, but rather that a combination of small changes that reinforced each other, which included better metal tools, superior plows, the cultivation of more varied crops, and the use of fertilizers.[12] These resulted in the steadily expanding food supply that allowed economic diversification away from the manorial economy to take place.[13] Moreover, this rise in output coincided with an expanded availability of coinage, which was used not only for commerce but also for manorial and feudal dues. Logically enough, the ability to sell extra food gave landlords incentives to produce more, as well as leading inevitably toward the increased commercialization of the European economy in general.[14]

The most obvious beneficiaries of this economic change were the towns and their inhabitants, which had been of scarce significance in most parts of northern and Western Europe during the early Middle Ages. From the eleventh century onward, crossroads hamlets and small village market centers grew in both population and wealth. Within these towns, workers and merchants earned incomes in money, which they could use to pay wages, buy supplies, and expand their businesses. As merchants transported a wider variety of goods to sell in ever-expanding markets, town and regional specialization took place. By the end of the twelfth century, a process of **systemic social change**—a chain reaction of changes in one aspect of society that led to changes in other aspects—was underway, with increased business activity involving more and more parts of the population and reaching further and further afield.[15]

Thus, the growth of towns and a new sort of town-based culture to go along with it were key elements of the High Middle Ages.[16] The inhabitants of such towns were known as **bourgeoisie** (that is, "people of the walled town"). They were a diverse group of individuals that included skilled artisans, shopkeepers, merchants, and eventually, wealthy professional people and financiers. However, what they had in common was more important than their differences: all of the bourgeoisie were dependent on the growing money economy, and they occupied the positions that allowed it to operate. Although they were technically members of the Third Estate, the bourgeoisie did not fit into the conventional medieval estate system, being neither peasants nor nobles. Instead, they represented a new sort of medieval person, one that was new not just in terms of occupation and residence, but also in terms of outlook and values. The towns where they lived quickly developed their own laws and institutions, and continued to attract ambitious newcomers from the countryside. Within the protective walls of medieval towns, the bourgeoisie would be at the forefront of European social chance for centuries to come.

Soon, European merchants, workers, and officials were regularly journeying along roads, rivers, and even the open ocean. Advances in shipbuilding, tool-making, construction, and navigation made travel easier and safer. New business techniques such as insurance, accounting, and letters of credit—most of them introduced from the more urbanized and commercial parts of Italy—facilitated business transactions of larger and larger scope. By the end of the thirteenth century, European cargo ships were traveling back and forth between the Mediterranean, Atlantic Ocean, and the Baltic Sea, while overland trade—almost nonexistent in the tenth century—had become commonplace. The commercial

Image 4.1 The fortified town of Carcassonne, Southern France, built in the
thirteenth century

© JLImages/Alamy

networks linking towns throughout the continent injected energy into all areas of
European life, since they allowed for the exchange of not just goods and money,
but of ideas as well.

A steady rise in the power of centralized political structures accompanied the
growth of towns and the emergence of the bourgeoisie. Monarchies began to compete successfully for power with the church and the nobility, in their quests to
create more efficient and powerful governments that featured bureaucratic administrations and sizable royal armies.[17] During the High Middle Ages, struggles over
taxation and legal authority brought the kings of England and France, and the Holy
Roman emperor in Germany, into several bitter conflicts with popes. By the end of
this era, the papacy had been forced to make significant concessions, which damaged
its prestige and authority in the process. At the same time, kings took away much
of the independence of lesser and local nobles, often by force of arms. The nobility,
as a group, became more directly dependent—militarily, politically, and economically—on the monarchs who sat at the top of the feudal system, as the traditional
decentralization of the feudal system gave way to more cohesive and efficient political structures under the control of **national monarchies**, where local authority gave
way to a centralized authority in the person of the king or queen.[18]

In hindsight, it is perhaps unsurprising that kings and the bourgeoisie would
find common cause. The growth of towns benefited immensely from the stability

and order that powerful kingships could provide. In turn, towns could provide monarchs with many of the things they needed most: dependable sources of tax revenue, soldiers for their armies, and the skills and capital of the bourgeoisie. Increasingly, kings and princes in Germany, England, France, and the Low Countries granted royal charters to existing towns, making them independent from feudal control, and they even founded many new ones as an effective means of expanding their influence through their realms.

As the High Middle Ages progressed, many towns evolved into real cities, becoming centers of royal administration, commerce, early industry, and education. Even the church recognized the growing centrality of town life: religious orders founded the first European universities, which energized the culture even further. During the same period, the skylines of European towns were graced by the construction of the first Gothic cathedrals, which stood as impressive testaments to Europe's growing wealth, ingenuity, and vitality. While the countryside remained agricultural, isolated, and traditional, the towns and cities became commercial, cosmopolitan, and dynamic engines of social change.

A Traditional Society Begins to Change

After the fall of the Roman Empire, Europeans had achieved a precarious sort of stability through the establishment of the estate system, the unifying influence of the church, feudalism, and manorial agriculture. The structure of this society reflected its sacred ethos, which interpreted the world according to divinely inspired, orderly, hierarchical principles. It was a highly traditional culture, which encouraged individuals to accept the *status quo* and view their eternal salvation as more important than their material comforts. It is for this reason that, although life itself was often tenuous, Europeans viewed change suspiciously, and had few incentives to either question authority or to find new ways to improve the conditions of life.

With the arrival of the high medieval period, starting in about the middle of the eleventh century, an expansion of the food supply gradually reawakened the forces of social change in Europe, which affected economics, politics, social organization, and culture. This systemic change represented the beginning of a movement toward modernization, one which would take Western civilization in directions that no society in world history had ever gone before.

Notes

1 Clifford Backman, *The Worlds of Medieval Europe* (New York: Oxford University Press, 2003), 175–76.
2 Robert S. Hoyt and Stanley Chodorow, *Europe in the Middle Ages*, 3rd ed. (San Diego: Harcourt, Brace, Jovanovich, 1976), 228.
3 Marc Bloch, *Feudal Society*, vol. 2, trans. L. A. Manyon (Chicago: University of Chicago Press, 1961), 320–24
4 R. W. Southern, *The Making of the Middle Ages* (New Haven: Yale University Press, 1953), 115–17.
5 Georges Duby, *Rural Economy and Country Life in the Medieval West*, trans. Cynthia Postan (Columbia: University of South Carolina Press, 1968), 34.

6   Backman, *Worlds of Medieval Europe*, 162.
7   Southern, *The Making of the Middle Ages*, 156–60.
8   Duby. *Rural Economy and Country Life*, 113–22.
9   Hoyt, *Europe in the Middle Ages*, 212, 218; Backman, *The Worlds of Medieval Europe*, 176–81.
10 Hoyt, *Europe in the Middle Ages*, 225–27, 236–37.
11 Duby, *Rural Economy and Country Life*, 197–231.
12 Ibid., p. 65–111; Robert S. Lopez, *The Commercial Revolution of the Middle Ages, 950–1350* (New York: Cambridge University Press, 1976), 36–48.
13 Lopez, *The Commercial Revolution of the Middle Ages* 56.
14 Duby, *Rural Economy and Country Life*, 126–65.
15 Lopez, *The Commercial Revolution of the Middle Ages*, 48–60.
16 Hoyt, *Europe in the Middle Ages*, 263–71.
17 Backman, *The Worlds of Medieval Europe*, 283–96.
18 Hoyt, *Europe in the Middle Ages*, 406–13.

Suggested Readings

Backman, Clifford R. *The Worlds of Medieval Europe*. 3rd. ed. New York: Oxford University Press, 2014.

Bloch, Marc. *Feudal Society*. Vol. 2. Translated by. L. A. Manyon. Chicago: University of Chicago Press, 1961.

Cook, William R., and Ronald B. Herzman. *The Medieval Worldview*. 3rd ed. Oxford: Oxford University Press, 2011.

Duby, Georges. *Rural Economy and Country Life in the Medieval West*. Translated by Cynthia Postan. Columbia: University of South Carolina Press, 1968.

Holmes, George. *Oxford History of Medieval Europe*. Oxford: Oxford University Press, 2002.

Lopez, Robert S. *The Commercial Revolution of the Middle Ages, 950–1350*. New York: Cambridge University Press, 1976.

Southern, R.W. *The Making of the Middle Ages*. New Haven: Yale University Press, 1953.

5 The Late Middle Ages and the Transformation of Medieval Society

John McGrath

Key Terms

anomie, demographic, invisible hand, scholasticism, standard of living

During the High Middle Ages, most parts of Western Europe benefited from relative stability compared to the disruption and insecurity of the previous age of migrations and invasions. Between around 1050 and 1300, population grew steadily, creating a society that featured a quite distinctive and often sophisticated culture, with admirable accomplishments in every area of life.

Politically, the establishment of the first royal monarchies in France and England (in the tenth and eleventh centuries, respectively) provided both increasingly stable forms of rule and a sense of popular unity. This intensified in the thirteenth century, as Kings Edward I of England (r. 1272–1307) and Philip IV of France (r. 1285–1314) built on this base to create efficient political states that featured bureaucratic administrations and relatively consistent monetary systems and legal codes. Other parts of Western and central Europe, such as the Netherlands and the numerous German states that comprised the Holy Roman Empire, followed the lead of France and England and turned toward more rational and secular political systems of their own.

Even as armed conflicts between states persisted—often, as in the case of England and France, on the basis of conflicting feudal claims—the economy of Europe picked up momentum during the thirteenth century. Towns and cities grew rapidly to become centers of commerce and specialized manufacturing, becoming dependent upon overland, river, and maritime trade. The Crusades that had begun in the late eleventh century had enabled the Italian city-states of Venice and Genoa to emerge as commercial intermediaries that linked Europe to the larger Mediterranean world, while Italian financiers created the basic structures of capitalism (see following chapter). By the end of the century, large businesses such as banks, trading companies, and manufacturing concerns were spreading throughout the continent, featuring increasingly complex and efficient financial practices, often with investment and protection by royal governments.

In terms of culture, the unifying influence of the Church of Rome could be felt almost everywhere in Europe by the thirteenth century, aside from a few contested areas in Iberia and in the East. In order to actively fight heresy, spread the Gospel,

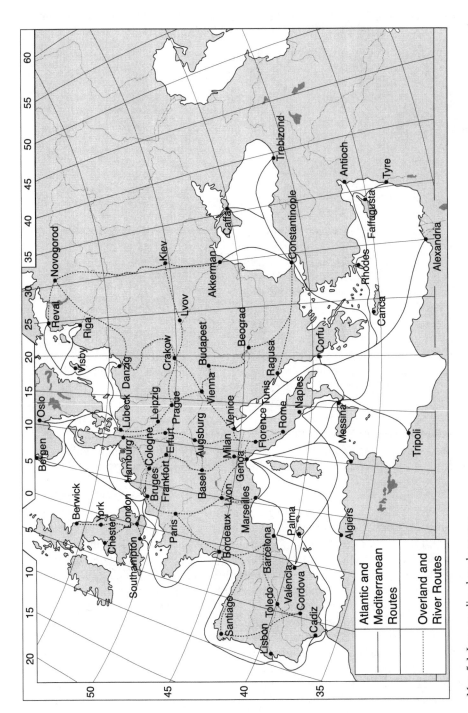

Map 5.1 Late medieval trade routes

Adapted from Wikimedia Commons Image

and help the poor, the papacy oversaw the foundation of two influential new orders of regular clergy, the Dominicans and Franciscans. These organizations were instrumental in the establishment of the first universities, which included programs of study in law and medicine, as literacy became, for the first time, accessible to the more privileged members of the rising bourgeoisie. At the same time, more regular cultural and trade contacts with the Middle East and North Africa had resulted in the rediscovery of much classical learning, such as the works of Aristotle and Plato, which encouraged European intellectuals to pursue increasingly practical and secular areas of thought.

The Beginnings of Decay

Because of these developments, high medieval Europe featured a vigorous society that had steady population growth, rising prosperity, and a certain amount of social mobility. Yet, as European society approached the fourteenth century, we can see some troubling signs. In fact, late thirteenth-century Europe was already experiencing an economic slowdown that can be traced to the fact that, by then, almost all available cropland, even marginal areas, was under cultivation, and the continued population growth could not be matched by an increase in food output.[1] Food shortages and rising grain prices translated into social problems for towns and cities that had become crowded with recent immigrants from the countryside, as crime and civil disorder increased. Meanwhile, the growing power of monarchs, princes, and town governments meant higher taxes and more autocratic rule. Such circumstances tempered the optimism of the age, as did the emergence of difficulties within the church, especially at the top of its hierarchy. During the last decade of the thirteenth century, the papacy was beset by scandal and internal disagreements. All of these situations set the stage for a sequence of crises that threatened the very survival of the European civilization that had taken root during the High Middle Ages.

The problems surrounding the papacy exploded right after the beginning of the century, in the biggest challenge to its authority that the church had yet faced as an institution. In France, the highly ambitious Philip IV contested both the church's legal authority and its ability to collect taxes within his kingdom. The culmination of an escalating series of confrontations between Philip and Pope Boniface VIII came in 1303, when the former dispatched a group of knights to Italy to capture and beat the elderly pope, who died a few weeks later after his release. Through additional intimidation, Philip's machinations assured the election of a Frenchman, Pope Clement V, as Boniface's successor, followed by the relocation of the seat of the church to the city of Avignon in southern France. While presiding in Avignon amid great wealth and splendor, Clement and his immediate successors remained under the watchful eye, and indirect control, of the French throne for more than seventy years. This was the beginning of what was known as the Avignon Papacy, or, as German religious reformer Martin Luther dubbed it, the "Babylonian Captivity" of the church.

Naturally, this did great damage to the prestige and influence of the papacy and the church in general. While the popes were "held hostage" in Avignon, other

European monarchs followed Philip's lead, and demanded a greater role in church affairs within their own realms, reducing both its legal authority and revenue stream. Ultimately, when the papacy finally returned to Rome, different coalitions of kings and princes backed the accession of rival popes, which resulted in the Great Schism of 1378, when two and later three rival claimants to the papacy emerged, each having been "elected" by a different group of cardinals. It would not be until 1417 that a single acknowledged pope would head the church. By then, the papacy had endured more than a century of conflict, which severely and permanently damaged its prestige and power, both politically and in terms of popular attitudes. The beginning of the Avignon Papacy started the fourteenth century on a note of crisis, and symbolized the victory of secular power over sacred power in European life.

Other troubles followed close on the heels of religious crisis. The existing economic and **demographic** situation set the stage for great problems during the second decade of the fourteenth century, when a series of cold and rainy summers led to crop failures and famine in many parts of Western Europe. For much of the Third Estate, mere hunger became outright starvation, both in the towns and in the countryside. Though the famines ended in 1322, they had caused profound social and economic damage. Economic expansion in the towns slowed or halted, profits and investment suffered, and all classes paid the price.

Not long afterwards, long-simmering tensions between the kingdoms of France and England finally erupted. Through inheritance and marriage, English kings had long held vast territories in western France, including some of the wealthiest areas of Europe, as fiefs. Legally, this meant that the English kings were vassals of the kings of France, which became a source of great resentment. This finally boiled over during the 1330s, when a crisis over the French royal succession allowed King Edward III of England to claim the French throne for himself, on the basis of earlier marriages between the French and English royal families. This provided a pretext for armed conflict, and the result was what is known today as the Hundred Years' War, which was fought intermittently until the mid-fifteenth century. This struggle was characterized primarily by large scale English raids into France that besieged cities and devastated the French countryside, and it drew in a variety of other European states as allies and as providers of mercenary forces.[2]

Meanwhile, the European intellectual world was also experiencing a period of turmoil and change.[3] Early in the fourteenth century, the Italian scholar Marsiglio of Padua attacked the authority of the pope in secular affairs, and encouraged others to criticize the church's role in politics. Shortly afterwards, the English scholar William of Ockham cast doubt on the established Catholic theological position of **scholasticism,** which presumed that God had created an orderly universe that could be understood through the application of human reason. Ockham seemed to question whether humans could ever truly understand the will of God, a profoundly disturbing shift that undermined his society's prevalent sacred ethos and ideology; all of a sudden, the perfect unity of Christendom seemed to be far less certain for a growing number of more freethinking Europeans.[4] The weakness of the papacy during its residence in Avignon made it difficult for the church to effectively defend itself against the new ideas expressed by Marsiglio, Ockham, and others. Instead, in response to its troubled financial straits, it had begun to institute a number of money-making schemes that damaged its reputation further. Indeed, all of these factors helped to further undermine the "Age of Faith" of the High Middle Ages, and by mid-century, the European worldview might be more accurately described as the "The Age of Skepticism."

The Black Death and Its Consequences

For all of these destabilizing factors, the worst was yet to come, and, in late 1347, it arrived with a horrifying suddenness that shook European civilization to its very foundation. This ultimate crisis—and one of the most significant developments in European history—was the arrival of the deadly epidemic known as the Black Death. Believed to be a flea-borne bacterial infection known as the bubonic plague, it was carried rapidly through Europe by rats, and infected a European population that lacked any natural immunity to it. Upon exposure, most human victims died within three days, covered in horrid putrefying boils. The plague traveled inexorably through county after county and town after town, leaving piles of corpses in its wake. In only three years, it killed as much as a third of Europe's population—and it recurred several more times in the next sixty years. Its repercussions would be felt for centuries.[5]

In the short run, the Black Death created mass panic and hysteria, made worse by the inability of either secular or religious authorities to understand either its causes or whether there was any remedy. To many, it seemed that the plague was the wrath of God visited upon a sinful populace, while others believed that it must be the work of Jews, foreigners, witches, or the devil himself. People barricaded themselves into cellars, burned down entire neighborhoods, and underwent bizarre rituals of religious purification in vain attempts to escape the scourge. Commerce came to a standstill, and rationality took a back seat to fear and hopelessness.

This sudden **demographic** catastrophe had critically important long-term economic effects, as well. The sudden removal of up to a third of the population necessarily had a massive impact on the operation of the economy, forcing the **invisible hand** of supply and demand to adjust to greatly altered circumstances. For one thing, with fewer mouths to feed, demand for food plummeted, and this meant a sharp decline in the prices of food, especially grain, in the marketplace. The result seems somewhat ironic in light of the magnitude of the catastrophe: simply put, most people had to devote less of their income to food, which made the survivors of the Black Death relatively wealthier than those who came before them.

Moreover, the reduced number of surviving peasants in the countryside found themselves, rather abruptly, less vulnerable to the power of their landlords. Rural landowners were forced to adapt to the fact that peasant labor was far scarcer, and to keep their serfs from fleeing into the towns, they had to begin paying them in wages and granting them more freedom and better living conditions. What this meant was the virtual demolition of the institution of serfdom in most parts of

Disease and History

In 1976, the historian William H. McNeill published an extraordinarily original work of history, in which he outlined the impact of infectious disease on the history of human societies. In *Plagues and Peoples*, he made a compelling case that many civilizations in the past, including Han China and the Roman Empire, were dramatically affected by diseases that had wide repercussions on economic, political, and cultural systems.[1] While many of McNeill's assertions of cause and effect were somewhat speculative, advances in science since that time have enabled later historians to follow up on this line of analysis, and better appreciate the role of disease on human affairs.

Differing susceptibility to diseases among different groups of people had a massive impact on such historical developments as the Atlantic slave trade, the rise and fall of Chinese dynasties, and the migrations of different groups of people. As evolutionary biologist Jared Diamond has explained, trade routes such as the Silk Road that have connected European, Middle Eastern, and Asian societies have also enabled the spread of germs, helping the people connected to it, directly and indirectly, to develop more resistance to many epidemic diseases.[2] Since McNeill's time, it has been firmly established that the introduction of such Old World diseases as smallpox, measles, and influenza killed far more Native American peoples than did European violence and cruelty.[3] But the impact of disease has not been entirely disastrous. Historians now widely recognize that the demographic impact of the Black Death in the fourteenth century had an immense influence on the process of European modernization, contributing in the long run to a more vibrant society.

Notes

1 William H. McNeill, *Plagues and Peoples*, (Chicago: University of Chicago Press, 1976).
2 Jared Diamond, *Guns, Germs, and Steel* (New York: Norton, 1999), especially pages 169–204.
3 Noble David Cook, *Born to Die: Disease and New World Conquest, 1492–1650*. (Cambridge: Cambridge University Press, 1998).

Western Europe.[6] The need to pay for labor had a further consequence: rural landowners—usually the church and the nobility—had to make their manors more commercially oriented and improve their efficiency. In many cases this meant a move toward more specialized and less labor-intensive activities, such as replacing grain cultivation with sheep raising, and the abandonment of the most marginal farmland. At the same time, there were also clear incentives to adopt labor saving technologies, such as improved plows and fertilizers. In all of these ways, the demographic crisis actually had long-term benefits that led to more efficiency and productivity in Western European agriculture.[7]

In part because of the breakdown of the traditional manor system, towns and cities recovered even more quickly from the Black Death than the countryside, even though they had suffered higher casualty rates because of their population densities. Rural survivors, enjoying fewer restrictions on their freedom, migrated in steady numbers to the towns, where employers had to offer higher wages to a smaller labor pool. Upon arrival, these new urban residents were able to enjoy an even higher real income than previous town dwellers, due to the decline in the cost of food and lowered demand for housing. And as was the case with rural landowners, business owners in the towns and cities also had incentives to invest in labor-saving technology, which, in the long run, played an important role in the development of new manufacturing techniques and more efficient transportation.[8] More generally, this influx of new people contributed to a breakdown of tradition and the diffusion of many new ideas of all sorts.

In this way, we can see that the Black Death dramatically transformed the economic equilibrium that characterized much of the High Middle Ages, by launching a sequence of social and economic changes that would have a huge long-term impact on the way that Western Europeans lived. The economy itself became more market driven, there was considerably heightened opportunity for the ambitious, and towns and cities became much more prominent in all areas of European life.

There was a significant shift of power, as well. The late medieval crises only intensified the efforts of national monarchies to centralize their power through the creation of royal bureaucracies, court systems, and armies that had begun during the High Middle Ages. Most kings and princes began to regard their noble vassals as obstacles to their power, and as a result, the landowning nobility, already hard hit by the disintegration of the manor system, was forced to accept more limited influence over the territories they held as fiefs.

Further reinforcing these changes were major shifts in cultural attitudes, especially in regard to views of authority. The church as an institution had already lost much of its authority as a result of the Avignon Papacy and Great Schism, and its actions and inactions in the wake of the plague only worsened its public image. When a terrified population turned to its traditional spiritual leaders for guidance and help, there was often none to be found, as the clergy was no more able to halt the destruction than was anyone else; neither lofty cardinals nor humble village priests could explain the nature of the catastrophe that had arrived. On the local level, Europeans openly questioned the practices of the church and its officials, and some people had begun to question some of the most fundamental Christian principles, such as papal infallibility and the practice of the sacraments.

Less acceptance of traditional authority and a crumbling of the traditional social structure had results that, in hindsight, seem entirely unsurprising. The most favored classes in society, with their authority and livelihoods threatened, tried without success to stem the tide of change. But when rural landlords attempted to restore their manorial power and privileges, this provoked fierce reaction from the peasantry, including broad-based uprisings in France during the late 1350s, related to the disruption of the Hundred Years' War, and in England during the 1380s. Meanwhile, urban workers in Florence responded to unemployment and pay reductions with a bloody uprising of their own in the 1370s, and violent outbreaks among workers and the urban poor took place in other cities and towns.[9] Even the fiercest backlashes by traditional authorities could not change the fact that the new realities created by the Black Death had made the less privileged orders unwilling and unable to revert back to the feudal and manorial *status quo*.

The Late Middle Ages and Rapid Social Change

An outstanding example of the shifts in society and culture can be seen in Geoffrey Chaucer's *Canterbury Tales*, written during the 1380s in the then-emerging English language. The various characters who take part in the pilgrimage to Canterbury represent a spectrum of new and more specialized occupations, both secular and religious: the Franklin, the Manciple, the Reeve, the Pardoner, the Wife of Bath, and many others are characters whose places in society would not have been possible in the previous century. But, more importantly, the attitudes and values of these characters had shifted dramatically from those of their high medieval forebears: their tales reveal them as selfish, vain, occasionally violent, and obsessed with death, lust, power, and wealth. Though Chaucer's social commentary is subtle and often understated, his characters seem almost a living embodiment of the corruption inherent in St. Augustine's *City of Man*.

Moreover, in the visual arts, there was a striking departure from the pious religiosity of paintings and sculpture. Gory crucifixion scenes and the grim and fantastic imagery of artists such as Hieronymous Bosch replaced the simple and rather static depictions of the Madonna and Child that dominated high medieval painting and sculpture. It was during this era that the Grim Reaper and the Four Horsemen of the Apocalypse made their first appearances, reflecting the preoccupation of Europeans with suffering and death.[10]

In both the literary and artistic expression of the late Middle Ages, one can see how, just a few decades into the plague era, the Christian Paternalistic Ethic was, if not completely dead, at least mortally wounded. Social change had been rapid and seemingly out of control in a society whose ethos had stressed conformity. The traditional pillars of high medieval society, feudalism and manorialism, were at the point of extinction. Not only had ambitious monarchs curtailed the power of the church as an institution, but the latter's evident impotence during the Black Death severely discredited it as a moral guide for many people of all classes.

It is not surprising, then, that such profound change within a traditional society spawned irrational and unusual cultural reactions. Late medieval Europeans became desperate to find answers to their myriad problems, turning to new and foreign ideas, such as religious cults, magic, and witchcraft. Meanwhile, kings, local officials, the remnants of church authority, and even just disorganized mobs fought back against such perceived threats to the moral order, resulting in widespread persecutions of "heresies" and disobedience of all sorts. It is no exaggeration to describe the late Middle Ages as an era dominated by *anomie* and its predictably unfortunate social consequences.

The dawn of the fifteenth century brought little relief, and perhaps its most outstanding feature was widespread, often savage, warfare. The Hundred Years' War continued its bloody course, featuring larger and larger armies. In central Europe, a combination of religious dissent and incipient Bohemian nationalism led to the vicious Hussite Wars, originally directed against the political and religious authority of the Holy Roman Empire, but quickly spiraling out of control. To the east, the Muslim Ottoman Turks expanded through the Balkans, then seized the city of Constantinople in 1453 and put an end to the Orthodox Christian Byzantine Empire; for the next two centuries, the Turks remained a genuine and constant threat to sweep further west. In Italy, even as the Renaissance reached its zenith, the city-states were victimized by foreign invasion and civil strife, creating the problems that Niccolò Macchiavelli implored his prince to overcome through the use of decisive statecraft. However, even Machiavelli's ideas were not enough, and Italy's worsening instability caused its economic and cultural decline during the sixteenth century.

As these and smaller conflicts took place, the military role of mounted knights declined in favor of large armies that employed increasingly destructive weaponry, such as the artillery that made its first European appearances in the late fourteenth century. As the nobility's traditional role of military leadership became less and less relevant, the key to success on the battlefield increasingly depended upon infantry, and this in turn relied upon the ability of monarchs to tax their subjects so that they could pay for, and equip, huge forces of commoners, often of the mercenary variety. The creation of larger armies, possessing more deadly technology and directed by ruthlessly ambitious monarchs, propelled fifteenth-century European states toward violence on a far larger and more frightening scale than anything experienced in the high medieval period.[11]

Changing Times and Changing Fortunes

With all of its problems, one can see the late medieval period as a transitional era, as Western Europe began to move toward a tentative new sort of equilibrium. The two traditional elite estates of the high medieval period—the church and the feudal nobility—faced insuperable economic, political, and social challenges that cost them their positions at the top of the social stratification system. The sacred ethos that supported their privileges was in retreat, as self-interest became more of a social norm for an increasingly diverse population.

Meanwhile, other groups were able to adapt better to the challenges of the fourteenth century and were actually able to improve their lot. The towns recovered both their populations and their vitality within a couple of generations, and their increasingly diverse populations started to enjoy a higher **standard of living,** a surprising level of personal liberty, and real social mobility. National monarchies centralized and rationalized their financial, legal, and administrative systems and expanded their power and authority. Even rural peasants were largely freed from the onerous restrictions of serfdom, and no longer inhabited a universe of rigid conformity. By the age of Machiavelli and Luther in the early sixteenth century, Europeans were not yet truly "modern," but the crises of the late Middle Ages had set the bow of their ship firmly in that direction. Though they would encounter contrary winds and rough seas during the coming centuries, by then, they were irrevocably committed to a destination.

Notes

1 Worthwhile discussions of the problems of this era can be found in Clifford R. Backman, *The Worlds of Medieval Europe* (New York: Oxford University Press, 2003), 369–94 and also John Kelly, *The Great Mortality* (New York: HarperCollins, 2005), 53–72.

2 The standard and most accessible account of this conflict is Christopher Allmand, *The Hundred Years War: England and France at War c.1300–c.1450* (Cambridge: Cambridge University Press 1988).

3 On the intellectual and religious crises of this age, see Charles B. Schmitt and Quentin Skinner, eds. *The Cambridge History of Renaissance Philosophy* (Cambridge: Cambridge University Press, 1988), 396–409, 474–78; also, Backman, *Worlds of Medieval Europe*, 388–90.

4 Schmitt and Skinner, *Renaissance Philosophy*, 474–78; Backman, *Worlds of Medieval Europe*, 388–90.

5 Among others, two excellent reasonably concise histories of the impact of the Black Death are Kelly, *The Great Mortality*, and Robert S. Gottfried, *The Black Death* (New York: Free Press, 1983).

6 This did not happen to an appreciable extent in most of central and eastern Europe, where manorial restrictions were often increased on peasants; this is widely attributed as a critical difference in the subsequent social development of Western Europe compared to eastern Europe. Gottfried, *Black Death*, 137.

7 Kelly, *Great Mortality*, 45–6; David Herlihy and Samuel K. Cohn, Jr. *The Black Death and the Transformation of the West* (Cambridge: Harvard University Press, 1997), 49–50.

8 Herlihy and Cohn, *Black Death*, 49–53.

9 Gottfried, *Black Death*, 98–103; Backman, *Worlds of Medieval Europe*, 379–80.

10 Gottfried, *Black Death*, 89–93.

11 Backman, *Worlds of Medieval Europe*, 383–87.

Suggested Readings

Allmand, Christopher. *The Hundred Years War: England and France at War c.1300–c.1450*. Cambridge: Cambridge University Press, 1988.

Campbell, Bruce. *The Great Transition: Climate, Disease, and Society in the Late Medieval World*. Cambridge: Cambridge University Press, 2016.

Gottfried, Robert S. *The Black Death*. New York: Free Press, 1983.

Herlihy, David, and Samuel K. Cohn, Jr. *The Black Death and the Transformation of Europe*. Cambridge: Harvard University Press, 1997.

Kelly, John. *The Great Mortality*. New York: HarperCollins, 2005.

6   The Italian Renaissance

Kathleen Callanan Martin and
John McGrath

Key Terms

Christian humanism, civic humanism, communes, humanism, printing press

As noted previously, the experience of the Italian peninsula during the Middle
Ages had differed from that of the classic medieval society of the north. While the
Roman Empire stagnated during the several hundred years after the time of
St. Augustine, its subject provinces outside of Italy lost much of their regular
contact with Rome, and as a result, these regions tended to become politically
independent and culturally disconnected from Roman culture. However, this was
much less true in Italy, where there was more cultural, economic, and political
continuity, and where many Roman cities and towns survived and even prospered
during the early Middle Ages. Despite the instability caused by invasions of
Vikings, Muslims, Huns, and Lombards, among other groups, the trade links
between the Italian peninsula and other parts of the Mediterranean world were
never completely severed, and Italian towns carried on semi-regular trade with
Greece and the Byzantine Empire, the Middle East, and North Africa. During the
early Middle Ages, though they were relatively poor compared to their trading
partners, these towns were able to maintain a commercially based economy with
a significant degree of regional and labor specialization. This was primarily true
only in the northern and central parts of the peninsula, since during the Middle
Ages and even afterwards, feudal states outside of Italy controlled Southern Italy
and Sicily, and these areas remained more rural and less developed than the north.

Medieval Italian City-States

Thus, by the arrival of the High Middle Ages around 1000 CE, towns remained
the foundation of northern Italian life, and some of them had populations in the
thousands of residents. For the most part, they developed similar political
structures, notably councils known as **communes**, that were composed of the
most prosperous and illustrious families. These families were (or became) landholding nobility, but this was a type of nobility unknown in the rest of Europe.
Though such people frequently possessed large properties in the countryside, they

usually lived in the towns, which allowed them to pursue livelihoods based on commerce, manufacturing, and rental incomes. Also, a greater proportion of the common people lived in towns, and they relied on urban occupations such as skilled and semiskilled crafts that paid them wages. These towns enjoyed a monetary economy, where wealth was a significant status factor, which offered opportunities for social advancement. As the medieval era progressed, the towns and their rural hinterlands tended to consolidate, becoming larger and fewer, and evolved into a few dozen "city-states" by the onset of the Renaissance in the mid-fourteenth century.[1]

In general, the High Middle Ages brought prosperity to Italy, especially after the beginning of the Crusades to the Holy Land in the late eleventh century. These Crusades stimulated Italian overseas trade through the establishment of commercial outposts in the relatively prosperous Near East. In particular, the twelfth century saw the rise of two powerful Italian maritime states, Venice and Genoa. During the High Middle Ages, these two rivals created intricate trade networks throughout the Mediterranean world, which included permanent Venetian and Genoese merchant colonies as far away as Morocco, Tunis, Alexandria, Syria, Constantinople, and the shores of the Black Sea. Trade in goods flowed in both directions, as these Italian commercial empires served as the critical intermediaries between the economies of northern and Western Europe, on the one hand, and the markets of the Byzantine and Islamic worlds, on the other. Italian cities themselves began to specialize in the manufacture of luxury textiles, including silk, that were much in demand elsewhere, and the merchant classes, in particular, experienced rising levels of wealth, prestige, and political power.

One critical development during the Middle Ages was that Venice and Genoa, later joined by other Italian states such as Florence and Milan, were responsible for the birth of the earliest forms of European capitalism. To promote both maritime and overseas commerce with Europe and the Mediterranean world, their merchants—who were often nobles—came up with a number of important innovations. They developed sophisticated accounting and financial methods that facilitated trade and investment by enabling the creation of trading companies, banks, maritime insurance, and stock exchanges, which allowed the Italian city-states to thrive during the High Middle Ages. As huge Italian financial and manufacturing concerns, such as the Medici and Bardi banks, began to invest in businesses of all sorts, diversify their operations, and amass tremendous amounts of investment capital, the Augustinian restraint on the accumulation of wealth steadily evaporated.[2]

Within these city-states, an Italian culture emerged that was quite distinct from that of the more rural and feudal north of Europe, as well as from the southern regions of Italy. Politically, there was a tradition of involvement in political affairs by various interest groups, including craft guilds and merchants' associations. The social and economic system gave incentives for urban residents of different ranks to acquire education, skills, and capital, which allowed social mobility and the creation of a more competitive and dynamic atmosphere. The reliance on foreign trade, moreover, resulted in a considerable amount of cultural diffusion, and the

Capitalism

Capitalism is an economic system that relies on private investment into economic enterprises for the purpose of achieving a profit in the future. It relies upon a legal recognition of private property, over which the investor can make free decisions about buying and selling.

Karl Marx's *Capital* made a distinction between the economic roles of workers and investors in a capitalist economy. Workers exchange their labor for wages, which they can then use to purchase the necessities of life, such as food and shelter. In contrast, investors use their existing capital, acquired by previous profits, to purchase goods, which could then be resold for a profit. Thus, instead of receiving money as payment for work, they used money to create more money, without actually creating anything material through labor.

Modern capitalism, featuring large businesses, complex technology, and an economy of scale, relies heavily on capital investment for economic growth. Medieval and Renaissance Italians developed new sorts of business practices and institutions that greatly facilitated capital investment, such as banking, accounting, stock exchanges, credit, and insurance, all of which continue to play a central role in the operation of today's global economy. During the early modern and modern eras, these elements promoted both economic growth and increasing economic complexity, while making the welfare of each individual increasingly dependent upon the performance of the larger capitalist economy.

populations of the Italian city-states became relatively tolerant of new ideas and even other religions. At the same time, the people in these city-states also developed strong self-identities and fierce senses of civic pride.

Italians were hardly immune to the crises of the fourteenth century, such as the Avignon Papacy, the economic slowdowns starting in the 1290s, and the Black Death (the last arriving in Italy via a Genoese merchant vessel coming from the Black Sea in 1347). However, these various problems, collectively, helped move the Italian city-states in the direction of modernity. The relatively rapid repopulation of the larger Italian cities after the Black Death brought new blood and new ideas into these environments. Meanwhile, as declining food prices raised the standard of living, the relative shortage of labor contributed to both higher wages and innovations in labor saving technology. This is not to imply that the problems of this era had no negative effects, but it is clear that the vast social changes of this troubled period disrupted traditional ways and forced Europeans, in Italy and elsewhere, to consider new practices and outlooks that were more appropriate for a changing world.[3] In the fertile soil of Italian society this ushered in what we now refer to as "The Italian Renaissance," beginning in the middle of the fourteenth century.

Renaissance Humanism: The Foundation of a New Ethos

Humanism, a defining element of the Renaissance, was both an educational approach and an intellectual outlook. The Italian Renaissance is often considered to have started during the middle of the fourteenth century with the career of Francesco Petrarch, who is also regarded as the first major humanist. Petrarch was a scholar who devoted his studies to classical literature and philosophy, especially the intellectual inheritances of the Romans, and his writing included histories and poetry, written in both classical Latin and the developing Italian vernacular language. He and contemporary early humanists emphasized the interconnectedness of all branches of knowledge, and revamped the educational system in a conscious attempt to produce worldly, socially aware leaders for their society.

As opposed to the traditional medieval view of life on earth as full of trials and tribulations, humanism came to recognize and celebrate the value of human existence and promote an appreciation of the surrounding natural world. However, humanists were not anti-religious; they tried to blend the secular and rational approach of classical writers with the positive, virtuous aspects of Christianity. With the rediscovery of classical learning, Renaissance scholars and artists felt that they had not one but two—largely compatible—approaches with which to understand their world, and this mixture came to typify the overall emphasis of the Italian Renaissance.[4]

By the 1400s (referred to by contemporaries as the *quattrocento*), humanism had spread to become an essential part of the Italian ethos, especially among the higher ranks of society. It was also during this century that the wealthy city-state of Florence emerged as the leading center of Renaissance culture. Florence had a long tradition of political republicanism, and the humanistic outlook began to dominate its civic life as well as that of other thriving Renaissance capitals such as Milan, Ferrara, Mantua, Venice, Padua, and Rome. Much of the reason for this was the active encouragement of the leading families who themselves had enjoyed humanistic educations; high nobles and wealthy merchants alike were determined to give their city-states glorious reputations as centers of cultural achievement. Encouraging people to take pride in their families and communities, leaders such as the Medici sponsored public festivals that featured parades, artistic performances, and tournaments. In Florence and elsewhere in Italy, humanism brought a new, more optimistic view of life that was absorbed by all classes. The connection between the flourishing humanistic outlook and this active and celebratory approach to public affairs is often referred to as **civic humanism**.

It was in the visual arts, however, that the qualities of humanism found their strongest expression. Both leading families and government bodies made it a priority to beautify their cities through the active patronage of Renaissance artists and architects. In particular, painting, sculpture, and architecture abandoned the somber tones of medieval artistic styles, and began to innovate and experiment with new techniques and methods, that frequently blended Christian and classical themes together. City-states competed among themselves to attract the most creative artists of all sorts, generously compensating them for creating dazzling art that glorified the wealth and sophistication of the city-states. For the first time since the classical age, "artists" attained a prestige and fame that carried them above the status of mere "artisans" or craftspeople, and elevated them into the elite ranks of society.[5]

The Medici Family: Wealth, Power, and Prestige in the Florentine Republic

Perhaps no family better represents the Italian Renaissance than the Medici, who rose from relatively humble merchants to become the dominant force in Florentine politics and European banking. Cosimo de Medici (1389–1464) inherited a prosperous family business that had already moved beyond trade to money lending, which still violated Church laws against the charging of interest but could be practiced discreetly with the help of various polite fictions about the nature of the transaction. Under Cosimo's leadership the Medici Bank became the largest in Europe (and probably the largest which had ever existed up to that time), with branches in most large Italian cities as well as in places like London, Cologne, Geneva, and Antwerp among many others. Their banking system not only advanced credit when it was needed for commercial or government purposes but also greatly facilitated international trade, since a properly executed note from a Medici representative in London, for example, could be redeemed at any other outpost of the Medici banking empire. The size and international reach of the Medici Bank put it in the perfect position to achieve the greatest prize of all when the Medici became the pope's bankers in 1420. One observer has commented that this made them "not only the most successful commercial enterprise in Italy, but the most profitable family business in the whole of Europe."[6]

Cosimo used this financial power shrewdly. He made astonishing amounts of money, and he also made sure that powerful men from whom he might one day need a favor were in his debt. He used his wealth to ensure that he would always have more influence than anyone else on the republican Florentine government, using any means necessary including well-placed loans, outright bribes, and public popularity cultivated through generous gifts to religious institutions and public charities. A learned man educated in the humanist tradition, Cosimo always preferred to exercise his power discreetly and remain in the shadows.

Not so his grandson Lorenzo (1449–1492), known to history (and even in his own time) as Lorenzo the Magnificent. Lorenzo was less interested in banking than his grandfather and less reticent about flaunting his power and wealth. A scholar, accomplished poet, and art connoisseur, he enlarged the family collections at great expense and gained a glorious reputation as a patron of artists and scholars. He ensured his family's position by arranging advantageous marriages for his children and other relatives and ensuring that several family members become cardinals. (His son Giovanni, a cardinal at sixteen, became Pope Leo X, the adversary of Martin Luther. His nephew Giulio later became Pope Clement VII.) All of this cost a great deal of money, and Lorenzo left the family bank poorer than he had found it. But he definitely found the glory he sought.

A list of the artists who received major commissions from the Medici family or were supported by them as pensioners reads like a "Who's Who" of Renaissance art: Donatello, Fra Lippo Lippi, Fra Angelico, Botticelli, Michelangelo, Leonardo da Vinci, and Raphael. Members of the Medici family supported the work of both Copernicus and Galileo, as well as commissioning many translations of classical literature. They built a magnificent library in Florence to house one of the best manuscript collections in the world, making it available to scholars from all nations. The Medici also exemplify the ceaseless power struggles of the era, involved as they were as perpetrators or victims of conspiracies, assassinations, conflict with the papacy, shifting international alliances, and numerous wars among the Italian city-states. This was the world described so evocatively by Machiavelli in *The Prince*.

Machiavelli: Realism and Power

Nobody has ever written about the exercise of power with fewer illusions than Niccolò Machiavelli (1469–1527), who served the Florentine Republic as an efficient functionary and as an able ambassador. In his lifetime Italy saw little peace. The city-states sought to enlarge their territories at each other's expense, while riots and factions disturbed their internal governments as well. (In 1478, for example, a conspiracy of families opposed to the Medici attempted to assassinate Lorenzo de Medici and his brother Giuliano while they attended church services in the cathedral; since they failed to kill Lorenzo, weeks of rioting and bloody repercussions ensued. This incident was far from unusual.) France, Spain, the Holy Roman emperor, and the papacy competed for supremacy on the Italian peninsula, while states like Florence formed ever-shifting alliances with each other and with the major players in this drama. Pope Julius II himself led his armies into battle on some occasions, determined to ensure the independence of the Papal States from outside interference. War is never pleasant, but these wars, fought primarily by mercenary armies paid for in part by looting, brought with them enormous devastation and misery.

Machiavelli was proud of the Florentine Republic and regarded republican government as best in every way. But he was not sentimental about it; his political analysis takes a clear look at the ways in which popular rule has been subverted or defeated, cataloging the disadvantages, as well as the advantages, of the republican form of government. Machiavelli was concerned, not with how power should be exercised, but with how it is exercised—how it is gained, how it is kept, how it is lost. His survey of historical examples has been called amoral and unprincipled; in a sense, it is. When, in *The Prince*, he counsels that a ruler probably should not be virtuous but should take care to look virtuous, he could not possibly be taking a more different view from that of St. Augustine. But in his own lifetime he could see all around him the disastrous results of ineffective government; this prompted him to the view that good policy must be the result of studying, not the Bible, but history. It is not for nothing that he is called the father of political science.

"The most relentlessly curious man in history": Leonardo da Vinci

Involved in every aspect of the life of the Renaissance was the man one expert on the period has called "the most relentlessly curious man in history."[7] Leonardo da Vinci (1452–1519) was prominent as an artist, a scientist, an inventor, and a civil engineer. Not only the Medici but many of the great patrons of the era commissioned works of art from Leonardo. City governments sought his help in designing stronger fortresses to protect their cities, or better weapons to breach the defenses of their opponents. His imagination was teeming with inventions, some of which could never have worked and some of which were quite practical. Leonardo was never content to do things in the usual way if he could imagine a better one, and the results were sometimes unfortunate. His experiments in new formulas for paints made some of his loveliest murals begin to fade prematurely; *The Last Supper*, for example, has been a conservator's nightmare ever since it was painted. But his refusal to be satisfied with what was already known pushed him to expand the limits of both knowledge and imagination. Risking serious legal consequences, he performed dissections on human cadavers and recorded his findings in a series of breathtaking anatomical drawings that can still impress in the era of electron microscopy. He saw no reason why man might not someday fly, and designed a series of machines he believed could make that possible. A true humanist in every sense, Leonardo truly believed that nothing was beyond man's competence if he could imagine it.

The Renaissance Spreads North

During the 1400s, what is sometimes called the "Northern Renaissance" started to take hold in European areas outside Italy, including Germany, the Netherlands, France, England, and Spain. In these places, because of both sociocultural differences and the later date, the Renaissance had a different flavor than it had in Italy. To begin with, these parts of Europe were more rural and agricultural, and feudalism was more prevalent in political systems. As noted elsewhere, the late medieval crises had damaged both manorial agriculture and the feudal system, while the locus of the power and cultural life swung to the towns, which soon recovered to experience relative prosperity and dynamism. During the course of the fifteenth century, towns such as Frankfurt, Lyon, Ghent, and London became economically specialized and reliant upon trade, and within their fortified walls, an educated class of bourgeoisie was starting to enjoy a higher standard of living than they ever had before.

But it was not until the mid to late fifteenth century that cultural diffusion carried the outlooks and attitudes of humanism from the Italian city-states into the towns of the northern parts of Europe, and by that time, certain important elements were in place that Italy had been lacking. One was the beginning of oceanic trade and exploration to Africa, Asia, and the Americas, which was causing Europeans to rethink their place in the world, both in figurative and literal senses. Another was that the late fifteenth century saw the invention of the **printing**

press, which made possible, for the first time, an economically feasible means of producing printed literature, on a wide range of subjects, for a growing literate population in the towns.

Perhaps most significantly, many communities in the north possessed a high degree of popular piety, which, somewhat ironically, coexisted with widespread anticlericalism. While the vast wealth of the Catholic Church had provoked resentment in many places, at the same time, the traumas and rapid change of the preceding centuries had left a spiritual void. Thus, when humanistic thinking arrived in the north from Italy during the fifteenth century and afterwards, it pushed northern intellectual life in a somewhat different direction. While humanism in both Italy and the north stressed open-mindedness and the use of reason, many educated northerners also became determined to reform the church toward what they believed were simpler, more direct forms of worship that they believed to be more consistent with early Christianity.

One of the defining elements of the Northern Renaissance, then, was an intellectual movement known as **Christian humanism**. By the sixteenth century, scholars such as Erasmus of Rotterdam and Thomas More in England were publishing works for the reading public, translated into many different languages, that both directly and indirectly criticized the practices of the Church. Both Erasmus and More, as well as many others in France, Switzerland, Spain, Germany, and elsewhere, urged their readers to practice a more ethical, less hypocritical brand of Christianity modeled on New Testament virtues of kindness, peace, tolerance, and mutual respect. Ultimately, this development set the stage for the Protestant Reformation during the sixteenth century.

The Northern Renaissance also saw an artistic and literary flowering, though, again, one that had a rather different tone than the Italian masters. Artists such as Albrecht Dürer, Matthias Grünewald, and Hieronymous Bosch created gruesome, violent, apocalyptic images, while others like Peter Brueghel the Elder and Jan van Eyck captured the essence of everyday life in the dynamic towns and cities of Europe. In France, Spain, and England, writers such as François Rabelais, Michel de Montaigne, Miguel de Cervantes, and William Shakespeare experimented with new forms of literature and are regarded as pioneers of the Northern Renaissance.

A New Ethos

The Italian Renaissance was a watershed in European history, because, for the first time in centuries, a significant number of people were able to cast off the conformist, traditional, religiously based ethos of their medieval inheritance. Sparked by the dramatic social changes of the fourteenth century, the educated elites in Italian city-states pioneered an intellectual approach that stressed, simultaneously, both a look back at the classical heritage and also a willingness to experiment, and this outlook quickly found expression in the monumental accomplishments in the visual arts.

As the Renaissance evolved during the *quattrocento*, and later spread to the northern parts of Europe, its new values influenced the outlooks and lives of an increasing number of people, and the Renaissance viewpoint affected the very ethos of the society. In contrast to the sacred, somewhat fatalistic outlook of traditional medieval society, Renaissance Europeans adopted a strikingly less passive view of the purpose of human life, one that contained new, mutually reinforcing elements. People during the Renaissance became not only willing but even eager to solve their problems, and began to use reason and practical thinking to do so. While there was undoubtedly a strong secular component to this attitude, it was not anti-religious; it would be more accurate to say that this secular view added to and enhanced the previously sacred perspective on human life and its possibilities. This meant, in practice, more freedom and innovation, as first expressed in the ideas and creations of Renaissance scholars, writers, and artists.

The Renaissance also radically transformed Europeans' sense of where they stood in history. Increasingly, they saw themselves as standing on the threshold of a "rebirth" that would not only recapture the glory of the classical past, but might even exceed it by applying both Christian virtues and the new attitude of innovation and experimentation. No longer preoccupied with sin and damnation, people in the Renaissance expressed considerable optimism about human capabilities—and about the future. This, arguably, was its most enduring legacy.

Though the literary and artistic creations of this age are nothing less than extraordinary, one should not necessarily conclude that the Renaissance represented some sort of a "Golden Age." Most people, even in prosperous and dynamic cities like Florence and Antwerp, were burdened as they had always been with the challenges of making a living and providing for their basic needs. Moreover, one must recognize that the changes taking place in European society were both products of, and contributors to, an era of considerable disorder and instability that was giving way to political despotism even during the *quattrocento*. Even so, the accomplishments of this age set the foundation for the massive and wide-ranging changes that would take place later. In subsequent centuries, as the Reformation, Scientific Revolution, and Enlightenment unfolded, each affected more and more Europeans and brought about an increased level of material change. Thus, although the Renaissance was largely limited in its scope to the intellectual and artistic worlds, it established a critical foundation for the modernization of European society.

Notes

1 On the evolution of Italian city states, see Daniel Waley, *The Italian City Republics*, 3rd ed (New York: Longman, 1988), especially 32–87.
2 George Holmes, *The Oxford History of Medieval Europe* (London: Oxford University Press, 1988), 229–235; Robert S. Lopez, *The Commercial Revolution of the Middle Ages, 950–1350* (New York: Cambridge University Press, 1976), 84–113.
3 A concise summary of the long-term transformations brought about by the Black Death can be found in Robert S. Gottfried, *The Black Death* (New York: Free Press, 1983), 129–60.
4 A useful explanation of humanism can be found in Jennifer Speake and Thomas Bergin, *Encyclopedia of the Renaissance and Reformation*, rev. ed. (New York: Facts on File, 2004), 246–247; also, De Lamar Jensen, *Renaissance Europe: Age of Recovery and Reconciliation*, 2nd ed. (Lexington, MA: Heath, 1982), 121–22.

5 Roger Osborne, *Civilization: A New History of the Western World* (New York: Pegasus, 2006), 211–12.
6 Christopher Hibbert, *The House of Medici: Its Rise and Fall* (New York: Harper Perennial, 1974), 37.
7 Kenneth Clark, *Civilisation: A Personal View.* (New York: Harper & Row, 1969).

Suggested Readings

Caferro, William, ed. *The Routledge History of the Renaissance.* Oxford and New York: Routledge, 2017.

Clark, Kenneth. *Civilisation: A Personal View.* New York: Harper & Row, 1969.

Gottfried, Robert S. *The Black Death.* New York: Free Press, 1983.

Hibbert, Christopher. *The House of Medici: Its Rise and Fall.* New York: Harper Perennial, 1974.

Holmes, George. *The Oxford History of Medieval Europe.* London: Oxford University Press, 1988.

Jardine, Lisa, *Worldly Goods: A New History of the Renaissance.* New York: Norton, 1996.

Jensen, De Lamar. *Renaissance Europe: Age of Recovery and Reconciliation.* 2nd ed. Lexington, MA: Heath, 1982.

Lopez, Robert S. *The Commercial Revolution of the Middle Ages, 950–1350.* New York: Cambridge University Press, 1976.

Najemy, John N. *Italy in the Age of the Renaissance, 1300–1550.* London: Oxford University Press, 2005.

Osborne, Roger. *Civilization: A New History of the Western World.* New York: Pegasus, 2006.

Speake, Jennifer and Thomas B. Bergin, eds. *Encyclopedia of the Renaissance and Reformation.* revised ed. New York: Facts on File, 2004.

Waley, Daniel. *The Italian City Republics.* 3rd ed. New York: Longman, 1988.

7 The Reformation

Susan Hagood Lee

Key Terms

corruption, egalitarianism, excommunication, indulgences, Inquisition, nationalism, pluralism, simony, *sola fide*, *sola scriptura*, technological innovation, theocracy

European society underwent profound change in the sixteenth century as charismatic leaders challenged the legitimacy of prevailing authority. Religious reformers proposed a new **egalitarianism** based on the idea that all are equal before God. If their preaching had been confined to a small audience—the local monastery or parish church—their views might have been snuffed out and forgotten. However, literacy had expanded greatly in the late Middle Ages due to the demands of urban commerce for educated employees. Technological innovation had reduced the cost of printing, making books, pamphlets, and other printed material readily available. With this new affordable medium, the message of religious reform spread rapidly across Europe, thanks to enterprising printers and literate consumers. Rising nationalism and the corruption of church officials threw more fuel on the religious bonfire. With these ideological, technical, economic, and social changes, many responded with heartfelt fervor to the movement that came to be called the Protestant Reformation.

The prevailing religious authority that the reformers challenged was the powerful Church of Rome. The church provided valuable social cohesion after the fall of the Roman Empire, and believers across Europe looked to the authority of the pope for guidance in daily life, marriage, war, peace, and eternal salvation. During the late Middle Ages, however, the institution entered a period of crisis that left it vulnerable to challenge. Starting in the early fourteenth century, the scandals of the Avignon Papacy and the Great Schism called into question the very legitimacy of the Church. **Corruption** was widespread, with religious officials looking to their own enrichment rather than the benefit of their flock. Cardinals and even popes took mistresses and placed their children in high church office. In the corrupt practice of **simony**, the wealthy could buy bishoprics for family members without regard to qualification or religious devotion. In another corrupt practice known as **pluralism**, some bishops held several positions at once, earning income

Protestantism

The term "Protestant" originated in a dispute in Germany in 1529 when the legislature of the Holy Roman Empire, the Diet, voted that the Lutheran faith should be suppressed. Several German states and free cities had become Lutheran and they objected to the majority edict. They wrote their views down in a Letter of Protest, asserting their right as independent states and cities to decide matters of religion. From that point forward, the religious reformers were called Protestants.

The Protestant reformers had some beliefs in common. They rejected the authority of the pope and affirmed the Bible as the highest religious authority. They agreed that salvation was by faith alone, not by good works such as donating money to the church. They believed in the priesthood of all believers. However, there were many issues on which the reformers differed: whether infants could be baptized, the meaning of the ritual of Holy Communion, and the role of bishops, among others. Initially, there were four branches of Protestant churches: Lutheran, Reformed (Calvinist), Anglican, and Anabaptist. Over time, these groups splintered over various doctrinal matters, producing hundreds of Protestant denominations. Today the term is used broadly to mean any Christian church that is not Roman Catholic or Eastern Orthodox.

The decentralized multiplicity of Protestant churches is in sharp contrast to the centralized Roman Catholic Church headed by the pope, the single most important Christian figure today.

from each position while neglecting to carry out the actual duties. Meanwhile, the church had been unable to offer comfort or explanation for the widespread devastation of the Black Death. Under the shadow of such corruption, the pope's prestige was greatly tarnished, and by the late fourteenth century, even church officials criticized the practices of their ailing institution.

The crisis in church authority took place at the same time that Europeans were becoming more educated and willing to question authority. With the revival of trade in the late Middle Ages and Renaissance, cities grew in wealth and influence, and the bourgeoisie who lived there became more prominent in European society. They developed secular schools outside the church, controlled by municipal or secular authorities, to provide young people with the reading, writing, and math skills needed in commerce. At the same time, **technological innovation** brought about new capabilities with Johannes Gutenberg's invention of movable type in the mid-fifteenth century. The publishing industry blossomed and enterprising printers provided books and other publications eagerly sought by a newly literate public. These developments exposed Europeans to new ideas, encouraged them to think for themselves, and prepared the cultural soil for wide-ranging changes.

Precursors of the Reformation

The themes of the Reformation were set out as early as the fourteenth century in response to church corruption. A professor in England, John Wyclif (c.1330–1384), was angered by the flagrant materialism and wealth of the Church and began to teach an egalitarian message: ordinary people can obtain salvation from their sins by reading the Bible for themselves without need of clergy. The official Bible of the church was written in Latin, the language of clergy and scholars across Europe. To encourage ordinary people to read the Bible, Wyclif and his associates translated it into English and taught that all church teachings should be measured against the standard of the Bible. Wyclif's followers, the Lollards, preached Wyclif's message to the common people while living simple lives of poverty in deliberate contrast to church officials. However, when impoverished peasants responded to Wyclif's egalitarian ideas and revolted against their landlords in 1381, the movement was discredited and persecuted. Wyclif's English Bible was banned throughout Britain and further English translations were solemnly forbidden.

Nevertheless, Wyclif's ideas of egalitarianism inspired others, including a professor in Bohemia (roughly today's Czech Republic) named Jan Hus (1369–1415). Like Wyclif, Hus rejected the special role given the clergy in the church and railed against the corrupt sale of **indulgences**, letters of pardon issued by the pope that granted penitents less time in purgatory. An emerging sense of **nationalism** drew the Czech nobility and native Czech churchmen to Hus's cause since they resented the power of foreigners in the Bohemian church. Hus was summoned to a church council where, despite a promise of safe conduct from the Holy Roman emperor, he was declared a heretic and burned at the stake. Enflamed by both religious passion and nationalist anger at the emperor, Bohemians broke away from the Roman church and defiantly established their own independent Bohemian church. As a result, for two decades much of central Europe was torn by warfare among armies challenging both political and religious authority.

Wyclif and Hus pursued their reforming agenda before Gutenberg's invention of movable type and were restricted in the reach of their message. After the technological advance in printing, subsequent reformers were able to spread the egalitarian creed much more effectively. Erasmus of Rotterdam (1466–1536), a Christian humanist who deplored the moral corruption of the church, took full advantage of the new technology. He had received his education from an egalitarian Dutch lay religious order, the Brethren of the Common Life, who taught that laity (those who were not church officials) could attain the same high level of spirituality and holiness as ordained clergy. Erasmus became well known in Europe by writing satirical attacks on corrupt priests who flagrantly violated their vows of celibacy and poverty.

Like Wyclif and Hus, Erasmus believed that the Bible should be freely available to all people, not just to the clergy, so they could read it for themselves. "I would to God that the ploughman would sing a text of the Scripture at his plough and that the weaver would hum them to the tune of his shuttle," he wrote.[1] Erasmus, himself the son of a priest, believed that the church should return to the original source of Christian faith, the Bible. The official version of the Bible was called the Vulgate, a Latin translation by Jerome in the fifth century. Erasmus collected the books of the New Testament in the original Greek and with the help of a Swiss publisher printed them with his own Latin commentary in 1516. Erasmus translated some Bible passages differently from Jerome and, in doing so, challenged key beliefs of the Roman church. For instance, in a passage about Mary's pregnancy with Jesus, Jerome's translation had described her as "a virgin," an important source for the church's belief in the virgin birth of Jesus. Erasmus translated the same Greek word as "a young woman," which suggested an entirely different inter-pretation.[2] Erasmus's New Testament was read eagerly all over Europe as literate lay people sought to understand the Christian faith for themselves without the mediation of the official church hierarchy. Although Erasmus never broke with Rome and saw rational scholarship as the best way to bring about reform in the church, his trenchant satire directed at corrupt church officials and his pioneering work in Biblical translation created the conditions that allowed Martin Luther, the founder of the Protestant Reformation, to find a favorable audience. As his contemporaries colorfully noted, "Erasmus laid the egg which Luther hatched."[3]

Martin Luther

Martin Luther (1483–1546), a German monk, was the first egalitarian reformer to break away from the Roman church. Luther was born in the German town of Eisleben, Saxony, the son of a prosperous mine owner. As a young man, Luther studied law to pursue a secular career, but his life changed when he was nearly struck by lightning in a violent thunderstorm. Terrified at the prospect of dying and going to hell, Luther vowed that he would become a monk if he survived. True to his word, he entered an Augustinian monastery in 1505. Luther continued his education as a monk, obtaining a doctorate and becoming a theology professor at the newly founded University of Wittenberg in Saxony.

Despite his advanced education and position, Luther struggled with the church's theology, especially its views on salvation. The church taught that to be forgiven one's sins and gain entrance into heaven, one must earn merit through good works while on earth, and that the ultimate good work was devoting one's life to God as a monk and priest. But even ordained, Luther did not feel worthy of God's love and agonized over the possibility that he could be condemned to eternal hell for his many sins. To Luther, God seemed a demanding and merciless taskmaster, impossible to please.

Luther came to doubt that any person had enough goodness to merit God's grace. No matter how hard a person tried, he or she could never be perfect, since every new day brought new opportunities to sin. When his spiritual advisor suggested he turn away from his overwhelming preoccupation with sin and focus on biblical studies, Luther agreed to offer a course on the Bible at his university. One biblical passage struck him with particular force, "The just shall live by faith."[4] It was as though a second lightning bolt hit him. Luther concluded that it was not by good deeds that a person finds salvation. God does not weigh up merit like some heavenly accountant; rather, God freely grants salvation to the faithful. People find peace of heart through trusting in God's goodness and mercy. Salvation comes by faith alone, Luther decided. Like the reformers before him, Luther's new views were egalitarian: individuals did not need intervention by church officials to be saved; they could find salvation on their own through faith.

With this new egalitarian perception of salvation, Luther became increasingly critical of the church's teaching and corrupt practices such as selling indulgences. The theory behind indulgences was that saints had more merit than they needed to enter heaven, and the pope had the right to distribute the surplus merit to persons of his choosing. It was customary for the penitent to give an offering to the church on the occasion of the granting of an indulgence. Technically, one did not buy indulgences, but the custom made it seem that the church was selling them. In Luther's mind, the appearance of awarding indulgences for money was completely corrupt.

Luther's disgust with the corrupt practice came to a head when Pope Leo X issued a new round of indulgences to finance the construction of St. Peter's Basilica in Rome. The pope sent John Tetzel to Wittenberg in 1517 to distribute the letters of indulgence and collect the customary fees, and Luther decided to challenge the legitimacy of the practice. He formulated a comprehensive list of points of disagreement about indulgences—his *Ninety-Five Theses*—and posted them on the Wittenberg church door. The theses included the argument that no one could earn salvation through good deeds or through offerings to the church, a direct challenge to prevailing ideas.

At that point, the new printing technology entered the picture once again. An enterprising printer obtained a copy of Luther's theses, written in Latin, and translated them into German, the language of the common people. Many Germans knew how to read as a result of the availability of inexpensive books from the Gutenberg press, and Luther's theses were an instant best seller. Many viewed Luther as a German patriot standing up to the foreign pope in far-away Rome. They liked the egalitarian implications of salvation by faith alone, without making payments to the church or bowing to clerical authority.

As Luther's thought developed, he published even bolder arguments, pressing his egalitarian ideas. The Bible became the sole authority for Luther, the standard to measure all church practices, and he urged believers to read the Bible for themselves. The importance of the Bible and the centrality of faith led to the two rallying cries of the Reformation: *sola fide* (by faith alone) and *sola scriptura* (by Scripture alone). These two bedrock Protestant principles displaced the Roman church hierarchy—the pope, cardinals, bishops, and priests—that had been the ironclad source of religious authority. If one could read the Bible for oneself and please God solely by faith, why have an elaborate and expensive church bureaucracy? The church taught that priests served as necessary intermediaries between God and the laity, but Luther asserted that all believing Christians were priests themselves and didn't need an intermediary. Luther pointed out that only two sacraments were mentioned in the Bible, baptism and Holy Communion, and he rejected the church's five other sacraments. He argued that the priest had no special power to transform the bread and wine of the Mass into the body and blood of Christ. And since the Bible did not mention monasteries or priestly celibacy, Luther rejected both; later, he left his monastery and married a former nun, Catherine of Bora.

Pope Leo X realized that Luther's ideas were a dangerous challenge to the legitimacy of church authority. He responded vigorously by sending Luther a papal bull of **excommunication**, the highest spiritual penalty in the church. Luther ceremoniously burned it, an open act of defiance. Charles V, the Holy Roman emperor and an ally of the pope, ordered Luther to appear before his legislature, the Diet, meeting at Worms in the German Rhineland. In a packed chamber, Luther refused to recant his writings and the emperor ruled that he was guilty of heresy. The pope demanded that Luther be sent to Rome for immediate execution, but Prince Frederick of Saxony, founder of the University of Wittenberg, didn't want to see his professor turned over to the pope and granted Luther safe haven in his territory. The pope was furious but had little power to impose his will on the autonomous states of Germany. While hiding in Saxony, Luther translated the Bible into German, allowing the many Germans who did not know Latin to read the Scriptures for themselves. For the first time, ordinary Germans had access to the sacred knowledge that had been available to the clergy alone. It was a giant step toward religious equality for the common person and a significant affirmation of German nationalism.

Some who eagerly heard Luther's egalitarian message were peasant farmers in the German states. German peasants lived in serfdom under the burden of subservience and traditional payments to their lords. When Luther challenged the

Image 7.1 Martin Luther at the Diet of Worms, 1521

© Falkenstein Heinz-Dieter/Alamy

religious authority of the church, the peasants concluded that the secular authority of the nobility was in question. Why should Christian people live in virtual slavery to their noble masters when they were all one in Christ? In 1525, peasants all over Germany revolted against their noble overlords, demanding an end to serfdom. The nobles appealed to Luther whose preaching they blamed for the peasant unrest. Luther was unsympathetic with the peasant revolt and shocked by its violence. His egalitarianism extended only to religion, not to politics. Luther himself was grateful to the noble Prince Frederick who had saved him from the pope's revenge, and he remembered how John Wyclif's reforms had been undermined by his peasant followers' political revolt. With these considerations, Luther refused to support the peasants and agreed with the nobility that the revolt should be put down. In a brutal crackdown, some 100,000 peasants were killed across the German states. It was a crushing blow to the peasant class that had looked to Luther as its champion.

The Swiss Reformation

A contrasting reform took place in the Swiss city of Zurich, a politically independent city in the Swiss confederation not governed by nobility. The church's authority there was challenged by Ulrich Zwingli (1484–1531), a priest who was greatly influenced by the ideas of Erasmus and Luther. While pastor of the largest church in Zurich in 1522, Zwingli rejected the customary practice of fasting when he approved the eating of sausages by a local printer during Lent.[5] This "affair of the sausages" launched Zwingli into public view as a reformer willing to stand up to the church. Zwingli opposed clerical celibacy and rejected the traditional Mass, arguing that it was only a memorial meal, not a sacred re-enactment of Christ's sacrifice. To air the differences between Zwingli and the Roman hierarchy, the city council held a series of debates presided over by the city magistrates. The council affirmed Zwingli's teachings and forbade the celebration of the Mass, ordering all preachers in Zurich to rely on the Bible as their sole authority. It was a resounding repudiation of the pope's authority and an affirmation of the authority of secular government, even over religious matters.

In the ferment of new ideas about the Christian faith, others in Zurich rejected the church's practice of baptizing infants. They believed that baptism was valid only if the person assented personally to baptism, and infants could not assent. This group was called the Anabaptists or re-baptizers, since the first adults they baptized had already been baptized as infants. The city's political leaders opposed the practice of adult baptism, but the Anabaptists rejected their authority over religious matters, claiming that church and state ought to be entirely separate. During the 1520s, the Anabaptists suffered great persecution in Zurich and elsewhere for ideas that were considered heretical, even by other rebels against church authority such as Zwingli.

As Zwingli's reforms spread through several Swiss cantons and nearby Germany, they provided an alternate reform to Luther's ideas. Eventually, prominent followers of both reformers tried to create a united front against the powerful

Roman church. In 1529, a meeting of many leaders of the reform movement took place in Marburg where Luther and Zwingli debated their ideas and came to broad agreement on everything except the ritual of Holy Communion. Nonetheless, the meeting did not unify the reformers enough to take a common stand against the Roman church. When Swiss cantons loyal to the pope attacked Zurich in 1531, Zwingli and 500 defenders of the city were killed on the battlefield. On hearing the unhappy news, Martin Luther dismissively sniffed that "all who take the sword will die by the sword."[6] The strong-minded independence that prompted Luther to challenge the pope prevented him from unifying the opposition through alliances with other reformers.

Calvinism

In nearby Geneva, a charismatic leader from a younger generation was inspired by both Luther and Zwingli. John Calvin (1509–1564) was a French lawyer versed in humanist learning who was forced to flee his native France due to his reformist views. In 1536 Calvin published *The Institutes of the Christian Religion*, a carefully reasoned analysis of the human condition and the need for church reform. Calvin rejected the nationalist views of other reformers and espoused a sweeping universal religious view. Where Luther addressed himself to Germany and Zwingli to Switzerland, Calvin wrote for all of Europe. With a lawyer's reasoning skill, he defended Luther's idea that salvation comes from faith alone, not from good works. Calvin agreed with Luther that God knows in advance how each person will respond to God's grace and asserted that every person is predestined to either heaven or hell, salvation or damnation. Since most would turn away from God's demanding standards, only a few would be saved, a small proportion of humanity Calvin called the elect, who would succeed in leading a holy life through all trials and tribulations. Even more than Luther, Calvin emphasized the solitary individual face to face with God, without any church intermediary.

Calvin challenged not only the legitimacy of the church but the authority of the state as well. He believed that a Christian country must be governed by God's rules, not by the will of a monarch. Luther had been obedient to state authorities such as Prince Frederick of Saxony who sheltered him from the pope. But Calvin saw Luther's deference to the state ruler as unacceptable. Calvin believed that the state should follow rules set out by the religious authorities. The independent city of Geneva invited Calvin to test his ideas of the model Christian state, and under Calvin's leadership, Geneva became a **theocracy**, a state governed by religious authorities. A committee of clergy and elders imposed strict rules enforced by the city council: all residents of Geneva were expected to be active members of the church and to lead a sober life dedicated to God. Frivolous entertainments such as dancing, card-playing, gambling, and drunkenness were forbidden, as were ostentatious displays of wealth (to stay in business, the jewelers turned to watchmaking!) Churches were stripped of their images, statues, and stained glass as distractions from the Word of God, while traditional devotions such as fasting, vows, pilgrimages, and prayers for the dead were prohibited. Sundays were spent in church listening to lengthy sermons on reformed Christian doctrine. Those who did not want to comply left or were expelled.

To publicize his ideas, Calvin turned to the resourceful printing industry that had made such a difference for Luther. He enlisted the assistance of reformist printers who had been banished from France for printing Bibles in the vernacular French. The French printing industry found a new home in Geneva and soon Calvin's writings were distributed throughout France and beyond by a dedicated and daring group of pastors who had been personally trained by Calvin.[7] People eager to live in a reformed Christian state streamed to Geneva, the new Protestant Rome, and the city swelled with religious immigrants, including many who later returned to their home to spread Calvin's teachings. Among these was a Scottish preacher, John Knox (1513–1572), who founded the Presbyterian Church in Scotland. Other Calvinist centers sprang up throughout France, where the reformers were called Huguenots, as well as in England and the Netherlands, the latter controlled by Catholic Spain. In all of these places, Calvinism became associated with political disobedience and even outright rebellion as it found a growing audience among nobles, bourgeoisie, and peasants who had grievances against their traditional rulers. By the 1560s, when serious civil warfare erupted in France and the Netherlands, Calvinism had become firmly established as a religion of revolutionaries, spawning generations of martyrs unafraid to die for their religious principles. This gave Reformation era warfare a level of fanaticism and savagery that would not be seen again until the twentieth century.

Anglican Reform from Above

The Protestant Reformation came to England for very different reasons than Germany and Switzerland. The English king Henry VIII wanted to protect his kingdom from a war of succession like the fifteenth-century Wars of the Roses. His children by Catherine of Aragon had all died in infancy except a girl, Mary, and Henry did not believe a female heir would be acceptable to the English people. The only previous female heir, the twelfth-century Matilda, had fought unsuccessfully for her rights to the throne, setting off a bitter succession battle.[8] Henry needed a son and appealed to Pope Clement VII for an annulment of his marriage, a common practice for monarchs in such distress. Unfortunately for Henry, though, the pope was temporarily imprisoned by the Holy Roman Emperor Charles V, Catherine's nephew, and did not offer him any hope. In desperation, Henry had his own Archbishop of Canterbury Thomas Cranmer declare his marriage to Catherine invalid, and he married Anne Boleyn, a young lady-in-waiting. When the pope excommunicated Henry for his bold disobedience, the English Parliament declared that the English church was independent of Rome, with the King as its supreme head. The English people supported the break from Rome since they had long resented the dominance of a foreign pope over their own English affairs. Yet while Henry wanted control of the English church, he did not want to change its theology and continued such Roman practices as clerical celibacy. Nonetheless, he appropriated the substantial and valuable monastic lands, selling them to wealthy laity.

Protestant ideas came to England through Henry's wives. During Anne Boleyn's brief three-year reign, she encouraged bishops sympathetic to church reform and promoted the publication of Bibles in English and in French. When Anne—alas!—produced only a daughter, Henry moved on to another wife (there were six in all), Jane Seymour, who finally gave Henry a son. Edward VI came to the throne in 1547 at the young age of nine and his uncle Edward Seymour actively promoted religious reform. Under Edward VI, Archbishop of Canterbury Thomas Cranmer wrote a church manual, the *Book of Common Prayer*, setting out an English reformation somewhat between the Lutheran and Calvinist positions. When King Edward died young, Catherine's daughter Mary succeeded him as the first reigning Queen of England. She proved unpopular when she took energetic steps to restore the English church to Rome. She revived the Catholic Mass and executed reform bishops such as Thomas Cranmer by burning them at the stake. Such excesses earned her the nickname Bloody Mary, and reformers not caught in her web fled to Zurich and Geneva.

With violent political battles over religious affiliation, England risked descending into civil war. But a charismatic leader emerged who forged a pragmatic compromise between church and state. Queen Mary died after a five-year reign and Elizabeth, Anne Boleyn's daughter, ascended the throne. Unlike her short-lived half-siblings, Elizabeth I reigned for forty-five years and solidified England as a Protestant nation. Reformers returned to England from the Continent and argued for a clean break with Catholic practices, a church modeled after Zwingli and Calvin. But Elizabeth was wary of going too far with reform. She saw armed conflict on the Continent between Protestant and Catholic countries and wanted to avoid more religious violence. She knew that the Protestant reformers were active mostly in cities and that the majority of the English people, the rural farmers, were sympathetic to traditional Catholic practices. To create a national church for everyone, Elizabeth forged a *via media* or Middle Way, a mixture of Protestant and Catholic beliefs and practices. She kept the traditional structure of a hierarchical church governed by bishops, so important to the legitimacy of royal rule. She retained the ancient liturgy with church vestments, candles, and stained-glass windows, all rejected by Zurich and Geneva reformers. But she insisted on the use of English as the language of the liturgy and allowed clergy to marry. The Scriptures were affirmed as the standard of Christian belief, and salvation was by faith alone. Elizabeth's revised *Book of Common Prayer* struck a careful balance. Catholic practices that had spurred the Protestant reforms such as indulgences, the veneration of saints, and the belief in purgatory were completely rejected. This Elizabethan Settlement gave great religious and political stability to England though some opposition remained among the Calvinist Puritans and nobles who remained faithful Catholics.

Catholic Counter-Reformation

The Church of Rome did not stand still while Protestant reformers such as Luther, Zwingli, Calvin, and Cranmer established independent churches. Many loyal

Catholics such as Erasmus recognized the corruption of the church and the need for reform. A Dutch pope, Adrian VI, a friend of Erasmus educated by the Brethren of the Common Life, admitted to a German Diet in 1523 that the problems in the church began at the top with a corrupt papacy.[9] Adrian unfortunately died too soon to bring real reform. A subsequent pope, Paul III, appointed a commission that condemned the corrupt practices of simony, pluralism, and nepotism that had discredited the church hierarchy. In the main, however, the Roman church's response to the Protestant movement was to oppose and repress reformers as heretics. Pope Paul IV blamed the free-wheeling printing industry and the ready availability of Protestant books. To restrict the spread of reformist ideas, he initiated an *Index of Prohibited Books* in 1559 listing all books deemed heretical by the Catholic hierarchy. Even moderate criticisms of the Church of Rome, such as those by Erasmus, were banned, and printers in Catholic countries could no longer publish books listed on the Index under pain of excommunication.

The Roman Church exerted even more forceful responses to the Protestant rebels in its attempt to reclaim religious legitimacy. The **Inquisition** was a system of church courts that prosecuted and punished heretics. It operated most effectively in lands controlled by Spain, though a Roman Inquisition was established in Italy as well. The purpose of the Inquisition was to root out Protestant sympathizers in countries where Catholicism was still dominant. The Spanish Inquisitors conducted their proceedings in secret and used torture to obtain confessions, and they were widely feared. The Inquisition was effective at suppressing open efforts at reform but it earned the Roman church a fearsome reputation for reactionary ruthlessness.

A more positive response to the Protestant movement was the rise of saintly individuals who emphasized the need for spiritual devotion and personal reform. The most important was the Spanish ascetic Ignatius Loyola (1491–1556) a soldier from a noble background. Loyola was forced by war injuries to give up his dreams of knightly combat, and he became convinced that God wanted him to be a spiritual knight devoted to the church.[10] In a gesture of surrender to the will of God, he offered his sword to the Black Madonna at the shrine of Montserrat near Barcelona and vowed to put on the armor of Christ. After months of religious reflection, he wrote the *Spiritual Exercises*, a guide to confrontation with personal sin and spiritual growth. Loyola wanted to convert distant peoples to Christianity and gathered a group of followers in a new religious order, the Society of Jesus, in 1540. His religious brothers, known as Jesuits, took the monastic vows of poverty, chastity, and obedience as well as an unusual fourth vow, to go without question or delay wherever the pope might send them for the mission of the church.

The Jesuits believed that true reform of the church would come through individual rather than institutional change. The problem with the church was not its theology, as Luther had charged, but the failure of individuals to live up to the standards of the church and their ignorance about Catholic belief. The Jesuits set about educating the faithful, setting up schools and colleges across Europe to produce a knowledgeable Catholic elite. Loyola was deeply committed to the

Roman church as the visible manifestation of Christ and wrote in his *Spiritual Exercises*, "What seems to me white, I will believe black, if the hierarchical church so defines."[11] Luther had rejected personal effort to merit salvation, but Loyola affirmed the need for individuals to strive for holiness. The vigorous work of the Jesuits in educating a new generation of Catholics brought reform and renewal to the Church of Rome through individual achievement.

European political realities required a stronger response to the Protestant challenge than long-term education and spiritual growth, however. The Holy Roman Emperor Charles V had to deal with a rapidly disintegrating empire as the states under his rule were choosing religious sides. Many of the German states had gone over to Luther. Charles impressed upon Pope Paul III the importance of calling a council to resolve Luther's charges against the church and bring Lutherans back into the Church of Rome. The pope delayed, remembering how often church councils had opposed papal authority. Nonetheless, Paul III finally authorized a council in the city of Trent in the Italian Alps. The Council of Trent met in three sessions between 1545 and 1563, addressing the theological and ethical charges of Luther. Much to Charles's distress, reconciliation with Protestants was not foremost on the agenda for the cardinals and bishops. Instead, they affirmed traditional church teachings with only an occasional nod to Luther. While the councils acknowledged the importance of Holy Scripture as a source of Christian faith, they maintained the traditional position that only the church hierarchy could properly interpret the meaning of Holy Scripture. They asserted that church traditions were not innovations, as Luther had charged, but an unwritten heritage from the apostles who had received them from Christ himself. Despite conservative theological positions, the Council of Trent was notably successful at reforming the worst abuses of church discipline.

The Council of Trent closed the door to reconciliation with the Protestants and drew up the lines of battle. On all the key points of Luther's challenges, the Council reaffirmed the traditional Roman position. The Council of Trent created the modern Roman Catholic Church, set against the proliferating Protestant churches: Lutheran, Calvinist, and Anglican. While the Protestant movement broke into independent churches, some along national lines and others along doctrinal ones, the Council of Trent preserved the structural unity and theological solidity of the Church of Rome. Renewed and reinvigorated, Roman Catholics were poised to wage the wars of religion that followed the Council of Trent into the following century.

Conclusion

The changes associated with the Protestant Reformation brought about a dramatic shift in European authority. The Church of Rome, the dominant authority in medieval Europe, lost its pre-eminent place as individuals responded to the Protestant message of equality before God. The Reformation succeeded in its challenge to Rome for a variety of reasons. Early reformers such as Luther enjoyed political protection motivated both by religious sentiment and by growing nationalism with its resentment of a foreign pope. The free cities of Zurich and Geneva provided space for religious experimentation, allowing Zwingli and Calvin to gain a foothold and try out their ideas, while protecting the printers who were so instrumental in the spread of the reform message. The English people wanted national self-determination and readily supported Henry's break with Rome.

The Reformation affirmed the possibility that individuals could influence their own destiny even on matters as important as eternal salvation. It dramatically reduced the power of the institutional church, not only the pope in Rome but also local bishops and priests. Ordinary people no longer had to defer to the clergy for religious comfort but could turn to the source, the Holy Scriptures, themselves. The access of the laity to religious knowledge represented an enormous power shift in European society. When faith became sufficient for salvation, traditional hierarchies lost their power over ordinary people.

Yet this power shift created a deep divide in Europe that helped to propel the forces of social change during the coming centuries. The Reformation undermined European social cohesion, presided over by the church, that had been taken for granted in the Middle Ages. Europeans were faced with a new dilemma: when individuals could think for themselves and make their own decisions, what could bring unity and social order? The sense of common purpose and vision that had permeated Europe in the Middle Ages would not easily be replaced.

Notes

1 Tony Lane, *Harper's Concise Book of Christian Faith* (San Francisco: Harper & Row, 1984), 113.
2 Diarmaid MacCulloch, *The Reformation: A History* (London: Penguin Books, 2003), 101.
3 Lane, 113.
4 *The Holy Bible, King James Version*, Romans 1:17.
5 Roland H. Bainton, *The Reformation of the Sixteenth Century* (Boston: Beacon Press, 1952), 84.
6 John B. Payne , "Zwingli and Luther: The Giant vs. Hercules," *Christian History* 1984 , accessed February 20, 2017, www.christianitytoday.com/history/issues/issue-4/zwingli-and-luther-giant-vs-hercules.html.
7 Robert Kingdon, *Geneva and the Coming of the Wars of Religion in France, 1555–1562* (Geneva: Droz, 1956) remains the authoritative work on Calvin's evangelization strategy.
8 Carter Lindberg, *The European Reformations* (Cambridge: Blackwell, 1996), 317.
9 Ibid, 338.
10 Ibid., 346.
11 Ibid., 349.

Suggested Readings

Bainton, Roland H. *The Reformation of the Sixteenth Century*. Boston: Beacon Press, 1952.
Kingdon, Robert. *Geneva and the Coming of the Wars of Religion in France, 1555–1562*. Geneva: Droz, 1956.

Lane, Tony. *Harper's Concise Book of Christian Faith*. San Francisco: Harper & Row, 1984.

Lindberg, Carter. *The European Reformations*. Cambridge: Blackwell, 1996.

MacCulloch, Diarmaid. *The Reformation: A History*. London: Penguin Books, 2003.

Mullet, Michael A. *The A to Z of the Reformation and Counter-Reformation*. Lanham, MD: Scarecrow Press, 2010.

Murphy, Cullen. *God's Jury: The Inquisition and the Making of the Modern World*. Boston: Houghton Mifflin Harcourt, 2012.

Roper, Lyndal. *Martin Luther: Renegade and Prophet*. New York: Random House, 2017.

Weir, Alison. *Henry VIII: The King and His Court*. New York: Ballantine Books, 2002.

Wright, Jonathan. *God's Soldiers: A History of the Jesuits*. Garden City, NY: Image Books, 2005.

8   Commerce, Cities, and Capitalism

John McGrath

Key Terms

capital, capital-intensive manufacturing, economic dependency, economic development, global economy, liberty, "putting-out system," regional economic specialization

During the High Middle Ages, Europeans had envied the wealth and sophistication of Asian and Middle Eastern civilizations. Italian trade with the eastern Mediterranean, stimulated by the Crusades, had connected the European economy to the extensive Asian trade networks that stretched all the way to China. While this gave Europeans access to useful and valuable goods from the east, Europe was comparatively poor and its participation in such early international trade was relatively minor. Moreover, Europeans' understanding of these societies was limited, since they knew them mostly indirectly through travelers' tales and legends of questionable accuracy; as a result, their attitudes toward non-Christians were characterized by suspicion and fear.[1]

Europe's insularity began to wane during the thirteenth and fourteenth centuries, as Europeans took the initiative in expanding their interactions with the outside world. Trade, as it frequently has in history, provided much of the impetus. Despite the problems of the late Middle Ages, advances in both maritime technology and financial practices made it easier for merchants to do business farther and farther afield. The rise of the powerful Italian trading states of Venice and Genoa created regular links with the Middle East and North Africa. Further north, the emergence of banks and trade associations energized trade in the Baltic and Atlantic regions. In turn, the growth of complex financial enterprises, such as the Medici Bank, and the protection and sponsorship of royal governments facilitated such developments. The expansion of commerce promoted economic diversification and regional specialization, highlighting the role of towns and cities as commercial centers.

By the Renaissance era, such **economic development** had made much of Europe dependent on trade for even basic and necessary commodities. While Europe's cities had begun to produce finished goods, notably textiles, for export to markets in the Middle East and North Africa, their inhabitants were becoming reliant on inter-regional and international imports of goods that were unavailable locally, including spices and manufactured products such as cotton cloth, paper, and ceramics. Even in the countryside, complete economic self-sufficiency was becoming rarer as a monetary economy became more pronounced.

The Beginnings of a Global Economy

However, as the economy of Europe evolved to become more complex and reliant on commerce, certain critical external developments began to disrupt its operation. Of particular importance was the expansion of Muslim power in the eastern Mediterranean, notably the rise of the Ottoman Empire, which made trade in this region more hazardous and expensive. Almost simultaneously, European merchants and monarchies alike had begun to suffer from a shortage of precious metals, especially gold, that placed them at a distinct trade disadvantage with societies to their south and east. Additionally, the ravages caused by the Black Death, as well as the wars and civil unrest of the late Middle Ages, slowed economic activity even further.[2] Difficult access to the two critical commodities of gold and spices posed a problem for the continued growth of the European economy. A shortage of the former reduced the purchasing power of European merchants, while the latter, necessary for preserving and flavoring food, became more expensive as Muslims asserted control over Middle Eastern and North African marketplaces.

The urban bourgeoisie and the royal monarchies, the same two groups whose fortunes had risen during the late medieval era, cooperated to provide a solution to this problem. The merchant community, in Italy and elsewhere, was always eager and able to fund promising ventures that might bring a profit. Meanwhile, even by the beginning of the Renaissance, most European monarchs recognized that healthy economies contributed to the power and stability of their realms, and thus they too saw the value of finding easier access to gold and spices. The logical alternative was establishing more direct access to the regions further east where such goods originated, enabling them to bypass the Muslim-controlled areas.

This meant the exploration of the oceans and the creation of entirely new trade links, and by the fifteenth century, Europe possessed both the will and the means to carry out these goals. The economic motives coincided with others, such as a desire to spread Christianity, monarchies that were eager to expand, and the genuine geographical curiosity that Renaissance humanism was encouraging. Certain important technological advances in ship-building and navigation, the results of both investment-driven innovation and cultural borrowing, provided the means.[3]

Two relatively new kingdoms, Portugal and Spain, became the first to explore and trade out into the Atlantic Ocean and beyond. During the fifteenth century, Portuguese mariners relied on both government and merchant investment to sail south along the west coast of Africa. Gradually expanding their reach, they built coastal trading forts that gave them access to gold, ivory, and slaves for importation back to Europe, and this trade provided profits that could be invested in new ventures. The Portuguese continually refined their maritime technology and navigational abilities, while contributing a great deal of new geographical knowledge.

Before the end of the fifteenth-century Portuguese vessels had rounded the tip of southern Africa and established a direct maritime route to the wealthy commercial cities of India. During the decades that followed, large, heavily armed Portuguese fleets used superior naval firepower to almost literally blast their way into the middle of existing Asian trading networks.[4] Seizing control of certain strategic points, they set up a series of militarily protected trading posts that stretched around the edges of the Indian Ocean as far as Southeast Asia, China, and Japan. These outposts became the foundation of a direct and profitable Portuguese commerce in spices and other valuable Eastern cargo. This trade transformed a tiny kingdom of slightly more than a million people into a remarkably wealthy and powerful state; equally importantly, the Portuguese success demonstrated the advantages that might be gained from taking a more energetic role overseas.

Meanwhile, Portugal's rival, the newly united Kingdom of Spain, had been dispatching ships westward out into the Atlantic, colonizing the Canary Islands and trading in northern Europe. Christopher Columbus, the son of a Genoese textile merchant, had established a successful career in Atlantic and Mediterranean seaborne commerce. While living in Lisbon, Portugal, he had become an expert in navigation and geography, and had heard sailors' reports of further islands that lay far to the west. Motivated by a complex combination of geographical theory, a hunger for gold, and Christian mysticism, Columbus developed a plan to reach "the Indies" by sailing west. Though he underestimated the circumference of the world, his previous experience sailing the Atlantic had revealed westward flowing currents and winds, which suggested to him he might reach the fabled kingdom of Japan after only a few weeks of sailing west from the Canary Islands.[5]

For more than a decade, various European monarchs rejected Columbus's appeals for financial support for his project. However, in 1492, Ferdinand and Isabella, the king and queen of Spain, who had previously turned him down, completed the conquest of the last Muslim city in the Iberian Peninsula, and by then had also become anxious about the newly found Portuguese route into the Indian Ocean. They provided Columbus with the means to outfit three ships for his momentous first voyage, and upon his return from the Caribbean, Ferdinand and Isabella made a formal claim to these territories. Even while uncertainties remained about the nature of this "New World," the Spanish crown began to sponsor permanent settlements, hoping to establish a trade in gold, spices, and other valuable goods. Before the end of the fifteenth century, both a papal decree and a diplomatic treaty formalized the division of the globe between Spain and Portugal, and both kingdoms were intensifying their overseas empire-building efforts.

The benefits in what soon became known as "America" were not as immediate as those enjoyed in the Indian Ocean. For almost thirty years, the Spanish outposts in the Caribbean remained largely unprofitable backwaters, but this changed suddenly in the 1520s and 1530s, when the conquests of Cortez and Pizarro, in Mexico and the South American Andes respectively, revealed wealthy societies and sources of precious metals. This energized both private and public interest, and the Spanish crown constructed a highly bureaucratized colonial system in order to control the territories it claimed. From the mid-sixteenth century onward, soldiers, adventurers, missionaries, administrators, and merchants—as well as African slaves—flooded into Spain's Central and South American colonies. Soon, fleets of heavily armed ships were hauling massive quantities of treasure, mostly silver, back to Spain to support the expanding Spanish European empire and pay for its frequent wars. Even by the 1570s, Spanish ships were sailing regularly across the Pacific Ocean to link the New World with Spanish possessions that had been established in the Philippines.[6]

Other European nations quickly recognized the advantages of overseas trade and colonization, and soon the English, French, and the Dutch were competing for a share of the presumed riches available around the globe. Even before the end of the seventeenth century, Europeans had conquered and/or established permanent outposts in virtually every latitude and longitude, including India, Brazil, Indonesia, East and West Africa, the Caribbean, the Persian Gulf, the

Image 8.1 Spanish galleon, sixteenth century

© INTERFOTO / Alamy

Canadian Maritimes, and China. Sugar, cotton, tobacco, dyes, silks, spices, slaves, lumber, furs, and ceramics were just a few of the earliest commodities they imported back to Europe and sold in foreign marketplaces. Even as different European powers fought native populations—and each other—to expand their overseas interests, Europe became the hub of a global maritime trade network that moved goods and people around the world. Though modest in scale at first, this marks the foundation of the first **global economy**, where different parts of the world were hooked into a connected system of production and commerce. This global economy would become more dominant and complex over the next five centuries.

These first two colonizing nations, Portugal and Spain, established the European pattern of empire-building by creating powerful formal institutions to regulate and control the process. Through royal licenses and monopolies, private entities— usually banks and wealthy merchant companies, often of foreign origin—were encouraged to invest in profit-making ventures under government sponsorship. While such investors took the initiative, and assumed much of the risk, the royal governments administered and directed this commerce for the benefit of their kingdoms, and often protected and promoted it with military force. Later, other European powers developed their own versions of these private/public partnerships as European control of the seas expanded.[7]

As mentioned above, there were many motives behind what has been called "The Age of Discoveries," and they varied both among the different participants and over time. These included the pursuit of profit, the desire to spread European culture and Christianity, diplomatic and strategic advantage, individual quests for adventure and fame, and genuine Renaissance inquisitiveness. But whatever the particular intentions and accomplishments of individuals such as Columbus, Magellan, or Hudson, they all added up to the creation of a network of ocean highways that connected, however tenuously, almost all of the settled parts of the earth that could be reached by sea.

"Spain's Century"

Although there were similarities in the ways that European states went about the process of overseas expansion, each did so under unique conditions, both at home and abroad, which affected their differing experiences with modernization. Spain provides a case in point. During the sixteenth century, this kingdom emerged as the dominant power in Europe and had seemed to contemporaries to be the prime beneficiary of the "Age of Discoveries." However, the Spanish experience demonstrates that the link between overseas dominion and economic development is not simple.

Charles V of the Habsburg dynasty became king of Spain in 1516, and by the 1520s he had inherited an enormous collection of territories that included Spain, Austria, present-day Belgium and the Netherlands, much of Italy, and several German states. In 1530, he was elected as Holy Roman Emperor, and the territories that he also ruled in America exceeded, in terms of land area, all of his European possessions put together. Thus, Charles controlled not only the lion's share of the wealthy parts of Europe, but by mid-century, when the export of New World silver to Spain began in earnest, the Spanish royal treasury had access to a seemingly unlimited supply of precious metals. Although Charles's abdication in 1556 resulted in the detachment of most of the central European Habsburg possessions, in 1580, Portugal and all of its overseas territories were joined to the Spanish dominions as the result of a dynastic struggle.

On paper, this made Spain the wealthiest and most powerful monarchy on the face of the earth. It seems remarkable, then, that by the late sixteenth century, the Spanish empire was facing financial collapse, which became a reality during the next century; after this time, Spain, bankrupt and impoverished, would never again be a major world power. How could this be, in a society that possessed almost unimaginable amounts of wealth? In hindsight, Spain's problems provide a useful lesson about the nature of economic growth.[8]

A main part of the answer has to do with the fate of the silver and gold that made its way into Seville every year aboard the royally controlled "silver fleets." Having been formed into bars and ingots in the New World, most of this treasure passed into the hands of the financiers and merchants—many of whom were foreigners—whose loans had underwritten the shipping, mining, ranching, settlement, and military activities that were instrumental in the development of New World resources. Much of what remained went to the merchants who possessed royal licenses—generally monopolistic—over different portions of the American economy, such as the cattle, silk, and wine trades. Finally, about 20 percent of the New World treasure went directly into the royal treasury as the so-called "king's fifth."

While the payouts received often amounted to enormous profits on investments, much of it left Spain almost immediately upon arrival. In particular, an increasing portion flowed into the coffers of German and Italian banks, especially the Fugger financial empire that served as the Habsburgs' bankers. Much of the rest was used for consumption, as the merchants and nobles who had privileged roles in the American trade spent their profits lavishly on the palaces, fine clothing, carriages, and artwork that they felt was necessary to display their status. However, most of these extravagances were neither made in Spain, nor made by Spaniards, because Italians, French, Dutch, and Germans dominated the luxury trades. What this meant was that as this American wealth arrived in Spain, much of it quickly departed again for other destinations. In this way, the economies outside of Spain wound up benefiting the most from all this American treasure.

It can be argued that the treasure retained by the Spanish crown had an even less constructive fate. The possession of such a huge empire meant that Spanish kings had to devote a tremendous amount of resources to defending it and keeping it under their control.[9] The menace presented by the Ottoman Turks in central Europe and the Mediterranean was only one threat that needed to be countered through enormous military expenditure. By the 1560s, the Reformation had also promoted conflicts in several Habsburg possessions, such as the wealthy Netherlands, while political and social disorder also plagued other Habsburg dominions. The result was that during the entire course of the sixteenth century, Spain was never truly at peace; in fact, for most of the century, the kingdom was directly involved in at least two major wars. What this added up to was the unfortunate reality that, by the time the Spanish crown got its hands on its share of the American treasure, they already owed it all to bankers—in Germany, Italy, and the Netherlands—because they had been borrowing from them to equip their armies and navies. The kings of Spain were not the first rulers, nor would they be the last, to learn a fairly simple lesson: no matter the century, war is a horribly expensive undertaking.

What happened to the American treasure coming into Spain may have been wasteful enough, but what is equally important is what did *not* happen to it: neither the private nor public sector in Spain invested much of it into the domestic economy. The growth and administration of empire relied largely on foreign investment **capital** and skills, and largely as a result the Spanish economy had weak financial institutions and few opportunities for entrepreneurial business owners. Despite the massive imports of treasure, Spain remained a society with a small bourgeoisie, few homegrown businesses, little domestic manufacturing, and, especially after mid-century, an economic system that was utterly dependent on the more sophisticated economies of Europe. Spain became a society with a few tremendously wealthy people, and a great mass of impoverished, unskilled, and illiterate peasants, while their towns and cities experienced high levels of unemployment. The royal government itself was constantly on the edge of bankruptcy, and continued to raise taxes on subjects already staggered by a rising cost of living. In a sense, sixteenth century Spain was a kingdom that had access to a tremendous amount of money, yet it possessed very little real wealth. Ultimately, it was the bourgeoisie elsewhere who wound up with this treasure, and they were the ones who used it to create genuine economic development.

Capitalism and Economic Specialization

During the High Middle Ages Europe had played merely a relatively minor role in a long-established trans-Asian chain of trade. By the early seventeenth century, economic, political, and cultural developments had placed Europe at the center of a global economy. From headquarters in growing cities such as Antwerp, London, and Bordeaux, royal governments and powerful financial enterprises exerted an increasing level of control over this system and had a profound influence on the modernization of European society.

One of the most noticeable and important shifts was an acceleration of the **regional economic specialization** that had first begun to appear in the medieval era. The demographic crises of the late Middle Ages had already greatly influenced Europe's economic structure, as larger, more capital-intensive enterprises began to replace self-sufficient enterprises like the manor system and village artisans. As commerce and trade intensified between the fourteenth and seventeenth centuries, different regions in Western Europe began to focus even more on particular products and industries, varying according to available natural, human, and financial resources. This specialization, in turn, promoted the emergence of larger, more complex economic and financial entities that became the backbone of what was essentially a different sort of economy.

One particularly important change took place in the organization of manufacturing. Since the Middle Ages, textiles, especially woolen cloth, had been the foundation of Europe's manufacturing sector. By the sixteenth century, increased trade, investment, and innovation had allowed this industry to evolve into something far more complex. Different parts of Italy, England, the Low Countries and Northern France began to produce specialized types of textiles and textile products: cotton cloth, silk stockings, luxury tapestries, and many diverse wool products. These found markets both within and outside of Europe.

Much of this textile output was produced in a new arrangement, known as the **"putting-out system,"** that emerged during the late Middle Ages. Entrepreneurs with capital purchased raw materials, usually wool or cotton, and then paid workers to use their own home looms and equipment to perform different stages of the production process, such as spinning and dyeing, while retaining ownership of the materials.[10] In this method of production, there was a clear distinction between those who invested the money and those who performed the labor, and these early capitalists could sell the finished products and reinvest the profits that came from the difference between their expenses and their revenues. The putting-out system, also known as "cottage industry," relied on the availability of start-up capital, insurance, reliable transportation, and economic demand for such goods, each of which had been made possible by the evolution of the European economy over the previous centuries. Over the course of the Early Modern Period, such **capital-intensive manufacturing** became a powerful engine of economic growth, creating the conditions necessary for the Industrial Revolution.

Eventually, less developed areas both within and outside Europe were drawn into the expanding global economic network. For instance, the hinterlands of Spain and England, unable to compete with the towns in textile production, concentrated on sheep raising and wool production, which were less labor intensive than growing wheat and less capital intensive than manufacturing. Rural areas of the Mediterranean began to specialize in fruit growing, while the lumber industry in the Baltic region expanded. Large parts of central and eastern Europe began to export wheat and other cereals in large quantities to Western towns that had previously relied on their surrounding regions for such food staples. Meanwhile, products from overseas, such as sugar and cotton in the sixteenth century and many other commodities by the seventeenth, added to the diversity of the products purchased and consumed by Europeans. What this all meant was that, by the seventeenth century, few parts of Europe remained economically self-sufficient, while many other parts of the globe were becoming **economically dependent** on Europe, no longer self-sufficient and reliant upon European commerce, expertise, and trade. Traditional economies evolved to become specialized parts of a larger international economy, a process that continued into the Industrial Revolution and beyond.

Urban Growth and the Bourgeoisie

This internationalization of the European economy could not fail to have a massive impact on European life. One of the most important effects was that it intensified the ongoing process of urbanization that had begun during the medieval era. By the sixteenth century, and expanding beyond, European cities assumed a far greater role in economic life, in politics, and in Europe's cultural world. The populations of the biggest cities in Europe grew tremendously during the sixteenth century, transforming the importance and roles of regional capitals. Seville became the headquarters of New World commerce; Lisbon, and later Antwerp, controlled the international spice trade; while Paris and London evolved from agricultural marketplaces into centers of manufacturing, finance, politics, and culture. Such cities experienced tripling and quadrupling of their populations into the hundreds of thousands of residents.[11]

Some of this can be explained by a higher standard of living, especially cheaper food and more disposable income. But this accounts for only part of this population growth; an equally important cause was a new sort of immigration. While medieval and late medieval towns had attracted new residents from the surrounding countryside, people came into these Early Modern cities and towns from further afield, from other parts of Europe and even from outside of Europe. These newcomers were responding to the economic demand for skilled workers and artisans, like metalsmiths, printers, and shipbuilders, as well as for educated professionals of all types, such as lawyers, officials, and entrepreneurs. They brought their skills, their new ideas, and their money with them, increasing the economic vitality of the growing cities. Because of more efficient monetary systems and financial institutions, capital flowed from one place to the next, stimulating employment, creating new inventions and business methods, and leading to more and more profits, for more and more people who were looking for new places where they might invest their wealth.

Logically enough, this urban dynamism also had political and cultural effects. To expand and modernize, royal political administrations required educated officials and access to finance, which prompted many monarchies to relocate their administrations to urban areas. The schools and universities that educated such officials and other professionals expanded, while new ones were created. Meanwhile, in the largest European cities, the influx of educated and wealthy new residents representing different cultures and religious traditions broke down what remained of the traditional *gemeinschaft* culture. Inevitably, the mainstays of the earlier medieval system—the church, feudalism, and the manorial system—survived in the cities only as cultural relics. In such places, by the seventeenth century, capitalism, rationality, and individualism had established firm roots in a changing society that was increasingly dominated by a varied and upwardly mobile bourgeoisie. The modern world of industrialization and the nation-state would spring from these roots.

Capitalism, Protestantism, and Modernization

Another clearly identifiable pattern that emerged during the Early Modern Period was a shift in economic balance. The economies of the southern parts of Europe—notably Spain, Portugal, and Italy—began to decline in the late sixteenth and early seventeenth centuries. Meanwhile, the northern parts of Europe experienced significant economic growth, both in relative terms and in real terms, and this economic change would be accompanied by a similar shift in political and military power.

The observer might also notice that in the south Roman Catholicism remained, often literally, the law of the land; for various political and social reasons, the Protestant Reformation never got a foothold in Iberia and Italy. In contrast, many parts of the north, like England, Germany, the Netherlands and France, developed either multireligious societies or followed Protestantism. It was the latter places that took over the economic leadership of Europe during the sixteenth century and beyond.

For the German sociologist Max Weber, this development was no coincidence. He argued that the emergence of Protestantism helped to encourage certain new cultural values that affected economic behavior. Specifically, the new religious ideas contributed to a new ethos—what he called the Protestant Ethic—that promoted hard work, savings, personal integrity, and self-confidence. According to Weber, in the long run, during the late sixteenth century and beyond, these new economic behaviors stimulated the growth of capitalism as an economic system.[12]

Though his point appears logical, proving the cause and effect between capitalism and Protestantism is quite difficult. Since Weber's time, historians have argued about the nature of the relationship between these two important features of Early Modern Europe. Did Protestantism in fact encourage capitalism, and if so, how and why? Alternatively, as many Marxists have suggested, perhaps it was the other way around: that the rise of capitalism encouraged Protestant beliefs that were less critical of the accumulation of wealth than the Christian Paternalistic Ethic had been.

Whatever their perspectives, most historians would admit that, in reality, the relationship between these two elements of social change was rather more complicated than either of these prescriptions might suggest. This is because there were some other notable changes during the sixteenth century that also factored into the equation. One was the spread of literacy, promoted by the development of the printing press during the fifteenth century. By the early sixteenth century printing technology had become efficient enough to produce books by the thousands. This lowered their cost, and books became affordable to many more people than just the very elite classes. It has been persuasively argued that both the production and consumption of typographic material (that is, books and other typeset reading materials) made a vast contribution to social change. Though its impact was often subtle and long term, it affected both private and public life in different ways by promoting rationalism, bureaucracy, capitalism, tolerance, and social mobility. It greatly facilitated cultural diffusion by making it much easier for the public to gain access to new ideas in a permanent and consistent format. In the long run, printing and literacy affected practically every area of European life, serving as a powerful engine in the movement toward modernization.[13]

There can be little doubt that this increased literacy stimulated both Protestantism and capitalism. Luther, Calvin, and other early Protestant leaders based much of their reformed theology on their own studies of the Bible and the works of early Christian scholars. They argued that their own interpretations were superior to those presented by the Roman Church, which, they argued, had been distorted over the centuries, and they encouraged their followers to read the Scriptures for themselves. Luther's German Bible, for example, was designed to enable literate Germans to experience the word of God firsthand.

Meanwhile, the spread of increasingly complex record keeping and bureaucratic procedures frequently made literacy an absolute necessity for those engaged in both private and public enterprise. It can hardly be surprising, then, that those who already possessed the skill of literacy—and thus enjoyed more options in an increasingly modern society—were more likely to follow the suggestions of Protestant theologians who urged them to read the Holy Word for themselves. On the other hand, it is equally unsurprising that early converts to Protestantism had incentives to learn reading and writing, which in turn contributed to their own personal success in an increasingly capitalistic, competitive society. In other words, literacy was becoming more of a social norm than an exceptional skill, and both religious change and economic development contributed to its proliferation.

Yet another element of modernization, one discussed above, reinforced the links among literacy, Protestantism, and capitalism during the Early Modern Period. This was the increasingly important role of cities, which provided an environment where each of these other three developments could flourish. As they had already done during the Middle Ages, but even more so, cities in the Early Modern era attracted concentrations of people with increasingly diverse back-grounds and ideas, while providing critical economic and cultural links with the wider world. As cities prospered, and these factors reinforced each other, they contributed a more vibrant and dynamic way of life throughout Europe.[14]

What all of this began to add up to was the realization of a critical legacy of the Renaissance, one that contradicted much traditional medieval thinking. Renaissance humanists had promoted the idea that human life could be worthwhile and even improved, while a corollary of this conviction was the idea that the lives of individual human beings mattered. As medieval towns grew into modern cities, a new social attitude developed: that freedom for the individual was beneficial, instead of a challenge to the Will of God. Before the end of the sixteenth century, there were even numerous people who were arguing—in print—that personal **liberty**, the freedom to do as one chooses, was a God-given right. To point out what is probably obvious, most of these people were educated members of the urban bourgeoisie.

The sixteenth and seventeenth centuries saw an intensification of the process of modernization that had begun centuries earlier. Social change had brought capitalism, Protestantism, literacy, and urbanization to many parts of Western Europe. Even in strongly Catholic regions, the collective and fatalistic mentality promoted by the Christian Paternalistic Ethic was in retreat, especially in the burgeoning towns and cities. Individualism, perhaps the most critical element of modernization, and the one that binds the rest together, was for the first time becoming a widely accepted social norm. In this way, Western Europe became the first major civilization in world history to experience this change.

Freedom and Liberty

These words are often used interchangeably as synonyms, since the English language has inherited these words as cognates from, in the first case, Germanic language ("*frei*" in German) and in the second, Romance language ("*libertas*" in Latin). Although the use of the latter word is at least a few thousand years old, the meanings today of "freedom" and "liberty" are broader than they were originally.

In ancient Rome, *libertas* generally referred to the state of not being a slave. In the European Middle Ages, "liberties" referred to freedom from certain feudal and manorial obligations for many classes of people, such as town dwellers, that were formally granted by monarchies or local nobles. England's *Magna Carta* in 1215 recognized the rights of many noble landowners from unlimited royal power over their affairs. This freedom *from* authority is what the philosopher Isaiah Berlin termed "negative freedom," since it was freedom *from* some specific type of restriction.

During the Early Modern Period, what Berlin called "positive freedom" emerged, referring to specific rights to actively do something, such as freedoms of occupation, religion, or participation in political affairs. French leaders during the Revolution, in documents such as the *Declaration of Rights of Man and Citizen*, used it to mean that individuals had both the right not to be oppressed by arbitrary justice or excessive taxation, and also specific rights to action, such as speech and religion.

In more modern times, the meaning of both words often depends upon context, but generally speaking, a "free" society is one in which the individual has both negative and positive freedoms. British political philosopher, John Stuart Mill, in his influential work *On Liberty* (1859), reasoned that a person's freedom of action should be unlimited unless it interfered with someone else's rights, while freedom of expression should be virtually unlimited. He recognized that creativity and innovation were ever more necessary to confront the new challenges of a world undergoing significant social change, and saw liberty as an essential element of a modern, progressive society.

Notes

1 A solidly researched and interesting view of Europe's relationship with the non-European world in the High and late Middle Ages is J. R. S. Phillips's *The Medieval Expansion of Europe* (Oxford: Oxford University Press, 1988).
2 On late medieval European society and the non-European world, see William D. Phillips, Jr., and Carla Rahn Phillips *The Worlds of Christopher Columbus*, (New York: Cambridge University Press, 1992). 1–81; and Felipe Fernández-Armesto, *Before Columbus: Exploration and Colonisation from the Mediterranean to the Atlantic, 1229–1492* (Philadelphia: University of Pennsylvania Press, 1987).

3 J. H. Elliott, *The Old World and the New, 1492–1650* (Cambridge: Cambridge University Press, 1992).

4 A useful modern study of Portuguese discoveries and empire building is Malyn Newitt, *A History of Portuguese Overseas Expansion 1400–1668* (London: Routledge, 2005).

5 On Columbus's career in its historical context see Phillips and Phillips, *The Worlds of Christopher Columbus.*

6 A reasonably concise account of the growth of the Spanish empire in the New World can be found in Henry Kamen, *Empire: How Spain Became a World Power, 1492–1763* (New York: HarperCollins, 2003), 95–149.

7 A useful discussion of the process of empire building can be found in G. V. Scammell, *The First Imperial Age: European Overseas Expansion, 1400–1715* (London: Unwin Hyman, 1989)

8 Over the last eighty years there have been many interpretations of the problems of the sixteenth-century Spanish economy, and some of the arguments are quite complicated. While causes and effects are controversial, there is unanimity that the failure of domestic capital investment was in the long run disastrous and prevented economic development. One fascinating new study is Elvira Vilches's *New World Gold: Cultural Anxiety and Monetary Disorder in Early Modern Spain* (Chicago: Chicago University Press, 2010); for a nuanced global interpretation, see Immanuel Wallerstein, *The Modern World System I: Capitalist Agriculture and the Origins of the European World Economy in the Sixteenth Century* (New York: Academic Press, 1974), especially 164–221; Jaime Vicens Vives's, *An Economic History of Spain* (Princeton: Princeton University Press, 1969) remains a solid overview.

9 On the challenges Spain faced see Kamen, *Empire,* 285–329.

10 Wiesner-Hanks, Merry, *Early Modern Europe, 1450–1789* (New York: Cambridge University Press, 2006), 418–23.

11 H.G. Koenigsberger, George L. Mosse, and G.Q. Bowler, *Europe in the Sixteenth Century,* 2nd ed. (London: Longman, 1989), 30–7; Wiesner-Hanks, *Early Modern Europe,* 243–49.

12 Weber's *The Protestant Ethic and the Spirit of Capitalism* was first published as a series of essays in 1904–1905, and has since appeared as a book in numerous editions.

13 The classic work on the impact of publishing on modernization remains Elizabeth Eisenstein's *The Printing Press as an Agent of Change* (Cambridge: Cambridge University Press, 1979).

14 R. A. Houston, "Colonies, Enterprises, and Wealth: The Economies of Europe and the Wider World in the Seventeenth Century," in *Early Modern Europe: An Oxford History,* ed. Euan Cameron (Oxford: Oxford University Press, 1999), 137–70.

Suggested Readings

Eisenstein, Elizabeth. *The Printing Press as an Agent of Change.* Cambridge: Cambridge University Press, 1979.

Elliott, J. H. *The Old World and the New, 1492–1650.* Cambridge: Cambridge University Press, 1992.

Fernández-Armesto. Felipe. *Before Columbus: Exploration and Colonisation from the Mediterranean to the Atlantic, 1229–1492.* Philadelphia: University of Pennsylvania Press, 1987.

Houston, R. A. "Colonies, Enterprises, and Wealth: The Economies of Europe and the Wider World in the Seventeenth Century." In *Early Modern Europe: An Oxford History.* Edited by Ewan Cameron. Oxford: Oxford University Press, 1999.

Kamen, Henry. *Empire: How Spain Became a World Power, 1492–1763.* New York: HarperCollins, 2003.

Koenigsberger, H. G., George L. Mosse, and G. Q. Bowler. *Europe in the Sixteenth Century.* 2nd ed. London: Longman, 1989.

Phillips, J. R. S. *The Medieval Expansion of Europe.* Oxford: Oxford University Press, 1988.

Phillips, William D. Jr., and Carla Rahn Phillips. *The Worlds of Christopher Columbus.* New York: Cambridge University Press, 1992.

Scammell, G. V. *The First Imperial Age: European Overseas Expansion, 1400–1715.* London: Unwin Hyman, 1989.

Vilches, Elvira. *New World Gold: Cultural Anxiety and Monetary Disorder in Early Modern Spain.* Chicago: Chicago University Press, 2010.

Vives, Jaime Vicens. *An Economic History of Spain.* Princeton: Princeton University Press, 1969.

Wallerstein, Immanuel. *The Modern World System I: Capitalist Agriculture and the Origins of the European World Economy in the Sixteenth Century.* New York: Academic Press, 1974.

Wiesner-Hanks, Merry, *Early Modern Europe, 1450–1789.* New York: Cambridge University Press, 2006.

9   The Centralization and Rationalization of the Political State

John McGrath

Key Terms

absolutism, "balance of power," bullionism, constitutional monarchy, "Divine Right," economy of scale, federated republic, infrastructure, mercantilism, separation of powers, "tax farmers"

While long-term economic and social forces helped to redefine the role of government during the Early Modern Period, more immediate circumstances also spurred political change, reinforcing the movement toward more concentrated forms of authority. During the Reformation era, religious divisions within and among European states, often intensified by ethnic, social, and economic differences, challenged even the most powerful monarchs to keep a firm grip on their subjects. This gave many European rulers another reason to increase the size, power, and efficiency of their administrations. The result was a new form and style of political organization known as **absolutism**.[1] Typically, absolutism "introduced standing armies, a permanent bureaucracy, national taxation, a codified law, and the beginnings of a unified market."[2] Together, these elements rationalized and centralized political authority, representing a significant step in the modernization of the political state.

These new structures and policies were justified on the basis of new ideologies that marked a distinct shift from the traditional medieval concept of authority. In contrast to the largely decentralized feudal system where successive levels of nobility ruled in accordance with local customs and practices, absolutist monarchies began to enjoy, at least in theory, total and absolute power over all their subjects. Such power was often supported by the religious concept of **"Divine Right,"** the idea that God had specially selected the royal families and endowed them with extraordinary qualities with which to lead their kingdoms. In this view, the machinery of absolutist government became merely the instrument through which such rulers exercised their supreme will. Their subjects, who had grown increasingly impatient with the insecurity that had accompanied the Reformation, largely accepted this new arrangement, since it provided badly needed stability and order.

Absolutism as a Remedy for Instability: England and France

England and France had been two of the first kingdoms to create effective national monarchies during the High Middle Ages. In response to Reformation-era turmoil, the rulers of both kingdoms modified already relatively sophisticated political systems by steadily expanding and strengthening them over the course of the sixteenth century. In doing so, they created the first absolutist governments.

The end of the Hundred Years' War saw England embroiled in a violent domestic power struggle among competing branches of the royal family, known as the Wars of the Roses (1455–1485). Ultimately, Henry Tudor emerged as the victor and took the throne as Henry VII. To prevent further instability and to secure power for himself and his successors, he began a process that placed more power in the hands of the monarchy and replaced much local and customary authority.[3] His son Henry VIII's creation of the national Anglican Church can be seen as only one aspect of this process, which, as it developed over more than a century, involved the creation of new royal administrative, legal, and financial institutions and practices.

This process culminated under Henry VIII's youngest daughter, Elizabeth I, who took the throne in 1558 after the brief and divisive reigns of her two immediate predecessors. Faced with domestic religious conflict, financial difficulties, and foreign threats, Elizabeth's response had to be both firm and practical. She improved the efficiency of the government through internal reforms and by delegating authority to capable, trustworthy individuals. To minimize religious division, she implemented distinctly secular policies that balanced the more conservative supporters of the Anglican Church against the reform-minded "Puritans," English subjects who had converted to continental varieties of Protestantism. During her forty-five-year reign, she vastly strengthened her subjects' loyalty to the kingdom and to herself through the cunning employment of imagery and propaganda. Although military expenditures strained her royal treasury, when she died in 1603 Elizabeth bequeathed to her successors, the Scottish Stuart dynasty, a stronger royal government that ruled over a more united populace. Unfortunately, this unity was not to last.

Meanwhile, in France, the reigns of three weak kings after 1559 had allowed almost forty years of intermittent but ferocious religious civil war between Catholics and Calvinists, known as the French Wars of Religion. The accession of King Henri IV in 1589 marked a turning point, as this Protestant prince was willing to convert to Catholicism in order to win the loyalty of his subjects, and subsequently proclaimed an official policy of religious toleration. He used his personal popularity and highly competent and dedicated ministers to return the Kingdom of France to peace and prosperity before the end of the century.[4]

Though Henri's reign ended prematurely in 1610 with his assassination by a Catholic fanatic, his successors, Louis XIII and Louis XIV, followed up on his accomplishments. Louis XIII's chief minister, the Cardinal Armand-Jean du Plessis, known as Cardinal Richelieu, significantly reorganized the structure of royal government, creating a hierarchical system of bureaucratic authority that he could control from the top. He continued the steady growth of the size of the royal government; royal courts, a centralized government treasury, and royally appointed officials began to replace local and traditional authority. Richelieu also created a network of spies and informants who kept him aware of developments throughout the entire kingdom, and who enabled him to identify those whose loyalty to the French crown was questionable. In foreign policy, he followed a pragmatic approach designed to weaken the power of France's traditional enemy, the Habsburg dynasty that ruled Spain, Austria, and the Netherlands.

The full accession of King Louis XIV in 1661 resulted in what many consider to have been the ultimate example of absolutist rule.[5] Determined to quell any possible resistance from quarreling noble factions, Louis expanded the power of his government by increasing the size of his government and army, supported by higher taxes. Notably, to manage his expanded state, Louis relied on the talents of educated bourgeoisie, instead of either churchmen or the nobility, as had been the usual practice. For example, his most powerful minister was Jean-Baptiste Colbert, a trained accountant who was the son of a clothier, who rose through the ranks of the royal state on merit, instead of through personal or political connections. Colbert directed French royal finances for two decades and immensely strengthened France's colonial interests and maritime capabilities. In doing so, he developed many of its mercantilist policies (discussed below), while gaining a reputation for financial wizardry. Louis XIV's reign represents the culmination of the growth of royal bureaucracy: from 1505 until 1664, the number of salaried employees of the French Crown increased almost sevenfold, from 12,000 to over 80,000.[6]

From the beginning of his reign, Louis XIV consciously cultivated a public image of himself as almost a semi-deity, and enjoyed popularity and even awe among the masses. To reinforce this image, he moved the center of his government outside Paris to the town of Versailles, where he constructed an enormous and spectacular chateau. Here he could both conduct affairs of state and keep an eye on the nobles, whose presence he required at his court, and whose power he was determined to minimize. Though he probably never uttered the widely cited quote "I am the state," he acted with a boldness and decisiveness in both domestic and foreign affairs that demonstrated an almost complete disregard for restraint.

Other European monarchies, such as Austria, the larger German states, and Spain, followed the lead of France by embracing absolutism during the seventeenth and eighteenth centuries. Each constructed a larger and more centralized political system, with variations according to circumstance, and adopted mercantilist economic policies. Increasingly, such governments relied on rational planning, instead of tradition, to create news laws, policies, and institutions that helped them maintain control and order. In each case, even in many Protestant states, they justified their power on the basis of "Divine Right."

By the end of the seventeenth century, the only two major states in Europe that had not adopted and intensified absolutism were the Netherlands and England. The former achieved independence from Spanish rule and became a **federated republic**—a formal union of a number of largely independent states—that prospered mightily from overseas trade; rather uniquely, the Dutch government promoted commercial freedom and opposed mercantilist forms of state control. England, known as Great Britain after its formal union with Scotland in 1707, became a **constitutional monarchy**, as outlined below. Even so, the English national government increased its size and authority over the course of the seventeenth century, and mercantilist economic policies provided the foundations for Great Britain's growing overseas empire.

The Thirty Years' War

By the early seventeenth century, more than 300, separate, mostly German-speaking states, large and small, comprised the Holy Roman Empire that extended over much of central Europe. Since the Middle Ages, these states had exercised a significant measure of independence from their nominal and elected Catholic overlord, the emperor. During the Reformation, some of these states had become Lutheran or Calvinist, while others remained faithful to Rome. This religious diversity made political unity impossible while causing considerable tension and disorder. By 1618, these inflammatory conditions provoked the most destructive war yet seen on the European continent, known as the Thirty Years' War.[7]

This conflict began locally, when a religiously influenced rebellion against the authority of the emperor erupted in the state of Bohemia, but soon other states within the empire entered to support one side or the other. The war escalated further during the 1620s, as the leaders of practically every sovereign state in continental Europe eventually decided that their involvement might lead to some political or economic advantage, and it became a continent-wide conflagration. Though most of the fighting took place in central Europe, especially Germany, military campaigns of unprecedented size ravaged parts of Italy, the Low Countries, France, and the Baltic States.

Not only did the scale of the warfare expand, so too did the political complexity, and the original causes of the war were soon practically irrelevant. By the mid-1630s, it had become nearly impossible to construct a peace agreement that would satisfy each of the dozens of belligerents—so the armies continued to fight, even without any evident goal. Meanwhile, many of the participating governments had run out of money due to the ever-rising military costs, and their unpaid mercenary armies marauded virtually at random through the countryside. Besieging cities and burning villages, they left vast areas almost completely depopulated, while starvation and disease took a terrible toll on the civilian populations.

At long last, in 1648, a series of treaties ended the war for most of the combatants, and this marked the end of large-scale religious conflict between European states. From this point on, governments pursued largely secular foreign policies and engaged in what became known as **"balance of power"** diplomacy, by forming alliances with each other that would discourage enemies from starting hostilities. As well, the demands of conducting major military efforts had forced many of the participating monarchies to expand both their taxation and their political administrations; after the end of the war such kingdoms as France,

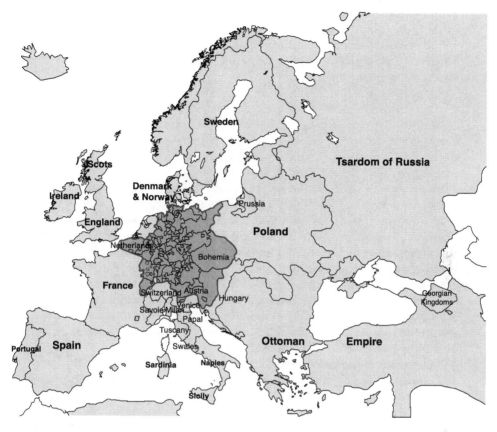

Map 9.1 Europe, 1648

Austria, Denmark, Sweden, and the rising German state of Brandenburg/Prussia, made these changes permanent. For these reasons, one can see the Thirty Years' War as contributing to the process of political modernization. Even so, the sheer destructiveness of this conflict provoked one historian to judge it as "morally subversive, economically destructive, socially degrading, devious in its course, futile in its result . . . [it is] the outstanding example in European history of meaningless conflict."[8]

State Finance and Mercantilism

The Thirty Years' War forced virtually every European state to increase the size and effectiveness of its standing (permanent) army, which required them to pay, transport, and supply larger numbers of troops. Moreover, the evolution of military technology also necessitated more expenditure per soldier; by the Thirty

Years' War, warfare had become more capital intensive, relying on an array of gunpowder weapons as well as larger fortifications and warships. As a direct result, by the beginning of the eighteenth century, the percent of state revenues for the military ranged from 25 percent in peace up to more than 80 percent during wartime. In the words on one historian, the state "became, in effect, a military institution in its own right."[9]

As Early Modern governments became more powerful, they also increased their control over their kingdoms' economies. An important aspect of absolutism were economic policies known collectively as **mercantilism**, which gave the state a larger direct role in the economy in the interest of strengthening the overall kingdom.[10] It represents a move toward a command economy that maximized **economy of scale** (see Chapter Twelve) and undermined the role of tradition in European economies. As it did so, mercantilism helped protect and encourage the accumulation and investment of capital that was critical to promoting the economic growth that took place in the seventeenth and eighteenth centuries.

As a result, the size and responsibilities of the nonmilitary aspects of government also expanded. Added to the higher cost of military, the mushrooming royal bureaucracies, legal systems, and **infrastructure** expenses made it essential that government revenues expand as well. This, of course, required more and higher taxation. As absolutist states extended their power, they instituted all sorts of new taxes and fees, including sales taxes on essential materials such as salt, "head" and "hearth" taxes that amounted to per-capita charges, and even taxes on land ownership.

Necessarily, the process of tax collection itself became more bureaucratized and efficient, with the appearance of centralized royal treasuries and finance ministries. Under Cardinal Richelieu, the French government subcontracted tax collection by allowing private citizens to bid for contracts as **"tax farmers."** What this meant in essence was that in exchange for the payment of a fixed sum representing the taxes owed by a province or town, such individuals—who were usually financiers with access to large amounts of capital—received a royal license to collect as much as they were able, usually over and above the sum they had given the state. Tax farming became an investment, one that was often extremely lucrative for both the state and the investor.[11]

However, as the overall tax requirements rose, so too did the number of individuals exempted from taxes. While European nobles were traditionally immune to taxation, the growth of the royal state meant that an increasing number of ambitious individuals became members of the nobility and/or became royal officials, giving them tax privileges as well. This meant that the poorer members of society wound up shouldering most of this expanding tax burden. With better recordkeeping, an expanded bureaucracy, and more soldiers and police to quash peasants' and workers' revolts, royal treasuries were consistently able to increase the amounts they collected. But even so, the delicate balance between revenues and expenditures could be quickly upset by the outbreak of warfare, which happened frequently during the late seventeenth and the eighteenth century. Many absolutist states began selling bonds and borrowing from financiers to pay for their growing expenses, as the financial structures of royal governments continued to become more complex during the eighteenth century.

Much of the early development of mercantilism can be traced to the spread of overseas trade and empire-building, as discussed in the previous chapter. As early as the fifteenth century, monarchs and their ministers had started to measure their "wealth" in terms of the amount of precious metals, or bullion, circulating within the kingdom. This principle, known as **bullionism**, encouraged royal treasuries to find ways to reduce the flow of bullion, or precious metals, out of the realm while increasing the amount that came into it; a widely held assumption was that the wealth of the kingdom could be measured by the amount of money in circulation within it. (see box)

One almost universal mercantilist policy was the taxation of imports, to discourage subjects from buying foreign goods and thus sending bullion outside the kingdom. Mercantilist policies guided the administration of colonial systems so that more "wealth" flowed toward the "home country" than toward the colony. For example, mercantilist governments usually forbade colonial subjects from buying foreign goods. In some cases, they even prevented colonies from producing many needed commodities themselves, which forced them to buy manufactured goods from the "home country," often at monopoly prices. Such practices contributed not only to the sorts of dissatisfaction that spurred the American Revolution, but also established a pattern of uneven economic development that persists even today, long after the dissolution of European colonial empires.

Mercantilist policy also called for direct government support of certain industries considered critical to the economic, military, and political power of the state. To avoid a dependence on foreign goods, domestic businesses in key industries such as manufacturing, shipping, and armaments were often granted or sold licenses and monopolies to operate under royal directives, and sometimes enjoyed direct government investment. Such privileged enterprises generally benefited from both an economy of scale and a lack of competition, and these arrangements amounted to a monopoly partnership between the state and private business owners where both entities prospered. The profits that often accrued from this sort of mercantilist protection helped many businesses to accumulate capital that could be used for reinvestment and future expansion. In the long run, mercantilist policies can be credited with helping rising industries—especially technologically dependent manufacturing—become firmly established in many European countries. In these sorts of arrangements, mercantilism both provided opportunities for ambitious entrepreneurs and investors, especially the wealthiest members of the bourgeoisie, and also directly promoted the long-term economic modernization that absolutist rulers desired for their states.

Stuart England

The only large European state to avoid major involvement in the Thirty Years' War was England, which experienced its own transformations over the course of the seventeenth century. Under the kings of the Stuart Dynasty, political, social, and religious divisions created a civil war, and its aftermath saw the emergence of the first modern constitutional monarchy.[12] The different path taken by England would have immense consequences for the future of Western development.

According to traditional law, English kings were required to call the institution of Parliament for approval of any new laws and taxes. However, by the 1600s, one of its two branches, the elected House of Commons, was dominated by wealthy, largely Calvinist, landowners, a social class known as the landed gentry. Members of the House of Commons found their interests increasingly at odds with those of the Scottish Stuart kings who had followed Elizabeth Tudor, and throughout the first part of the century, serious disagreements over religion, taxation, and military spending provided an obstacle to the continued expansion of royal power. In 1641, these issues came to a head with the outbreak of the English Civil War, between separate armies fighting on behalf of Crown and Parliament.

After several years of campaigning, the Parliamentary forces emerged victorious under the innovative military leadership of Parliamentarian Oliver Cromwell, and they even captured King Charles I, who was executed for treason in early 1649. However, little consensus emerged among the victors on how to manage affairs of state. An experiment with parliamentary rule created only government paralysis, followed by several years in the 1650s when Cromwell headed what has been called a "Puritan military dictatorship," but which was equally ineffective in solving England's mounting problems. One significant result of this troubled period was that its political frustrations fueled remarkably fertile debate, featuring the publication of many influential and often novel political arguments. Among the most significant of these was *Leviathan*, by Thomas Hobbes, former tutor to the king, who advocated a strong central government to ensure order and security. Notably, *Leviathan* was based on reason and logic, as opposed to the Divine Right argument that justified many continental absolutist monarchies.

Cromwell's death and the further deterioration of effective political leadership led to popular calls for a return to kingship. In the Restoration of 1660, the executed king's son, Charles II, returned from exile on the continent to take the throne, and for the most part, he worked constructively with Parliament. But when he was succeeded by his brother James II in 1685, the Calvinist-dominated Parliament recoiled from the new king's Catholicism and pro-French sympathies, mobilizing yet another rebellion against the monarchy. This time, though, events were carefully managed, and the nearly bloodless Glorious Revolution of 1688 forced James to flee and handed the kingship to William of Orange, ruler of the Netherlands, who was married to James's daughter Mary. However, Parliamentary leaders had attached a condition to the arrangement: William was required to sign the English Bill of Rights, which acknowledged the supremacy of Parliament in managing most domestic affairs.

One of the major figures involved in this transfer of power was the philosopher John Locke, whose *Second Treatise of Government* of 1689 provided a rebuttal to Hobbes's *Leviathan*. In the *Second Treatise*, which is universally regarded as one of history's most important works of political philosophy, Locke argued that a **separation of powers**, where the monarchy and an elected legislature served as checks on each other's power, was necessary to avoid the dangers of tyranny. Not coincidentally, the Glorious Revolution had just created such an arrangement, giving England a division of powers between the king and Parliament.

Early Modern Europe and the Absolutist Age

Historians often refer to the two and a half centuries between the Protestant Reformation and the French Revolution in 1789 as the Early Modern Period of European history. By the beginning of this era, the main elements of modernity had already been established in most parts of Western and central Europe. Building on this foundation, monarchies employed increasingly efficient methods of securing their power and imposing order on their kingdoms; as they did so, the absolutist form of government helped to promote and even accelerate the further spread of modernity. In particular, it fostered the rationalism, political centralization, and bureaucratization that together provide a reasonably complete definition of what absolutism actually was. In addition, it enabled early modern governments to regulate and direct the increasingly complicated economic systems that became the foundations of a global economy.

For the most part, monarchs ruled such states with the active cooperation of some or all of the elite social classes, whether noble or bourgeoisie, who possessed the talents and resources needed for more modern and efficient governance. Such elites had evident positive incentives, material and otherwise, to attach themselves to the centers of power. As assemblies of notables, royal advisors, military officers, or government functionaries, the upper classes hardly needed to be bludgeoned or threatened into assuming their new roles as instruments of the royal will. Although occasional revolts and lesser types of resistance took place during the Early Modern period, these were more the exception than the rule. For the most part, during the absolutist age the interests of the highest social orders largely coincided with, instead of conflicting with, the interests of the expanding royal state, and this helped to maintain the social order that the crises of the Reformation era had disrupted.

This new arrangement necessarily extended throughout the social system, as persons of all ranks adjusted to living in a monarchy with more unified administrative, economic, and legal systems. As this happened over centuries, the medieval corporate ethos adjusted to become something significantly different: the acceptance of the monarchy as the rightful head of a distinctive entity, one that bound subjects together in a sense of mutual obligation. All subjects, inevitably, developed some sense of common interest with other subjects of that kingdom, and a self-identity based on a common loyalty to the crown.

Thus, during the sixteenth, seventeenth, and even eighteenth centuries, we can detect a broad pattern of mutually reinforcing developments. Despite significant variations from case to case, we can see the decisive establishment of European overseas trade and colonies, the formation of larger armies that were engaged in more frequent warfare, the growth of cities, and a more specialized money economy. Each of these important steps was connected as both cause and effect to the growth of absolutism and mercantilism. Whatever the particular ideological justification for absolutist rule, during the Early Modern Period, local and traditional authority steadily gave way to a more centralized legal/rational authority, reinforcing the mutual dependence of the ruler and those over whom he or she ruled.

While it would be anachronistic to call this "nationalism," we can consider it a type of "protonationalism" that set the stage for the age of the nation-state in the nineteenth century. Moreover, the relative stability and rationalization of government during the absolutist age laid a steady foundation for the economic, social, and intellectual growth that stimulated other elements of modernization during the eighteenth century and beyond.

Economic Growth

Economic growth is a quantitative term that expresses the increase in the value of the goods and services produced by an economy over time. Comparing one period to another, such as one year to the next, the rate of growth serves as one indicator of the health of an economy.

During most of the Early Modern Period, the field of study that we call economics did not yet exist. As absolutism developed, royal governments generally increased their control over such elements as taxation, the money supply, customs duties, and frequently even prices and wages, through a largely unsystematic collection of policies known as mercantilism. It was largely assumed that the amount of precious metals in circulation within a kingdom was the best indicator of a healthy economy. Thus many of these policies were what we today would call protectionist, since they were designed to stimulate domestic production, under the assumption that different states were competing with each other for a finite amount of wealth. Mercantilist policies varied from place to place, but were usually designed to discourage imports and encourage exports. This was because it was widely believed that purchasing foreign-produced goods would result in "wealth," in the form of precious metals, departing the kingdom and enriching economic competitors.

It was only in the Enlightenment that intellectuals such as the French Physiocrats and Adam Smith questioned the validity of this assumption. The latter's *Wealth of Nations* (1776) contributed greatly to a redefinition of the title subject, pointing out that wealth could be measured more meaningfully as a function of the frequency of economic transactions—how often money changes hands—instead of as the amount of money in circulation. While the supply of money within an economy may affect the willingness of individuals, businesses, and governments to use it for production, consumption, and investment, it is what these entities do with the money available that is a more meaningful reflection of the strength of an economy.

Today, modern nations typically use a measure known as Gross Domestic Product, or GDP, to measure economic growth. It is generally calculated as the total of consumer spending, business investment, and government expenditure over a given period.

Notes

1 A solid general study of absolutism is John Miller, *Absolutism in Seventeenth Century Europe* (London: Palgrave Macmillan, 1991). More concise explanations can be found in Geoffrey Parker, *Europe in Crisis: 1598–1648* (New York: Wiley Blackwell, 2001), 54–66, and Merry Wiesner-Hanks, *Early Modern Europe 1450–1789* (New York: Cambridge University Press, 2006), 285–325. Perry Anderson's *The Lineages of the Absolutist State* (London: Verso, 1974) remains a standard interpretation of absolutism.
2 Anderson, *Lineages*, 16.
3 Among the numerous studies of Tudor England, a very solid scholarly work is John Guy, *Tudor England* (New York: Oxford University Press, 1990). See also Wiesner-Hanks, *Early Modern Europe*, 303–09.
4 On developments in France under Henri IV and Louis XIII, see William Beik, *Absolutism and Society in Seventeenth Century France* (Cambridge: Cambridge University Press, 1985), Wiesner-Hanks, *Early Modern Europe*, 297–303, and Anderson, *Lineages*, 90–100.
5 Numerous excellent studies of the Sun King include John B. Wolf, *Louis XIV* (New York: Norton, 1974), a detailed and thorough work; and Rich Wilkinson, *Louis XIV* (New York: Routledge, 2007), which is shorter and more accessible, and contains numerous entertaining anecdotes.
6 Geoffrey Parker, *Europe in Crisis*, 44.
7 Now regarded as the standard work on this confusing war is Geoffrey Parker's *The Thirty Years War*, 2nd ed. (London: Routledge, 1997), which has supplanted C. V. Wedgwood's *The Thirty Years War* (New York: Doubleday Anchor, 1961).
8 Wedgewood, *The Thirty Years War*, 506.
9 Parker, *Europe in Crisis 1598–1648*, 72; Steven Gunn, "War, Religion, and the State" in *Early Modern Europe: An Oxford History*, Euan Cameron ed., (London: Oxford University Press, 1999), 110–19.
10 The classic work on mercantilism is Eli Heckscher, *Mercantilism*, 2 vols., (London: Bradford and Dickens, 1962). See also Immanuel Wallerstein, *The Modern World-System II: Mercantilism and the Consolidation of the European World-Economy, 1600–1750* (New York: Academic Press, 1980), and Anderson, *Lineages*, 35–42.
11 Beik, *Absolutism and Society in Seventeenth Century France*, 245–78.
12 In the crowded field of historical writing on the Stuart era, Barry Coward's *The Stuart Age*, 3rd ed. (London: Longman, 2003) is recommended.

Suggested Readings

Anderson, Perry. *Lineages of the Absolutist State*. London: Verso, 1974.

Beik, William. *Absolutism and Society in Seventeenth Century France*. Cambridge: Cambridge University Press, 1985.

Cameron, Euan, ed. *Early Modern Europe: An Oxford History*. London: Oxford University Press, 1999.

Coward, Barry. *The Stuart Age.*, 3rd ed. London: Longman, 2003.

Guy, John. *Tudor England*. New York: Oxford University Press, 1990.

Heckscher, Eli. *Mercantilism*. Two volumes. London: Bradford and Dickens, 1962.

Miller, John. *Absolutism in Seventeenth Century Europe*. London: Palgrave Macmillan, 1991.

Parker, Geoffrey. *Europe in Crisis: 1598–1648*. New York: Wiley Blackwell, 2001.

Parker, Geoffrey. ed. *The Thirty Years' War*. 2nd ed. London: Routledge, 1997.

Wallerstein, Immanuel, *The Modern World-System II: Mercantilism and the Consolidation of the European World-Economy, 1600–1750*. New York: Academic Press, 1980.

Wiesner-Hanks, Merry E. *Early Modern Europe, 1450–1789*. New York: Cambridge University Press, 2006.

Wilkinson, Rich. *Louis XIV*. New York: Routledge, 2007.

Wolf, John B. *Louis XIV*. New York, Norton, 1974.

10 The Enlightenment

John McGrath

Key Terms

deism, enlightened despotism, enlightened self-interest, "Invisible Hand," natural laws

The Enlightenment was a period of European intellectual and cultural development that began in the late seventeenth century and lasted through the eighteenth century. Building on the foundations established by the Renaissance and Scientific Revolution, the Enlightenment encouraged Europeans to view their world from a more rational, goal-oriented perspective, setting the stage for much of the massive social change that took place in the late eighteenth and nineteenth centuries. People during the Enlightenment often referred to their era as the "Age of Reason."

Science and Reason

The Scientific Revolution that had begun in the late sixteenth century was a critical stage in the modernization of Europe, since it emphasized the systematic study and observation of natural phenomena. This allowed scholars like Descartes and Galileo to develop theories and general principles that could be applied to the natural world. Because of the printing press, such ideas could be compared and debated, but although their discoveries were important in the history of scientific inquiry, early scientists comprised a somewhat isolated intellectual community. In comparison, the Enlightenment featured wider participation by the rapidly growing community of literate and educated people of all sorts, who were pursuing a much wider spectrum of topics. They focused especially on the nature of humanity and human societies, in order to develop **"natural laws,"** that is, principles of human behavior that might be useful in creating a better society. During the Enlightenment, such scholars' efforts led them into many fields of inquiry, including education, philosophy, technology, politics, criminology, music, literature, and even the beginnings of sociology and economics.

The Scientific Revolution had helped to discredit the narrow Christian explanations of the nature of humanity, the earth, and the cosmos. Instead, it promoted the sense that some sort of rational benevolent force had created the world, a perspective that is often called **deism**, which became an essential foundation of the Enlightenment approach to the pursuit of knowledge.[1] A frequent analogy demonstrating the concept of deism is "God as clockmaker;" many scholars held the conviction that had God created the universe as an entity that operated somewhat like a machine, according to rationally designed principles of cause and effect. Enlightenment scholars largely devoted their efforts to uncovering these principles and applying them in ways that would benefit humanity.

On the whole, the Enlightenment demolished the blind acceptance of tradition as a guiding principle of life. In marked contrast to the medieval era, with its emphasis on faith and obedience, many Europeans began to question customary methods, institutions, and authorities of all sorts. As one historian expressed it:

> Armed with science, reason, and empirical facts, the Enlightenment saw itself as engaged in a noble struggle against the constricting medieval darkness of Church dogma and popular superstition, tied to a backward and tyrannical political structure of corrupt privilege.[2]

Optimism, Knowledge, and Skepticism

Many historians would consider the first major Enlightenment figure to be the Englishman John Locke, because of his more optimistic view of human capabilities compared to common previous outlooks. Convinced that an individual's thinking and behavior were shaped by experience, instead of determined by birth, Locke promoted the influential idea that people could use reason to educate themselves and improve their societies.[3] In 1689, the year after England's Glorious Revolution, he published his *Two Treatises on Government*, which judged absolutism to be an irrational way of organizing a political state, and even a dangerous one, since it could so easily turn into tyranny. In the *Second Treatise*, Locke constructed a supremely rational argument in favor of a separation of powers in government, where an elected legislature could act as a check on monarchy, and he further asserted that the prime responsibility of political power was the protection of the God-given rights of life, liberty, and property.

Locke's ideas, and those of other early Enlightenment figures, stimulated the next generations of educated Europeans to follow the path of reason. As the eighteenth century progressed, the movement grew and spread, as Enlightenment-inspired thinking began to dominate intellectual discourse throughout the Western world, including France, Holland, Italy, Scandinavia, Spain, Germany, and even the British colonies in America. By this time, technological improvements in printing had enabled the publication of more affordable books, pamphlets, and magazines on a wide variety of subjects, for an increasingly educated and literate population. Throughout Europe, cafés, bookstores, private clubs, and scientific societies provided environments where educated people could mingle to debate ideas.[4]

Empiricism

The empirical approach to learning emphasizes sensory experience as a means to knowledge. It is the foundation of the scientific method, where hypotheses and assumptions can be tested against evidence gained from the observation of phenomena, such as the results of experiments.

During the Scientific Revolution and Enlightenment, intellectuals began to express skepticism of any "truths" that could not be demonstrated as valid. John Locke was an early proponent of the empirical approach, asserting that the human mind at birth is a *tabula rasa*, or "blank slate," and that all knowledge and ideas are the products of one's experiences. This contrasted with traditional views that the world contained "innate truths" that could not be proven but which must be accepted, such as beliefs that certain phenomena are evil, impossible, or inevitable, even if such conclusions could not be supported with evidence. Locke and other Enlightenment figures insisted that any given idea must be supported empirically if it was to be accepted as true.

During the eighteenth century, the Kingdom of France soon achieved recognition as the cultural capital of Europe. There, leading intellectual figures known as *philosophes* ("lovers of learning") achieved celebrity status.[5] Especially in Paris, a "salon culture" evolved where Enlightenment scholars of many backgrounds gathered regularly in the houses of wealthy sponsors, especially noble women. One of the most influential early *philosophes* was a French aristocrat, the Baron de la Brède et de Montesquieu, who was among the first to examine the dynamics of human societies from a comparative perspective. He recognized that each society had unique needs and resources available to it, and he investigated how these factors could influence the development of distinctive cultures, laws, and institutions. Montesquieu's 1748 *Spirit of the Laws* has been described as the first serious study of political science and sociology; in this important work, he followed and expanded upon Locke's argument in favor of a balance of differing political powers.[6]

Undoubtedly the most famous and influential of the *philosophes* was the Frenchman François-Marie Arouet, known by his pen name of Voltaire.[7] Starting in the 1730s, until his death in 1778, he authored hundreds of separate works in various genres, including poetry, social history, essays, and fiction. For most of his career, Voltaire lived in exile from France, due to his attacks on privileged interests such as organized religion and monarchical governments. Younger Enlightenment figures practically worshipped Voltaire, to the point where he has often been called "the Grandfather of the Enlightenment."

Voltaire urged his readers to look objectively at their societies, and to be skeptical of what traditional authority defined as proper and right. He considered the abuse of power to be a particular problem, and he became a champion of tolerance of all sorts. While he was more socially and politically conservative than many other Enlightenment figures—such as Jean-Jacques Rousseau, with whom he quarreled bitterly—he possessed an optimism that with some effort, people's lives could be made better. Yet at the same time he warned against overly idealistic expectations. The novel *Candide*, written in 1759, illustrates nearly all of Voltaire's main criticisms of society.[8] As the title character journeys through a world featuring a seemingly endless number of cruelties, he wonders why human beings seem to insist on creating such avoidable evils as war, persecution, and slavery. As in many of his other works, Voltaire employs satire and irreverence in *Candide* to make his points, poking fun at practically everything, including the Enlightenment itself.

Probably the most ambitious project of the Enlightenment was the *Encyclopedia*, edited by the multitalented *philosophes* Denis Diderot and Jean d'Alembert.[9] Envisioned as a collection of all the world's knowledge, it eventually appeared in twenty-eight volumes between 1751 and 1772, and its almost 72,000 total articles were authored by the leading intellectual figures of Europe, including Voltaire (anonymously) on religion and other topics, Montesquieu on politics, and Rousseau on music and political economy. While the *Encyclopedia* proclaimed itself objective and neutral, all of its contributors were favorable to the principles of intellectual freedom, and the articles tended to be critical of both monarchy and organized religion. Though it was officially banned in France by royal decree in 1759, it continued, in large part because it had many supporters at the royal court, and, in fact, the wives of some of the king's ministers regularly hosted the *Encyclopedia* editors in their salons.

A Diversity of Viewpoints: Rousseau and Smith

Despite such attempts to consolidate the new learning, as time went on the Enlightenment promoted an ever greater diversity of ideas, promoting more and more argument and debate, some of it quite serious and profound. A good illustration of the difficulty in generalizing about Enlightenment thinking can be seen in comparing the contributions of two eighteenth century figures, the Frenchman Jean-Jacques Rousseau and the Scotsman Adam Smith. While they shared certain fundamental assumptions concerning the rationality of human beings and the possibility of progress, they arrived at quite different conclusions about what should be done.

Rousseau, a largely self-taught intellectual from a rather humble background, saw a just and moral society as the highest aspiration of humanity, but lamented that artificial "civilization," with its emphasis on private property, encouraged greed and inequality.[10] He possessed a great optimism that people could do better, arguing that for real enlightenment to be achieved, people must recognize their dependence on each other. A society that could encourage sympathy for one's fellows and make the common welfare the highest priority, would be, by his definition, a virtuous one. He lamented the greed and abuse of power that he saw in eighteenth-century France, which he believed retarded social progress toward a more "enlightened" society. Rousseau's view of human nature and his emphasis on virtue, as expressed in his works *Discourse on Inequality* (1754) and *The Social Contract* (1762), made him a transitional figure between the Enlightenment and the Romantic era that took root in the late eighteenth century. After his death, during the French Revolution, his ideas energized such revolutionary leaders as Jean-Paul Marat and Maximilien Robespierre to undertake massive changes in French society.

Smith, a professor of moral philosophy in Glasgow, Scotland, was likewise concerned with human nature. However, Smith believed that people were most effectively motivated by **"enlightened self-interest,"** the ability to rationally understand what was best for themselves in the long term, which could overcome impulses for the immediate satisfaction of human desires. This, he argued, could be a powerful instrument for creating a more humane and happier society.[11] His most famous work, *The Wealth of Nations* (1776) argues that restraints on economic competition posed by mercantilist controls and the emergence of monopolies hindered economic growth. Individuals were motivated by a rational desire to compete with one another in order to better their economic standing, and if the political state would allow the **"Invisible Hand"** of supply and demand to operate with a minimum of interference, the result would be increased productivity and material progress. Both his view of human nature as essentially rational and his explanation of cause and effect on a society-wide level demonstrate important elements of the Enlightenment approach to understanding the world. Smith's thinking reflects many of Locke's convictions about human capabilities, as well as providing much of the foundation for the ideology of Classical Liberalism that would emerge in the next century.

In a sense, Smith promoted a principle that was the complete opposite of Rousseau's: he argued that if individuals could work toward their own self-interests, the result would be an improvement in the common welfare. In contrast, Rousseau had contended that citizens who put the common welfare ahead of their own selfish desires would personally benefit from their membership in a virtuous society. While this may not seem like a major difference, it has great implications for the sorts of laws, institutions, and social structures that each thought would work the best.

A Rational Ethos

It is difficult in a brief space to do justice to all of the accomplishments achieved by Enlightenment thinkers, in various parts of Europe, over a span of more than a century. Different places, such as Italy, Germany, Scotland, Spain, and Holland developed distinctive Enlightenment themes and approaches that often clashed in substance and style, and provoked a constant give and take of ideas. Perhaps the single unifying element is best expressed through the frequent assertion that the Enlightenment was "not so much a specific set of opinions or beliefs as an attitude of mind."[12] Encouraging lofty scholars and casual readers alike to question conventional wisdom, this attitude became firmly entrenched in the Western cultural outlook and played a major role in promoting social change in all areas of life.

One does not have to look very hard to see that, even in the eighteenth century, Enlightenment ideas directly contributed to material improvement in many European societies. In many absolutist states, including some of the most backward and repressive, these new perspectives were used to reform some of the more counterproductive elements of absolutist and traditional societies; such efforts have sometimes been called "Enlightened Absolutism" or "**enlightened despotism.**" Additionally, Enlightenment thinking motivated people to come up with new and useful ideas in all sorts of fields, from politics to education to science to literature, helping to make European society more innovative and dynamic.

Elsewhere, the impact of the Enlightenment was significant in another way. While new ideas promoted optimism, they also helped to undermine the traditions, customs, and social norms that had helped bind the society together, and the Enlightenment unleashed changes that were difficult to rein in. Beginning in the late eighteenth century, the Enlightenment's encouragement of skepticism played a central role in the profound political and social upheavals that occurred in North America, Europe, and Latin America.[13] During this critical era, for the first time, a critical mass of people had started to believe that, by making the best use of their abilities, they could shape the destinies of their societies as never before. Though there was often fierce disagreement about what direction to take, this, too, was an important step in the creation of modern society.

Notes

1 Norman Hampson, "The Enlightenment," in *Early Modern Europe: An Oxford History*, ed. Euan Cameron (Oxford: Oxford University Press, 1999), 269–74.
2 Richard Tarnas, *The Passion of the Western Mind* (New York: Ballantine, 1991), 312.
3 Ibid., 333–36.
4 Roger Osborne, *Civilization: A New History of the Western World* (New York: Pegasus, 2006), 306–11.
5 A good brief study of the central role of France and Paris is Frederick B. Artz, *The Enlightenment in France* (Kent, OH: Kent State University Press, 1968).
6 Ibid., 57–65.
7 Ibid., 66–82.
8 On *Candide*, see Peter Gay, *The Enlightenment: The Rise of Modern Paganism* (New York: Norton, 1965), 197–203.
9 Artz, *Enlightenment in France*, 88–98; Osborne, *Civilization*, 311.
10 Artz, *Enlightenment in France*, 130–50.
11 On Smith, see Robert L. Heilbroner, *The Worldly Philosophers*, 7th ed. (New York: Touchstone, 1999), 42–74.
12 Hampson, "The Enlightenment," 289.
13 Gay, *The Enlightenment*, 127–207.

Suggested Readings

Artz, Frederick B. *The Enlightenment in France*. Kent, OH: Kent State University Press, 1968.
Gay, Peter. *The Enlightenment: The Rise of Modern Paganism*. New York: Norton, 1965.

Hampson, Norman. "The Enlightenment." In *Early Modern Europe: An Oxford History*. Edited by Euan Cameron, Oxford. Oxford University Press, 1999.

Heilbroner, Robert L. *The Worldly Philosophers*. 7th ed. New York: Touchstone, 1999.

Hyland, Paul. *The Enlightenment*. London: Routledge, 2003.

Osborne, Roger. *Civilization: A New History of the Western World*. New York: Pegasus, 2006.

Outram, Dorinda. *The Enlightenment*. Cambridge: Cambridge University Press, 2013.

Pagden, Anthony. *The Enlightenment: And Why It Still Matters*. New York: Random House, 2013.

Tarnas, Richard. *The Passion of the Western Mind*. New York: Ballantine, 1991.

11 The French Revolution

John McGrath

Key Terms

constitutional monarchy, deputies, general will, nationalism, republican, tribunals

July 14, 1789: At about ten o'clock on a warm summer morning, about 900 residents of Paris, mostly men from the nearby working-class St. Antoine district, congregated in the shadow of the venerable fortress known as the Bastille. Two officials from the Paris Town Hall had just gone inside, to discuss the fate of the large quantity of gunpowder that had recently been moved there.

The crowd was hungry and nervous. In recent days, there had been unsettling reports from the royal palace at Versailles, where the newly elected body known as the Estates-General was trying to resolve the kingdom's financial problems. King Louis XVI had removed the popular Minister of Finance, Jacques Necker, and in Paris, where civil disorder had already been common for several months, this news had provoked several violent clashes between royal troops and local residents. Many Parisians now believed that Louis was intent on reasserting his control of the city, perhaps by ordering foreign mercenary troops to seize it. Hastily organized into militias under the command of city officials, they were becoming desperate to find the means to defend Paris from a possible attack by their own king. Although they possessed cannon, muskets, and ammunition, they lacked gunpowder, and they knew that more than 250 barrels now lay within the massive walls of the fortress.[1]

In the minds of many, the Bastille was a hated symbol of royal despotism, having served as a prison for numerous enemies of the absolutist state. As the situation in Paris had deteriorated in recent weeks, it remained a defiant outpost of the king's power. While the city officials inside pressed for the release of the gunpowder, the hours passed, the heat rose, and the crowd waiting outside grew more restless. At half-past one, several men, apparently acting independently, climbed on top of a perfume shop next to the fortress's front gate and from there cut the chains that held up the drawbridge. Without warning the massive platform slammed down with an earsplitting crash, killing a man standing below it.

Like many other pivotal events in history, what happened next was fueled by misperception and confusion. The members of the crowd, taken by surprise, experienced a few minutes of uncertainty before assuming—wrongly—that the Bastille's commander had ordered the gate to be lowered as a means of inviting them inside. And so, with enthusiastic shouts, men began streaming across the bridge. They were largely unarmed.

However, the royal troops inside the courtyard were equally confused. They could only conclude the worst: that the members of the approaching mob were forcing their way in. Vastly outnumbered, but with muskets and cannon already loaded, the soldiers opened fire with a deadly hail of projectiles that halted the approaching surge of cheering men.

Faced with such unexpected, withering, fire, it did not take long for the onrushing men to come to an ugly, though again erroneous, conclusion: that this had been a trap carefully crafted by the treacherous King Louis. Now enraged, they set about besieging the fortress, reinforced by Paris militiamen and deserting royal troops who had rushed to the scene. By three-thirty, after about ninety of their number had been killed, the attackers had maneuvered cannon opposite the Bastille's main gate, which forced the defenders to surrender.

The capitulation failed to quench the mob's fury. Men swarmed through the fortress, looking for gunpowder, more weapons, and rumored political prisoners they were determined to liberate. (Of the last, they were sorely disappointed, as only seven prisoners were being held there, and all of them were either petty criminals or insane.) By late afternoon, the Bastille's commander was marched to the nearby Town Hall, where the disorderly crowd killed and decapitated him and another official. Their heads were placed on pikes, which were carried at the head of an impromptu parade. As the procession moved through the streets of Paris, throngs of celebrating civilians joined in, along with various units of soldiers and police. Near the front marched the seven liberated prisoners, who included one elderly man who believed that he was Julius Caesar.

News of the episode—often wildly inaccurate and exaggerated—raced through Paris, from neighborhood to neighborhood, from house to house, and from shop to shop. Except for a few members of the privileged classes, almost all of the city's residents took to the streets to cheer or join the grisly procession, which lasted well into the night.

Paris was now in open rebellion against royal authority, and there could be no turning back. From this point on the forces of change would propel French society into the unknown.

Social Change and Revolution

Literally thousands of books have been written about the French Revolution, which attests not only to its importance, but also to its complexity. From the summer of 1789 through the final defeat of Napoleon at Waterloo in 1815, French society underwent transformations that defy easy generalizations. A nation of close to thirty million people had thrown off the yoke of absolute monarchy and plunged into unknown territory, and as unexpected events seemed to provoke further unexpected events, the Revolution attained a life of its own. The French

Revolution is one of the defining events in the emergence of what we call the "modern world." What, then, were the conditions that created it?

A useful way to answer this is by examining this episode in a context of social change and modernization. In France, the eighteenth century had been a time of long-term, gradual internal and external change, punctuated by sudden crises, which had disrupted familiar ways of life and created insecurity and uneasiness for many people within the kingdom. To many men and women in the kingdom, conventional solutions to their problems appeared inadequate, and indeed, as time went on and the sense of dissatisfaction deepened, the conventional solutions often seemed to be part of the problem itself. By July 1789, a sequence of emergencies had pushed France's population beyond the breaking point, encouraging confused, angry, and fearful people to violently reject traditional authority. In all of the chaos and uncertainty that ensued, leaders emerged who offered new solutions, which themselves created new problems, and gave rise to other leaders who offered yet more new ideas. The result was incessant conflict, both within and outside of France, and the French Revolution continued until it had run its bloody course and overwhelmed most of a continent. It left in its wake new structures and ideas that remain essential parts of the modern world as we know it.

A Society in Transition

A hundred years before the fall of the Bastille, France had seemed the epitome of stability under King Louis XIV, the "Sun King," who ruled from his palace at Versailles with the iron hand provided by a relatively efficient absolutist political state. Though heavy taxes and warfare were constant burdens on the French people, the machinery of government succeeded in providing the political control that it had been designed for. King Louis dealt effectively with the occasional revolt by peasants, dissident nobles, or Protestants, and could even boast of great public support. However, when he died in 1715, he bequeathed to his great-grandson, Louis XV, a state that was already weakened by diplomatic isolation, financial problems, and the abuse of power.

During Louis XV's long reign (1715–1774), the royal government became even more complex, inefficient and corrupt, which dramatically magnified the longstanding problem of how to make tax revenues support royal spending. But despite the fact that his government was constantly on the edge of financial insolvency, Louis XV tried only halfhearted reforms of government structure and policies, and he accomplished nothing positive or lasting. Meanwhile, the society around him continued to change, becoming more diverse and unstable.

One main force of this change was the economic development that took place in the eighteenth century, which, though impressive by some measurements, had been quite uneven. While the average standard of living in France rose steadily, not everyone benefited equally. Mercantilist policies had helped many French cities, such as Bordeaux, Lyons, and Rouen, to become world-class industrial and commercial centers. However, agriculture, long the backbone of the French economy, lagged behind, hindered by a confusing array of local laws and customs.

Despite an occasional attempt by the royal government to centralize and rationalize the state and its economy, most of rural France stubbornly maintained traditional ways. Some historians speak of the existence of two different French economies, one tradition-bound and stagnant, and the other dynamic and innovative. [2]

The absolutist state, arising as a solution to the turbulence of the Reformation era, had been designed to provide stability. Yet, somewhat ironically, its success in doing so encouraged the economic growth that fueled this destabilizing social change, and the eighteenth century saw rising economic and social complexity in France that continued to evolve at an accelerating rate. This change wreaked havoc on the social stratification system, and inevitably, many came to resent their perceived victimization by other groups. By 1789, the sense of collective purpose that had been fostered by the absolutist state had largely evaporated, as different social groups saw themselves in competition with other groups for wealth, power, and status. [3]

Historically, the first two estates, the clergy and the nobility, enjoyed privileges that included access to political power and exemption from most taxes. The uneven modernization of the eighteenth century complicated that picture. Doctrinal and political disagreements paralyzed the Catholic Church as many people within France viewed it as the possessor of undeserved privileges and wealth. Meanwhile, a new nobility of state officials and bureaucrats, whose origins were bourgeois, had gained noble titles through royal favor, strategic marriages, or even monetary purchase, which blurred the distinctions at the high end of the stratification system. As a group, the nobility became much more diverse, with great differences among them in financial status, political power, and values. As the elite orders struggled for privilege, this created a great deal of social tension and animosity at the top levels of society. [4]

Economic change had brought similar changes to the rest of the social system, as well. Many bourgeoisie had amassed great wealth, through the manufacturing and finance that mercantilism had stimulated, while the fortunes of others declined in the face of foreign competition. While French cities provided great opportunities for the ambitious, they also became home to a growing mass of unskilled, impoverished commoners. The French working class came to include many different sorts of workers, with various levels of skills and incomes, ranging from self-employed artisans, to workers in huge factories, to domestic servants, to indentured laborers. In the meantime, the social situation in rural areas—where a large majority of the population still resided—was also in transition. Even peasant farmers had become a quite diverse group, varying from well-off independent landowners to laborers whose conditions approximated medieval serfdom, depending largely on the province and its local laws and customs. Throughout the kingdom, taxes fell disproportionately upon the poorest of the king's subjects, while tax collectors, known as tax farmers, were among the wealthiest people in France.

Since the age of the Sun King, a great deal had changed in popular attitudes, as well. The Enlightenment was spreading deeply and broadly through Western Europe, and in many respects, its nerve center was the city of Paris. Despite

French government censorship, new voices emerged that called for the public to reexamine the nature of their society, and to consider new solutions for a changing world. Such new ideas reached many more people than ever before; in France, literacy rates had almost doubled between 1715 and 1789, so that perhaps 40 percent of the total population was literate by the outbreak of the Revolution. This meant that in French cities such as Paris, a majority of the adult population, including many working-class people, could and did read, and also that literate peasants could be found even in the most backward rural areas. People at all levels of the social ladder were becoming receptive to the new ways of thinking—based on logic and reason, instead of tradition—promoted by the Enlightenment. [5]

It was not just the most popular Enlightenment literature, such as the *Encyclopedia* or the best-selling works of Voltaire, that altered the outlooks of the king's subjects. Late eighteenth-century France also witnessed a virtual explosion of printed newspapers, pamphlets and leaflets that stimulated public interest in news and current issues. While some of this literary output was learned and informative, much was not. By the reign of Louis XVI, starting in 1775, the publication of pamphlets and broadsides, published in violation of censorship laws, were increasingly effective in promoting skepticism and even hostility toward the government.[6] Especially popular were cheaply printed pieces that crudely attacked members of the royal family; scandalous literature that depicted Queen Marie Antoinette as a sexually insatiable imbecile comprised almost an industry in itself. As one scholar put it, the scurrilous publications that became so popular and widespread during the 1780s "severed the sense of decency that bound the public to its rulers," through "a common denominator of irreligion, immorality, and uncivility."[7] Thus, written material, in addition to "enlightening" the French population, also contributed to a pervasive cynicism that undermined respect for authority.

Under the absolutist system of Louis XIV, people had largely understood what was expected of those in their social rank, and whatever their status, they had shared a respect for the king as his obedient subjects. But by the late eighteenth century the social realities had changed so dramatically that it was hard to determine even what ranks existed, never mind what their appropriate behaviors were. Moreover, any sense of belonging to a collective whole with a common purpose was disintegrating. Contempt for their king had become one of the only unifying factors among the diverse people of this fast-changing society.

Even by the time he wrote *Candide*, forty years earlier, Voltaire had hardly been exaggerating the antagonisms that existed in France when he wrote:

> Except during supper, when people are relatively gay and accommodating, the rest of the time is spent in trivial quarrels: Jansenists against Molinists, men of *parlement* against men of the Church, men of letters against men of letters, courtiers against courtiers, financiers against the people, wives against their husbands, relatives against relatives; it is an eternal war.[8]

Probably not even Voltaire understood just how literally true this would turn out to be.

The Crisis of the Monarchy

When Louis XV's son inherited the throne, as Louis XVI, he possessed some evident intentions to improve the situation. But he soon found that this was no easy task, as his efforts to restore order to royal finances with Enlightenment-inspired reforms failed for a variety of political and economic reasons. Initiatives to modernize the tax system met with firm opposition from powerful interest groups, including the king's own ministers and the law courts, who saw their authority threatened by the proposed changes. Meanwhile, France's military support for the American war of independence had forced the crown to take on huge levels of unmanageable debt.

Louis XVI also inherited an unwinnable situation regarding the price of bread, which, due to the fact that its cost made up about half of the total expenditure of most French households, was the most inflammatory political issue during the second half of the century.[9] Traditionally, the crown enforced a certain maximum price on bread as a way of serving the welfare of its subjects; however, during the eighteenth century, while the French population grew, the level of grain production stagnated, both because of a reliance on traditional farming practices and the fact that the maximum prices took away farmers' incentives to innovate and invest in agriculture. As time went on, urban populations often complained that the prices were too high, while rural farmers complained that prices were too low; whatever price the royal government decided on, it angered one group or the other, and often both at the same time. Inevitably, production diminished, while bread prices crept upward due to scarcity. One important long-term consequence of this state of affairs was that it spurred public anger against the already-mistrusted royal government and its officials, who were widely believed—perhaps with some justification—to be conspiring to profit from the situation. Worse, when a series of bad harvests occurred in the 1780s, an already difficult political and economic problem became a genuine crisis, as actual starvation appeared in some cities when there was no bread available at any price.

Meanwhile, the expenses of military spending, government salaries, and the costs of maintaining the royal household continued to rise, necessitating more and more tax revenue to pay for it. However, traditional privilege had given immunity from taxation to the first two estates, the church and the nobility, while many of the wealthiest members of the bourgeoisie had been buying offices and noble titles that gave them immunity as well. All of these groups resisted any suggestions that they should pay a share of taxes, which only embittered the less privileged classes.[10] However, aside from expanding the tax base, the only other way that the royal government could meet its financial obligations was through borrowing from wealthy financiers and foreign banks. This provided only short-term relief, and in the long run proved disastrous, because as the total debts of the royal government rose, so too did the interest rates that the crown had to pay.[11] Even five years into Louis XVI's reign, the expansion of government debt had grown beyond all practical levels, and as privileged interest groups blocked all attempts at reforming the financial system, it appeared that a declaration of royal bankruptcy was the only possible option.

By the mid-1780s, the crisis had become serious enough, and widely recognized enough, that Louis was persuaded by his advisors to summon a meeting of the Estates-General, an ancient institution that in past centuries had served as an advisory body to the king. The intention was to come up with government reforms, especially of taxation, that would solve the financial crisis and at the same time gather public support for further reforms.[12] As representatives of the three estates of the clergy, nobles, and commoners—chosen by elections held throughout France—assembled at Versailles in early 1789, the economy was on the brink of disaster. Meanwhile, bad weather and resulting food shortages were causing breakdowns of civil order in the cities, including Paris, just a dozen miles from Versailles.

However, before the pertinent issues even came up for consideration, the Estates-General found itself in serious disagreement about procedural issues, especially voting, a situation made worse by the king's contradictory statements concerning how much authority he would allow the assembly to have. In mid-June, out of anger and frustration, the 600 representatives of the Third Estate, joined by some members of the clergy and nobility, proclaimed themselves the legitimate authority in France as the National Assembly. Defying the king's orders to disperse, they asserted their intention to transform the absolute monarchy into a **constitutional monarchy** with a division of powers. In order to prevent the clergy and nobility from completely losing influence, Louis ordered the representatives of the first two estates to join those of the third, and by the end of the month, a 1,200-member National Assembly was in place at Versailles.[13] Yet neither the extent of this new body's power nor the king's intentions were clear. Such were the immediate circumstances that preceded the seizure of the Bastille.

The Great Fear, the Declaration of Rights of Man and Citizen, and the October Days

The violent uprising in Paris on July 14 created widespread uncertainty throughout the entire kingdom as to who or what controlled the country. While the National Assembly at Versailles claimed to represent legitimate authority, many suspected that the king was plotting to destroy it by force of arms. In Paris, city officials defiantly rejected royal commands, but their relationship with the National Assembly remained problematic. In most parts of France, it was a legitimate question as to who was directing various administrative, military, and police bodies. Rumors abounded of conspiracy, revolt, invasion, and persecution.

The period of confusion that followed was aptly referred to as "The Great Fear," since no one could be sure of what was happening around them and widespread panic was often the consequence. In an age where the timely transmission of reliable news was impossible, rumors and misperceptions spurred violence and civil unrest, especially in rural areas, during late July and August of 1789. In particular, a persistent belief that the nobles were arming groups of criminals to attack local villages provoked peasants in many places to rise against noble landowners. Large parts of France approached anarchy.

The National Assembly, somewhat legitimized by the king's halfhearted and probably insincere recognition, devoted its efforts to coming up with a set of principles to guide the creation of a reformed government. With significant input from the Marquis de Lafayette, a hero of the American Revolution who was in charge of the Paris militia, a subcommittee composed the *Declaration of Rights of Man and Citizen*, a manifesto of principles that were intended to be the basis for a full constitution. Relying on the Enlightenment ideas of Locke and Rousseau, the product that emerged in August was rather vague, but it was dedicated, as its title suggests, to the principle of individual rights and freedoms. It was immediately printed and distributed widely, and become a symbol of the transformation that had taken place. By then, the word "revolution" had gained wide currency throughout France, but what it meant was not yet clear.[14]

A constitutional monarchy would require cooperation between an elected assembly and the king, but it was difficult to know what limitations on his power Louis would accept. In recent months, he had demonstrated a talent for changing his mind unexpectedly, and as the weeks went along the situation remained tense. By October, high bread prices provoked an angry demonstration by Parisian women, who marched on Versailles, accompanied by Lafayette's militia. After a brief and bloody confrontation with the king's guards, they forced the king and the rest of the royal family to move to Paris, with the National Assembly following shortly thereafter. After these so-called "October Days," events in Paris largely dictated the course of the Revolution.

The Constitutional Monarchy

From Paris, the Assembly—now known as the Constituent Assembly—tried to make constitutional monarchy into a reality. Through the Declaration, it had already legally limited the king's power, abolished privileges of birth, and asserted the right of the people to determine their own form of government. By the end of the year, the Assembly had begun to focus on more immediate, less theoretical issues, and initiated a number of significant administrative reforms concerning elections, justice, taxation, finance, commerce, and government structure.[15]

One especially divisive issue—which would remain so throughout the Revolution—was the future role of the Catholic Church. The overwhelming majority of the French population was Catholic, including many deeply conservative believers, but the church's traditional privileges made it an obvious target for reform-minded politicians. As early as the fall of 1789, the Assembly began to limit church income and confiscate its property, culminating in July of 1790 with comprehensive legislation known as the Civil Constitution of the Clergy, which essentially made the church a department of the political administration. These initiatives deeply offended many loyal Catholics, especially in the provinces, and the Assembly's perceived attack on religion provided the basis of the first widespread resistance to the new government.[16]

Even during the first year of existence, the early optimism of the Constituent Assembly began to wane. Since it was composed of members, known as **deputies**, from all three estates and from every part of the country, there were vastly different perspectives and it was never easy to gain consensus about any issue. As the Assembly made a determined effort to carry out its self-appointed tasks, there were already deep political factions among the representatives, largely based on different interpretations of the proper role of the Assembly itself and the amount of power the king would retain in any future constitutional arrangement.

Such political divisions were fueled, moreover, by the freedom of the press guaranteed by the Declaration, which had ended government censorship and promoted a tremendous expansion of political literature and a rapid politicization of the reading public. Related to this was the formation of formal and informal political clubs, where educated people met to debate issues, develop lobbying strategies, and compose political literature to influence public opinion. Increasingly, these clubs came to represent different interest groups and viewpoints, and they maintained important ties to political groups in the provinces. Even by 1790, such clubs, which included the reform-minded Jacobins, had begun to serve as power bases for active and aspiring politicians. The first factions that emerged within the Assembly reflected affiliations with these clubs, which evolved into *de facto* political parties.[17]

From late 1789 into 1791, the Constituent Assembly soldiered on with the burdens of maintaining order while working on a constitution. Yet even their undeniable accomplishments could not provide political and social tranquility. Unlike the case of England's Glorious Revolution in 1688, the events of 1789 had not achieved a popular acceptance of a new *status quo*. Disagreement, mistrust, and antagonism remained, and were even intensifying, among the people of France.

Civil Society Disintegrates

By early 1791, the most immediate threats to stability came from the conservative elements intent on defending the privileges of the church, nobility, and monarchy. Since the summer of 1789, the king had generally cooperated with the Assembly, but within a year he had begun to publicly express his displeasure with the actions it had taken in regard to the church. Meanwhile, some local leaders in the provinces, often in alliance with the clergy, were actively undermining the Paris government's authority by refusing to obey it. And angry nobles, both those who had fled to neighboring countries and those who had remained, were vowing to raise armies to reverse the Revolution.

In particular, rumors abounded that the queen's Austrian relatives and their allies might provide military forces to help the king and conservative factions regain political power. The truth to these rumors seemed to be confirmed when, in June of 1791, Louis and his family attempted to secretly flee Paris, evidently with the intention of meeting up with Austrian troops at the border of the Netherlands. Largely due to their own sheer incompetence, they were caught, returned to Paris under heavy guard, and reinstalled in their palace there as virtual prisoners.

The "flight to Varennes," as it became known, convinced many people that the king was a potential counter-revolutionary who could not be trusted. This increased the power of the factions in the Assembly who advocated the creation of a **republican** form of government, that is, an elected legislature operating without a king. Protests against Louis and his supporters took place, including an episode in Paris where the National Guard, controlled by moderates, massacred republican demonstrators. Meanwhile, the rulers of several European nations, including Austria, were enraged by the treatment of the royal family after their failed escape. Even those foreign leaders who had little sympathy for the king feared instability in France, and diplomatic relations between the Assembly and its neighbors rapidly deteriorated.

Republic

The term "republic," referring to a form of government, has been used differently in different places and at different times. The word's origin is Latin, dating from the Roman Republic: *res* ("thing") + *publica* ("of the people"), and the defining principle has been that the government's prime responsibility is to the collective "people."

Since the appearance of the term in classical Rome, the term was applied to a variety of political bodies, most notably medieval Italian city-states, the Netherlands after independence from Spain, and the English Commonwealth under Oliver Cromwell. The most important characteristic they shared was the absence of a king, and this is the element that was most salient for the leaders who formed the first French Republic in 1792. With the removal and later execution of King Louis XVI, the republic's sovereign power resided in the National Convention, a body of elected legislators.

Republics that have appeared in history have had presidents, prime ministers, or other leaders who have been elected or appointed. Many have varied considerably from earlier types, and have included autocracies (the "Republic of Zaïre"), communist states ("Soviet Republics"), and federations of smaller states (the "Republic of South Africa"). It is difficult to argue that all that have claimed the name have maintained the original principle, and some of these have paid precious little attention to the welfare of "the people."

To make matters even worse, 1791 had been another year of disappointing harvests, which increased turmoil in the cities even further. Working class wage earners, with jobs scarce and prices high, resented the fact that the Revolution had done little to benefit them, and had complained that it had just replaced one group of privileged elites with another; after all, the principles outlined in the Declaration, such as freedoms of assembly and expression, meant little to people who lacked enough to eat. In Paris, working people known as *sans-culottes*—referring to their

:k of the stylish knee-length trousers worn by the wealthy—began to organize
eir own neighborhood political associations and emerged as an influential and
unpredictable political factor. Gathering outside the Assembly's meeting hall on a
daily basis, they pressured the Assembly toward more radical actions by threatening
the deputies as they entered and departed, swayed by the exhortations of extremist
leaders known as *enragés* ("the mad ones"). While some members of the Assembly
despised the *sans-culottes* as a dangerous mob, others were more sympathetic, and
advocated reforms that were designed to help the poorer members of society who
felt overlooked by the Revolution.

With France seemingly threatened by conservative reaction from both within
and without, the Jacobins both gained more power and became fiercely republican
in their aims, gaining political and popular support at the expense of the Girondin
faction that had sponsored many of the reforms of the previous year. The Jacobin
leadership included some of the most influential and well-known personalities of
the Revolution. Among them was Georges Danton, the headstrong and outspoken
Assembly leader who rejected compromise and directed his efforts toward
turning France into a republic. Jean-Paul Marat, a multi-talented firebrand, used
his newspaper *The Friend of the People* to advocate increasingly harsh penalties
against anyone sympathetic to the privileged classes; Marat's dramatic and
inspiring prose transformed him, in the minds of many people, into the living
voice of the Revolution. Meanwhile, Maximilien Robespierre, a lawyer by training
and disciple of Jean-Jacques Rousseau's philosophy, emerged as the chief strategist
of Jacobin policies.

The leadership of such men was largely responsible for a polarization of opinion
that put moderate politicians into an uncomfortable position between pro-
republican factions and supporters of a return to monarchy. Even though the
king was persuaded to approve the long-awaited constitution at the end of
the summer of 1791, the political middle ground was fast disappearing. According
to the procedures outlined by this constitution, a new, somewhat smaller assembly
known as the Legislative Assembly was elected, and it was largely dominated
by the Jacobins. The Jacobins' resistance to compromise grew more pronounced
as the *sans-culottes* became more influential, and reports of foreign threats raised
public fears.[18]

War, Republic, and Terror

In early 1792, two and a half years after the outbreak of Revolution and only a
few months after the birth of the Legislative Assembly, all of these problems
seemed to collide and hurl France toward even further extremes. In April,
ongoing diplomatic hostility with neighboring monarchies resulted in a French
declaration of war against Austria. However, the French army was underprepared,
especially because many of its noble officers had fled the country, and the beginning
of the conflict went badly. As war hysteria gripped the nation, the radical Paris
Commune seized power in the capital with the support of the Jacobins and the
sans-culottes, demanding not just political equality, but equality of wealth as well.

As crowd violence in Paris surged out of control, the Commune set up revolutionary **tribunals,** specially created courts, to seek out traitors, and began employing the guillotine for carrying out sentences of death. In August, when French armies failed to prevent Austrian troops from entering France, an angry demonstration against the king's possible support for the enemy led to a bloody confrontation at the royal palace where hundreds were killed. With public sentiment in Paris, if not necessarily elsewhere, now firmly in favor of a republic, the Legislative Assembly removed the king from any remaining political role and called for the election of a new republican legislature, known as the National Convention, to cope with the emergencies of warfare.[19]

Even as this new body was being created through another round of elections, further French military defeats in September of 1792 sent Paris crowds into an uncontrollable frenzy, leading to the cold-blooded massacre of 1,300 imprisoned clergymen and other supposed counter-revolutionaries in Paris. By December, the king was brought to trial for his apparent complicity with foreign armies, and he was found guilty of treason. He and his queen went to the guillotine in 1793, which shocked and angered conservatives both inside and outside the country. By then, even though the fortunes of war were improving, paranoia was widespread, and violence of all sorts had become the social norm in many, and perhaps most, parts of France.[20]

The National Convention intended to develop a new republican constitution, but until that was accomplished, it claimed the right to act without restraint. The Jacobins, benefiting from an appeal to patriotism and the support of the *sans-culottes*, attained a near-monopoly on power. To deal with the threats surrounding

Image 11.1 The execution of King Louis XVI, 1793

© Mary Evans Picture Library / Alamy

them, they instituted a command wartime economy, created a military draft, and also established the Committee of Public Safety, an appointed twelve-member body designed to provide more efficient executive power. By late 1793, Robespierre largely controlled the Committee, and used it and the revolutionary tribunals to hunt out all whose loyalties were suspect, according to his standards of moral purity. Robespierre believed that he and the Jacobins were upholding the **general will** of the people—a concept popularized by Rousseau's writing—in the struggle against forces of counterrevolution, and saw those who hesitated to fully support their cause as enemies of the republic.[21]

By that time, however, there were many groups who had serious disagreements with the Jacobins, including dissatisfied *sans-culottes*, radical *enragés*, moderate deputies, former royal officials, army officers, provincial leaders, and loyal Catholics. With the war effort being the obvious priority, the Jacobins took severe steps against these "enemies of the Revolution," and their methods—often referred to as the Reign of Terror—provoked equally determined resistance. Revolts against the Convention's power broke out both in large cities and rural areas, often encouraged and even supported by foreign enemies. The most notable uprising took place in the Vendée region of western France, where Catholic peasants, aided by dissident nobles, fought a guerrilla war that was ultimately crushed by the Revolutionary Army. Out of a total population of around 800,000 in the Vendée, it is conservatively estimated that 200,000 civilians died during the fighting, and close to the same number of soldiers, before the region was "pacified."[22]

The Jacobins and the leaders of the National Convention were not satisfied with simply eliminating enemies. Inspired by Rousseau's ideas, they also undertook to change the cultural landscape of France by eliminating traces of the feudal past.[23] They instituted a revolutionary calendar that had new months and a Year One beginning in September 1792, as well as introducing the metric system as the basis of a new system of keeping time. A "de-Christianization" campaign abolished church holidays, encouraged worship of the "Goddess of Liberty," and created a "Festival of the Supreme Being" as a major public celebration. The political leadership even formally legislated changes to speech, such as requiring people to address each other as "citizen," instead of the less democratic term "monsieur" ("my lord"). These efforts often approached the absurd, such as changing the rules of checkers to forbid the practice of "kinging" pieces that reached the last row. The Jacobins' attempt to erase the "corrupt" past and replace it with "correct" revolutionary thinking seems an eerie precursor to Mao's Chinese Cultural Revolution 170 years later.

As French military victories increased and the fear of invasion lessened during the summer of 1794, public support for the Jacobins' extreme policies weakened. In July (the revolutionary month of Thermidor), leaders in the Convention, in what was probably a pre-emptive strike designed to save themselves from charges of treason, denounced Robespierre and some of his closest allies. By then, because of Robespierre's uncompromising methods—which included the execution of his friend and colleague Danton—not even the *sans-culottes* or the Paris Commune was willing to protect him, and he and several of his associates went to the guillotine. This ended the Reign of Terror, as the Convention not only dismantled the revolutionary tribunals and stopped the mass executions, but also purged the remaining Jacobin leadership and dealt severely with *sans-culotte* agitation.[24]

This "Thermidorean Reaction" left the government as a republic, and in 1795 a new constitution provided for a two-chamber legislature and most executive authority in the hands of a rotating five-member committee known as the Directory. In effect, power passed back to the propertied bourgeoisie, who concentrated their efforts on conducting the war, a task that they carried out reasonably competently for the next four years with relatively little internal opposition.[25]

Revolutionary War and Napoleon

A number of factors can explain the success of the French armies that began in late 1792.[26] For one thing, their officer corps had matured and benefited from a more democratic policy of advancement by merit, regardless of social class, instead of reserving the highest ranks to nobles. The Jacobins' military draft, moreover, greatly expanded the size of the army, and after 1792 French forces began to overwhelm smaller opponents on the basis of sheer numbers. Their opponents, meanwhile, were hampered by both a tendency to underestimate French military capabilities and a lack of coordination among their own various forces.

Perhaps the most important reason for French success, though, was that both officers and enlisted men in the Revolutionary Army had started to believe that they were fighting for an important cause. Initially, the troops fought desperately to save their homeland from foreign enemies of the Revolution, which gave them a sense of united purpose, and most historians would agree that the French Revolutionary Wars provided the forge out of which was fashioned a powerful new phenomenon known as **nationalism**. Because of this, their morale and effectiveness was considerably higher than that of the largely mercenary armies against whom they were fighting. Yet this advantage carried over even after the safety of French borders was assured, as the French troops began to see themselves as liberators who were spreading revolution and democracy to less enlightened parts of the Continent. As time went on, at least part of the French military success can be attributed to the fact that, in many of the territories they invaded, local populations were won over by the rhetoric of liberation, and often aided the French armies against their own rulers.

Even as early as 1795, the young Corsican general Napoleon Bonaparte won public acclaim through his battlefield victories. Employing aggressive, innovative strategies and tactics, he gave the French people the young, energetic, and charismatic hero that they needed. Napoleon was also calculating and ambitious, and used his political connections to seize his opportunities while he negotiated the political minefields of revolutionary France.[27] Leading his armies against changing coalitions of European opponents, he never lost a major battle between 1795 and 1812, and positioned himself brilliantly by helping a new, more concentrated form of government known as the Consulate seize power from the

Directory in 1799. By manipulating politicians and crowds alike, Napoleon emerged as a virtual dictator, and in 1804, had himself crowned emperor.

The years of struggle had made the French people especially vulnerable to Napoleon's charisma, and few leaders in history have been more successful in dazzling the masses with promises of glory and empire. Although Napoleon gained much support from his claim to be the defender of Revolutionary principles, his most important priorities were domestic stability and foreign conquest. He preserved most of the Enlightenment-inspired reforms that had taken place, and even added to these, with broad initiatives in banking, industry, and national education. Perhaps his most impressive accomplishment was the creation of the Napoleonic Code, the first truly unified and egalitarian legal system in Europe, which formalized and rationalized an unprecedented number of aspects of life. He also healed the rift between the Revolutionary government and the church, a masterful move that cemented popular support for his regime.

During the era of the empire, almost all of continental Europe came under the direct or indirect rule of France. In conquered areas, French armies brought elements of liberation, including social and legal equality, limited political democracy, and rational bureaucracies. Unwittingly, they also unleashed the forces of nationalism, which eventually energized numerous conquered peoples to remove the French. After his disastrous invasion of Russia in 1812, where his "Grande Armée" was nearly annihilated by starvation, disease, and freezing weather, Napoleon was unable to maintain his control over the rest of his European conquests. By 1815 he was defeated for the final time at Waterloo in today's Belgium.

The Legacy of the French Revolution

Although France's victorious opponents returned France to a monarchy in 1815, the Revolution and its wars had fatally wounded absolutism as a form of government, and the legitimacy of kingship would be on the defensive, in France and elsewhere in Europe, throughout the nineteenth century. This tumultuous era had transformed "liberty, equality and fraternity" from revolutionary slogans into cherished principles of civic life, and ever since we have struggled to implement them in a practical way. We can see the French Revolution as an essential step in the development of the modern state, giving us a remarkable array of new ideologies, forms of political organization, and types of government power. Together with the economic transformations brought about by the Industrial Revolution, the entire structure of European society would change dramatically during the nineteenth century.

One of the most enduring effects of the Revolution was more abstract: its effect on how individuals saw themselves in relation to the larger society. The French Revolution encouraged people to believe that they no longer had to patiently accept the hand that they had been dealt at birth, as the idea emerged that people could—and even must—control their own destinies. To a much greater extent than ever before, people of all walks of life started to feel that they could question the *status quo*, and this more skeptical and less passive outlook has become an essential part of modern society.

Though the French Revolution has inspired generations of people throughout the world to make their world freer and more equitable, it also provides some cautionary lessons. As Martin Luther had discovered, and countless other revolutionaries have learned since, it is one thing to tear down an existing system, but quite another to agree on what to put in its place. In France, it may have been true that the destruction of the Old Regime in France was inevitable, and many have even argued that it was admirable. But once this process was underway, the people of France found themselves at odds with each other about what direction to take next; after 1789, the course of events was largely determined by a bewildering combination of developments, imperfectly understood and beyond the control of any individual or group. As one historian wrote, "the French Revolution had not been made by revolutionaries. It would be truer to say that the revolutionaries had been created by the Revolution."[28]

It is only in hindsight that we can impose some sort of order on the course of the French Revolution. Social change inevitably creates new realities and new ideas, which themselves promote more change, and the French Revolution opened up entirely new possibilities, both for France and for societies everywhere. Though 1789 remains a largely symbolic date, there is a great deal of validity to the assertion that the "modern era" began with the French Revolution.

Notes

1 The most complete English-language, historical rendering of the fall of the Bastille is found in Simon Schama, *Citizens: A Chronicle of the French Revolution,* (New York: Knopf, 1991), 363–406.

2 Schama, *Citizens,* 183–99; William Doyle, *Origins of the French Revolution,* 2nd. ed. (Oxford: Oxford University Press, 1991), 31–2.

3 Jeremy D. Popkin, *A Short History of the French Revolution,* 3rd ed. (Upper Saddle River, NJ: 2002), 11–15, Schama, *Citizens,* 112–21.

4 Popkin, *Short History,* 8–9; Doyle, *Origins,* 16–25.

5 Doyle, *Origins,* 78.

6 Robert Darnton, *The Literary Underground of the Old Regime* (Cambridge: Harvard University Press, 1982), 199–209.

7 Ibid., 204, 207.

8 Voltaire, *Candide,* trans. and ed. Daniel Gordon, (Boston: Bedford/St. Martin's: 1999) 94–5.

9 The monumental work of Steven Kaplan, including *Bread, Politics, and Political Economy in the Reign of Louis XV* (The Hague: Martinus Nijhoff, 1976), is the most thorough on this critically important though often neglected topic.

10 Sylvia Neely, *A Concise History of the French Revolution* (Lanham, MD: Rowman & Littlefield, 2008) 55–6; Popkin, *Short History,* 8–9.

11 J. F. Bosher's *French Finances 1770–1795: From Business to Bureaucracy* (Cambridge: Cambridge University Press, 2008), building on his own earlier research and many new discoveries, contributes major insights on the often-messy subject of French government debt and taxation.

12 Popkin, *Short History,* 22–3.

13 A clear explanation of the often-confusing sequence of events that led to the establishment of the National Assembly is provided by Neely, *Concise History*, 55–69.

14 Popkin, *Short History*, 36–43; Schama, *Citizens*, 442–43.

15 Neely, *Concise History*, 95–101.

16 Popkin, *Short History*, 51–2.

17 Neely, *Concise History*, 120–24; Popkin, *Short History*, 53–4.

18 Popkin, *Short History*, 44–5.

19 Neely, *Concise History*, 155–62.

20 Ibid., 164–73.

21 Ruth Scurr's *Fatal Purity: Robespierre and the French Revolution* (New York: Metropolitan Books, 2006) is an excellent recent work that captures Robespierre's influences and outlook exceptionally well.

22 Neely, *Concise History*, 206.

23 Popkin *Short History*, 86–7; Neely, *Concise History*, 197–203.

24 Popkin, *Short History*, 97–105.

25 Neely, *Concise History*, 221–30.

26 Ibid., 233.

27 On Bonaparte and the Empire, a useful summary can be found in Neely, *Concise History*, 241–248; of the many excellent studies on Napoleon's career, Robert B. Asprey's two volume *The Rise and Fall of Napoleon Bonaparte* (Boston: Little, Brown, 2000, 2002) is recommended.

28 Doyle, *Origins*, 213.

Suggested Readings

Asprey, Robert B. *The Rise and Fall of Napoleon Bonaparte*. 2 vols. Boston: Little, Brown, 2000, 2002.

Bosher, J. F. *French Finances 1770–1795: From Business to Bureaucracy*. Cambridge: Cambridge University Press, 2008.

Darnton, Robert. *The Literary Underground of the Old Regime*. Cambridge: Harvard University Press, 1982.

Doyle, William. *Origins of the French Revolution*. 2nd ed. Oxford: Oxford University Press, 1988.

Kaplan, Steven. *Bread, Politics, and Political Economy in the Reign of Louis XV*. The Hague: Martinus Nijhoff, 1976.

McPhee, Peter. *Liberty or Death: The French Revolution*. New Haven: Yale University Press, 2016.

Neely, Silvia. *A Concise History of the French Revolution*. Lanham, MD: Rowman & Littlefield, 2008.

Popkin, Jeremy D. *A Short History of the French Revolution*. 3rd ed. Upper Saddle River, NJ: Prentice Hall, 2002.

Schama, Simon. *Citizens: A Chronicle of the French Revolution*. New York: Knopf, 1991.

Scurr, Ruth. *Fatal Purity: Robespierre and the French Revolution*. New York: Metropolitan Books, 2006.

Voltaire. *Candide*. Edited and translated by Daniel Gordon. Boston: Bedford/ St. Martin's, 1999.

12 The Industrial Revolution

John W. Mackey

Key Terms

agricultural revolution, consumer capitalism, consumer goods, division of labor, extractive industries, factory system, great migration, heavy industries, industrial pollution, labor movement, labor supply, Luddites, public health movement, Second Industrial Revolution, separate spheres, transportation revolution, unions, urbanization

Perhaps no other historical development has had such massive and far-reaching effects as the Industrial Revolution. It introduced new methods of production and an array of new products, while transforming the nature of work for vast numbers of people. It created new social classes and vast new fortunes, and instigated a rapid increase in urbanization. It greatly enhanced the speed of transportation and communication, and it altered the relationship between the West and the non-Western world. Industrialization also transformed our environment in profound ways, even ultimately altering the earth's climate. And the Industrial Revolution created new, deadlier tools and methods of warfare.

The Industrial Revolution is described by economists Robert L. Heilbroner and William Milberg as "a *great turning period* in history, during which manufacturing and industrial activity became primary forms of social production."[1] Historians generally agree that this great turn toward industry and the factory system had its origins in the mid to late eighteenth century, and was in full force by the mid-nineteenth century. A later period, between about 1870 and the eve of the First World War, is often described as the **Second Industrial Revolution**, and it was marked by the development of electricity, new types of engines, and new chemicals and industrial materials.

This revolution began in Great Britain, matured there rather rapidly, and spread to Western Europe and the United States throughout the course of the nineteenth century. While it is impossible to pinpoint the exact factors that caused the Industrial Revolution, there were a number of conditions present in eighteenth-century Britain that made this transformation possible.

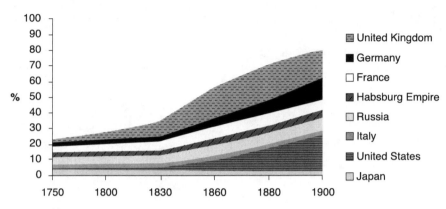

Figure 12.1 Relative share of world manufacturing output, 1750–1900

Adapted from Wikimedia Commons Figure

The Origins of the Industrial Revolution in Britain

After a tumultuous seventeenth century, Great Britain enjoyed relative stability and prosperity in the eighteenth century, when the beginnings of the Industrial Revolution took hold. Britain had comparatively stable and effective government institutions, a growing economy aided by a system of banking and credit, and a developing market economy.[2] As a result, the economic and political conditions for the accumulation of capital and economic development were in place. In addition, British institutions like the Royal Society, founded in 1660 to propagate science, and especially the Royal Society for the encouragement of Arts, Manufactures, and Commerce, founded in 1754, promoted experimentation and innovation in technology and production. Thus, Britain provided a more hospitable environment for economic change and invention than most nations in the eighteenth century.

Britain also had an available and relatively mobile **labor supply** in the eighteenth century. Britain, like much of Europe at this time, experienced a population boom. Several factors, including an increasing food supply created by the rise of new, more efficient agricultural techniques, help explain this population growth. Indeed, Britain, and much of Europe generally, is said to have experienced an **agricultural revolution** in the eighteenth century, in which more sophisticated crop rotation, enclosure of land that was formerly held in common, new animal breeding techniques, and improved farming equipment greatly increased yields. In addition to a growing food supply, a decrease in diseases like the plague and smallpox, and earlier marriages may also have been significant contributors to population growth.

The available supply of labor in Britain was not only growing in eighteenth-century Britain, but relatively mobile, as well. Under the manorial system, peasants were tied to the land in a form of unfree labor that was highly exploitative, but stable. By the eighteenth century, however, the enclosure movement left many farm laborers seeking whatever employment they could find, without ties to a manor or lord. Enclosures were efforts by landowners to privatize and enclose their land, eliminating traditional common lands, and gearing agriculture toward the market rather than local family and village production. Therefore, eighteenth-century Britain had both a growing population and a significant number of landless laborers seeking a living. These factors meant that a ready supply of mobile and cheap labor would be available to work the factories, mills, and mines of the Industrial Revolution.

Britain also benefited from geographical factors that helped make industrialization possible. Transportation networks were strong, as Britain had a relatively developed canal and road system, in addition to many port cities and a long history of seafaring trade. This helped facilitate the movement of goods, people, and raw materials necessary for industrial growth. Britain also had large deposits of both iron ore and coal, two of the key ingredients in the mechanization of production. Iron was used to make machinery, and, especially after the 1850s, transformed into steel, which was crucial to the construction of railroads, cities, factories, and countless other structures of the industrializing world. Coal, along with coke, which is a substance made from super-heated coal, were the fuels most responsible for firing the steam engines and blast furnaces of the Industrial Revolution.

Most of these characteristics were not unique to Great Britain. But Britain's particular combination of these factors helped create the conditions under which significant economic and technological changes could occur. Taken together, these changes are what we call the Industrial Revolution.

The Nature of the Industrial Revolution

Perhaps the simplest way to distinguish the pre-industrial world from the industrialized world is by looking at common, everyday products; before the Industrial Revolution they were made by human hands, and ever since, they have increasingly been made by machines. The much-discussed automation of manufacturing in the twenty-first century is best seen not as a novel phenomenon, but as a continuation of a process that began in the Industrial Revolution. In a pre-industrial age, the vast majority of average people would have owned or had access only to products—clothing, a few tools, some cooking implements—that were made by hand, and probably made locally, and perhaps even made by someone they knew. But the products a middle-class Westerner might own today—a computer, a car, clothes, a cell phone, a television, sporting goods, furniture—were likely all made by machines, in factories run by people the purchaser of the products will never know, perhaps thousands of miles away. Such is the legacy of the mechanization of production and the global expansion of industrial capitalism.

The Mechanization of Production and Transportation

Mechanization involves at first enhancing, and then largely replacing the power of nature (human bodies, animals, wind, and water) with the power of machines.

These changes greatly increased the speed and efficiency of production. Several inventions in the eighteenth century (the spinning jenny, the spinning mule) increased the productivity of the textile industry in Britain, by multiplying the power of humans, water, or animals. And as textile producers came to see that it was more efficient to bring large numbers of workers together in the same place to operate machinery than to rely on production by individuals in their homes, the **factory system** was born.

Time, Factories, and the Protestant Ethic

The advent of factory work meant a workday based not on the rhythms of nature or the rising and setting of the sun but on carefully recorded time. When the machinery started up, it was important for everyone to be there and ready to work, so punctuality was essential. Stopping the machinery for anything other than necessary repairs was inefficient and reduced productivity, so in the early factories breaks were few. Leaving expensive machinery idle for holidays and festivals seemed wasteful to manufacturers, and so these interruptions to the work week became progressively fewer—and leisure time accordingly less. Increasingly, time was money, and for many people this constituted a major change in the way they experienced their lives.

Workers showed considerable resistance to this loss of control over their lives and work, but the need for wage labor won out. In addition to economic pressures, this change was probably also encouraged by the Protestant emphasis on hard work and discipline. In England the Puritans, the largest and most influential of the Calvinist sects, preached that wasting time was sinful, and this emphasis was increasingly shared by the Methodists and other Evangelical groups as well. Max Weber's view that the attitudes of Protestantism in general and of Calvinism in particular facilitated the rise of modern industrial capitalism is very relevant here. Since some critics have mistakenly concluded that Weber saw Calvinism as the *cause* of capitalism, rather than as something that helped it on its way, it is interesting to note that the celebrated English labor historian E. P. Thompson agreed with this perspective, describing Puritanism as "the agent which converted men to new valuations of time."[1] While Weber was more inclined toward cultural arguments, and Thompson, a Marxist, was more inclined toward economic arguments, each man understood that changing ideas and changing economic factors both matter in bringing about change.

Note

1 E.P. Thompson, "Time, Work-Discipline, and Industrial Capitalism," *Past and Present Society* 38 (1967): 95.

Even more striking changes to the production process accompanied the widespread use of the steam engine during the nineteenth century. James Watt, a Scottish engineer, is credited with making the necessary improvements to steam engines that eventually made them widely applicable for industrial uses. Watt patented his new steam engine in 1769, and by the early to mid-nineteenth century, advanced steam engines were in extensive use in industry and transportation.

Machines powered by coal or wood-fired steam power no longer relied as much on human muscle, and did not need to be located near water sources. As engine-powered mechanization grew, production grew ever faster, larger in scale, and cheaper. Therefore, industrialists whose factories were most technologically advanced and efficient enjoyed a comparative advantage in the growing capitalist marketplace. Cottage industries and small handcrafters could not compete with the power of the mechanized textile industry and its growing factories. The mechanization process and the factory system that largely started in the textile industry would also transform the production of countless other products, and the addition of steam power helped to create a massive, indeed revolutionary change in human societies.

Just as steam power transformed the speed of production, it greatly increased the speed at which people and their cargoes could travel, creating a **transportation revolution**. Industrialization and transportation also enhanced each other; new industrial technologies and materials led to faster, more widespread transportation networks, which in turn helped move products to new markets more quickly, fueling industrial growth. Before the use of steam engines, a land traveler and his or her cargo could move only as fast as a horse could pull a carriage or rail car. The creation of steam-powered locomotives, however, spectacularly transformed the speed and efficiency of travel and the distribution of freight. Thus, one of the hallmarks of the industrial age was the construction of extensive railroad networks in Europe, the United States, and numerous regions of the world that had been colonized by Europeans.

Like land travel, boat and ship transportation was also revolutionized by the steam engine. Before the industrial revolution, natural forces—the strength of people, horses, or winds—limited the speed and consistency of water transport. But steam-powered boats, equipped with a power source independent of such natural forces, greatly enhanced the movement of goods and people. Rapid industrialization in the United States, for example, was aided by the steamboats that carried people and cargo on its rivers in the early to mid-nineteenth century. Practical and effective oceangoing steamships took longer to develop, but by the late nineteenth century, steam travel on the seas became much more rapid, effective, and commonplace. Steamships were vital in transporting goods and raw materials over vast distances as the Industrial Revolution became more and more global, and more intertwined with European empires.

The Second Industrial Revolution (ca. 1870–1914)

A number of important economic and technological developments in the late nineteenth and early twentieth centuries cause many historians to see this period as a Second Industrial Revolution. This revolution is perhaps best seen not as a separate event, but as an expansion of the technological changes of the Industrial Revolution into new directions. New inventions, new fuel power sources, and new materials differentiate this later period from the earlier decades of the Industrial Revolution.

For example, while coal and iron were crucial to the early Industrial Revolution, oil and steel came to be more important in the later period, and would continue to be basic components of industrial societies in the twentieth century. While an advanced process for making steel, a strong and highly useful alloy consisting primarily of iron ore, was developed before this later period, steel production became increasingly crucial in the late nineteenth century. It became a key component in the construction of cities, factories, military hardware, and transport systems. Similarly, the invention of the internal combustion engine, along with the development of commercial drilling, made oil a crucial fuel of industrialization. And in addition to more widespread construction of railroad networks, the Second Industrial Revolution contributed oceangoing steamships, as well as automobiles and airplanes powered by internal combustion engines, to the revolution in transportation.

The era between about 1870 and 1914 was also marked by the development of electricity, the wireless telegraph, and the chemical industry, as well as by changes in the nature of industrial capitalism. While heavy industries (iron, steel, machines, etc.) dominated much of the nineteenth century, and continued to be crucial to industrial societies, **consumer capitalism** became more widespread near the turn of the twentieth century. Britain, in particular, began to gear more of its production toward **consumer goods**—designed to be bought by everyday people—than ever before. As a result, department stores and mail-order catalogs proliferated in this period, and businesses came to realize that there was great profit in catering to the consumption desires of the middle class and skilled workers.

The Impact of the Industrial Revolution: The Changing Class System

The traditional European class system, rooted in feudalism and manorialism, did not disappear overnight, but wherever the Industrial Revolution took hold, it transformed the social class system. Two new classes were created by industrial capitalism—the property-owning bourgeoisie or "middle" class, and the proletariat, or working class. For economists like Karl Marx, the development of these two new classes was the leading development of the nineteenth century. In industrial society, Marx argued, one's class position is determined by one's "relationship to the means of production;" members of the bourgeoisie own and/or control the means of production, while the members of the proletariat do not. An individual proletarian, who owns no capital, has only his labor to sell, and subsists on hourly wages.

The European bourgeoisie was not entirely new during the nineteenth century, of course (see Chapter 8). But a new, *industrial* bourgeoisie was on the rise.

During the Industrial Revolution, fortunes were increasingly linked to the factory system, the raw materials and fuel that supported it, and the financial capital that allowed it to expand. As a result, the industrial bourgeoisie emerged as the dominant class of the nineteenth century, flush with the profits of a rapidly expanding industrial economy. The richest members of the bourgeoisie did not entirely *replace* the aristocracy, however; in many cases, they *merged* with it through marriage. A marriage between a son of aristocratic lineage and the heiress to an industrial fortune, for example, could be beneficial to both parties, as the aristocratic family could gain the financial benefits of industry, while the bourgeois family could acquire the gentility of aristocratic title.

The Industrial Revolution also altered the lives of the laboring classes. As industrialization spread and grew, the industrial proletariat began to replace the peasantry as the class whose labor created the wealth of nations. As the rural, agricultural society of Europe was transformed into a more urban, industrial one, the majority of manual labor was increasingly performed in factories and mines by a new working class.[3]

Thus, the old estate system of Europe, and the manorial and feudal ties that bound it together, was being supplanted by a new, more individualistic social system. Traditional rural and village life, arguably based on what German sociologist Ferdinand Tönnies called *gemeinschaft*, or "community," was marked by its smaller scale, an emphasis on primary relationships, and an orientation toward the needs of the group. By contrast, the social class system and mass society that accompanied industrial capitalism created what Tönnies called *gesellschaft*, or "society." The new society was larger in scale, less personal, based more on secondary or transactional relationships, competitive, dominated by the money economy, and marked by a much more complex division of labor.

The Nature of Work

As the bourgeoisie began to supplant the aristocracy as the wealthiest, most economically dynamic class in industrializing Europe, it changed the nature of ruling-class life. The aristocracy was a class whose authority and power were rooted in land ownership and an ancestry with a martial past, but it was in large part a class of leisure. An aristocrat, as a gentleman of leisure, was largely defined by what he did *not* do—work. The industrial bourgeoisie was a different sort of class, defined not by leisure but by commercial or professional achievement. Bourgeois values of hard work, thrift, efficiency, self-discipline, and innovation were the hallmarks of the "new men" who emerged at the top of the economic ladder in the nineteenth century. [4] The culture of the industrial bourgeoisie was also marked by a distinct, male-dominated gender code, sometimes referred to as **separate spheres**.[5] The public sphere of business, politics, and property ownership was said to be a male domain, while women were expected to remain largely confined to the home, or domestic sphere.

The work of the laboring classes changed drastically as a result of industrialization. For centuries, the majority of European society was made up of a toiling peasantry, landless and overworked. In addition to the peasants, European villages were home to small handcrafters, who produced the products of everyday life in their modest shops. As industrialization spread, the lives of the working class were still grindingly difficult, but in new ways. Instead of plowing and sowing, or cobbling and hand-weaving, the new industrial working class increasingly labored in mechanized factories and mines.

Industrial working conditions, especially before the late nineteenth century, were generally brutal. Factories were often crowded, hot, loud, poorly ventilated, and dangerous. Working hours were long, breaks were few, and child labor was common, as factory owners and managers in a competitive environment emphasized profit far above worker comfort and safety. In the coal mines, which quite literally fueled the Industrial Revolution, conditions were even worse. The lack of industrial regulation regarding safety, working hours, and job conditions meant that early industrial workers often risked their health, or even their lives, every day on the job.

Not surprisingly, many members of the new industrial proletariat found the changing nature of work disturbing. Handcrafters, accustomed to traditional forms of production, the guild system, and a certain degree of personal control over their labor, found themselves driven out of business by faster, more efficient factories. Unlike the world of small, familial handcraft shops, the new industrial economy was based on an increasingly complex **division of labor**, which required workers to complete specific, repetitive tasks that left them feeling like anonymous cogs, alienated from the products of their labor. The new industrial workplace was less personal, more subject to change, and less rooted in familiar tradition than its pre-industrial counterpart.[6]

Some workers, angered by the threat of industrialization to their traditional forms of production and their livelihoods, attempted to fight back. Famously, textile workers in England, known as the **Luddites**, formed a secret society dedicated to putting a stop to the sweeping changes in the textile industry in the early nineteenth century. They issued demands to mill owners and sometimes destroyed machinery, but were ultimately unable to stop the changes that accompanied the mechanization of cloth production.

Industrial workers who came to the factory from an agrarian background also found life in the new mills and mines unsettling. Centuries of folk traditions were ingrained in rural life, and these traditions, like work itself, followed the rhythms of nature. The work of peasants and small farmers followed familiar cues—sunlight and darkness, the changing of seasons, weather conditions, and the like. Conversely, industrial life was governed by factory discipline. Rather than to the needs of crops and livestock, workers now had to respond to dictates of the time-clock and the factory boss.[7] Both former craftspeople and former agricultural workers found the highly regimented demands of industrial work discipline unfamiliar and oppressive.

The nature of the industrial workplace led to the development of the modern **labor movement**, and eventually to the associated rise of socialist and labor-oriented political parties. British workers who saw their traditional livelihoods threatened and believed themselves to be exploited attempted to form **unions** in the late eighteenth century. Property owners, capitalists, and the British government feared these "combinations" of workers would promote instability, violence, and social revolution. Thus, Britain passed the Combination Acts from 1799 to 1800, which made workers' unions illegal, and defended the property and privilege of the capitalist class.

Unions operated secretly, outside the law, until the Combination Acts were repealed in 1825 (though full legal recognition for unions did not exist until workers won the right to strike in the 1870s). After repeal, trade and labor union organization grew in Britain, as well as in other industrializing regions and nations. Unions operated under the premise that while individual workers were powerless against exploitative capitalists, a unified front of workers could bargain for higher wages, more reasonable working hours, and better working conditions. And in industries and regions where union organization was strong, wages and working conditions did improve over time. But even after the legalization of unions, the organization of labor remained beset by challenges. Throughout the nineteenth century, business owners harassed union organizers, employed strike breakers, and sometimes took illegal actions to break unions or to prevent them from forming.

While wages of the working class remained pitifully low throughout the early decades of industrialization, their lot eventually improved somewhat. Debates about living standards of early industrial workers continue amongst historians, but it is clear that in the second half of the nineteenth century, wages and living standards of average industrial workers in Britain improved significantly.[8] Unskilled and semi-skilled laborers still remained near the bottom of a still highly stratified society, however, as the top 20 percent of people in industrialized societies earned over half of their nation's incomes during much of the nineteenth century.

In addition to the hard-won benefits gained by labor unions, reform and state regulation of the industrial economy gradually helped curb some of the worst abuses of the industrial workplace. For example, the Factory Acts were a series of laws regulating factories in Britain passed at various points, starting in 1802 and continuing over more than a century. However, in many cases, the provisions contained in these acts may seem modest at best. The Factory Act of 1847, for example (the long-awaited Ten Hours Act), established a maximum working day in textile factories of ten hours for women and for children between ages thirteen and eighteen. To the extent that working-class life improved as industrial societies matured, it was government intervention and labor organization—not the invisible hand—that played the major role.

Urbanization and Impact on the Environment

Just as industrialization transformed production, transportation, the class system, and the nature of work, it profoundly altered our natural and human-made environments. As industrialization grew, it brought with it a great wave of

Image 12.1 Women workers, textile factory, nineteenth-century England

© Classic Image / Alamy

urbanization. From the late eighteenth century on, enormous numbers of people migrated from small villages and rural areas into rapidly growing cities. The migrants were drawn by the possibility of finding factory work, which was increasingly located in urban areas. Before the invention of the steam engine, mills were generally dependent on water power, and were thus restricted to locations that provided appropriate river access. But steam-powered machinery allowed factory owners to build their facilities in cities, taking advantage of the concentration of people (to provide labor and possibly markets), better transportation and supply networks, and closer proximity to other businesses.

European cities had a long history as religious, cultural, commercial, and political centers. But the growth of the factory system created something new— industrial cities. The new urban centers were often almost entirely dependent upon industry, and in some cases, a single industry. Whereas London, for example, had long been a market town, a religious center, a bastion of culture, and the seat of royal authority, the cotton-producing city of Manchester, in northern England, owed its rise to prominence entirely to the rapid growth of the textile industry. Elsewhere, other cities grew rapidly around their industries; in the United States, the location of Pittsburgh, Pennsylvania near coal fields and supplies of ore that fueled iron foundries and steel mills, helped it grow rapidly from a tiny village into a mighty industrial center.

The pace and scale of urbanization in cities like Manchester and Pittsburgh, to name just two, were astounding. Manchester's modest population of about 20,000 in the 1770s exploded to over 300,000 by about the mid-nineteenth century. Pittsburgh was an insignificant settlement around a military fort in 1800, claiming a population of only about 1,500 people. By 1900, the "Steel City" was one of the world's great heavy industrial cities, and its population had grown by over 320,000. Industrialization caused some other cities to grow even faster. Between 1840 and 1890, the American city of Chicago, Illinois grew from a small town of fewer than 5,000 people to a giant urban center of over one million inhabitants. And throughout the course of the nineteenth century, the percentage of the population in industrializing nations living in urban areas more than tripled.

As the populations of industrializing cities grew, so did their problems. Simply put, nineteenth-century industrial cities were crowded, filthy, and unsanitary in the extreme. Cities were unable to handle the rapid influx of new inhabitants, who were often forced to live in quickly and shoddily constructed row houses that were crowded, poorly ventilated, and featured only shared outhouses as sanitary facilities. A lack of public provision for sewage and sanitation meant that city streets were often filled with the stench of human and animal waste and rotting garbage. And the conditions of industrial cities were more than just unpleasant; in the 1830s and 1840s, for example, thousands died in cholera epidemics in British cities from contaminated water. The shocking conditions of cities led to a **public health movement** in industrialized countries, which convinced governments to act. By the second half of the nineteenth century, government initiatives helped supply more acceptable drinking water, sanitation, and sewage systems in industrial cities. While the conditions of urban areas gradually became less deadly, they still tended to be crowded and dirty places.

It was not only urban environments that were affected by industrialization. The Industrial Revolution represents nothing less than a turning point in the human relationship to our environment, as it was built upon massive alterations to our land, air, and water. Two of the main components of industrialization were tremendous quantities of coal and iron ore. In other words, factory production and the transportation revolution both relied on extractive industries for fuel and basic materials. **Extractive industries**, like coal mining or oil drilling, involve *extracting* these elements from the earth, which causes tremendous impacts on both the land and water. It is no coincidence that areas of the earth blessed with valuable reserves of coal, oil, iron ore, copper, and other materials needed for industrial development have suffered severe and often long-lasting environmental damage.

Not only the mining of coal, but also the burning of huge quantities of coal in factories, mills, locomotives, steamships, residences, and other buildings also led to significant environmental damage. Industrial cities were often thick with coal smoke; indeed, the famous "London fog" of legend was a product not just of weather, but of the smokestacks and chimneys that filled the city's skyline. **Industrial pollution** of the air and water, along with destruction of the land from extraction, are among the lasting legacies of industrialization.

Globalization and Western Dominance

The Industrial Revolution caused a veritable re-ordering of the global economic system. Western nations, especially those that industrialized earliest and most thoroughly, became far wealthier relative to the rest of the world than they had ever been. When Europe was still a pre-industrial, agricultural region, there was little global economic stratification *between* nations—virtually every nation in the world had a relatively poor majority, and a small, wealthy elite. Thus, the largest differences in wealth in the pre-industrial world were between the rich and poor *within* any given nation. But the massive profits of industrialization caused Europe and the United States to become the wealthiest societies to that point in history, many times wealthier than non-industrialized areas of Asia, Africa, and Latin America. The global legacies of this uneven development are still in place today.

Industrialization coincided with the massive expansion of European empires (see Chapter 8), and the imperialists of the nineteenth century were determined to make their colonies profitable. Various regions of the non-Western world were viewed as potential sources of raw materials and as captive markets. Since Britain controlled India, for example, it could force its products on the Indian market, prevent India from erecting any kind of protective tariff, and eventually drive many its manufacturers out of business. It was not only the speed and efficiency of industrial production that caused Western nations to profit greatly during this period; European imperialists were also in a position to "rig the system" in their favor.

Between about 1840 and 1914, Europeans also produced two exports in huge quantities—people and capital. A **great migration**, the largest movement of people in history to that point, resulted from the rising population and changing economies of Europe. Rising populations in the nineteenth century meant increased competition for jobs and scarce land resources, and the efficiency of industrial production rendered the skills of numerous craftspeople obsolete. As a result, millions of small landholders and craftspeople emigrated from Europe to the Americas, Asiatic Russia, Australia, and New Zealand.

During the period roughly corresponding with the Second Industrial Revolution, Europeans sent not only their people but their investments abroad as well. Foreign investment increased dramatically during this period, as Western capitalists sought higher profit margins in as-yet undeveloped regions of the world. Higher rates of return on investment insured that capital continued to flow out of industrialized Europe until the world economy was devastated by World War I.

The industrialization that started in the textile mills of northern England spread rapidly across Europe and North America, and eventually transformed the non-Western regions, too. Comparing the world in 1800 with the world in 1900, after about a century of industrialization (a very short period in human history), the immense transformation of the world becomes apparent. In industrialized regions, the size and nature of cities changed dramatically, a new class system was established, new forms of production predominated, machines became a crucial part of life, the nature of work for the majority of people changed, new products and inventions were everywhere, transportation was revolutionized, and the environment was altered dramatically. And taking a wider perspective, a new kind of profound global inequality resulted from the fortunes compiled by the Western nations and their exploitative empires.

The Industrial Revolution occurred during a time of great competition, not only between capitalists, but between European nations, as well. The nineteenth century was marked not only by economic changes, but by ideological ones, too. Thus, fueled by economic aspirations but also by nationalist ideologies and imperialist ambitions, European nations created a competitive international environment that would lead to massive war by 1914. And, thanks to the technological advancements of industrialization, new kinds of weapons would make that war bloodier and more disastrous than any before.

Notes

1 Robert L. Heilbroner and William Milberg, *The Making of Economic Society* (Upper Saddle River, NJ: Prentice Hall, 2002), 100.
2 Some historians have also suggested that a lack of regulation and interference in the economy by the British government also helped fuel the innovation that led to industrialization. Periods of rapid industrialization in nations like Germany and China, however, suggest that *laissez-faire* policies are not a necessary precondition for industrialization.
3 E. P. Thompson, *The Making of the English Working Class* (New York: Pantheon, 1964).
4 Anthony Wiener, *English Culture and the Decline of the Industrial Spirit, 1850–1980* (Cambridge: Cambridge University Press,1981).
5 See Lenore Davidoff and Catherine Hall, *Family Fortunes: Men and Women of the English Middle Class, 1780–1850* (Chicago: University of Chicago Press, 1987).
6 A renowned study of the changing nature of work is Peter Laslett, *The World We Have Lost* (New York: Scribner, 1965).
7 For a classic study of the transformation of time and work discipline that accompanied the industrial revolution, see E. P. Thompson, "Time, Work-Discipline, and Industrial Capitalism," *Past and Present*, no. 38 (1967), 56–97.
8 E. J. Hobsbawm, "The Standard of Living During the Industrial Revolution: A Discussion," *Economic History Review* 16, no. 1 (1963), 119–34.

Suggested Readings

Briggs, Asa. *The Age of Improvement, 1783–1867.* London: Longman, 1965.
Davidoff, Lenore, and Catherine Hall. *Family Fortunes: Men and Women of the English Middle Class, 1780–1850.* Chicago: University of Chicago Press, 1987.
Heilbroner, Robert L. and William Milberg. *The Making of Economic Society.* 7th ed. Upper Saddle River, NJ: Prentice Hall, 2002.
Hobsbawm, E. J. *The Age of Capital, 1848–1975.* New York: Scribner, 1975.
Hobsbawm, E. J. "The Standard of Living During the Industrial Revolution: A Discussion." *Economic History Review* 16, no. 1 (1963).
Kemp, Tom. *Industrialization in Nineteenth-Century Europe.* New York: Longman, 1985.

Laslett, Peter. *The World We Have Lost*. New York: Scribner, 1965.

Thompson, E. P. *The Making of the English Working Class*. New York: Pantheon, 1964.

Thompson, E. P. "Time, Work Discipline, and Industrial Capitalism." *Past and Present*, no. 38 (1967).

Thompson, F. M. L., ed. *The Cambridge Social History of Britain, 1750–1950*, 3 vols. Cambridge: Cambridge University Press, 1990.

Wiener, Martin J. *English Culture and the Decline of the Industrial Spirit, 1850–1980*. Cambridge: Cambridge University Press, 1981.

13 Classical Liberalism and the Bourgeois State

Kathleen Callanan Martin

Key Terms

Classical Liberalism, comparative advantage, franchise, free trade, *laissez-faire*, representative government, separation of powers, "tyranny of the majority," Utilitarianism

Writing in 1911, prominent English liberal L.T. Hobhouse proclaimed that liberalism is "saturated with the conviction that the unfettered action of the individual is the mainspring of all progress."[1] This is the underlying principle uniting a set of apparently diverse political and economic ideas that began to evolve in the eighteenth century and became the most influential ideology in the Western world during much of the nineteenth: the fervent belief that, "The more the individual receives free scope for the play of his faculties, the more rapidly will society as a whole advance."[2] This ideology, which differs in significant ways from the liberalism known to Americans in the twentieth-first century, is customarily called **Classical Liberalism**.

Europe in the late seventeenth century was a significantly different culture from medieval Europe, and many of the changes that had taken place raised the status of the individual as opposed to the group. Protestant theology emphasized the responsibility of the individual for his own salvation, while the breakdown of manorial agriculture and then of the guild system increasingly made each man an independent economic actor as well. The Scientific Revolution of the seventeenth century had offered dramatic proof that man could use his faculties to understand the world around him and thereby gain more control over it. If Newton could understand the movement of heavenly bodies and Harvey the circulation of blood, might not mankind be able to solve the riddles of human interaction and find optimal ways to govern its affairs? The great thinkers of the Enlightenment certainly thought that this was possible, and they tried to lead the way. Most important of all, perhaps, was the Enlightenment's optimistic view of human nature. A political philosopher who sees man as a hopeless sinner, or as a person likely to behave as badly as he can, will believe that it takes a very strong and vigilant government to prevent crimes, lawlessness, and even general chaos. Man must be closely governed for his own good. A political philosopher who sees man as inclined to good behavior, or at least not inclined to bad behavior, can imagine a world in which government can often leave people alone without dire consequences. This view of government—the liberal view—is one that the Enlightenment made possible.

A New View of Government

The most important contributors to liberal political thought agreed with each other in all of the most fundamental matters. Each had his own contributions to make, but their differences were largely differences of emphasis, rather than of basis premises. Political philosopher John Locke (1632–1704) advanced the idea that government can only be based on the consent of the governed, must protect the rights of the individual, and should be so organized as to divide power among several branches, rather than concentrating it in one person or institution, which would inevitably lead to abuse. His political writings, in particular his *Second Treatise of Civil Government,* built upon the experience of the English Civil War and Interregnum to advocate a constitutional monarchy responsible to a **representative government**. It is important to keep in mind that representative government and democracy are not the same thing. Democracy means, "rule by the people." In a democracy, every citizen would be entitled to have a voice in every decision. This would be extremely cumbersome in a large country, probably impossible. Representative government is not democracy; it is a system in which citizens elect legislators to represent them in making decisions. Locke was certainly no democrat. He expressly disapproved of democracy, not only for practical reasons, but because he felt that only people with a fair amount of property should take part in government.[3] Locke, in fact, placed a great deal of emphasis on property as the most important right that government must protect, along with freedom of worship, publication, and speech. He looked forward to a world in which social and economic progress would result from the energies of free people, unfettered by arbitrary government. His ideas had a tremendous influence on European political thought, and that influence was undoubtedly increased by the success of the American Revolution, whose founding documents everywhere reflect Locke's influence.

The French political thinkers Montesquieu and Tocqueville further developed these ideas of liberty and representative government. Both men were born into aristocratic families, but they preferred limited representative government in the English tradition to the absolutist monarchy of France. Certainly, they shared Locke's concern for property rights and freedom of opinion. In his most famous work, *The Spirit of the Laws* (1748), Montesquieu made a strong case for constitutional government based on the idea of the **separation of powers**, the deliberate division of governmental powers among several bodies so as to prevent too much power from falling into the hands of any one person or institution, thus threatening liberty. (This is why the US Constitution provides for executive, legislative, and judicial branches.) While Locke had assumed the virtues of this arrangement, which was characteristic of the British government tradition, Montesquieu made a strong theoretical argument for its importance in any type of government seriously committed to the preservation of freedom. Alexis de Tocqueville vehemently agreed with this idea but was concerned that representative government was no guarantee of freedom for the individual, even with carefully separated powers. Like Locke, he felt that it would be inappropriate for uneducated men of no property to be involved in government, and he worried that too much emphasis on equality might be a threat to liberty.

Democracy in America, published in two volumes in the 1830s, is a chronicle of Tocqueville's travels in the newly formed United States and his reactions to his experiences there. He admired much of what he saw, but he felt that too much democracy inhibited, rather than advanced, liberty. "I know of no country," he wrote, "in which there is so little independence of mind and real freedom of discussion as in America."[4] This was due to what he called "the **tyranny of the majority**"—the force of public opinion in a polity where ultimate authority resides in the people. While in the unreformed absolutist regimes of continental Europe it was a repressive government that inhibited freedom of thought and speech, in egalitarian America unwillingness to be different from one's fellows had the same effect, possibly to a greater degree. In any system of government, therefore, there must be some kind of limit to what can be demanded from the citizen if freedom is to be preserved. "Unlimited power is in itself a bad and dangerous thing. Human beings are not competent to exercise it with discretion."[5] The logic of Tocqueville's argument suggests that government must be limited by some kind of inviolable guarantee of individual rights, one of the most fundamental political concepts in the liberal tradition. It also suggests that quick decisions based on outbursts of vehement public opinion should always be suspect in a society that values the rights of the individual. Democracy and freedom, in this view, are somewhat incompatible.

Another influential source of ideas on social improvement somewhat at odds with the Lockean tradition came from the great English eccentric Jeremy Bentham (1748–1832), who founded the school of thought known as **Utilitarianism**. A perfect exemplar of Enlightenment skepticism, he was by nature disinclined to adhere to any idea or practice simply because of its antiquity. Utility means usefulness. In Bentham's view, only policies that work well and are conducive to human progress and happiness are useful, and therefore worth pursuing. While he shared the reluctance of Locke to coerce people or to tell them what to think, Bentham tended to stress the public good, rather than individual rights, in his social thought. The best way to assess the desirability of any given policy or law was to assess its utility: it must be workable in practice and must give the most possible benefit to the greatest possible number of people. Otherwise it was an unjustified intrusion on the activities of individuals and probably would not achieve its purpose.

These, then, are the most important political ideas of Classical Liberalism: it seeks reform in the interests of limited, constitutional government that is representative in nature and respects the rights of the individual, guarding against abusive office holders as well as against "the tyranny of the majority" in order to secure the public welfare in the least coercive way possible.

With the success of the American and French Revolutions, the political ideas of Classical Liberalism came to be more and more widely discussed by educated Europeans. People who felt oppressed by the old order came to hope (as people who felt attached to the old order came to fear) that liberal reforms were the wave of the future, that they would inevitably sweep across Europe bringing progress (or mob rule) to even the least Enlightened areas. Among the strongest supporters of Classical Liberalism were members of the bourgeoisie, professionals and businessmen who had no political role in the absolutist monarchies and who wanted recognition of their rights to think, worship, and conduct business as they saw fit, free from the restrictions of censorship, established religion, and mercantilist economic regulation.

Political Economy

The fundamental economic ideas of Classical Liberalism derive, for the most part, from the work of Adam Smith (1723–1790). Smith, too, shared the optimistic Enlightenment view that mankind could use reason to understand and improve the world. Just as Isaac Newton had changed the way educated Europeans thought of the solar system, postulating that it was a self-regulating mechanism rather than an unfathomable mystery, Smith intended to show that there were natural laws dictating the action of the economy as well. Understanding those laws, and acting in accordance with them, could yield a higher standard of living than unnecessary and inefficient mercantilist interference in the economy could ever provide. Like liberal political ideas, Smith's preferred economic policies are designed to set the individual free to achieve what he can in life, unencumbered by unnecessary government supervision or regulation. In *The Wealth of Nations*, published in the very year of the American Revolution (1776), Smith extolled the virtues of a market economy in which economic activity is motivated by individual self-interest and regulated, not by the government, but by competition. In such an economy, the natural ebb and flow of market forces will determine outcomes, as self-interested individuals do what seems best in the pursuit of profit. This freedom would not, Smith argued, benefit greedy individuals at the expense of the society as a whole:

> Every individual is continually exerting himself to find out the most advantageous employment for whatever capital he can command. It is his own advantage, indeed, and not that of the society, which he has in view. But the study of his own advantage naturally, or rather necessarily, leads him to prefer that employment which is most advantageous to the society.[6]

The impartial forces of the market reconcile all interests.

Much of Smith's great book is a protest against what he saw as the arbitrariness, economic ignorance, and general ineffectiveness of mercantilist economic policies.

Smith did not deny that governments should care about the economic well-being of their people. He merely asserted that mercantilist policies did more harm than good. Protected monopolies did not provide consumers with the best goods at the best prices; they shielded incompetence and actually raised prices, since firms with no competition can charge whatever they like for their products. Why shield domestic producers from competition with foreign producers who make a better or cheaper product? Why not let people follow their own inclination to make money and let competition sort out the rest?

As Smith wrote, England was in the early stages of industrialization. The entrepreneurs who were driving this process were frustrated by government rules and regulations that they saw as burdensome, and indignant at the privileged status of licensed traders like the British East India Company, which enjoyed the sole right to import goods from South and East Asia into Britain. For obvious reasons, they found Smith's ideas very appealing. (In assessing the popularity of these ideas, it is important to bear in mind that Britain was the first country to industrialize and therefore was in a very strong position to compete with its trade rivals. Classical Liberalism was always more popular in the English-speaking world than elsewhere, and with good reason.) As the business sector of the British economy grew, more and more people came to favor Adam Smith's preferred policy of **free trade** unencumbered by taxes, monopolies, or restrictions on imports and exports. This "system of perfect liberty," as Smith called it, would stimulate economic growth and deliver the best goods at the best prices for consumers, while allowing individual businessmen and consumers to do as they pleased.[7] Manufacturers campaigned in particular against the so-called Corn Laws, which aimed to protect British farmers by placing a tariff on imported grain, thus keeping the price of bread artificially high. The manufacturers were acting, as good disciples of Smith, in their own self-interest rather than out of concern for the poor, since it is not possible to pay workers less than the cost of survival. High bread prices necessarily meant high wages. The repeal of the Corn Laws by Parliament in 1846 represented a significant victory for liberal economic thought.

As more and more parts of Europe came under the sway of market economies, and as the tide of industrialization swept across Europe and North America, the economic ideas of Classical Liberalism gained more adherents among businessmen and professionals outside Britain. Just as the success of the American and French Revolutions seemed to make a good case for political liberalism, the growing economic success of Britain and the United States seemed to make a good case for economic liberalism. Like liberal political thought, liberal economic thought offered members of the bourgeoisie more freedom from governmental restraint and an enhanced position in society as the agents of progress. They could make a new, better world for everyone (and considerable profit for themselves) if only the government would stand back and let them do it.

Smith's description of free trade as the "system of perfect liberty" highlights the close connection between the political and economic ideas of Classical Liberalism. They work very well together and form a coherent ideology because they all place a strong emphasis on the freedom of the individual to do whatever he feels is in his own best interest. In political terms, this means representative government and respect for individual rights. In economic terms, it means a policy of *laissez-faire*, or of leaving people alone to pursue their own self-interest. Both sets of ideas imply that the best government is the least government; government should intervene in the activities of the individual only when there is a compelling public reason to do so.

This insistence that the government had best leave well enough alone and keep its hands off the economy became axiomatic in the emerging discipline of Political Economy, as economics was called in the early period of its existence. Adam Smith is rightfully known as the father of economics, but the political economists who followed his lead made their own contributions to this school of thought. British political economist David Ricardo (1772–1823) argued that since the division of labor and specialization yield higher productivity, international specialization should be seen as desirable, not as a source of anxiety about foreign competition. In Britain, for example, the climate would make production of oranges or tea prohibitively expensive; in the production of these commodities Spain and China have a **comparative advantage** over the British. On the other hand, industrializing Britain could now produce large quantities of cotton cloth much cheaper than either Spain or China because of the capital investments that British firms had made in new technology. Why not let each country's economy do what it does best? This idea, of course, greatly enhanced the perceived advantages of free trade. British political economist Thomas Malthus (1766–1834) is best known for his *Essay on the Principle of Population*, which asserted that population will always expand to use (and overtax) the resources available. On this basis Malthus argued that attempts by the state to help the poor were, while well intended, counterproductive, because by helping the poor to survive they encouraged the growth of population. Only so much food could be produced; beyond this limit, starvation would result. Even if this were not true, as more people chased the same number of jobs, market forces would cause wages to decline, making the lot of the poor worse rather than better. Therefore, Classical Liberals opposed relief for the poor on principle.

The logic of Classical Liberalism (and arguably the economic self-interest of its adherents as well) prompted nineteenth-century liberals to take many political positions that come as a surprise to contemporary Americans accustomed to contemporary American liberalism. In the nineteenth century, liberals vehemently opposed legislation intended to reform the appalling working conditions of the early factories. They fought hard against the legalization of labor unions, prohibition of child labor, attempts to shorten the very long work day, and efforts to make factory work less dangerous, all in the name of *laissez-faire*. These laws would inhibit freedom of contract between the employer and the employee, they argued, unjustifiably interfere with the economy, and put manufacturers at a disadvantage relative to their foreign competitors. On the same grounds they opposed slum clearance, building codes, and regulation of the purity of food and drugs. For most of the nineteenth century, British liberals opposed campaigns to widen the franchise, giving the vote to more than the small minority of propertied people (all of them male) who were eligible to vote at the start of the century. (The **franchise** is the legally recognized right to vote.) Because they shared Tocqueville's fear of mob rule, and because they knew that factory employees were less enthusiastic about the supremacy of *laissez-faire* policies than their employers were, liberals favored restricting the right to vote to men of property. It is for these reasons that it was always the Conservatives, rather than the Liberals, who granted successive enlargements of the British parliamentary franchise, and that the first establishment of health insurance and unemployment compensation in Europe came in distinctly conservative Germany rather than in liberal Britain.

John Stuart Mill

The harmony of the political and economic ideas of Classical Liberalism is most evident in the person of economist and political philosopher John Stuart Mill, undoubtedly its most eloquent spokesman. John Stuart Mill (1806–1873) was the son of Jeremy Bentham's friend and disciple James Mill and, as a child, knew Bentham personally. Well educated at home by his demanding father, Mill undoubtedly read more widely and thought more penetratingly than most men of his or any other time. After a nervous breakdown early in life, Mill carefully re-examined all of his most cherished views and was never inclined to take any idea on authority or by custom. (Unlike most of his contemporary male liberals, for example, Mill argued forcefully for the right of women to be accepted as full adults and given the vote. Otherwise sympathetic observers attributed this eccentric view to his marriage to feminist Harriet Taylor.) For the ideas that did pass his intense scrutiny he was an ardent and effective advocate. In his *Principles of Political Economy* (1848) he clearly explained the concepts of *laissez-faire* economics, making a strong case for this approach to economic policy as the foundation of liberty itself, relying as it does on the achievements and energies of the unrestrained individual. *On Liberty* (1859) still ranks today as the finest argument ever made for allowing the fullest possible personal freedom to each and every individual. Infringing on the natural right of the individual to worship as he wishes, to read, say, and publish whatever he likes, and in general to do whatever he wants to do cannot be tolerated, Mill says, on grounds of unpopularity, perceived immorality, or even of possible harm to the individual himself. (In this last instance, of course, Mill permits exceptions for children and the insane, but only for them. Man has a right to risk harm to himself if he wishes to do so.) Only harm to others can make a valid excuse for encroachments on liberty. True to his Utilitarian upbringing, Mill does not rest his case on the natural rights of the individual alone. Society itself, he argues, is better off if all ideas can be heard and discussed, whether they are right or wrong. The greatest good of the greatest number demands the free play of the marketplace of ideas. In the end, the best ideas will triumph, provided people have sufficient practice in sifting through the available arguments so as to find the ones that legitimately convince. Even bad ideas and falsehoods, therefore, have utility and must be tolerated.

> That mankind are not infallible; that their truths, for the most part, are only half-truths; that unity of opinion, unless resulting from the fullest and freest comparison of opposite opinions, is not desirable, and diversity not an evil, but a good, until mankind are much more capable than at present of recognizing all sides of the truth, are principles applicable to men's modes of action, not less than to their opinions.[8]

Clearly Mill did take seriously the idea of the tyranny of the majority. He argued that toleration of unpopular, even obnoxious opinion is essential to a free society and that its absence indicates a society that does not value freedom sufficiently. But he had faith in education and the free flow of ideas to create a safe climate for full participation by the many, rather than merely by the few. Liberty and democracy, perhaps, need not be at odds after all.

At the midpoint of the nineteenth century, the political and economic ideas of Classical Liberalism seemed to a growing number of people, particularly to middle-class people in Europe and America, to be an inevitable force that would bring progress to the entire world. Hobhouse summarized this vision superbly when he described liberalism as "a movement of liberation, a clearance of obstructions, an opening of channels for the flow of free spontaneous vital activity."[9] Yet by the end of the century Classical Liberalism was an ideology under siege. Even some of its most ardent supporters, Mill included, had begun to wonder if freedom without substantial equality is truly possible, since the poor must take whatever terms the rich choose to offer them. Capitalism, it seemed, was surpassingly good at production, but at distribution it seemed considerably less successful. To the right, the growing forces of militant nationalism opposed liberal views, to the left, the growing forces of socialist and communist movements. Even in Britain, the land of its birth, by the start of World War I the standard of the future appeared to many to have passed into other hands.

Classical Liberalism and Progressive Liberalism

The subject of this chapter has been Classical Liberalism, which differed in many ways from the type of liberalism most familiar to people today. The change is not total: today's liberalism, in countries like Canada and the United States, still places a very high value on the political ideas of its ancestor. It sees the authority of government as deriving from the consent of the governed and favors representative governments that respect the civil rights of the people. Contemporary progressive liberals also, unlike socialists, still favor the free enterprise system and the operation of the market as the best basis of a prosperous society.

But John Stuart Mill's concerns, late in his life, about the compatibility of human dignity and vast social inequality came to be shared by more and more liberals as time passed. Do large differences in the resources available to children of different social classes make the idea of equal opportunity questionable? Does basing how much education a person receives on how much that person's family can afford indicate a lack of respect for the essential dignity and rights of everyone? Do differences in wealth mean differences in how much justice is available to the individual, or in how much attention the government pays to his or her views? And even in the realm of economics, do completely unregulated markets produce the very monopolies that Adam Smith condemned in the days of mercantilism—this time as a result of competition, rather than of government favor? In the period after Mill's death, many liberals came to share his concern that a capitalist market economy is much better at producing wealth than at distributing it fairly, and that society may need to step in to make sure that all of its members have the opportunity to enjoy a decent life, develop their abilities, and have their voices heard. In the words of Isaiah Berlin, "Freedom for the wolves has often meant death to the sheep."[1] And it is this perspective which sets contemporary Progressive Liberalism apart from the Classical Liberalism of the nineteenth century.

Note

1 Isaiah Berlin, *Four Essays on Liberty* (London: Oxford University Press, 1969) xlv–xlvi.

Notes

1 L.T. Hobhouse, *Liberalism* (London: Oxford University Press, [1911] 1964), 44.
2 Ibid., 34.
3 Christopher Hill, *The Century of Revolution* 1603–1714 (New York: W.W. Norton & Co., 1980), 255.
4 Alexis de Tocqueville, *Democracy in America* (New York: Alfred A. Knopf, Inc., [1835] 1945), 273. In any standard edition of this work, the discussion of the "tyranny of the majority" is to be found in Volume I, Chapter XVI.
5 Tocqueville, 270.
6 Adam Smith, *The Wealth of Nations* (New York: Bantam Dell, [1776] 2003), 569–70. In any full edition, this discussion is to be found in Book IV, Chapter II.
7 Smith, 770. In any full edition, this can be found in Book IV, Chapter VII, Part III.
8 John Stuart Mill, *The Basic Writings of John Stuart Mill: On Liberty, The Subjection of Women and Utilitarianism* (New York: Classic Books of America, [1859] 2009), 62–3. This passage comes from *On Liberty*, Chapter 3.
9 Hobhouse, 28.

Suggested Readings:

Briggs, Asa. *Victorian People: A Reassessment of Persons and Themes 1851–1867.* Chicago: University of Chicago Press, 1970.
Heilbroner, Robert L. *The Worldly Philosophers: The Lives, Times and Ideas of the Great Economic Thinkers.* New York: Touchstone, 1999.

Hobhouse, L.T. *Liberalism*. London: Oxford University Press, [1911] 1964.
Mill, John Stuart. *On Liberty*. New York: Classic Books of America, [1859] 2009.
————*The Subjection of Women*. New York: Classic Books of America, [1869] 2009.
————*Utilitarianism*. New York: Classic Books of America, [1861] 2009.
Smith, Adam. *The Wealth of Nations*. New York: Bantam Dell, [1776] 2003.
Tocqueville. Alexis de. *Democracy in America*. 2 vols. New York: Alfred A. Knopf, Inc.,
    [1835] 1945.

14 Karl Marx and the Socialist Response to Capitalism

Kathleen Callanan Martin

Key Terms

alienation, communism, materialism, socialism

As the Industrial Revolution and the ideas of liberalism spread out across Europe during the early nineteenth century, not everyone was happy about the changes that ensued. Landed aristocrats and members of the upper clergy, of course, were concerned about the possible loss of the privileges they enjoyed under the old order. For many working people, too, the tide of change was worrisome. Cities began to grow quickly and haphazardly as workers streamed in from the countryside looking for jobs; the inhabitants of their overcrowded, disease-ridden slums endured a truly miserable (and often short) existence. Conditions were no better at work, as people worked extremely long hours under dangerous conditions for very low pay and lost their jobs abruptly during downturns in trade. The abolition of guild privileges may have been good for the growth of the economy in the long run, but in the short run it was experienced as a disaster by craftsmen who lost their independence, status, and sometimes their comfortable standard of living as well.[1] And of course liberals, with their fervent belief in *laissez-faire* and minimal government, actively opposed laws intended to ameliorate any of these problems. To them it seemed obvious that a system of political liberty and a self-regulating economy would yield the most progress in the end. To many workers, who could not meet the property requirements for the vote and who desperately needed improvement in their living and working conditions, this seemed like an alliance of the propertied against the defenseless workers. They were attracted, therefore, to the growing body of ideas called **socialism**.

Socialism is not a single doctrine that is easy to define. Since its origin in the early nineteenth century, many people with very different ideas have called themselves socialists. The movement is based on the political ideas of the Enlightenment. For most socialists, the most important of these ideas were the equality of all men and the potential to solve human problems by the application of reason. They valued cooperation over individualism, but they did not deny the value of the individual; they argued that each individual must be given an opportunity to develop to the best of his potential—clearly not a likely outcome for a malnourished, illiterate child

Communism and Socialism

All of the **communist** governments that have existed to date have declared themselves to be following the ideas of Karl Marx. According to Marx, in a communist society the means of production, distribution, and exchange of goods would be collectively owned, and collectively managed, for the good of all members of society. (The "means of production" are factories, mines, tools, and so on; the "means of distribution" are the network of stores, trucks, and so on by which goods reach individuals; the "means of exchange" include things like banks and wholesalers.) In pursuit of this goal, communist governments seized ownership of these assets and managed them through a central bureaucracy. The result was supposed to be a fairer society for everyone: "From each according to his ability, to each according to his need."[1]

Whatever the intentions of the revolutionaries may have been, we can say this: the reality of communist societies so far indicates that no close approximation of this ideal type has ever been achieved. The relatively primitive state of each of these economies when communist rule began, internal power struggles, the priority placed on the national security interests of the Soviet Union during the Cold War, and the difficulties of managing a large and complex economy through a central bureaucracy all played a role in this failure.

Socialism is much harder to define, because so many different people with so many different ideas have called themselves socialists. To the extent that generalization is possible, it is probably fairly accurate to say that most socialists accept the political ideas of liberalism but reject its economic ideas. Socialists approve of representative government and guarantees of civil rights, but they feel quite certain that considerable government involvement in the economy is necessary to make sure that no members of society are poor, uneducated, abused, and ignored by government. At a minimum, socialists favor welfare-state provisions and extensive regulation of industry; many of them also favor government ownership of at least some key parts of the economy. (A typical list might include transportation, extractive industries like mining and petroleum, and banks.) Unlike the government-owned command economy favored by communists, socialists prefer a "mixed economy"—part command, part market—with some state-sponsored enterprise and careful regulation of the rest.

Note

1 Karl Marx, *Critique of the Gotha Program* (1875) www.marxists.org/archive/marx/works/1875/gotha/

living in a pestilential slum. Surely, they argued, an increasingly enlightened and wealthy society can do better. Over time socialists have proposed a wide variety of means to this end, including government ownership, worker control, or collective regulation of some or all industries.[2]

Not surprisingly, in early nineteenth-century Europe the center of the socialist movement was the revolutionary city of Paris. But the ideas of socialism were widespread and tended to become increasingly popular in any given country as it began to industrialize. This popularity was given a substantial push in the year 1848, when Paris once again became the scene of a revolution, and a revolutionary wave seemed to be spreading across Europe.

A number of factors contributed to the wave of rebellions and revolutions that occurred in Europe in 1848, and the combination of them differed from one area to the next. Several consecutive years of bad harvests had raised the price of food considerably or, in some cases, caused severe famine. (The Irish Potato Famine is the most famous of these disasters; it caused the death by starvation of about a million Irish and sent even more across the seas to North America and Australia.) Combined with a business recession that swelled the ranks of the unemployed, this caused tremendous hardship to the poor. Many urban artisans were desperate to reverse the erosion of their status and income under the pressure of industrialization. Many middle-class professionals wanted political liberties of the kind enjoyed by their counterparts in Britain. In some areas, particularly in yet-to-be-unified Italy and Germany and in portions of the Habsburg Empire, nationalism also played a significant role in popular unrest. In various combinations, these issues fed the chain reaction of rebellion once the news of revolutionary Paris began to spread. Over the course of the year the Revolutions of 1848 affected most of Europe: Paris, Vienna, Prague, Hungary, the Papal States, Palermo and Naples, Munich, Berlin, Frankfurt, and many other areas. Even relatively stable and liberal Britain experienced, not a revolution, but a significant increase in popular protest against working conditions and agitation for extension of the right to vote to more people. While most of these revolutionary movements were in the end put down, often with great violence followed by an increase in repression of dissident views, for a time it looked like a mighty and irresistible tide of change was sweeping across Europe. And it was in the excitement of this moment that socialists Karl Marx and Friedrich Engels published their best-known book, *The Communist Manifesto*.

Karl Marx: The Man and the Ideas

Karl Marx was born in the city of Trier in the Rhineland in 1818, shortly after the Napoleonic occupation had brought revolutionary new ideas to this prosperous area of Germany. His father, an enthusiastic liberal and a respected lawyer who raised his son on the classic works of the Enlightenment, had converted to Protestantism to avoid the legal inequalities imposed on Jews. Like many fathers, he wanted his son to follow in his footsteps, so Karl Marx studied law at the University of Berlin. It was there that he encountered the philosophy of Hegel, very much in vogue in German intellectual circles of the day, and changed his focus from law to philosophy. He received his PhD in philosophy from the University of Jena in 1841. But by the time his dissertation was accepted Marx's growing concerns about the social issues of the day had become stronger than his interest in teaching philosophy. "The philosophers have only interpreted the world in various ways;" he wrote in his *Theses on Feuerbach*, "the point, however, is to change it." [3]

Thus began Marx's career as a crusading radical journalist and editor, during which the legal authorities of several countries suppressed his publications and ejected him from the country on short notice. Marx and his family were in turn expelled from Paris, Brussels, and Cologne. In each place, he made the acquaintance of the local socialists and other radicals and familiarized himself with their ideas. And in each place the legal authorities took a very dim view of the newspaper or journal in which these views were expressed, deeming it a threat to the *status quo*. During these years Marx made quite a few enemies and several friends, the most important of whom was his closest friend, Friedrich Engels (1820–1895).

Engels, too, was German, the son of a very prosperous cotton textile manufacturer. His pious father, a Protestant evangelical, was displeased by his son's attraction to frivolous pursuits like dueling, poetry, and radical politics at the university. The remedy for this was to be immersion in the family business; after a period of training Engels assumed management of the Manchester branch of his father's firm. This gave Engels a very comfortable income but did not cure him of his interest in radical causes. In fact, he used his early years in Manchester as the basis for research on the living and working conditions of factory workers in this mushrooming city. His book *The Condition of the Working Class in England*, published in 1844, paints a disturbing picture of life in the city's teeming slums and smoky factories. Marx greatly admired this book; it helped to seal a friendship based on shared interests and ideas about the state of Europe in the early industrial age. Intellectually, Marx was very much the greater of the two, as Engels freely acknowledged, but Engels provided Marx with useful feedback in the development of his ideas and a much-needed supplement to his income, especially after Marx settled in England in 1849. When, in the heady days of the Revolutions of 1848, a small radical group calling themselves the Communist League wanted to publish a pamphlet of revolutionary goals, they entrusted the task of composing this to Karl Marx and Friedrich Engels.

Probably because of the atmosphere of the time, *The Communist Manifesto* strikes a far more militant tone than most of Marx's later writings. Subsequent Communist revolutions in Russia and China have caused many people to pay most attention to the vision of "the specter of Communism" said to be haunting Europe in the *Manifesto*'s opening pages. But even more influential, in the long run, has been Marx's analysis of history and of capitalism, of which this is the earliest coherent statement. True to his Hegelian roots, Marx saw the flow of history as a series of pitched battles between diametrically opposed forces. For Hegel, these forces were contending ideas. Marx, however, was a **materialist** and therefore believed only in things that could be perceived by the senses: tasted, touched, heard, seen, smelled, or felt. So, for Marx these opposed forces are classes whose economic interests are in conflict. "The history of all hitherto existing society," the *Manifesto* proclaims, "is the history of class struggles."[4] In any given era, there is an exploiting class, which owns the means of production, and an exploited class, which does not. The resulting class struggle is the engine of historical change. The struggle between the feudal aristocracy and the rising middle class, for example, brought about the French Revolution and the beginnings of the modern era. In turn, according to Marx, the contemporary struggle between the triumphant bourgeoisie and the industrial proletariat they have called into existence to work in their factories will in the end inevitably destroy the liberal capitalist order and usher in the era of **communism**, in which the means of production will be collectively owned and managed for the good of everyone. This will happen not because of the greed, malice, or heroism of individuals, but because that is simply the way history works. Capitalism will collapse not because of the actions of revolutionaries but because it has created an ever-growing class of proletarians whose interests cannot be reconciled to those of their employers. "What the bourgeoisie produces, above all, is its own grave-diggers. Its fall and the victory of the proletariat are equally inevitable."[5]

Karl Marx, Historical Sociologist

The importance of Marx's ideas is by no means confined to the later development of revolutionary groups calling themselves Communist. His approach to history and culture has had a considerable influence on the social sciences. It was Marx who prompted Europeans to consider how much impact material surroundings, economic standing, and cultural framework have on us as individuals. In fact, Marx clearly exhibited what American sociologist C. Wright Mills would later call "The Sociological Imagination," an ability to place individual lives within the context of wider social forces, to connect biography with history. "Men make their own history," Marx wrote:

> but they do not make it just as they please; they do not make it under circumstances chosen by themselves, but under circumstances directly encountered, given and transmitted from the past. The history of all the dead generations weighs like a nightmare on the brain of the living.[6]

Men may have free will, but they do not create the circumstances into which they are born. Nor can they create an infinite number of different cultures from the material reality in which they live. To Marx, an economic determinist, it seemed clear that the economic basis of any given society will govern the values, ideas, and social arrangements of that society. Members of hunter-gatherer bands cannot be individualists, nor can they live in vast cities. As the Industrial Revolution advanced, therefore, social change was inevitable. "The hand-mill gives you society with the feudal lord; the steam-mill, society with the industrial capitalist."[7]

To be sure, not all modern historians are economic determinists, but since Marx, few have denied that changes in a society's economic arrangements are likely to have a major impact on other aspects of the society.

The French historian Henri Lefebvre has suggested that Marx's greatest influence on sociology may have been his attention to ideology, "one of the most original and comprehensive concepts Marx introduced."[8] Marx argued that "The ruling ideas of each age have ever been the ideas of its ruling class."[9] These ideas justify the existing disposition of power and wealth in that society and therefore serve a purpose in maintaining the *status quo*. Ever since Marx, social scientists of many political persuasions have looked carefully at the religious, moral, and political ideas of a given society with the understanding that not everyone shares them and that they may serve the purposes of some groups better than others. From this perspective, too, systems of social stratification are studied as they actually function and are maintained, rather than as ideal blueprints of how society ought to be. Medieval concepts of society, for example, emphasized the God-given nature of the social order and the unimportance of riches and power in this life. These ideas were not only in harmony with traditional Christian thought but also far more conducive to maintenance of the existing system than to change in the interests of equality or fairness.

Another legacy of Marx is a concern for the **alienation** of modern man in the increasingly large and impersonal social arrangements of the contemporary world. This is one emphasis that Marx retained from his days as a philosopher; he often wrote of man's estrangement from himself in the working world, where the worker retains no control over his work and someone else profits from it more than the worker himself and his family. Crammed together in huge, impersonal factories and enormous, impersonal cities, man finds himself in a world where it seems that no connection exists between one man and another except for the "cash nexus" of "naked self-interest."[10] Since Marx's time, this progressive impoverishment of the inner life and emotional relationships of man as modernization takes place has been a continuing concern of many social analysts, socialist, liberal, and conservative alike.

Karl Marx, Economist

From the time of his arrival in England in 1849 until his death in 1883, Marx spent much of his time on a deep study of how capitalism arose, how it works, and what its future might be. He conducted much of his research in the Reading Room of the British Museum, reading all of the works of the classical political economists like Adam Smith and David Ricardo, their predecessors, and their followers. He plowed through voluminous statistics on the development of various industries throughout Europe and the world, the construction of railroads and canals, and the competition for expanded colonial empires, filling notebook after notebook with his findings. The result was *Capital*, never finished in Marx's lifetime and eventually published in three volumes. It was hardly an immediate success; it took four years for the first thousand copies of Volume I to be sold.[11]

It is enormously long, mind-numbingly detailed, and read by very few people. But it deserves more attention than it receives, especially since the fall of the Communist regimes of Russia and Eastern Europe, because Marx's track record in predicting the future development of capitalism has been disturbingly accurate.

Marx predicted that capitalism would experience a secular trend toward falling profits, as well as an ever-increasing scale of industry and resultant decrease in the number of firms. He predicted the increasing severity of the business cycle, leading to worldwide economic depressions and crises, each worse than the previous. (In 1883 this idea seemed rather absurd to many people; by 1930 it seemed frighteningly possible.) He predicted that governments would find it impossible to deal adequately with these crises because they had no reach outside their national boundaries and were too intimately connected with the dominant capitalist class to be objective in their approach. He predicted globalization, the erosion of local and even national culture over time, and the dominance of multinational corporations against which no individual government can stand. In all of these instances, his foresight has been impressive.

Finally, Marx predicted, despite the enormous wealth created by capitalism (and celebrated in the *Communist Manifesto*), eventually the entire system would come crashing down, a victim of its own success. At the time of his death Marx did not expect to see this happen soon, but he was no less convinced than he had been in 1848 that eventually we will find "The conditions of bourgeois society are too narrow to comprise the wealth created by them." [12] The enormous social forces of production would have to be controlled not by the few, as private property, but by the many, collectively. However much this prospect heartened Karl Marx, this is not a future to which most citizens of the developed world in the post-Communist era would look forward with pleasure. And yet his record as a prophet of capitalism indicates that Marx was a man who understood capitalism very, very well. If we are to understand it well enough to have some control over our own destiny in a capitalist world, prudence would dictate that we not ignore his insights.

Notes

1 In the medieval period, organizations of master craftsmen had arisen to set standards for training, recognition of master status, and quality of workmanship of the finished goods. These organizations were called guilds; only their members could engage in the craft they regulated.

2 For a sense of just how wide a variety of ideas have been proposed under the banner of socialism, see Michael Newman, *Socialism: A Very Short Introduction* (Oxford: Oxford University Press, 2005).

3 Karl Marx, *Theses on Feuerbach*, in *Selected Works of Karl Marx and Friedrich Engels* (New York: International Publishers, 1972), 30.

4 Karl Marx and Friedrich Engels, *The Communist Manifesto*, in *Selected Works of Karl Marx and Friedrich Engels*, 35.

5 *The Communist Manifesto*, 46.

6 Karl Marx, *The Eighteenth Brumaire of Louis Bonaparte*, in *Selected Works*, 97.

7 Karl Marx, *The Poverty of Philosophy*, cited in David McLellan, *Karl Marx: His Life and Thought* (New York: Harper & Row, 1973), 164.

8 Henri Lefebvre, *The Sociology of Marx* (New York: Pantheon Books, 1968), 59. This is the first American edition, translated from the French by Norbert Guterman.
9 *The Communist Manifesto,* in *Selected Works,* 54.
10 *The Communist Manifesto,* in *Selected Works,* 38.
11 McLellan, 353.
12 *The Communist Manifesto,* in *Selected Works,* 41.

Suggested Readings

Heilbroner, Robert L. *The Worldly Philosophers: The Lives, Times and Ideas of the Great Economic Thinkers.* New York: Touchstone, 1999

McLellan, David. *Karl Marx: His Life and Thought.* New York: Harper & Row, 1973.

Marx, Karl, and Friedrich Engels. *The Communist Manifesto.* In *Selected Works of Karl Marx and Friedrich Engels.* New York: International Publishers, [1848] 1972.

Newman, Michael. *Socialism: A Very Short Introduction.* Oxford: Oxford University Press, 2005.

15 Nationalism and Nations

John W. Mackey

Key Terms

anti-Semitism, authority, chauvinism, citizenship, latent force, liberal nationalism, nation-state, nationalism, physical force, racial nationalism, rational-legal authority, romantic nationalism, scientific racism, Social Darwinism, subjecthood

In addition to rapid industrialization, the nineteenth century was also marked by the popularity and wide dissemination of new ideologies. Especially in the Western parts of Europe, more concentrated urban populations, which were becoming increasingly literate, were drawn to systems of ideas that they believed promoted their interests and would help to bring about the sorts of progress that Enlightenment thinking encouraged. In addition to Classical Liberalism and early ideas of socialism, one of the most powerful of these ideologies was what we call **nationalism**. Though it came in several varieties and displayed a tendency to change over time, by the end of the nineteenth century, nationalism had emerged as perhaps the most powerful ideology yet to appear in Western society, intimately connected to the process of modernization. This process was accompanied by the birth of the **nation-state** in its modern form.

The Power and Authority of the Modern Nation-State

The modern nation-state is one of the most significant and powerful of all human institutions. The nation-state organizes the political lives of a given people in a particular land area over which it has sovereign jurisdiction. It creates laws that regulate behavior and judicial systems and punishments to deal with the violators of laws. The modern state also provides for a wide variety of human needs through the creation of bureaucracies and government agencies. While some states offer a high degree of personal liberty to their citizens, others are repressive or even totalitarian in nature; the latter are often met with anger, dissent, and resistance from their citizenry.

Although nation-states vary widely in the ways they govern, all successful states are able to function because they can wield power. Among the types of power identified by sociologist Max Weber is the power of **physical force**. Nation-states can use physical force to impose their will, and to that end they organize police and military services. Weber also argued that another type of power might be called **latent force**, or the threat of physical force. Nation-states utilize latent force as well; for example, citizens of a particular nation may be dissuaded from violating a law for fear of facing the physical force of the police. The state may benefit, then, from both the use of physical force and its looming possibility; physical force need not be in active operation to be effective as a tool of control.

But Weber believed that governing by physical force alone is not optimal or even efficient for a well-run state. Thus, modern nation-states govern on the basis of their authority. **Authority** is power that is presumed to be legitimate by those who are subject to it. Many modern states have created constitutional systems and institutions that provide the justification for the exercise of power, a type of authority Weber called **rational-legal authority**. Thus, in an effective modern nation-state, citizens participate constructively in their societies not merely because they fear the force of the state, but because they feel part of a legitimate system that is based on reasonably fair and rational principles.

Both the nation-state and its corresponding ideology, known as nationalism, are generally considered to have been products of the European nineteenth century. As the effects of the Enlightenment and the Industrial Revolution spread through the continent, nation-states and nationalism assumed various forms. But whatever the varying environments that surrounded them, Europeans increasingly began to identify with the concept of "the nation."

The Early Nineteenth Century: Liberal and Romantic Nationalism

As the century began, **liberal nationalism** was on the rise as a political force, and **romantic nationalism** sparked the imaginations of many newly patriotic Europeans, who began to identify strongly with a nation. Romantic nationalists usually defined the nation in terms of a shared history, as well as common language and customs. Historians credit the French Revolution with giving birth to both types of early nationalism. Revolutionary leaders such as the Jacobins emphasized the ideal of loyalty to the nation, and they defined the nation not as a class or ruling power, but as the French people themselves. According to the republican ideals of the Revolution, individuals were no longer to consider themselves loyal to a particular monarch or family, nor to a region or locality; the people of France were to be *citizens* of a republic, not *subjects* of a monarch. To be a subject, as the prefix "sub" would suggest, is to be under the power of a force higher than oneself. **Subjecthood**, therefore, implies inequality, obedience, and allegiance to a sovereign power superior to oneself. The more modern concept of **citizenship** implies equality, civil rights, and participation in the governance of the state. As Rousseau argued, citizenship obligated individuals to actively participate in their own governance, while absolutist rule based on blind obedience was equivalent to slavery.[1] The nationalism of the French Revolution was based on

Enlightenment values, active citizenship, representative institutions, and devotion to the concept of the people as the nation. French Revolutionary citizenship, however, was a gendered concept—only males were eligible for active participation in the Republic.

The Napoleonic Wars facilitated the spread of the nationalist spirit of the French Revolution. As Napoleon's armies marched through Europe in the early years of the nineteenth century, they brought their nationalist enthusiasms with them, encouraging the subjects of absolutist states to liberate themselves. Their message found a receptive audience, especially among peoples who saw themselves as a distinctive national or ethnic group under the control of a foreign power or within a multiethnic empire. Thus, enthusiasm for what is sometimes called liberal nationalism was unleashed across Europe. Liberal nationalists believed that the modern, constitutional nation-state was the ideal institution for the expression of the will of the nation and the safeguarding of individual liberty. They regarded absolutism as tyrannical and obsolete.

The old, conservative order in Europe resisted this spreading ideology, viewing it as a threat to stability, tradition, and the entrenched European power system. Liberal nationalism, an ideology of the rising bourgeoisie, was a threat to the traditional ruling triumvirate of crown, aristocracy, and church. But despite the conservative backlash that followed Napoleon's final defeat in 1815, liberal nationalism continued to gain momentum that could not be reversed. Critics found the old, conservative order increasingly incapable of meeting the needs and desires of modernizing societies, and enthusiasm for representative institutions grew accordingly. Minority populations in multiethnic empires in particular began to demand national self-determination, new institutions, and political independence.

One of the earliest victories for nineteenth-century nationalism took place in Greece, which had long been under the control of the Turkish Ottoman Empire. In 1821 Greek nationalist leaders asserted their right to nationhood, and by 1830 had gained the support of several major European states. Armed resistance forced the Ottoman Empire to recognize the independence of a new Greek nation-state. Throughout Europe, the Greek War of Independence was hailed as a victory of the unstoppable force of liberty against despotism, further energizing the movement.

In the following decades, other nationalist movements in Europe met both significant successes and abject failures. In 1848, an uprising in France provoked a chain reaction of rebellions in numerous other European nations (see Chapter 14). Though most of these failed, it was clear that nationalism had become a widespread popular force, as nationalist groups, often tied to youth movements, continued to demand national self-determination for their people. For example, the multiethnic Austrian Habsburg Empire was shaken by revolts of nationalist Germans, Hungarians, Poles, Czechs, Romanians, and Serbs, among others. Other nationalist revolutionary movements occurred in Ireland, the German states, and the Italian peninsula.

This liberal form of nationalism was dominant among nationalist political movements in the first half of the nineteenth century. But there existed other forms of nationalist sentiment in Europe, including what is often called romantic nationalism. While liberal nationalism was based on rational republican values, romantics stressed the uniqueness of a particular people and their history. They suggested that each people had a national essence, or a series of traits and qualities they believed to be inherent. Such an essence was not a rational phenomenon, but rather something more like a spiritual quality. German Romantics called this essence the *Volksgeist* or "spirit of the people." Romantic nationalism tended to emphasize the ancient or even timeless nature of the nation and its traditions, and of the historical unity of the nation. Historical evidence shows, however, that such assertions of national character were frequently based on exaggerated or even entirely mythical narratives, and many national "traditions" (like forms of "national dress") are in fact quite modern inventions.[2]

In stressing the inherent uniqueness of people rather than universal human principles, romantic nationalism commonly highlighted the differences between nations and peoples. Informed by romantic nationalism, the seemingly benign love of country and culture often evolved into **chauvinism**—"my nation is great" tended to become "my nation is superior to yours." Bigotry and stereotyping often accompanied romantic nationalism, inciting violence and conflict between states or between members of different national or ethnic groups within a state.

In the first half of the nineteenth century, nationalism, in both liberal and romantic expressions, inspired activists and revolutionaries from Greece to Ireland, and from Poland to Italy. And while these forms of nationalism differed, they could also operate together. In the latter half of the nineteenth century, however, nationalism in Europe changed in character. As the nationalism of this period helped form new European nation-states, it also came to be more closely associated with power politics, conservatism, and racism. Among the major events that accompanied the growth of nineteenth-century nationalism were the unification of Italy and the birth of the modern German nation-state.

The Late Nineteenth Century: Unification and Power Politics

Despite the efforts of liberal nationalists in the revolutions of 1848, at mid-century the Italian peninsula had remained a collection of separate states, many under the control of other European powers. Liberal and romantic Italian nationalists yearned for a unified state that would reflect their vision of the common culture and history of the Italian people. But it would take a series of bold political moves and military calculations to bring about a unified Italy.

While a number of factors contributed to the eventual success of Italian unification, the process was led by the military efforts and power politics exercised after mid-century by Count Camillo di Cavour, the Prime Minister of the Kingdom of Piedmont-Sardinia. His calculated alliances with great powers like France and Prussia enabled successful military campaigns against Austria and the forces of the papacy, with inspiring leadership provided by Giuseppe Garibaldi, a veteran of the failed nationalist uprising of 1848. Largely due to the vision and efforts of these two individuals, a new state emerged in 1861 as the Kingdom of

Italy, a constitutional monarchy under the leadership of the King of Piedmont-Sardinia. The final pieces of the puzzle were added during the next decade with the addition of Venice and the city of Rome. While republican liberal nationalists had provided some of the early sparks, the creation of modern Italy only succeeded through the use of military force and bold diplomatic maneuvering.

The other major political development during this period was the creation of a unified German state, which was composed of the varied collection of former principalities that had emerged from the Napoleonic Wars. The process of German unification is a good example of how nationalism became a force of the political right in the second half of the nineteenth century. Germany lacked political unity prior to 1871; before that year, no German nation-state existed. Yet "Germany" existed as a regional term, used to describe the places where the German-speaking people lived. German nationalists relied on this ethnic and linguistic consciousness in their efforts to consolidate a single political entity.

The key figure in the unification of Germany was the aristocratic Prussian chancellor Otto von Bismarck. The two large ethnically German states of Austria and Prussia were both potential leaders of any movement toward German unification. When Bismarck defeated Austria in the Austro-Prussian War of 1866, he created a Prussian-led confederation of Northern German states that became the precursor of a unified Germany. Then, by provoking another war, this time with France (the Franco-Prussian War of 1870–1871), Bismarck induced most of the remaining German territories to join his coalition, consolidating his leadership over the larger part of the German-speaking world.

This new Germany hardly resembled the fulfillment of republican liberal nationalist dreams. It was literally a German empire, complete with the first "German Emperor," Wilhelm I, while the Imperial Chancellor Bismarck controlled the levers of political power. In Bismarck's hands, the German state was powerful and conservative, retaining the traditional institutions of monarchy and aristocracy and attacking socialist movements and parties. The "Iron Chancellor" skillfully exploited German nationalist sentiments to promote the power of the state, while enacting reforms, including ambitious social welfare programs, that rallied popular enthusiasm among the masses. In Bismarck's Germany, nationalism became a phenomenon of the political right, as its conservative leaders appealed to national unity and loyalty to the state as alternatives to class loyalty and class conflict.

While the cases of Italy and Germany demonstrated how this phenomenon could unify states, nationalism could also be based on a separatist agenda. Irish and Hungarian nationalists in 1848, for example, wished to separate from a larger political entity (Britain and the Austro-Hungarian Empire, respectively) and enjoy self-determination in independent nation-states. They had limited success in each case; fully independent, separate Irish and Hungarian states would be a product of the twentieth century. Other situations were more complicated. In some parts of eastern Europe, for example, distinct ethnic groups had shared the same territory for centuries, often with one group dominating another. In such places, nationalist appeals frequently resulted not in newly unified, culturally homogenous states, but in political and social instability. Nationalist appeals in such places as

Romania and Serbia encouraged neighbors who had grudgingly learned to coexist to take up arms against each other to redress "historical wrongs." Such tensions contributed in a major way to the war that exploded in 1914.

Extreme Nationalism

During the same decades that brought about Italian and German unification, most forms of nationalism in Europe grew more zealous and militaristic. Extreme nationalists championed the superiority of their own people, while disparaging the people of other nations. Their views were increasingly influenced by the development of **Social Darwinism** and so-called **scientific racism**. Social Darwinists took Darwinian ideas about evolution out of their intended contexts, and commonly argued that history can be seen as a struggle among nations or peoples who display varying levels of sophistication or evolution. They trumpeted a far different message than Enlightenment liberals; while the latter spoke of human equality, nineteenth century Social Darwinists emphasized what they believed to be significant evolutionary differences between races and nations.[3]

Similarly, scientific racism held that it was possible to use scientific methods to identify biological differences among racial groups, and adherents to this movement promoted the concept of a world racial hierarchy. In a number of long-since discredited "scientific" studies, scientific racists claimed to illustrate the inherent superiority of the "white" race over African and Asian peoples. Such racial categories, which were in reality socially-constructed and politically-motivated myths, were accepted as natural and essential biological facts. These biological beliefs about the supposedly inherent natures of human groups, combined with mistaken Darwinist notions, helped create a distinctively racial form of nationalism as the nineteenth century wore on. **Racial nationalism** contended that human history is a clash between nations and/or races in which only the "fittest" peoples would survive. Racial and extreme nationalists celebrated war and conflict, arguing that the defeat of inferior peoples on the field of battle would cleanse the world of the weak and allow the strong to prosper. Thus, nationalists urged the masses to willingly sacrifice their lives for the greatness of their nation. The brutally violent racial imagery and glorification of war employed by such virulent strains of nationalism influenced twentieth-century movements like Nazism.

Extreme nationalism also became infused with **anti-Semitism** in the late nineteenth century. Prejudice, discrimination, and even waves of violence against Jews were not new in Europe at this time. But anti-Semitism, when linked with extreme forms of racial nationalism, began to take on a new character.[4] Extreme nationalists began to describe Jews as racially distinct and inferior to supposedly "authentic" Europeans. Unlike the anti-Semites of the Middle Ages, racial nationalists argued that Jews could not be "cured" or assimilated by converting to Christianity. They were presumed to be a foreign and inferior race of people whose presence contaminated the purity of the "national race." This particular form of racism found formal voice in anti-Semitic political movements and parties in Austria and Germany in the 1880s and 1890s, but was present elsewhere in Europe in various forms as well.

Nationalism and Identity

The concept of the nation-state has become essential in our modern political lives and the contemporary system of international relations. It emerged from the ideology of nationalism that first appeared in the wake of the French Revolution and Napoleonic Wars. The liberal nationalists of the early nineteenth century tended to argue that the modern state was the ideal institution to safeguard personal liberty and Enlightenment values. Concurrently, early romantic nationalists created works of art and literature, and started movements that grew from their belief in the inherent, distinctive, and ancient qualities of their people.

As the nineteenth century progressed, nationalism became more closely associated with the political right. As the German Chancellor Bismarck illustrated, conservative forces could harness or manipulate nationalist feelings to quell class conflict and strengthen loyalty to the state. Nationalism, then, was often pitted against socialism; while the socialist left tried to organize the workers of the world (or at least of Europe) based on their class position, the nationalist right appealed to national identity over class identity. In more extreme forms of nationalism, often connected to Social Darwinist, anti-Semitic, or racist ideas, the world was portrayed as a brutal clash of nations and/or races, in which only the strongest peoples would and should survive.

As a social phenomenon, the appeal of nationalism, even extreme nationalism, is understandable. Members of European societies that had been shaken by economic change and political stability faced severe crises of identity. The forces of urbanization, industrialization, secularism, rationalism, and skepticism had transformed social stratification systems, demolished traditional ways of life, and created complex, confusing new sets of social norms. Even while prosperity increased for the majority of people, the social fabric was disintegrating, in ways that worried observers like Émile Durkheim, Ferdinand Tönnies, and Max Weber. As individuals longed for something that might give meaning to their lives within the rapidly developing *gesellschaft*, nationalist ideologies seemed to fill the void. Nationalism would become one of history's most powerful forces. And while nationalism is based on a concept of unity among a people, it is also inherently divisive. By the twentieth century, the divisive character of European nationalisms would ignite conflicts that stand among the great disasters in all of human history.

Anomie

In his analysis of the social changes that come with modernization, a critical concern of the French sociologist Émile Durkheim was *anomie*. *Anomie* is the absence or breakdown of social norms and values. In a well-functioning society, there is a widely shared consensus about what kinds of behavior are acceptable (normal) and what kinds are not, about what is important and what is not. In stable traditional societies unified by mechanical solidarity, only exceptional situations like famine or war can pose a threat to this consensus. When a threat of this kind does not exist, the individual members have a clear sense of how they should behave, what they should hold sacred, who deserves respect, and what they can expect from life.

But the process of modernization brought with it increasingly rapid social change, and rapid social change is always destabilizing to the social order. Durkheim's concern was that the social changes brought about by increasing specialization of labor and the pressures of a market economy were weakening the social consensus. He worried that in the world of organic solidarity, in which people depend on each other's labor but do not necessarily have much in common with their neighbors, there would be less and less of an agreement among people about questions of morality or which values were most important. A multiplicity of occupations, income levels, educational experiences, and religious backgrounds might bring personal freedom, but they would also inevitably bring the potential for confusion, unhappiness, and conflict. A society with no clear consensus on these important matters is in a state of *anomie*, and this poses a clear threat to the welfare of humans, who are inherently social by nature.

Over the course of the nineteenth century, European societies became increasingly modern and increasingly anomic. Is it possible that the anxiety this created prompted more and more Europeans to turn to nationalism as a source of personal meaning and social solidarity?

One of the most important impacts of nationalism was that it helped to create a climate of competition and rivalry among the nation-states of the Western world. Such competition would have far-ranging effects and consequences. The nation-state system created the arms races, territorial disputes, alliance systems, and conditions for conflict that led to the great catastrophe of World War I. More immediately, the competitive rivalries among Western states that were fueled by nationalism also played out across the globe, as a rapid drive to create vast overseas colonial holdings that we call the Age of Empire.

Notes

1 Jean-Jacques Rousseau, *The Social Contract* (New York: Penguin Classics, 1968), 53–56.
2 For a thorough study of the creation of nationalist traditions, see Eric J. Hobsbawm and Terence Ranger, eds., *The Invention of Tradition* (Cambridge: Cambridge University Press, 1992).
3 For an in-depth explanation of the faulty science and biological determinism that fueled Social Darwinism and scientific racism, see Stephen Jay Gould, *The Mismeasure of Man* (New York: Norton, 1981).
4 See Donald L. Niewyk, ed., *The Holocaust: Problems and Perspectives of Interpretation* (Boston: Houghton Mifflin, 2003) and George L. Mosse, *Masses and Man: Nationalist and Fascist Perceptions of Reality* (New York: Howard Fertig, 1980).

Suggested Readings

Anderson, Benedict. *Imagined Communities: Reflections on the Origin and Spread of Nationalism*. London: Verso, 1983.

Breuilly, John. *Nationalism and the State*. Chicago: University of Chicago Press, 1994.

Gould, Stephen Jay. *The Mismeasure of Man*. New York: Norton, 1981.

Hobsbawm, Eric J. and Terence Ranger, eds. *The Invention of Tradition*. Cambridge and New York: Cambridge University Press, 1992.

Hobsbawm, Eric J. *Nations and Nationalism since 1780: Programme, Myth, Reality*. Cambridge and New York: Cambridge University Press, 1992.

Kohn, Hans. *The Idea of Nationalism: A Study in Its Origins and Background*. New York: Macmillan, 1961.

Mosse, George L. *Masses and Man: Nationalist and Fascist Perceptions of Reality*. New York: Howard Fertig, 1980.

Niewyk, Donald L., ed. *The Holocaust: Problems and Perspectives of Interpretation*. Boston: Houghton Mifflin, 2003.

Rousseau, Jean-Jacques. *The Social Contract*. New York: Penguin Classics, 1968.

Smith, Anthony D. *National Identity*. London: Penguin, 1991.

16 The Age of Empire

John W. Mackey

Key Terms

acculturation, imperialism, civilizing mission, cultural diffusion, decolonization, direct rule, indirect rule, nationalist movements, new imperialism, "Scramble for Africa," settler colonies, single-crop agriculture, "the white man's burden"

Historians consider **imperialism** a modern phenomenon, but one with historical roots in the Crusades of the Middle Ages and the creation of overseas trading networks in the Early Modern Period. During the second half of the nineteenth century, powerful Western nation states embarked on an energetic program of seizing and formalizing possession over much of the world, in what has often been called the "Age of Empire."[1] One critical difference from the earlier era of colonization was that the Industrial Revolution had given Europeans the technological and military advantages that allowed them to conquer and colonize non-Western lands, often quickly, easily, and brutally. This made the nineteenth- and early-twentieth-century process both qualitatively and quantitatively different from anything that had come before.

Motives for Empire

As in earlier efforts at overseas expansion, there were various motives and goals behind the Age of Empire. Among the most obvious were economic. In previous centuries, Europeans had sought to create colonies as potential sources of natural resources, slave labor, foodstuffs, or "exotic" products not available at home. As European economies developed during the mercantilist age, their colonial endeavors relied upon increasingly higher levels of capital investment to achieve economies of scale, and by the time of the Industrial Revolution, this had created new, even more compelling economic needs. Not only could colonial territories provide raw materials and labor for factories, but they could also serve as captive markets for industrial goods produced in the colonizing country. European imperialists sought markets in China for their textiles and for opium grown in India; they mined diamonds and gold in Africa; and everywhere colonizing powers sought profit and competitive economic advantage over other colonial

Image 16.1 British engineers like Isambard Kingdom Brunel, shown here
with the massive anchor chains for his new steamship, revolutionized
transportation and enabled the building of a vast empire

© Heritage Image Partnership Ltd / Alamy

powers. As a result, indigenous economies were often weakened or even destroyed, and Western-dominated investment-driven market systems took their place.

Proponents of imperialism, relying on the Classical Liberal arguments of David Ricardo and others, argued that it benefited colonizer and colonized alike by maximizing efficiency through comparative advantage. Though state involvement and monopolies were common features of this process, imperialism was often defended as the extension of "legitimate trade" across the globe. Others, however, attacked it as capitalistic exploitation, such as the Russian Communist revolutionary V.I. Lenin, who saw imperialism as the logical, and somewhat inevitable, expansion of capitalist profiteering beyond the industrialized world. He famously called it the "Latest Stage of Capitalism,"[2] arguing that as exploitation led to excess capital at home, capitalist economies would be driven to invest abroad in their quest for continued profits.

As critical as economic imperatives were, European cultural factors also supported imperialism. Westerners in the nineteenth century believed their centuries of progress had made their cultures, political institutions, and economies highly advanced in comparison to those of other societies. They often associated Western civilization with civilization itself, and, influenced by Social Darwinist arguments, they viewed African and Asian peoples as primitive, or in some cases even savage or barbaric. Therefore, colonizers often spoke of their duty to carry out a **civilizing mission** in their empires. This attitude suggests that not only the colonizer, but also the colonized had something of great benefit to gain from the growth of empires. The belief in the duty of so-called advanced Western nations to engage in a civilizing mission became known as **"the white man's burden,"** a phrase taken from the title of a poem about America's involvement in the Philippines by British poet Rudyard Kipling. The civilizing mission rested on the notion that non-white people were incapable of advancement and self-government, and needed help from supposedly civilized Westerners. A major component of this "civilizing mission," as in the earlier era, was the desire to spread Christianity.[3] A wave of missionary activity often followed conquest and the establishment of European rule, to help bring salvation to people whom European Christians regarded as "heathens" and potential converts. Many Europeans held a deeply patronizing but optimistic view that the "unfortunate natives" could change and advance if exposed to the civilizing influence of Christianity and Western culture. Building schools and hospitals as well as churches, missionaries considered it their duty to bring not only the Gospel but Western advancement and Western culture to the "backward" areas of the world.

The White Man's Burden

Rudyard Kipling's 1899 poem "The White Man's Burden" has come to be commonly viewed as the quintessentially imperial literary work. Kipling knew empire well, as he was born in British India and spent many years there, publishing numerous stories and poems, many on the theme of imperial adventure. He was among the most widely read British authors of his time, and he was awarded the Nobel Prize in Literature in 1907.

But his work is highly controversial. Kipling remains a popular and admired writer, yet his works are often considered to be riven with Victorian-era racism and patronizing imperialist attitudes. "The White Man's Burden" was written on the occasion of the Philippine-American War, and Kipling appears to be urging the United States to take its place among the world's imperial powers. The poem refers to colonized peoples as "captives," "sullen peoples," and perhaps most shockingly to contemporary readers, "Half devil and half child."

As the poem makes clear, however, Kipling saw empire as a sacrifice ("burden") to be borne by the colonizers, rather than, say, a crusade for riches and glory. There may be more ambivalence in the poem than one might first assume, or that the oft-repeated refrain "Take up the White Man's Burden" implies. As you read the poem, you may ask yourself the following questions:

- According to the poem, who benefits from imperialism?
- What sort of "reward" will the United States reap if it takes up this "burden"?
- What sorts of words does Kipling use to describe the colonizer and the colonized?
- In the context of this poem, what might the paradoxical phrase "savage wars of peace" mean?
- What do you think Kipling meant to imply by juxtaposing the "tawdry rule of kings" with the "tale of common things"?

The White Man's Burden
(*The United States and the Philippine Islands*)

Take up the White Man's burden—
Send forth the best ye breed—
Go bind your sons to exile
To serve your captives' need;
To wait in heavy harness,
On fluttered folk and wild—
Your new-caught, sullen peoples,
Half-devil and half-child.

Take up the White Man's burden—
In patience to abide,
To veil the threat of terror
And check the show of pride;
By open speech and simple,
An hundred times made plain
To seek another's profit,
And work another's gain.

Take up the White Man's burden—
The savage wars of peace—
Fill full the mouth of Famine
And bid the sickness cease;
And when your goal is nearest
The end for others sought,
Watch sloth and heathen Folly
Bring all your hopes to nought.

Take up the White Man's burden—
No tawdry rule of kings,
But toil of serf and sweeper—
The tale of common things.

The ports ye shall not enter,
The roads ye shall not tread,
Go mark them with your living,
And mark them with your dead!

Take up the White Man's burden—
And reap his old reward:
The blame of those ye better,
The hate of those ye guard—
The cry of hosts ye humour
(Ah, slowly!) toward the light: —
"Why brought he us from bondage,
Our loved Egyptian night?"

Take up the White Man's burden—
Ye dare not stoop to less—
Nor call too loud on Freedom
To cloak your weariness;
By all ye cry or whisper,
By all ye leave or do,
The silent, sullen peoples
Shall weigh your gods and you.

Take up the White Man's burden—
Have done with childish days—
The lightly proffered laurel,
The easy, ungrudged praise.
Comes now, to search your manhood
Through all the thankless years
Cold, edged with dear-bought wisdom,
The judgment of your peers![1]

Note

1 Rudyard Kipling, "The White Man's Burden," in *The Portable Kipling*, ed. Irving Howe (New York: Penguin, 1982), 602.

But as the nineteenth century progressed, and Social Darwinism and scientific racism became more widespread, Westerners became even more hardened in their attitudes and less optimistic that Africans and Asians could be "improved." A deeply patronizing sense of missionary zeal gave way to more racialized view of the world in the late nineteenth century, as Europeans came to believe that differences between peoples were inherent, biological, and unchanging. Yet as the twentieth century dawned and empires expanded, strategic considerations assumed more prominence. As European nations actively competed for overseas possessions, diplomatic tensions rose, heightening concern for the defensibility of the global trade routes that were the critical arteries of empire. Britain, France, Germany, and the United States, among others, sought places to establish military garrisons, fueling stations, and supply depots to protect and support both commercial and military traffic. Locations such as the Suez Canal, Singapore, and South Africa assumed enormous importance in the functioning of imperial systems, and for both politicians and military planners, securing their possessions from jealous imperial rivals became an essential priority.

The Global Reach of the New Imperialism

Between about 1870 and 1914, a great wave of colonization and growth of empires rapidly changed the world. Nineteenth-century nationalism fueled great rivalries among the powerful nation-states of Europe, while Germany and the United States began to take their places as competitive world industrial powers. Each great power sought the prestige of a vast empire, as well as the presumed economic benefits this would bring.

Before the nineteenth century, European contact with Africa had been mostly confined to coastal areas. During the course of the century, however, Western explorers, missionaries, and merchants began penetrating the interior of the continent, revealing great quantities of resources that might be exploited. As nationalistic fervor began to drive colonial competition ever more intensely, what became known as the **"Scramble for Africa"** commenced during the 1880s. To minimize future conflicts among themselves in the "Dark Continent," European representatives at the Berlin Conference of 1884–1885 literally divided up the continent with a map and a ruler, then set ground rules governing future colonial trade, settlement, and administration. By the eve of World War I, the nations of Britain, France, Belgium, Germany, Italy, Spain, and Portugal controlled nearly all of Africa; only Ethiopia, which had resisted Italian imperialist advances, and Liberia, a state founded for freed American slaves, remained independent. Many of the arbitrary and impractical colonial lines drawn at Berlin, which had largely ignored the traditional economies and settlement patterns of the local peoples, became the borders of the modern independent African nations that emerged after World War II.

By the late nineteenth century, Europeans had already possessed colonial footholds in Asia for centuries. But the Age of Empire expanded and intensified their control. Britain held the largest and most prestigious imperial prize in its control of the "subcontinent" of India, accomplished through the state-supported efforts of the British East India Company, the largest privately funded company of the age. Britain also claimed significant colonies in Southeast Asia. The French had established a presence in Indochina (present-day Vietnam, Laos, and Cambodia), the Dutch held lucrative colonies in the East Indies (present-day Indonesia), and the expanding Russian empire had extended its tentacles into Manchuria and central Asia. By the end of the century, the United States had taken control of the Pacific islands of Hawaii, the Philippines, and Guam in a wave of colonialism in the era that included the Spanish-American War. Meanwhile, the imperial powers had forced major trade concessions from the declining Chinese Qing Dynasty, helping to bring about its demise in the early twentieth century. In Asia, only Japan was largely successful in resisting foreign incursion. Modernizing on the Western model during the nineteenth century, Japan too became an imperial power, annexing Korea and Taiwan by 1910.

Western imperialism also touched other less-developed parts of the world, including Latin America and the Middle East, though often in a less formal manner. While European powers often recognized the independence of states, they were also able to enter into trade or diplomatic agreements that made sovereign nations economically, politically, and/or militarily dependent on one of the "Great Powers." For example, during most of the nineteenth century, British financial and trading firms came to dominate Brazilian exports of coffee, sugar, and cotton, making Brazil, in the minds of some, a *de facto* British colony. Other territories, including some that officially remained parts of the declining Ottoman Empire, became the focus of European competition for control of the resources they offered, such as petroleum, by the turn of the twentieth century. While European imperial powers did establish the occasional formal colony in these regions, for the most part Western dominance was less direct, though sometimes no less thorough. As empires competed with each other for far-flung resources, an increasing proportion of the world's population became entangled in the expanding global economy.

Imperial Administration

The creation of empire was based on the ability to impose authority, and empire-builders devised new institutions to carry out the tasks of governance and administration. Depending on the circumstances, they employed a variety of strategies to govern their overseas possessions. Under the system of **direct rule**, imperial officials assumed formal, unambiguous control over the colony. In this arrangement, the new rulers might hire the services of low-level native administrators, but the real power was in the hands of foreigners who acted as direct representatives of the crown or parliament back home. An example of direct rule was the enormous, diverse territory of French West Africa, where the French governor general in Dakar carried out the will of the government in Paris. Supported as necessary by French military forces largely composed of African troops, the governor general enforced justice and oversaw the operations of both large French trading companies and evangelization efforts.

Other imperial territories were governed by a system of **indirect rule,** where the colonizers ruled through arrangements with local princes, aristocrats, or other indigenous elites. While ultimate authority usually rested in the hands of the colonizing power, indigenous leaders were responsible for many elements of local

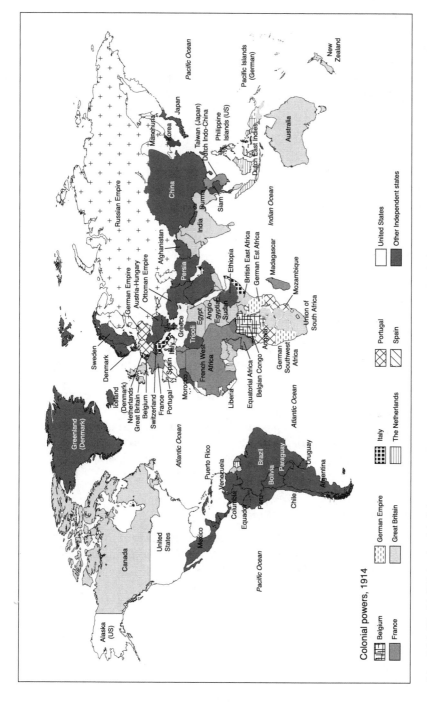

Map 16.1 World 1914 colonial claims

Colonial powers, 1914

Belgium

France

German Empire

Great Britain

Italy

The Netherlands

Portugal

Spain

United States

Other Independent states

Pacific Ocean

Alaska (US)

Canada

United States

Greenland (Denmark)

Mexico

Puerto Rico

Venezuela

Columbia

Ecuador

Peru

Bolivia

Brazil

Paraguay

Uruguay

Chile

Argentina

Atlantic Ocean

Iceland (Denmark)

Sweden

Denmark

Netherlands

Great Britain

Belgium

Switzerland

France

Portugal

Spain

Italy

German Empire

Austria-Hungary

Ottoman Empire

Greece

Morocco

French West Africa

Liberia

Equatorial Africa

Belgian Congo

Angola

German Southwest Africa

Union of South Africa

Egypt

Tripoli

Anglo-Egyptian Sudan

Ethiopia

British East Africa

German Est Africa

Madagascar

Mozambique

Afghanistan

Persia

Russian Empire

India

Burma

Siam

China

Manchuria

Korea

Japan

Taiwan (Japan)

Dutch Indo-China

Philippine Islands (US)

Dutch East Indies

Indian Ocean

Pacific Ocean

Pacific Islands (German)

Australia

New Zealand

administration and often kept much of their traditional social systems intact. An example of indirect rule would be Britain's relationship with Malay leaders, known as sultans, whose rule was strengthened by British advisers, investment, and military support. While local elites did most of the day-to-day work of governance, both the British and the sultans profited from exports of minerals and agricultural products. The advantage of the system of indirect rule was that it enabled colonial powers to both gain and maintain control without exhausting their own manpower and resources.

Settler colonies operated differently, and in some ways resembled the colonies established by Spain in Central and South America during the sixteenth and seventeenth centuries. In such places settler populations from the colonizing country had a hand in creating institutions of self-government, and they often displaced indigenous populations through forced resettlement or even genocide. However, a significant difference from the Spanish model was that, during the Age of Empire, the rise of modern racial ideologies usually meant stricter segregation of settlers and natives. Canada, Rhodesia, Australia, and New Zealand—all British colonial holdings—are examples of settler colonies. Such colonies were constructed according to a racial form of stratification, as citizenship was defined in racial terms, reserved for the white settler population.

Somewhat ironically, imperialism ultimately generated the forces that would bring it down. Colonial regimes and the inequality and oppression they brought created anger and resentment among indigenous peoples. As a result, colonial dominance encouraged previously separate peoples to unify against foreign rule, eventually creating **nationalist movements** seeking independence. For example, resentment of British colonial rule caused Indians, many of whom had little in common except a desire to be free of colonial domination, to unify in the Indian National Congress (INC) in 1885. The INC demanded and received a voice in the colonial administration, and later emerged as a leading voice for Indian independence. Similar nationalist movements developed throughout the colonized world, and in the twentieth century, they helped dismantle empires and create entirely new nation states in a process known as **decolonization**.

The Impact of the New Imperialism

The economic impacts of imperialism varied with the resources, demography, climate, and location of the colony. Since the dominant colonial powers orchestrated economic activity for their own benefit, without regard to the needs and traditions of indigenous peoples, the economic effects of imperialism were often brutally harsh and disruptive. Colonial economic imperatives interfered with or destroyed traditional patterns of trade, agriculture, herding, and commodity production. In some areas, colonial powers imposed **single-crop agriculture**, seizing land to create plantations for the growing of export crops. In other areas, mining operations caused waves of migration, as indigenous people often traveled great distances to take cash-based employment so that they could pay the colonial taxes imposed upon them by foreign powers.

The **new imperialism** served to reorder the global economy and social system. As a result of the vast extent of Western colonization and the dominant position of European interests and those of white settlers, colonialism imposed what might be called an international system of stratification. And because positions of power, authority, wealth, and opportunity were reserved for white populations and European nations, imperialism contributed to pervasive attitudes of racial superiority. Both the inequalities and the attitudes promoted by imperialism still linger in the twenty-first century. The process of decolonization in the twentieth century succeeded in removing formal colonial political power, but the legacies of racism, pervasive economic exploitation, and the transformation of whole cultures and societies have proved more difficult to reverse.

The intense and prolonged cultural contacts of imperialism resulted in a significant degree of social change. On the whole, because colonizing powers held the upper hand in colonial relationships, the impact of Western cultures on non-Western cultures was greater than the reverse, since Western cultures, beliefs, and social systems held higher prestige within the colonial order. Of course, it did work in both directions; new products, new types of employment, greater contact with non-Western people, and increased immigration into the West all contributed to significant social change. By the twentieth century, **cultural diffusion** could be found in the homes of both colonizer and colonized.[4] Englishmen enjoyed tea and tobacco from the empire while sitting in London, whereas Indians in Delhi often spoke English while wearing shirts made in Britain.

But the colonized often saw their cultures and societies transformed in a more thorough way than did the colonizers, as the sustained and profound forces of imperialism often led to **acculturation**. The influence of missionaries, Western-style education systems, and the dominance of the economic and political culture of the colonizer often transformed indigenous societies and cultures almost beyond recognition. As a consequence, non-Western people living in European colonies frequently wore Western clothes, spoke European languages, attended Christian churches, and worked in colonial offices or Western-owned businesses. Indeed, colonial penetration has been directly or indirectly responsible for the extinction of hundreds, and perhaps even thousands, of languages across the world, as well as the suppression of numerous native religions, and countless local customs and traditions.[5] By the time that many societies were able to assert their independence, the imperial legacy had already profoundly and irreversibly distorted traditional ways of life.

The age of imperialism grew out of great-power rivalries and competition, economic motives, and a Western desire to carry out what they saw as a civilizing mission. In a short span of about forty years, the European powers and the United States colonized nearly all of Africa, as well as a significant portion of Asia and the Pacific islands. Colonialism reordered the world economy, with the Western powers as the beneficiaries of African and Asian labor, resources, and markets at the expense of traditional indigenous economies. In effect, colonialism created a global form of stratification in which whites held the dominant position. Colonialism also brought profound changes to non-Western cultural systems and political structures. As it did so, the Age of Empire also created great tensions that would have an enormous effect on the twentieth century, by contributing to the rivalries that would bring about World War I, and by creating new forms of nationalism that would challenge the colonial system itself.

Notes

1 In his trilogy of books chronicling the "long" nineteenth century (1789–1914), influential historian Eric J. Hobsbawm divides the century into "The Age of Revolution" from 1789 to 1848, "The Age of Capital" from 1848 to 1875, and "The Age of Empire" from 1875 to 1914.
2 Vladimir I. Lenin, *Selected Works [of] V. I. Lenin: One-Volume Edition* (Moscow: Progress Publishers, 1968).
3 See Andrew Porter, *Religion Versus Empire?: British Protestant Missionaries and Overseas Expansion, 1700–1914* (Manchester: Manchester University Press, 2004).
4 For more on the impact of imperialism on the cultures of the colonized, see Frederick Cooper and Ann Laura Stoler, eds., *Tensions of Empire: Colonial Cultures in a Bourgeois World* (Berkeley: University of California Press, 1997).
5 Daniel Nettle and Suzanne Romaine, *The Extinction of the World's Languages* (Oxford: Oxford University Press, 2002).

Suggested Readings

Cain, P. J., and A. G. Hopkins. *British Imperialism: Innovation and Expansion, 1688–1914.* London and New York: Longman, 1993.

Cannadine, David. *Ornamentalism.* Oxford: Oxford University Press, 2001.

Cohn, Bernard S. *Colonialism and Its Forms of Knowledge.* Princeton, NJ: Princeton University Press, 1996.

Cooper, Frederick, and Ann Laura Stoler, eds. *Tensions of Empire: Colonial Cultures in a Bourgeois World.* Berkeley: University of California Press, 1997.

Hall, Catherine, and Sonya O. Rose, eds. *At Home with the Empire: Metropolitan Culture and the Imperial World.* Cambridge and New York: Cambridge University Press, 2007.

Hochschild, Adam. *King Leopold's Ghost: A Story of Greed, Terror, and Heroism in Colonial Africa.* Boston: Houghton Mifflin, 1998.

Hobsbawm, Eric J. *The Age of Empire, 1875–1914.* New York: Pantheon Books, 1987.

Marshall, P. J., ed. The *Cambridge Illustrated History of the British Empire, Vol. III: The Nineteenth Century.* Cambridge: Cambridge University Press, 1996.

Nettle, Daniel, and Suzanne Romaine. *The Extinction of the World's Languages.* Oxford: Oxford University Press, 2002.

Porter, Andrew. *Religion Versus Empire?: British Protestant Missionaries and Overseas Expansion, 1700–1914.* Manchester: Manchester University Press, 2004.

Said, Edward W. *Culture and Imperialism.* New York: Vintage, 1993.

17 The Great War

Benjamin E. Varat

Key Terms

abdication, blockade, convoy system, multinational empire, "No Man's Land," ultimatum

On June 28, 1914, in the Bosnian city Sarajevo, Gavrilo Princip, a nineteen-year old Serb nationalist, shot and killed Archduke Franz Ferdinand, heir to the Austro-Hungarian throne. His assassination set off a chain of events that led to the outbreak of a war in Europe that eventually resulted in the most costly conflict the world had ever suffered. Nearly forty million people, many of them civilians, would be killed, wounded, or missing by the time World War I ended.

What began as a European war ultimately spanned the globe. Men died fighting in Africa, the Middle East, South America, and Asia while Indians, Australians, South Africans, Canadians, Chinese, and Senegalese soldiers perished in the trenches of Belgium and France. Millions of troops from the United States played the decisive role in ending the war. The sheer breadth and scope of World War I presents a conundrum to those who study it: How did the assassination of an Austro-Hungarian archduke result in the most destructive war the world had yet seen?

Franz Ferdinand's death is only a small part of the answer to why the Great Powers chose the battlefield over diplomacy. Alliance systems, nationalistic ideologies, the decay of multiethnic empires, an arms race, and incompetent leadership all played some part in precipitating war. Add to this mix the destabilizing effects of industrialization and mass social change, and a picture emerges of the Great Powers standing on a precipice, needing only a small push to send them to their doom below.

Origins of the War

Untangling the origins of World War I begins in the Balkans, the region of southeastern Europe that today includes parts or all of the following countries: Turkey, Greece, Bulgaria, Romania, Albania, Macedonia, Serbia, Kosovo, Croatia, Montenegro, Slovenia, and Bosnia-Herzegovina.[1] A hodgepodge of national and religious divisions, the Balkans prior to World War I experienced a rising sea of nationalist fervor that led to occasional wars and threatened to tear apart the two empires in the region, the Ottoman and Austro-Hungarian. The two Balkan Wars of 1912 and 1913 had largely dismantled the European portion of the Ottoman Empire, increasing the size of several nation-states like Serbia, Bulgaria, and Romania, but ultimately the conflicts left even the victors unsatisfied. Practically every nation sought further territory, which political leaders justified by appeals to nationalism and reference to historical myths that told of some long-ago moment when all the people of this nation had lived together in a single state. With the Ottoman Empire clinging tenaciously to its last few square miles of European soil, the Balkan peoples turned their attention to the other multinational empire in their midst, Austria-Hungary.

The Austro-Hungarian Empire, the weakest of the Great Powers, was a **multi-national empire**, a political aggregation of distinct peoples generally broken down along ethnic and religious lines, whose varied subjects owed allegiance to the Habsburg family, a dynasty that had controlled much of central and eastern Europe as Holy Roman emperors since before the time of Martin Luther. In 1914, Emperor Franz Josef had already been in power for more than sixty-five years; he was a deeply conservative man who hated and feared the changes wrought by liberalism, industrialization, and especially ethnic nationalism. He and his advisors, increasingly insecure about their Great Power status, recognized the mortal threat national passions posed to the Austro-Hungarian Empire and did everything in their power to suppress it. Of particular concern were the ethnic Serbs, millions of whom lived under Franz Josef's authority, but who clearly preferred to join their brethren in the Kingdom of Serbia just to the east and south. Even before the turn of the century, illegal Serb nationalist organizations had operated within the empire, stirring up popular resentment and assassinating Austrian officials, sometimes with the active support of Serbia's government. Gavrilo Princip was a member of one such organization, the Black Hand.

This explosive situation raised tensions with another Great Power, Russia, whose tsar saw himself as the protector of all ethnic Slavs, which included Serbs as well as Russians. However odd it may seem that the Russian tsar, who also ruled a highly insecure, unstable multinational empire that included various ethnicities of various religious persuasions, should support ethnic nationalism, the fact remained that his support for Serbia placed Russia and Austria-Hungary on a collision course. By 1914, most observers saw war between them as inevitable. If this war occurred, it threatened to bring in the rest of the "Great Powers:" Germany, France, and Great Britain.

Culture and treaties bound Germany and Austria-Hungary closely together. These states, both ruled by ethnic Germans, had an alliance dating back to the early 1880s. The treaties establishing this relationship, which became known as the Triple Alliance when Italy joined it, stated that any attack on one member was considered an attack on all of them. In other words, if the Russians initiated hostilities with Austria-Hungary, Germany and Italy were obligated to declare war on Russia.

But it was even more complicated than that, since Russia too had alliances. A close one existed with France that dated back to the 1890s. Humiliated by the loss of Alsace-Lorraine to Prussia in 1870, the French were determined to regain the region, but German unification the following year had left France comparatively weaker than its new neighbor. This made an alliance with Russia, resentful of German policies in the Balkans and desperate to modernize, a logical step. Thus was born the Franco-Russian alliance. French money flowed into Russia to build railroads and help industrialize an empire that was still quite backwards. France had successfully rearranged the European chessboard; hereafter, Germany faced the possibility of a two-front war.

The last of the "Great Powers," Great Britain, was an obvious alliance partner for neither France nor Russia, and certainly not both. During most of the nineteenth century, Britain had tried to avoid continental entanglements, preferring to focus on its vast empire, which often led to conflicts with France and Russia, though seldom with Germany. But everything changed for Britain in 1897 when German naval advisors to Kaiser Wilhelm II convinced him that Germany needed a large navy to have its own "place in the sun." Aspiring to be a global power, Germany started building a large deep-water navy that would command Britain's respect and vastly increase German prestige. Apparently, none of the Germans considered that the British might see the building of a modern German fleet—whose apparent purpose was to challenge British naval supremacy—as a threat.

The British Parliament responded to German naval expansion by approving huge new naval expenditures of its own. Fear of Germany's rising power also led British leaders to accept an alliance with France in 1904 that overturned nearly a thousand years of Anglo-French conflict. Three years later a series of agreements created the alliance known as the Triple Entente, which allied the Russians with the British and French and divided the Great Powers of Europe into two antagonistic coalitions.

As discussed in earlier chapters, racial theories and nationalist fervor added further layers of tension. Social Darwinism gained wide popular appeal, especially in Germany, among people who completely misunderstood Darwin's theories of evolution and natural selection. Social Darwinists claimed that humans were naturally divided by distinct racial and physical characteristics into nations. War, they believed, was the natural state for nations, since it destroyed the weaker nations while only the fittest survived. Conflict also supposedly cleansed the nation of its weakest elements, those people somehow unfit to be part of the nation, whom the German historian Heinrich von Treitschke called "puny man."[2] The fact that no large-scale European wars had taken place since 1815 meant that such rhetoric was absorbed by citizens who had scarce knowledge of the nature of warfare, and even less sense of what it might be like when fought with industrial weaponry.

If war was the natural state for the nation, then the nation had to be strengthened at all costs. Toward this goal, youth groups devoted to the active life cropped up in the early years of the twentieth century. The *Wandervogel* in Germany and Boy Scouts in Britain were but two examples of new organizations focused on liberating young people, mostly boys, from the confines of their sedate bourgeois lives and giving them a vigorous regimen of group exercise and outdoor activities. Leaders of such organizations explicitly connected their efforts with building national unity in the face of shadowy foreign and domestic threats.

No one doubted that such threats existed, and war scares were common in the years before World War I. Balkan instability, alliance systems, aggressive ideologies, and the ongoing rapid social change caused by modernization left many in Europe so unsettled that war—by then an abstract concept tied somehow to heroism and national honor—seemed positively desirable. All these factors provided kindling for a European conflagration. Gavrilo Princip's bullets provided the spark that set it alight.

Mobilization: July 1914

The assassination of heir-apparent Franz Ferdinand in late June gave Austria-Hungary its excuse to finally act against the Kingdom of Serbia. Worried about Russian intervention, Austrian officials asked German leaders if they would support military action against Serbia. They responded affirmatively, promising to back Austria even if Russia entered the conflict. This "blank check" was a key development in the run-up to war for two reasons. First, it allowed Austria to act freely against Serbia without worrying about Russia's response. Second, the "blank check" in essence gave Austria control over whether or not Germany went to war, because an Austrian declaration of war on Serbia committed Germany to fight.

In hindsight, German leaders faced a difficult set of circumstances in 1914. By then, they feared that the European balance of power had shifted against them. Efforts to build a navy that could rival Britain's not only had failed—the British navy was still twice as large—but also left German finances severely strained. Meanwhile, Germany's potential enemies were only getting stronger. Russia was industrializing and each new year brought more railroads and a stronger military, while France, too, was increasing the size of its army. With Austria-Hungary, Germany's only real ally, destabilized by rising nationalist movements, 1914 appeared to many German officials as the last chance to weaken their enemies before the balance of power shifted in their favor. Diplomacy alone could not protect them, and Germany had shown little diplomatic skill in recent decades anyway. Thus the "blank check" was a means to bring war without having to assume responsibility for starting it. But the German strategy also ensured that once war came, it would involve all of Europe.[3]

The German war plan, known as the Schlieffen Plan, had been developed as a response to the Franco-Russian alliance of the early 1890s.[4] The alliance left Germany facing a two-front war: the Russians to the east and the French to the west. The Chief of the Imperial German General Staff in the 1890s, Count Alfred von Schlieffen, argued that Germany could counter this situation by defeating France before Russia was ready to fight. Schlieffen assumed that the Russians would take about six weeks for full **mobilization**, to organize and assemble their soldiers and supplies, leaving just enough time for the German army to destroy the French forces and take Paris before having to rush to the east to face the Russians. Therefore, the plan required the Germans to attack France the instant war broke out.

Since any delay in defeating France would leave Germany vulnerable to a Russian advance, Schlieffen wanted German forces to avoid the French defenses on the border with German-controlled Alsace-Lorraine. Instead, he planned to send the German army through neutral Belgium, which shared an unfortified border with France. Schlieffen believed this maneuver would surprise the French, throw them off-balance and ultimately lead to a quick surrender. While the breach of Belgian neutrality might bring Great Britain into the war, this possibility did not seem to worry Schlieffen. The British lacked a sizable army and its superior naval power would not matter in what, he calculated, would be a six-week campaign in the west. Moreover, once Germany defeated France, German troops would vacate Belgium, removing the British rationale for war. Schlieffen concluded that success on the Western Front guaranteed success on the Eastern Front; undistracted by a two-front war, the better-trained and better-equipped German forces would grind down the Russians even if the latter had more troops. The Schlieffen Plan was a gamble, but one the German leadership accepted, believing that no better alternative existed.

German officials, therefore, watched passively as Austria-Hungary presented an **ultimatum** to Serbia on July 23. As with any ultimatum, this one included a set of demands, related to Franz Ferdinand's assassination, and the Austro-Hungarians stated these demands had to be accepted within forty-eight hours or else they would declare on Serbia. In this case, however, what differed from traditional ultimatums was that Franz Joseph and his advisers fully intended for their terms to be rejected, allowing Austria-Hungary to declare war. Serbia nearly overthrew this plan when the Serbians surprisingly accepted most of the terms and asked for negotiations on the remaining ones. But Austria replied that the ultimatum was absolute and mobilization began for both countries on July 28, leading Russia to mobilize two days later. The German high command, on the verge of ordering full mobilization, suddenly recognized that France might choose to do nothing until Germany was fully engaged in fighting Russia. The Germans quickly sent an ultimatum of impossible demands to its enemies, insisting that the Russians must cease their mobilization and the French must both publicly announce their neutrality and hand over all border fortresses to Germany. Both countries had twelve hours to comply. Neither did.

In the industrialized Europe of 1914, military wheels moved faster than political ones; industrial societies could ready and deploy troops in hours, instead of weeks. Because military planners perceived speed of mobilization as so central to victory, all four of the Continental powers were getting their troops onto trains before announcing their declarations of war. Germany and France began to mobilize their armies on July 31 and German soldiers actually entered France on August 2, one day before the two countries officially went to war.

Regardless of when the actual declarations of war occurred, news of impending conflict provoked spontaneous celebrations in Paris, Berlin, St. Petersburg, and

Vienna. So many years of tension and fear made war seem almost a relief. Not all shared in the good cheer. British Foreign Secretary Sir Edward Grey remarked to a friend that "the lamps are going out all over Europe. We shall not see them lit again in our time."[5] World War I had begun.

The Guns of August 1914

Forty-eight hours after mobilization began, German soldiers entered France and also took over the Luxembourg railroads. On August 4, exactly on schedule, the German army attacked Belgium. As Schlieffen had expected, Britain declared war on Germany, bringing the last Great Power into the conflict.

Winston Churchill, First Lord of the Admiralty, immediately ordered the British navy to **blockade** German ports, using the British navy to cut off all access for German merchant shipping and its high seas navy between German ports and the rest of the world. Beyond this act Britain could offer little immediate assistance to Belgium or France. Most British troops were stationed thousands of miles away in Britain's colonial empire, and it would take weeks to deploy them back to Europe. In the meantime, the British government began calling on its young men to volunteer for the army. By 1916, recruitment efforts had yielded 2.5 million men, many of who became the core of the British Expeditionary Force (BEF).

While the British organized their war effort, the French army in mid-August went barreling into Alsace-Lorraine to meet well-fortified German troops, leaving much of the Franco-Belgian border undermanned. Then, when the German army swept deeper into Belgium and captured Brussels, French commanders frantically redeployed troops to meet the threat in the west. Schlieffen seemingly had planned well. Britain's lack of preparation and French strategic confusion appeared destined to bring Germany a quick victory.

Victory, however, slipped from German hands when two developments changed the trajectory of the war. First, on August 23, as German troops in Belgium approached the border with France, they ran into an unexpected storm of bullets around the city of Mons. Unknown to the German leadership, the first part of the BEF had arrived in France. Despite being significantly outnumbered, the British troops delayed the German advance for two days, time vitally needed for French commanders to move the French army. Second, Russia mobilized much faster than Schlieffen predicted. Just as the BEF was making itself known in southern Belgium, the German leadership received word of Russian divisions attacking Austrian and under-manned German forces across a broad front in eastern Europe.

The German high command panicked upon hearing of the Russian initiatives and immediately began moving men from the Western to the Eastern Front. This decision eventually proved the undoing of the Schlieffen Plan. Although the Germans quickly stabilized the east by defeating the Russian army at the Battle of Tannenberg in late August, the removal of hundreds of thousands of troops from the west left the German army too weak to carry out their strategy of defeating France quickly.

German forces in the west managed to sustain their momentum through early September. Front-line German units advanced to within thirty-five miles of Paris, close enough for their long-range artillery to hit the city. But this moment was the high-water mark for the German offensive. Further advances became nearly impossible because of the troop diversions to eastern Europe, the arrival of the British, ever longer supply lines, and troop exhaustion.

On September 5, 150,000 French and 70,000 British soldiers launched a major counterattack, in what became known as the First Battle of the Marne. It was a desperate struggle. When German units began breaking through the French line on the third day of fighting, threatening to capture Paris and put a quick end to the war, French reinforcements arrived from the capital in taxi cabs and rushed up to fill the gap in one of the most famous moments of World War I. Buoyed by the additional troops and the bravery of the taxi drivers, French forces launched a surprise nighttime attack on September 8 that broke the German line, forcing them to retreat.

The "miracle of the Marne" saved Paris, but Triple Entente troops were too cautious in pursuing the Germans, allowing them to stop their retreat after forty miles. Both sides began digging the network of trenches that characterized the Western Front and became the symbol of World War I. By the end of 1914, trenches extended almost 400 miles, from a sliver of British-controlled Belgium on the Channel, across northern France, and down to Switzerland. Despite millions of casualties, this line of battle changed little until 1918.[6]

Expectations on all sides had been for a quick war, where everyone would be home by Christmas at the latest, but the failure of the Schlieffen Plan led to a type of war few expected and no one desired. World War I would destroy a generation of young men and shatter the Enlightenment belief that humans were logical, rational creatures destined to perfect the world.

The Horror Begins: Trench Warfare

War had changed, but few generals noticed it. In the minds of the military planners, war was a test of national will in which armies were supposed to go on the offensive, attacking the enemy until he disintegrated or surrendered; fighting spirit mattered above all else. But they had it all wrong. Science and engineering, the core of the Industrial Revolution, now provided armies with heavy artillery, machine guns, poison gas, hand grenades, and flamethrowers. Artillery and machine guns, the iconic weapons of World War I, favored defenders, not attackers. Human flesh could not withstand shell and bullet.

In Erich Maria Remarque's classic World War I novel, *All Quiet on the Western Front*, the main character, Paul Baümer, says that the spade was the soldier's most important possession.[7] Soldiers quickly discovered that narrow trenches, up to twelve feet deep, protected troops best. They reinforced their trench walls with metal plates and lay sand bags across the top, front and back, to block shrapnel and protect the men shooting at the enemy from the elevated fire step. Steel doors and zigzag corners connected trenches so that they could easily be isolated and retaken if overrun by the enemy. Conditions inside the trench were appalling. Soldiers shared it with lice, rats, stagnant water, and dead comrades. Artillery shells roared overhead without end, punctuated occasionally by an enemy attack. Sleep was almost impossible.

Yet the trench was the safest place on the field of battle. While a trench held many horrors, the order to attack was even more terrifying. Attacks rarely achieved surprise, since they were usually announced by massive artillery bombardments. Generals, especially British and French, ordered hours and often days of advance shelling in the unshakeable but quite mistaken belief that doing so destroyed the enemy's trenches and the defenders within them. Intense shelling certainly rattled the enemy's nerves and a direct hit could destroy a trench, but the real effect of these long bombardments was to give the enemy time to reinforce the area to be attacked.

Once the artillery ceased and the attack whistles blew, soldiers leaped out of the trenches, desperate to get across as quickly as possible **"No Man's Land,"** the strip of land separating the two armies and their labyrinths of trenches by only a few dozen yards. The landscape, however, prevented quick movement. Artillery shells cratered No Man's Land, making running difficult, although the craters provided shelter from artillery. Barbed wire and unseen landmines added further obstacles to attackers running directly into streams of machine-gun bullets. Those attackers who managed to successfully navigate No Man's Land threw hand grenades into the nearest enemy trench, hoping to kill its defenders before jumping into it. Yet taking a trench often proved pointless; the enemy usually just fell back to the next line of trenches before striking back at the exhausted invaders. A successful counter-attack mirrored the original attack, except it was fought on the other side of no-man's land.

As the war progressed, both sides on the Western Front came up with new, ever more destructive weapons to end the stalemate. The Germans first used poison gas in April 1915 during an attack on British troops. A gray-green cloud passed over no-man's land and descended on the British who had no idea what it was until their lungs began collapsing. Panic ensued in the British lines and a massive gap opened as they fled. But German troops, hesitant to approach the gassed areas themselves, pursued slowly, and lost the momentary advantage. One ingenious British soldier, who recognized the gas as chlorine, took out a handkerchief, urinated on it, and pressed it to his mouth and nose, breathing normally. A chemical in the urine made the chlorine inactive; thus was born the first gas mask.

Gas attacks became a "normal" battlefield horror, one immortalized by Wilfred Owen, the famous World War I poet who died on the Western Front in 1918. His haunting poem, *Dulce et Decorum Est* describes a gas attack and the terrible death of a soldier unable to get his mask on in time.[8]

Gas! Gas! Quick, boys!
—An ecstasy of fumbling,
Fitting the clumsy helmets just in time;
But someone still was yelling out and stumbling,

Image 17.1 British troops advance during gas attack, 1917

© The Keasbury-Gordon Photograph Archive / Alamy

And flound'ring like a man in fire or lime . . .
Dim, through the misty panes and thick green light,
As under a green sea, I saw him drowning.[9]

Airplanes also played important roles on the World War I battlefields. Initially used for scouting, they soon carried machine guns and gravity-propelled bombs. Fighter planes fought battles in the sky while bombers added one more worry to the men trying to survive in the trenches. It was the airplane that first brought civilians into direct contact with the war, when each side began bombing industrial centers in an effort to undermine the enemy's war effort. The British, long protected by their navy and the English Channel, found the bombing especially traumatic.

But neither poison gas nor planes brought movement back to the battlefield. It was a British invention, the tank, that finally overcame the barriers of crater, mine, barbed wire, and machine gun. Initially, British military officials did not understand the potential of this new industrial weapon and only the intervention of the First Lord of the Admiralty, Winston Churchill, pushed the project forward. By replacing conventional wheels with so-called caterpillar tracks, the tank could navigate almost any obstacle and, if sufficiently armored, ignore machine gun fire. The first tank action took place during the 1916 Battle of the Somme, but with limited numbers and still largely untested, they had little effect on the fighting. Only in the last months of the war, after dramatic improvements in armor and firepower, did the tank finally change battlefield dynamics. It would take another world war to fully reveal the tank's significance.[10]

Only the Dead Go Home

Another relatively new weapon, the submarine, became the central feature of German naval strategy, largely from necessity. The British blockade of German ports left Germany's expensive navy useless and slowly strangled their war effort. Soldiers and civilians suffered all manner of shortages, compelling German military officials to attack Entente shipping with submarines (U-boats). This strategy hinged on forcing the British navy to withdraw the blockade in favor of protecting the merchant shipping on which the British war effort depended.

At first, German U-boats only sank merchant ships after giving the crew time to evacuate. This gentlemanly conception of warfare gave way in early 1915 to unrestricted submarine warfare, in which enemy ships were sunk with no prior warning. Considered illegal according to international law (as was the British blockade), the new German policy dramatically increased British shipping losses. This strategy, however, risked an international incident with the United States. American trade with Britain had increased tremendously since the war began, which meant merchant ships, either owned by US firms or at least carrying Americans on them, constantly passed through the German designated war zone around the British Isles. Civilian cruise ships also continued to operate between the United States and Britain. The undiscerning nature of unrestricted submarine warfare made it practically inevitable that a German submarine would sink a ship that had a large number of Americans aboard.

This happened on May 7, 1915 when a German U-boat fired a single torpedo into the *Lusitania*, a British passenger liner en route from New York City to England. The ship sank within minutes, killing 1,198 people, including 128 Americans. Outrage emanated from all over the world, most prominently from American President Woodrow Wilson, who threatened war if Germany continued their submarine campaign. Despite German protests that the *Lusitania* carried war material, the threat of American involvement cowed the German government into revising its submarine policy. For the next eighteen months, German submarines operated under far more restrictions, somewhat reducing tensions with the US, but also ensuring that the British blockade remained in place.[11]

Meanwhile, World War I continued relentlessly through 1915 and 1916, quashing hopes of a quick war, while drawing in new countries anxious for the supposed spoils that victory might bring. The Ottomans had entered the war in December 1914, as an ally of Germany and Austria-Hungary, in the hope of recapturing lost territory and glory from a defeated Russia. Italy, which had refused to honor its Triple Alliance commitment at the outbreak of the war, turned coat and joined the Entente in April 1915 with promises of territorial gains in southeastern Europe. Although neither addition significantly affected the outcome of the conflict, they did bring millions more soldiers and civilians into the inferno.

As the war in the trenches took its toll on the soldiers, another battle of sorts went on behind the lines, on the home front. Survival in World War I, to say nothing of victory, required not just the strategies of generals or the strength of soldiers, but also the perseverance of those far behind the lines. While millions of men fought in the trenches, millions of women took their place in the factories and fields, trying to provide for soldiers and civilians alike. Thus, the war effort in each country required the involvement of all a nation's citizens. In sum, economic production, the ability of political leaders to keep their people unified, and the endurance of entire populations would go a long way toward determining the winners and losers of World War I.

Social cohesion first began breaking down in Austria-Hungary and Russia. The incompetence of the Austrian high command forced the Germans to take greater control of the Austro-Hungarian army, undermining its morale. Austria-Hungary also suffered from major food shortages, due to the Allied blockade, leading to strikes and bread riots by the middle of 1916. A further blow fell in November that year when Emperor Franz-Josef died; only his presence had held together Austria-Hungary as a multinational empire well into the age of nationalism. Continued military reverses created even more desperation, and finally the empire began to crack open along national lines. Army desertions rose, nationalist parties emerged, and street violence spread across the country. As 1916 waned, the question of victory or defeat in World War I appeared increasingly irrelevant to Austria-Hungary, since neither outcome seemed likely to prevent its collapse.

By this time, Russia too faced collapse. Each battlefield failure further demoralized the Russian army and weakened morale at home. Poor planning, a still underdeveloped transportation system, and the Ottoman closure of the Turkish Straits in late 1914 slowly reduced the food available for Russia's major industrial centers. Food riots and street violence erupted by 1916, and Russia, like Austria-Hungary, lacked political leadership capable of handling the crisis. Tsar Nicholas II, while a man of some intelligence, possessed minimal leadership skills, often relying on his unbalanced wife and her spiritual adviser, the infamous Rasputin, for advice on running the war. By late 1916, with army desertion rates reaching catastrophic levels and growing industrial strikes threatening economic chaos, both the Russian war effort and Russia itself seemed on the verge of disintegration.

Russia's collapse would, of course, be good news for Germany, which desperately needed Russia's agricultural resources to feed a blockade-starved population. A German victory on the Eastern Front also would potentially free millions of troops for duty on the Western Front, tipping the balance of forces in the west enough in Germany's favor to make it victorious across Europe. Such hopes, however, would be not realized in 1916, as Russia held on in the east and trench warfare continued to take its terrible toll on the soldiers in the west.

More Than Man Can Bear: Verdun and the Somme, 1916

The year 1916 would be remembered for two battles, Verdun and the Somme River, which nearly destroyed the armies involved and left enduring scars on the landscape and people of Western Europe. The Battle of Verdun, a German effort to capture French fortresses 200 miles east of Paris, resulted in nearly 800,000 casualties, almost all German and French. Artillery did most of the damage to body and soul as literally tens of millions of German and French shells rained down on soldiers. Periodic infantry offensives, none of which resulted in anything beyond human destruction, punctuated the ubiquitous shelling. In December, after ten months of fighting, the front line was essentially unchanged. Only winter and the obscene casualty rate ended the battle.[12]

German and French troops pulled double duty in 1916, for the Battle of the Somme overlapped Verdun. What began as a British offensive in July developed into one of the bloodiest battles ever fought. More than a million soldiers—British, French, and German—were killed and wounded before winter mercifully ended the slaughter. On the first day alone, the British suffered nearly 60,000 casualties, most of which resulted from a pointless charge across No Man's Land. Without needing to aim, German machine gunners fired into the tightly massed British infantry, exacting such a terrible toll that many Germans refused to keep firing at retreating soldiers. When the battle ended in November, the British had gained less than a square foot of territory for every casualty.

There is no way to explain how traumatic the Somme was for the British, but one statistic offers some illumination. In 1917, about twenty-three million British, half the population, watched the silent film footage of the battle. This record number of viewers stood until 1977, when *Star Wars* surpassed it, and by then, Britain's population was sixty million.[13]

Royal Newfoundland Regiment

The Royal Newfoundland Regiment was a reserve Canadian infantry regiment founded in 1795 and, with some breaks along the way, it still exists today as part of the Canadian Army. Under British command, it fought in many battles during World War I, but it is most famous for being almost entirely destroyed on the first day of the Battle of the Somme, July 1, 1916. Shortly after the battle commenced, the Royal Newfoundland Regiment received orders to move forward against German positions due to a mistaken belief in the British high command that the initial attack had opened a gap in the German lines. A series of contradictory orders to other British and Canadian units resulted in the 780 officers and enlisted men of the Royal Newfoundland Regiment setting out alone into No Man's Land. German infantry across the way, having clear sight lines and no other enemy troops attacking them, fired their machine guns into the massed Canadians. Within twenty minutes they retreated, having made it about halfway across No Man's Land. At roll call the next morning, sixty-eight soldiers of the Royal Newfoundland Regiment were present. Today, a memorial exists near that halfway point, commemorating the terrible heroism of the 712 men killed or wounded, as well as the few who escaped physically unscathed.

America Enters the War and Europe Begins to Disintegrate

By the end of 1916, German officials had come to believe that time was not on their side, and they decided to resume unrestricted submarine warfare in the desperate hope that Allied shipping losses would end the war before the United States effectively entered it. German submarines did manage to inflict major damage on British merchant shipping, but the renewed attacks also sank American ships. American public opinion quickly turned bellicose, a shift intensified by misguided German diplomatic intrigues in Mexico. Although American President Woodrow Wilson had won re-election in 1916 at least partly on his promise that he would not send American soldiers to fight in Europe, growing anti-German sentiment forced him to declare war on Germany on April 6, allying the United States with the Entente powers. (The United States did not formally join the Entente; thus, the anti-German forces became known as the Allies). Events halfway around the world helped ease his decision. A few weeks before the American declaration of war, Russian Tsar Nicholas II had **abdicated**, irrevocably renouncing his monarchical authority. In his place came the unstable but nominally democratic Provisional Government (which lasted only until the fall of 1917), a far more palatable ally for Wilson and the United States.

Meanwhile, the implementation of a **convoy system**, in which clusters of ten to fifty merchant ships and troops transports joined with approximately twenty warships to cross the Atlantic, vastly increased the safety of ships carrying supplies and men arriving in Europe from the United States. As convoys zigzagged across the ocean, the warships used reconnaissance equipment to locate lurking submarines and then dropped high explosive depth charges to rupture U-boat hulls. With the American entrance into the war and the inauguration of the convoy system, the German gamble on unrestricted submarine warfare had failed.

Yet none of these developments led to victory for the Allies in 1917. Instead, the countries fighting on the Western Front suffered through more bloody, pointless battles until finally French soldiers mutinied, refusing to continue making suicidal attacks. By early June 1917, half the army had stopped taking orders, while sympathy strikes broke out among workers across France that further endangered the war effort. Only the appointment of a new French commander-in-chief of the army ended the mutiny. Meanwhile, the Russian Provisional Government collapsed in the autumn of 1917, enabling Vladimir Ilyich Lenin and the Bolsheviks, a small but rapidly growing Marxist party, to seize power and abruptly end most Russian involvement in the war.[14]

One Last Gamble: The Ludendorff Offensive, Spring 1918

During the winter of 1917–1918 Austria-Hungary slowly disintegrated, as did the Ottoman Empire, with the latter facing British-inspired rebellions in its Middle East possessions. Despite these setbacks for the Germans, they managed to achieve total victory on the Eastern Front in March 1918. The Bolsheviks signed a peace treaty that transferred a million square miles of Russian territory to Germany and took Russia out of the war for good. German military officials now saw their opportunity for victory on the Western Front. They transferred hundreds of thousands of troops there and began organizing what they hoped was a final victorious offensive. Their plan called for three million German troops to attack in northern France, to open a gap between British and French troops. The German army would then swivel toward the northwest, wipe out the British army, before sweeping back east to take Paris and conquer France. The Ludendorff Offensive, named for the chief of the imperial German general staff, would end the war and leave Germany the master of Europe. At least that was the plan.

The offensive began in March 1918, and for three months enjoyed success. German troops managed to cross the Marne River and threaten Paris for the first time since 1914. But that was as far as they got, and the cost had been more than 300,000 casualties. The American Expeditionary Force, now over a million men strong, played a major role in repelling the German threat. By late summer, an Allied counter-offensive retook all the territory Germany had captured the previous spring.[15] Once again the German generals had gambled and lost.

The war would soon be lost as well. In the east, Austria-Hungary could no longer field an army, the Ottoman Empire had largely ceased to exist, and the Russian Civil War disrupted German control of the territory they had won in eastern Europe. Germany itself began to fall apart; a naval rebellion and massive communist-directed protests made a revolution seem imminent. By late October, the Allies, with two million men and nearly unlimited supplies, had almost reached the German border. Nothing remained for Germany to do but surrender.

Rather than take responsibility for the defeat, Kaiser Wilhelm abdicated and fled to the Netherlands. On November 8 representatives from what remained of the German government met with the French to accept their terms. Although Kaiser Wilhelm and his generals had caused and lost the war, the civilian negotiators, the core of the future Weimar Republic, would ultimately take the blame.

The war ended on November 11, 1918 at 11:00 a.m. Almost eleven million soldiers and nearly seven million civilians were dead. More than twenty million soldiers had been wounded. The number of those psychologically and emotionally broken is unknown. The nations of Europe, whether victorious or defeated, lay in shambles. Before the end of the year, Woodrow Wilson had embarked across the Atlantic with his grand vision of peace forever. Citizens of the shattered societies of Europe desperately wanted to believe that the New World could teach the Old World how to live in harmony. It was to prove a forlorn hope.

Notes

1 James Joll and Gordon Martel, *The Origins of the First World War*, 3rd ed. (London: Pearson-Longman, 2007). Joll's book, recently revised by Martel, is an eminently readable, sophisticated analysis of why the war began.
2 Heinrich von Treitschke, "The New Nationalism and Racism," in *Readings in Social Theory and Modernization* edited by John McGrath, vol. 2, (New York: Learning Solutions, 2010), 207.
3 Fritz Fischer, *Germany's War Aims in the First World War* (New York: W. W. Norton & Company, Inc., 1967). When first published, Fischer's book evoked a storm of

controversy for his claim that Germany was largely to blame for causing the war. Subsequent scholarship has pretty much confirmed, with some modification, this so-called Fischer Thesis. For a summary of this scholarship see Joll and Martel's text referenced above: Joll and Martel, *The Origins of the First World War*, 1–9.

4 John Keegan, *The First World War* (New York: Alfred A. Knopf, 1999), 28–36.

5 G. J. Meyer, *A World Undone: The Story of the Great War, 1914–1918* (New York: Bantam Dell, 2007), 149.

6 Keegan, *The First World War*, 112–203; Captain B. H. Liddell Hart, *The Real War, 1914–1918* (Boston: Little, Brown and Company, 1930), 82–102.

7 Erich Maria Remarque, *All Quiet on the Western Front*, trans. A. W. Wheen (New York: Ballantine Books, 1929), 55–56, 104.

8 www.oucs.ox.ac.uk/ww1lit/collections/item/3303?CISOBOX=1&REC=5

9 Wilfred Owen, "Dulce et Decorum Est," The First World War Poetry Archive, www.oucs.ox.ac.uk/ww1lit/collections/item/3303?CISOBOX=1&REC=5

10 Meyer, *A World Undone*, 260–64; Remarque, *All Quiet*, 105–18; Liddell Hart, *The Real War*, 248–55.

11 Meyer, *A World Undone*, 289–91.

12 Alistair Horne, *The Price of Glory: Verdun 1916* (London: Penguin Books, 1962).

13 www.national-army-museum.ac.uk/exhibitions/theSomme/

14 Michael Kort, *The Soviet Colossus: History and Aftermath*, 7th ed., (New York: M. E. Sharpe, 2010); George F. Kennan, *Soviet Foreign Policy, 1917–1941* (Malabar, FL: Robert E. Krieger Publishing Company, 1960).

15 Keegan, *The First World War*, 372–414.

Suggested Readings

Hastings, Max. *Catastrophe 1914: Europe Goes to War.* New York: Alfred A. Knopf, 2013.

Hochschild, Adam. *To End All Wars: A Story of Loyalty and Rebellion, 1914–1918.* Boston: Mariner Books, Houghton Mifflin Harcourt, 2011.

Horne, Alistair. *The Price of Glory: Verdun 1916.* London: Penguin Books, 1962.

Joll, James, and Gordon Martel. *The Origins of the First World War*, 3rd ed. London: Pearson-Longman, 2007.

Keegan, John. *The First World War.* New York: Alfred A. Knopf, 1999.

Kennan, George F. *Soviet Foreign Policy, 1917–1941.* Malabar, FL: Robert E. Krieger Publishing Company, 1960.

Kort, Michael. *The Soviet Colossus: History and Aftermath*, 7th ed. New York: M. E. Sharpe, 2010.

Liddell Hart, Captain B. H. *The Real War, 1914–1918.* Boston: Little, Brown and Company, 1930.

MacMillan, Margaret. *The War That Ended Peace: The Road to 1914.* New York: Random House, 2013.

Meyer, G. J. *A World Undone: The Story of the Great War, 1914–1918.* New York: Bantam Dell, 2007.

Remarque, Erich Maria. *All Quiet on the Western Front.* Translated by A. W. Wheen. New York: Ballantine Books, 1929.

Winter, Jay, ed. *The Cambridge History of the First World War: Volume 1, Global War.* Cambridge: Cambridge University Press, 2016.

18 Europe between Wars

Jay P. Corrin

Key Terms

command economies, economic depression, economic nationalism, inflation, isolationism, mandates, protectionism, reparations, self-determination, tariffs

World War I turned out to be a watershed in European history. It produced a series of political, social, and economic crises that transformed the landscape of Western culture. Ten million military deaths robbed nations of their future leaders. Germany and France lost some 16 percent of their male populations; to put this in context, a comparable proportion of America's current population would be fifteen million adult males—and even in World War II, America's costliest conflict, the number of American dead was less than half a million. If this devastation was not enough, in 1918 the Spanish influenza epidemic began to sweep through a cold, hungry and weakened world, killing twice as many as had been taken in World War I.

Germany's civilians may have suffered the most during the war. Thanks to the British naval blockade, metal for armaments was in such low supply that the government had to expropriate from citizens kettles, cooking pots, brass ornaments, 10,000 church bells and even doorknobs. Food shortages led to near starving conditions for civilians. Bread, a dietary staple for many, had to be made from potato peels and sawdust. Such conditions meant that Germans lost 20 percent of their body weight during the war. Their Austrian civilian counterparts had it even worse.[1] These civilian deprivations in the German alliance help explain the deep and lingering anger associated with what was perceived to be a harsh, unfair peace treaty. Many historians have concluded that the war that prevented the Germans from overrunning Europe virtually assured a second try in 1939.

In addition to the human cost, this conflict ravaged Europe's economy. The Germans lost 22 percent of their national treasure, while the Italians lost 26 percent of their wealth and France 30 percent. The British had expended more capital on the war than they had invested in all previous industrial and financial undertakings. British war spending by 1918 had reached 70 percent of its gross national product, exceeding even what it would become in World War II. Unsurprisingly, by the end of 1918 Great Britain had ceased to be the world's banker and was instead, much like France, deeply in debt to the United States. The locus of world financial and industrial power shifted abruptly from Europe to America, a nation that was ill-prepared to assume the role of world leader.

The economic and social demands of waging a total war also had the effect of profoundly transforming capitalism. The liberal foundation of traditional capitalism was the idea that government should not engage in business activities and that the market mechanisms of supply and demand should regulate transactions. But even before 1914, increasing international competition had compelled governments to become more involved in their national economies by establishing **tariffs**—taxes on imported goods—to protect fledgling domestic industries and seeking new markets and raw materials by state-supported imperialist ventures. Once the war broke out, the belligerents needed to organize their economies more systematically, with an objective of "rationalizing" production to advance the nation's economic and military needs. Thus, state economic control only increased, as free competition was deemed too inefficient to respond to national emergencies. After the conflict ended, it was difficult for European nations to dismantle the bureaucratic institutions and mentalities that had managed their wartime economic systems, especially with the emergence of economic crises after 1919. The wartime shift to "planned" or **"command" economies** became permanent.

The economic challenge of reconstruction after the war was compounded by the imperative of dealing with huge national debts, which could only be ameliorated by higher taxes for years to come. All of its citizens were now faced with the prospect of declining economic and social development. Most significantly, no longer would Europe be the world's center of manufacturing, banking and overall economic power.

Peace Making

While the economic wreckage was unprecedented, the political situation was equally problematic. Given the wartime propaganda that demonized the enemy, it was very difficult if not impossible for the belligerents to draw up a satisfactory peace settlement. Fixed ideas, deep-seated angers, hatreds, and fears became obstacles to rational and judicious political judgment.

As the victorious powers gathered in Paris in the bleak winter of 1919 to draw up peace treaties, much of Europe was mired in chaos and suffering. Russia was in the hands of Bolsheviks, violent communist revolutionaries who had declared their intention to spread unrest throughout the world in order to destroy bourgeois democracy and capitalism. The German and Austro-Hungarian empires had collapsed, creating political vacuums that several revolutionary regimes struggled to fill.

The world placed much hope in the visionary determination of American President Woodrow Wilson, who arrived in Paris to great fanfare in January 1919 with a message that promised freedom and peace. Indeed, Wilson was convinced that his ideas on the subject would eliminate the need for future wars altogether. The mechanisms for achieving this noble goal were contained in his famous

"Fourteen Points," which, among other provisions, called for an end to secret treaties and secret diplomacy, which had been prime causal factors of World War I. He also called for freedom of the seas, ending barriers to international trade, armament reduction, colonial readjustments, the **self-determination** of nationalities, the promotion of democracy and, most important, an international organization to prevent conflict among states.

Unfortunately, Wilson ran into resistance in getting the victorious powers to accept his Fourteen Points. From the start, the Paris conference was crippled by conflicting goals and attitudes. The German delegates at the conference had hoped for moderation from British and French diplomats, in order to rebuild their nation along the lines of popular democracy, an experiment in government that had never been tried before in that country. But they were disappointed by the demands of their former enemies, whose political leaders were driven by the festering anger of their citizens, who insisted on German blood.

Wilson ultimately won support for what came to be called the League of Nations, a permanent international body in which states could discuss their interests and settle disputes without resorting to war. Yet this was among his few triumphs in Paris. The war in the West had been mostly fought on French soil, and French diplomats demanded that Germany should provide compensation to France for war damages and expenses, known as **reparations**, so that they could rebuild their own economy and repay the huge war debts they owed the United States; Britain, at least initially, made similar claims, and both nations were apprehensive about the threat a revived Germany might pose. Under pressure from French diplomats the Versailles Peace Treaty contained the infamous Article 231, which was called by the Germans the "war guilt clause." The article suggested that Germany had to accept full responsibility both for starting the war and making good on the losses and damage it had caused.[2]

This was clearly unfair and inflamed German public opinion. Arguably, the British and French had been as responsible as Germany for stumbling into the war, but of course the spoils always go to the victors. Almost immediately, the notion of "war guilt" provided an opening for extremist groups in Germany who aimed to overthrow the Versailles Peace Treaty, and even moderate Germans considered Article 231 a stain on their sense of national self-respect. Not only was the new German Republic burdened with the task of repaying unrealistic reparations, but the peace treaty also forbade the government from rebuilding an effective army and navy.

Furthermore, it deprived Germany of all her former overseas colonies, which were now called "**mandates**" rather than the politically incorrect "colonies," and were turned over to the victors. The Versailles Treaty was so severe that even the allies felt conflicted, and as time went on, they became increasingly unwilling to enforce its terms.

Although German diplomats resisted the harsher terms of the Versailles Treaty, they gave way after the Allies threatened to renew hostilities. The German statesmen who eventually signed the peace treaty would forevermore be damned for accepting such humiliation. This made it even more difficult for these politicians

The Treaty of Versailles and the "Stab in the Back"

The capitulation of German forces in November 1918, followed by Kaiser Wilhelm II's abdication and flight to Holland, hit the German nation with such shock that the public had difficulty accepting the reality of it all. The grim news was even more incomprehensible given the government's censorship of news and its propaganda campaigns to boost public morale by exaggerating German successes on the battlefields. Many of the public found the defeat so improbable that to blunt the impact they more easily accepted the "false fact" that the military had not really lost in combat but was rather done in—"stabbed in the back"—by cowardly traitors: corrupt politicians, war profiteers, communists, and Jewish defeatists.

In the midst of this psychological inability to accept defeat came Article 231 of the Versailles Peace Treaty, which blamed Germany and Austria-Hungary for starting the war. Germany and her confederates were obliged to accept the charge that they were the aggressors and therefore responsible for all the resulting losses and damages. The final cost for the carnage was a bill of some 132 billion gold marks to be paid to the victors.

The so-called "war guilt clause" combined with the canard of a "stab in the back" would have lethal consequences for peacemaking. It proved very challenging to get the German public to accept a return to prewar normality, especially when it appeared that the victors were not merely unfair but vengeful and out for blood.

to create a workable liberal democracy. German agitators who demanded a full repudiation of the treaty found a ready audience among people who had previously known only monarchical authority and state paternalism. And the new government, known as the Weimar Republic (named after the city in which the democratic constitution was drafted—the capital remained in Berlin), received little support from the victorious powers that had forced the treaty upon them, since within a few years it became clear that the allies had become more concerned about protecting the Continent from Soviet Bolshevism than they were about Germany. France and Britain came to see the efficacy of using Germany as a shield against revolutionary communism, and generally closed their eyes to the Weimar government's endeavors to circumvent the treaty's strictures on rearmament.

Thus, the Versailles Peace Treaty proved to be a disaster. The perceived unfairness of German reparations and the stigma of war guilt sowed the seeds of social, economic, and political unrest. The warnings of English economist John Maynard Keynes proved prophetic. He had warned that if Germany were not reintegrated into the European system, if its industrial potential went unrecognized, there could be no European-wide economic recovery. The ensuing economic difficulties would not be accepted mildly by those who suffered the most, said

Keynes, and these rumblings could well spawn revolutionary upheaval. This was lost on the minds of the peacemakers who were bent on keeping Germany down, and the world would pay dearly for this oversight in the years to come.

New Geo-Political Challenges

Although Wilson succeeded in convincing the reluctant European powers to accept the League of Nations, he failed to get US congressional approval, and the American government did not ratify the Versailles Treaty, although a separate peace agreement was signed between the US and Germany sometime later. Unfortunately, this meant that Washington would not participate in executing the terms of what became the Peace of Paris, leaving a financially weakened Britain and France with the Herculean task of carrying out and enforcing its terms. For the next few decades, as far as European statecraft was concerned, the United States once again retreated into splendid **isolationism**, mistakenly assuming that its people could remain shielded from foreign power politics by the breadth of its oceans.

In addition to dealing with Germany, Europe's statesmen had a number of other challenges. The map of Europe also had to be redrawn, both to weaken Germany and to fill the open spaces caused by the collapse of the Russian, Austro-Hungarian, and Ottoman Empires. This was complicated by the emergence, in Russia, of a communist regime bent on universal subversion. The ethnic-linguistic self-determination advocated by Wilson, along with a need to discourage communism, became the guiding principles in the creation of new nations, most of which were destined to be politically unstable and economically backward.

The regional conflicts these new nations engendered tore the Continent apart up through the 1990s. After 1919 Austria and Hungary were vastly reduced in size, and several territories once part of their empire became independent states. Serbia merged with Croatia and Montenegro to become Yugoslavia, while the new state of Czechoslovakia arose from the combination of Czech, Slovakian, and Ruthenian homelands. None of these ethnic and religious mixings proved very stable. German territorial claims to areas with large numbers of German speakers during the 1930s contributed directly to the Second World War; more recently, in the 1990s, Yugoslavia disintegrated amid wars of "ethnic cleansing." As the historian E. J. Hobsbawm observed, the old chickens of Versailles once again came home to roost.

The British and French were hardly better off. Their leaders were greatly disappointed when President Wilson made it clear that the United States expected them to rely on their own resources to recover from the war. The victors were deeply in debt to Washington, and the Americans, as good capitalists, expected to be repaid. In the spring of 1919 the US Secretary of the Treasury announced that all American government loans to its wartime allies would be terminated. The Europeans had expected either a cancellation of their American debts so as to allow their own economies to recover, or at least Washington's support for a recovery plan, along the lines of what later became the Marshall Plan that helped

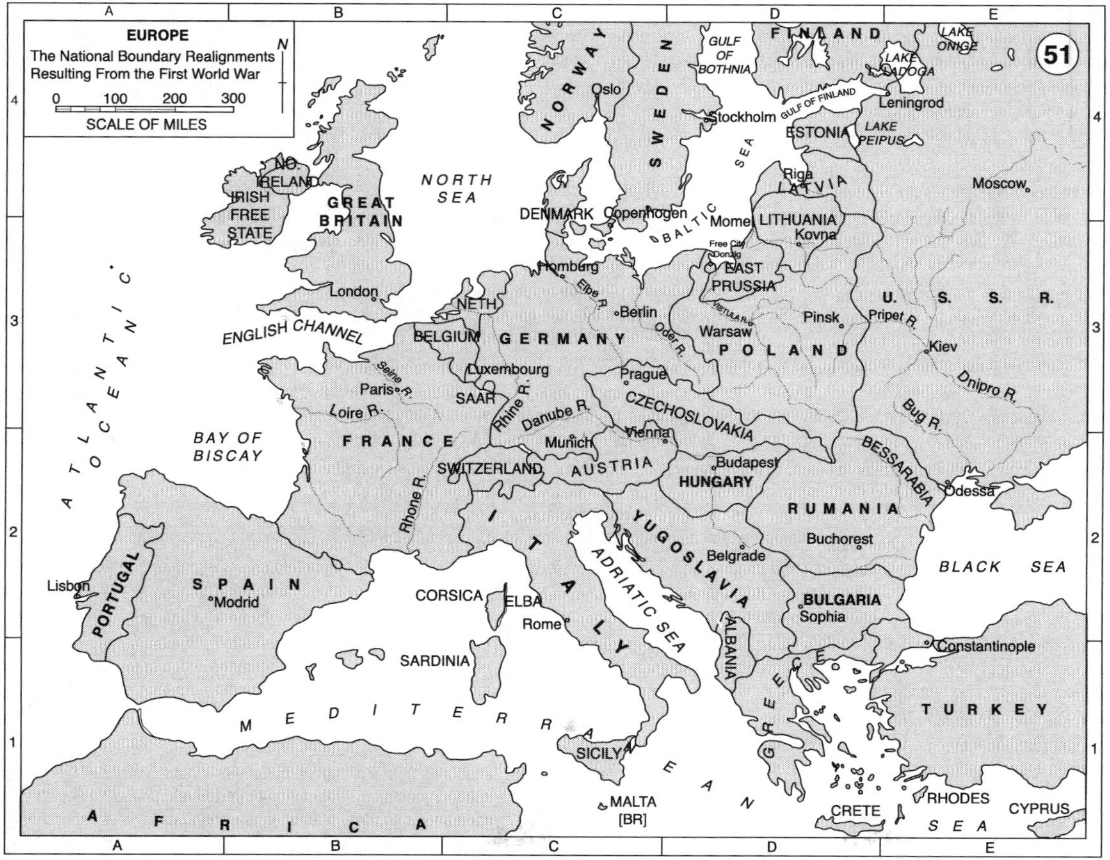

Map 18.1
Europe after the Peace of Paris, 1921

Europe recover from World War II. But the Americans believed in the free market, and any future European loans and credits would have to come not from American taxpayers but from private capitalists on Wall Street. The American return to what amounted to **economic nationalism** convinced the French to press even harder for reparation payments from Germany, so as to stimulate their own economic recovery and repay debts to the United States.

Cultural Despair

The Great War also brought about a transformation of Western culture. The beginning of the twentieth century had seemed to represent a full flowering of bourgeois liberal civilization. There were of course muted tones of pessimism and a handful of critics of middle-class mentalities (Friedrich Nietzsche, for example), but for the most part the century had opened with continuing faith in the progress made possible by democracy, liberal capitalism, and the contributions of science. Living standards had been improving everywhere on the Continent and political pluralism seemed to be carrying the day. Indeed, even large-scale war seemed a thing of the past.

But the unprecedented destruction of World War I and the consequent economic and political crises it produced led to radical changes in outlook and growing pessimism about the future. The cultural mindset of the post-war era was symbolized by a plethora of literary and artistic trends. As early as 1918, for example, the German philosopher of history Oswald Spengler published a widely-read book entitled *The Decline of the West*. Its central theme was that Western civilization was in an advanced stage of dementia and would soon die. Even the titles T. S. Eliot gave to two of his best-known poems captured the sense of impending doom, *The Waste Land* (1922) and *The Hollow Men* (1925). The latter concluded with the following lines:

This is the way the world ends
Not with a bang but a whimper[3]

"The Lost Generation" was a term used to describe many of the writers of the interwar years, several of whom became literary vagabonds, seemingly in search for a way of life that could give more meaning to a world in turmoil. Almost all the major literary figures of the era—D. H. Lawrence, Andre Gide, Ernest Hemingway, James Joyce, Robert Graves, T. S. Eliot—were marked wanderers who chose to live and write in other people's countries.

Since the secular religions of liberalism, democracy, and capitalism appeared to have failed, a number of intellectuals pursued "strange new gods" by embracing communism (Jean-Paul Sartre and Arthur Koestler) or its totalitarian counterpart, fascism (Ezra Pound and Wyndham Lewis). Still others returned to Christianity, as it appeared that the secular god of liberalism, with its belief in progress, had proven false. Many of these intellectuals (Eliot, Jacques Maritain, Karl Barth) found in original sin and Christian humility an antidote to the shallow morality of the pre-war liberals and socialists who believed in rationality and the perfectibility of man.

In art we find Dadaism, a nonsense word for a movement based on the conviction that everything was nonsensical. Here is a sample of how Dada expressed the incongruity of bourgeois life and the absurdity of the age in poetry:

The aeroplane weaves through telegraph wires and the fountain
    sings the same song.
At the rendezvous of the coachmen the aperitif is orange but the locomotive
    mechanics have blue eyes.
The lady has lost her smile in the woods. [4]

Dada soon gave way to Surrealism, a form of artistic expression that reflected Freud's sense of the irrational, the subconscious and the bizarre; its best-known practitioners were the painters Salvador Dali, Marc Chagall, Paul Klee, and Pablo Picasso. The balance and harmony of traditional classical music, which had expressed the rationality and order of a gentler and more humane world, were now replaced by new experiments in atonality. Arnold Schonberg, for instance, abandoned traditional scales for what was called the twelve-tone scale, music that sounded purely cacophonous to the uninitiated. Igor Stravinsky's world premiere of *Sacre du Printemps* (*Rite of Spring*) in 1913 sounded so outlandish to his audience that it provoked a full-scale riot. The police were called in and Stravinsky saved himself from a furious crowd by jumping through a window backstage. Yet Stravinsky's music was clearly anticipating the confusions and uncertainties of a new era. An advocate of this futuristic musical style wrote:

> The art of combining musical sounds reached its peak at the end of the nineteenth century. In the music of the future the sounds of our mechanical civilization—its machinery and crowded cities—will be subtly combined into an art of noises.[5]

Popular culture, on the other hand, reflected less despair and foreboding than it did escapism. When the world economic downturn set in by the 1930s, "the people" found solace from their angst in record-breaking airplane flights of Charles Lindbergh, the thrilling crime escapades of Bonnie and Clyde, and movie stars such as the dancing wonders of Fred Astaire and Ginger Rogers. This was when Walt Disney began creating an alternative reality in animal magic and dreamy escapist kingdoms inhabited by the likes of Mickey Mouse. On one level, all this represented the expansion of democratic culture to the common people. While elitists like T. S. Eliot found such attractions insipid, and popular culture itself cheapening, now the "little people" were on the rise, as mass newspapers and magazines with minimum intellectual content began to pander to rather mundane thrills and tastes. While these developments may have represented the expansion of popular democracy, some wondered if it was wise to feed the base impulses of the masses.

New Economic Challenges

Another major feature of Europe during the interwar years was the growing size and responsibilities of the political state. Since the functioning of its many bureaucracies required increases in taxes, it became obligatory for governments to expand voting and satisfy mass demands. Budgets began to expand to provide for security and public services. Big government and big industry merged together, and as manufacturing expanded so did its need for capital. Increasingly, cartels and oligopolistic organizations capable of amassing huge pools of capital came to dominate the market; these business enterprises in turn developed close affiliation with their respective governments. "The day of combination is here to stay," observed John D. Rockefeller: "Individualism is gone never to return."[6] What this also meant, especially in Europe, where state social welfare was more advanced, was that when economic conditions deteriorated the people held their governments responsible.

Europe's combatants had financed the cost of fighting the war through loans, all of which had to be repaid when the conflict ended, and their desperate monetary policies contributed to postwar **inflation**. For example, in France and Italy between 1913 and 1926, prices of most goods rose 250 percent or more. In France, much of the post-war reconstruction was supposed to be financed by loans, which were to be repaid from German reparations, and this led to a ninefold increase in public debt by 1926. This was especially devastating for those on fixed incomes, such as wage earners, creditors, and pensioners. Small businesses suffered as well, since they had to replenish their stock at higher costs. At the same time, governments had to increase taxes to pay for this mounting public debt. Adding to these problems was the fact that civilians who had purchased war bonds from their governments now were repaid with depreciated currency.

Britain, and France to a lesser extent, saw recovery through the restoration of international trade. Yet such recovery required the participation of Germany as a prosperous trading partner, and this was compromised by the collection of war reparations. Unfortunately, economic recovery proved to be a slow and painful process. During the war, the combatants had experienced difficulty in meeting their economic needs through their own productive capacities. After hostilities ended, the lesson taken from this was to strive for economic self-sufficiency. A spirit of **economic nationalism** swept the Continent, as domestic markets were closed to foreign products. The United States compounded the problem by imposing high tariffs that restricted the market for European goods. Such **protectionist** policies only served to retard the restoration of international trade.

The situation was far worse in the defeated countries, where currencies had largely collapsed. In Austria prices rose 4,000 times their pre-war level; in Hungary prices multiplied 23,000 times; in Poland 2,500,000 times. Germany's inflation was even worse. Their hyperinflation was due largely to France's and Belgium's decision in 1923 to invade the Ruhr, Germany's industrial heartland, because its government had fallen delinquent on war reparations, in this case by failing to deliver a thousand telephone poles. Without an army to resist the invasion, the

Weimar politicians commanded workers to resist by undertaking a general strike, and in order to compensate the workers the government simply printed money. This resulted in probably the highest level of inflation in world history, as prices rose by a multiple of a thousand billion. Money essentially became worthless, and many used it for fuel, since it was cheaper than purchasing wood or coal. This catastrophic situation was only relieved by American intervention, when short-term loans from US banks under the Dawes Plan stabilized the deutschmark.

Thanks to American intervention Germany for the next few years enjoyed not only social stability but even modest economic growth. Unfortunately, this "Indian summer" of quietude was abruptly shaken by the onslaught of a world-wide **economic depression**. The catastrophe was the consequence of a multitude of factors, including structural weaknesses in the US economy and careless speculation, which led to the crash of the American stock market and the insolvency of domestic banks and financial institutions. Wall Street responded by calling in loan payments from the German banks. The ensuing economic crash in Germany, a country already struggling to adjust to the requisites of democratic politics, was far more severe than anything that hit the American heartland. John Maynard Keynes's earlier prognostications of what could happen to men and women in the despair of economic loss proved tragically prophetic. As savings, jobs and hopes for the future vanished peddlers of extremist political views found ready audiences for their messages of hate.

Notes

1 See Adam Hochschild, *To End All Wars: A Story of Loyalty and Rebellion* (New York, Houghton Mifflin Harcourt, 2011), 311.
2 There was no specific language regarding a "war guilt clause" in Article 231, but the stricture was interpreted rather loosely as blaming the Kaiser and the German military for starting the conflict. The article was inserted in the treaty by an American delegate to the Reparations Commission in order to protect Germany against allied demands to pay all the costs of the war. Article 231 in fact declared Germany *morally* responsible for the war and its consequences but *legally* liable only for narrowly defined damages specified in the treaty. (See William Keylor, *The Twentieth-Century World: An International History* [New York: Oxford University Press, 1984], 85). The myth of the "war guilt clause" was employed with great effect by German governments up through the 1920s as a political tool to fan resentments against what it considered the injustices of the Versailles Treaty. Hitler used this myth with consummate success in overturning strictures on German rearmament.
3 T.S. Eliot, *Poems, 1909–1925* (London: Faber & Gwyer, 1925).
4 Roland N. Stromberg, *An Intellectual History of Modern Europe* (New York: Appleton-Century-Crofts, 1966), 380.
5 *The Art of Noise* (futurist manifesto 1923) by Luigi Russolo www.artype.de/Sammlung/pd/russolo_noise.pdf.
6 Quoted by Herbert J. Muller, *Freedom in the Modern World* (New York: Harper & Row, 1966), 50.

Suggested Readings

Aldcroft, Derek H. *From Versailles to Wall Street, 1919–1929.* Berkeley: University of California Press, 1981.

Aldcroft, Derek H. *The European Economy, 1914–2000.* London: Routledge, 2001.

Ambrosius, Gerold, and William H. Hubbard. *A Social and Economic History of Twentieth-Century Europe.* Translated by Keith Tribe and William H. Hubbard. Cambridge, MA: Harvard University Press. 1989.

Bessel, Richard, *Germany After the First World War.* Oxford: Oxford University Press, 1993.

Galbraith, John Kenneth. *The Great Crash, 1929.* Boston: Houghton Mifflin, 1961.

Hobsbawm, E. J. *The Age of Extremes: A History of the World, 1914–1991.* New York: Random House, 1994.

Hochshild, Adam. *To End All Wars: A Story of Loyalty and Rebellion.* New York: Houghton Mifflin Harcourt, 2011.

Keylor, William. *The Twentieth-Century World: An International History.* New York: Oxford University Press, 1984.

Kindleberger, Charles. *The World in Depression, 1929–1939.* Berkeley: University of California Press, 1986.

Silverman, Dan P. *Reconstructing Europe After the Great War.* Cambridge: Harvard University Press, 1982.

19 The Rise of Fascism

Jay P. Corrin

Key Terms

corporativism, eugenic science, fascism, martial law, statism, totalitarianism, *volksgemeinschaft*

Political and social unrest had haunted Europe long before the onset of the Great Depression. A good example of this can be seen in the post-war situation in Italy. Italy had fought on the side of the victors. Her contributions had been negligible yet losses severe, owing in large part to grossly incompetent field commanders. Compounding the misery was the nation's anger at being insufficiently rewarded at the peace conference with adequate spoils of war in terms of territorial gains. The Italian economy, weak even before 1914, had quickly slipped into a serious economic depression at the war's conclusion. The heavy war debt, high levels of taxation, rampant inflation, surging unemployment and food shortages brought Italy to the precipice of revolution. Workers went on strike and attacked factories, the unemployed rioted in the streets, and peasants seized large estates and destroyed property. Meanwhile, Italy's parliamentary politicians bickered and dithered while the nation moved closer to anarchy. Into this miasma of disorder stepped Benito Mussolini.

Mussolini (1883–1945) was the son of a fiercely anti-clerical blacksmith, and his early education had been disrupted by dismissal from a Catholic seminary for putting a knife in one of his classmates. After this, Mussolini became somewhat of a vagabond, skipping from one country to another to avoid military service. During these peregrinations he managed to pick up a smattering of socialist ideas and paid his keep by serving as a trade union organizer and left-wing radical journalist. Mussolini's political and cultural ideas were deeply influenced by George Sorel's *Reflections on Violence* and the writings of Friedrich Nietzsche. After numerous tirades against Italy's conquest of Ethiopia—socialists at the time were pacifist and anti-imperialist—Mussolini was arrested. After release from jail in 1912 he became editor of Milan's *Avanti* ("Forward"), the leading socialist newspaper in Italy. Yet with the outbreak of World War I he suddenly shifted his political orientation: Mussolini became an outspoken supporter of Italy's intervention in the conflict, which his socialist comrades vehemently opposed.

At this point Mussolini took on the role of an ultra-nationalist and joined the army, where he rose to the rank of corporal. A political opportunist, a thug and a braggart, Mussolini was also clever, dynamic, and ambitious, and perfected his skills as a demagogic orator.

After the war, Mussolini had hoped to recover standing with his socialist comrades in order to advance his political career, namely to become master of Italy. But when his former associates rebuffed him, he decided to move to the other end of the political spectrum by organizing an anti-socialist movement. He called this group the *Fascio di combattimento*, and his first recruits to what became the Fascist Party were ex-soldiers and unemployed youth. Because of the country's growing fear of Soviet-inspired communism, Mussolini soon attracted financial support from wealthy industrialists and landowners who found the thuggery of Fascist *squadristi* useful for breaking up strikes and bashing the heads of unruly peasants. Mussolini dressed his followers in black shirts, gave them discipline through military training and promised to bring order to the mess that was Italy. The Fascists became especially popular with those who feared disorder and a communist takeover, including some of the most powerful interests in Italy: the captains of industry, bankers, the urban middle classes, wealthy landowners and the Roman Catholic Church. Another significant dynamic that fueled Mussolini's movement consisted of young people. Fascist paramilitary activity and energetic, testosterone-fueled challenges to the establishment provided a window of liberation for young males, as well as females, to rebel against the strictures of Italian family discipline. The sociologist Michael Mann has argued that this age-cohort represented the first great political manifestation of the cult of youth, something up to this point largely overlooked by scholars of **fascism**.[1]

By 1921 Mussolini's party had 300,000 members and through the use of violence and intimidation won some thirty-five seats in elections to the Chamber of Deputies. The Fascists dreamed of Italy once again becoming a world power, claiming that the historical accomplishments of their Roman ancestors could supply the inspiration to make this a reality.

In the autumn of 1922, Mussolini's "Blackshirts" began to overthrow local governments in Milan and Bologna. This was accompanied by generous doses of street violence against those the Fascists accused of threatening the national order, such as communists, alleged communists, socialists, Christian socialists and even ordinary people whose version of reality differed from that of Mussolini. Besides using rubber truncheons and chains, the Blackshirts' instrument of choice was castor oil, since when taken in large quantities it produced violent spasms of vomiting and diarrhea.

The culmination of these activities occurred in late October when the Fascists undertook their famous March on Rome (Mussolini conveniently stayed safely at home) aimed at taking over the nation's government. Although the liberal-democratic coalition cabinet in Rome tried to secure itself by declaring **martial law**, suspending individual liberties on the basis of national emergency, the king refused to approve it, and when the cabinet resigned, the weak and distraught King Victor Emmanuel III appointed Mussolini his prime minister. Although he was given only temporary emergency power to restore order and initiate reforms, Mussolini forced through parliament a new law that permitted a quick national election. In yet another campaign of terror, replete with lethal doses of physical violence and castor oil, the Fascists claimed a majority of votes in a rigged election. By April 1924 their domination of Italy was complete.

But what was the Fascist program for reform? What ideology was to guide the Fascist political vision? Never had Mussolini articulated a positive set of ideas for reconstructing the country. He only claimed that Italy needed a spiritual revolution facilitated by a Nietzschean "will to power" to generate action against enemies of the state. In practice Mussolini presented himself as fascism personified: a chauvinist demagogue working up the crowds, a virile dictator shouting marching orders to disciplined soldiers (Mussolini liked to pose bare-chested for the cameras, much like his current authoritarian counterpart Russian dictator Vladimir Putin) and to youthful supporters in black-colored shirts who would beat up the weak and cowardly. The goal was to reconstruct the Roman Empire through force, with Mussolini as the new Caesar. How could this be done? Through war alone, said Mussolini, since it "brings up the highest tension, all human energy and puts the stamp of nobility upon the people who have the courage to meet it."[2] The message was clear: beware all those men with no chests!

Mussolini's Fascists promised to destroy the forces tearing away the fabric of Italian society—namely class struggle, democratic factionalism and financial greed—by seeking a third way between socialism and capitalism. The vehicle for achieving this objective was "**statism,**" a philosophy by which the state itself would transcend conventional politics and wield absolute power in the name of the people. As Mussolini put it in his efforts to further define fascism: "Everything in the state, nothing against the state, nothing outside the state."[3]

In order to legitimize his use of power Mussolini turned to the philosopher Giovanni Gentile to provide him with an ideology of fascism. Gentile wrote up the definition, which was widely published as Mussolini's own philosophy. What emerged was an eclectic and jumbled mix of ideas from a variety of sources, including Hegel, Nietzsche, Sorel, Treitschke and a number of other idealist writers who celebrated anti-rational impulses. Fascism glorified the use of force and war as the noblest of human activities, and it denounced liberalism, capitalism, democracy, socialism, and communism. Most significantly fascism deified the state as the supreme embodiment of the human spirit. The English writer G. K. Chesterton said that fascism was nationalism gone mad.

In 1925 Mussolini undertook an agreement with Italian industrialists and bankers that gave them privileges in return for supporting the Fascist Party. This partnership, which Mussolini called "**corporativism,**" was presented as the vehicle for ending class conflict. In reality, the arrangement simply assured the dominance of capitalism and the control of labor and professional groups. The so-called corporativist economic structure was to eliminate the free market and, through planning and management, reallocate resources for maximal efficiency. In practice corporativism was nothing more than a rhetorical mask to hide the creation of a command economy under the control of government and big business. Trade unions were abolished, except those controlled by Fascists. State propaganda went into high gear. Images of Mussolini were posted throughout the country; radio and films depicted him as "Il Duce," or "the leader." Although Mussolini was himself an atheist, he saw the necessity of cultivating the support of the Catholic Church. In February 1929 Mussolini settled all political problems with the church with an agreement that gave the pope sovereign control over the territory around St. Peter's Basilica and the Vatican. The Lateran Treaty recognized the role of the church in education and guaranteed the Italian marriage laws. The church, in return, was to recognize the Fascist regime and absent itself from politics.

Corporativism

Corporativism was Mussolini's plan to integrate professional, trade, and industrial associations into self-sufficient and self-governing corporate bodies. The corporations he claimed would serve as instruments to suppress excessive individualism, special interest groups, big business and finance, and governmental overreach for the national good of the organic state. This idea was originally outlined in Catholic social teaching as a critique of capitalism and socialism set out in Pope Leo XIII's encyclical *Rerum Novarum* (1891). Many in Britain, the United States, and other democratic countries initially gave Mussolini's experiment in corporativism wide support for the reasons explained above.

However, the liberating justification for Mussolini's project was mere window dressing, in large part designed to appeal to Catholic interests needed for support of his domestic agenda. In practice Mussolini submitted all these corporate bodies to the control of the state. The real purpose of all this was to serve as a means of rationalizing and thereby facilitating the Fascist Party's totalitarian control over the social order.

The Case of Germany

Varieties of fascism had considerable appeal throughout Europe. Mussolini's brand was the first of its kind and had considerable influence giving birth to imitators. The greatest triumph of the creed emerged in Germany. Adolf Hitler was inspired by his Italian counterpart, but he carried Mussolini's musings to a level of reality that literally altered the course of world history.

Adolf Hitler was certainly Mussolini's best pupil. He was born in Austria (1898) and did not become a German citizen until 1932. Son of an Austrian customs official with high social aspirations, Hitler lost his father at the age of fourteen and two years later his mother. The latter's passing was a severe blow, since Hitler was unusually attached to his overindulgent mother, whose death from breast cancer he blamed on her Jewish doctor. At the age of sixteen he dropped out of school and soon thereafter drifted around the cosmopolitan city of Vienna after being denied admittance to a local academy as an art student. These years were marked by poverty as Hitler refused any jobs of menial labor and survived sometimes in squalor by selling inferior-quality postcards and watercolors of his own making.

Vienna was the capital of the multiethnic Hapsburg Empire and was frequented by wealthy noblemen of eastern Europe driving through the streets in fashionable carriages, laborers of mixed nationalities attached to international Marxism, and successful Jews who had become assimilated to the German culture of the empire and occupied distinguished positions in business, banking, medicine, law, education, and journalism. Hitler hated them all, somehow convinced that their very existence was the cause of his own failures. He was also exceedingly race conscious. Considering himself to be of pure German blood, he looked down with disdain upon those he considered racial hybrids. Hitler's categories of hatreds were legion, including of course Jews (he was pathologically anti-Semitic), aristocrats, capitalists, socialists (especially Marxists), foreigners, people of "mixed breeds," and all those with physical disabilities (in his mind a potential source of gene pollution). Hitler's intense aversion to the cosmopolitanism of Vienna led him in 1913 to the German city of Munich, capital of Bavaria, where presumably he would find people of superior racial stock absent the stain of "mongrelization."

Life in more amenable surroundings still remained difficult and fraught with personal failure for this insolent drifter until August of 1914. Like so many other young people in Europe who felt isolated and alienated from what was considered the drab routine of peace, Hitler found that the onslaught of world war provided an exciting opportunity for the kind of action that could give life new meaning. Suddenly what was a lonely and impersonal existence was transformed by the passions of patriotism and conflict that roused in some individual soldiers a fresh sense of belonging in their search for something greater than the self. For many this "rain of fire and steel" lifted the individual out of isolation and merged him into a greater whole. Upon hearing about the outbreak of hostilities Hitler fell to his knees and thanked God for allowing him to live in such propitious times.

By all accounts Hitler was a worthy soldier but, like Mussolini, failed to rise any higher than the rank of corporal. As was the case with many other soldiers, when peace returned Hitler felt an emotional and moral let down, longing for the close companionship produced by trench combat that raised life to exalted levels of meaning. After discharge, he returned to the city of Munich, which at this juncture was a cauldron of political unrest. In 1919 a Bavarian Socialist Republic, with Munich as its capital, was declared with the active support of Moscow. The federal government eventually crushed this experiment in communism, but its legacy produced a deep aversion among many Germans to all forms of socialism, liberalism and democratic ideas. Bavaria itself swarmed with violent secret societies and paramilitary organizations led by frustrated former military officers who found the post-war peace settlement forced on Germany intolerable.

This was an environment that enabled Hitler to finally discover his true talent, which was not artistic but a unique ability to move crowds with demagogic speeches. He was given a job with the army's political instruction program to combat socialist and democratic propaganda among demobilized soldiers, with the aim of keeping alive their patriotic and military spirits. At the army's urging Hitler joined a small organization called the German Worker's Party. He soon took over as leader and changed the name to the National Socialist Workers' Party, whose members became known as Nazis, a name derived from the German pronunciation of the first two syllables of the word "national."

Germany after the war was socially and politically fractious owing to persistent economic problems and the unpopularity of its government, the fledgling democratic Weimar Republic. This was Germany's first experiment in participatory politics, which would have been a difficult undertaking even in the best of times given the country's tradition of monarchical paternalism. The post-war governing constitution was drawn up in the city of Weimar, which had been selected for this important event in part because it had been the home of two of Germany's most esteemed philosophers, Goethe and Schiller. The city also was one of the centers of eighteenth-century European cosmopolitanism and represented different values from the militaristic and authoritarian legacy of Berlin.

The Weimar Republic was in trouble from its birth after being saddled with accepting the harsh and unpopular Versailles peace settlement. Many Germans associated the government with humiliation and defeat, due in large part to the myth of a "stab in the back," the idea that the war was lost not on the battlefield but through a political sell-out by those who dominated the new republic. Right-wing groups spread rumors that communists and Jews associated with the Weimar leadership clique purposely had weakened the nation with its betrayal of the German military by prematurely signing an armistice. This negative image was compounded by the harsh peace terms: lost territory and people, restrictions on the military, and unfair reparations.

Attempts by the Weimar Republic to establish legitimacy and maintain social peace were undermined by repeated economic, political, and diplomatic crises in the 1920s. The country was plagued by a number of military threats from extremists on both the political right and left throughout the decade. Two of the republic's most promising leaders were assassinated, and a major source of social unrest was post-war inflation. However, once the inflation was reined in by American loans through the Dawes Plan of 1923, there was a substantial economic recovery and Germany experienced economic growth. Industrial output expanded, workers secured good wages, and the government expanded social welfare services. All this came crashing to the ground with the onslaught of global depression triggered by the American stock market debacle. US banks called in their international loans and the German economy collapsed.

It was the Depression that opened the door to the Nazis, who had previously remained small and ineffectual. Hitler earlier had managed to make a name for himself in 1923 when he was involved in the so-called "Beer Hall Putsch" against the Bavarian state government in Munich. This attempted coup failed, and Hitler was put on trial where he availed himself of the opportunity to air his extremist political views. Although he was given a five-year prison sentence, Hitler was pardoned after only a year, a reflection of the government's ambivalence about challenges to democracy. It was during this prison term that Hitler wrote

Mein Kampf (*My Struggle*), a rambling, bilious screed against communists, liberals, and Jews, and also a disjointed, confusing attempt to articulate a political philosophy. This turgid literary farrago became the bible of the Nazi Party. Today's audience would find it largely unreadable.

Once the Depression set in, the Nazi Party, which initially attracted unemployed soldiers and criminals, or as one historian put it "the gutter elite," stepped out of the shadows and attracted broader popular support. Hitler inveighed against the Treaty of Versailles, denouncing Weimar democracy for fomenting class struggle, division and weakness. He called for a "real democracy" of the German *Volk*, a pure master race who would be united as a vital force behind the leadership of a strong leader, the Nazi *Fuhrer*. Hitler also railed against unfair taxes, unearned incomes, the power of great trusts, land speculators, and above all the Jews, whom he accused of running both capitalism and international communism. Nazi doctrine, claimed Hitler, speaks for the German "little men."

The party performed well in the 1930 general election; its representation in the Reichstag national assembly increased from twelve to more than one hundred. For the next two and a half years, divisions within the government between social democrats, conservatives, liberals, Nazis, and communists paralyzed the government. The streets turned to mayhem as Hitler's paramilitary thugs or storm troopers known as the Brown Shirts battled communists. A new election in July 1932 produced a substantial increase in Nazi Reichstag seats. Finally, after numerous failed efforts to put together a stable government, the aged and near senile President Paul von Hindenburg appointed Hitler chancellor on January 30, 1933.

In this position of power Hitler called for another election in March, while unleashing the Brown Shirts to beat up the opposition in the guise of preserving public order from communist subversion. Some five days before the scheduled March fifth election, the Reichstag (Germany's legislative assembly) was set ablaze. Although it is likely that the Nazis themselves started the fire, Hitler blamed the communists for the crime and used his emergency powers as chancellor to outlaw the Communist Party. The Nazis still failed to capture the majority of Reichstag seats, but Hitler managed to win the support of several key conservatives from other parties, who thought they could control him once in power, and forced through the so-called Enabling Act, which gave him emergency dictatorial power for a period of four years. The dictatorship quickly became permanent. Hitler now put in place the domestic infrastructures that would rid the nation of its internal enemies, reorganized both the economic and social order, and launched a massive military buildup that created full employment and provided the requisite muscle for creating what he called the "Third Reich," an empire that would last for a thousand years.

Where did the Nazis find their audience? Initially they appealed to the demoralized and disenchanted, especially demobilized lesser army officers. Among Hitler's leading followers were Hermann Goering, a WWI air fighter ace and drug addict who became second in command.[4] Rudolph Hess, a humorless and rather stupid man, assumed command of Nazi political action. Ernst Rohm, a sexual pervert, was the leader of the S.A. (*Sturmabteilung*) or Brown Shirts. Other key Nazis included Julius Streicher, a pornographer and rapist who always appeared in public with a whip; Paul Joseph Goebbels, a club footed and acid-tongued chief propagandist, who was one of the few Nazis with a high level of education; and Heinrich Himmler, a former chicken farmer and failed fertilizer salesman given leadership of the S.S. (*Schutzstaffel*). All these men were supposed to represent the purity of the "Aryan race," a mythical people that appeared in the writings of Nietzsche and were believed to move the wheels of history. Hitler, on the other hand, had no illusions about the character of the men who became his leaders and followers. Such elements, he admitted, were unusable in time of peace.

> [B]ut in turbulent periods it is quite different . . . fundamentally, they were just overgrown children . . . . they were simply creatures, all of a piece . . . . from the beginning I knew that one could make a party only with elements like that . . . I especially looked for people of disheveled appearance. A bourgeois in a stiff collar would have bitched up everything.[5]

As the economy deteriorated, frustrated university graduates who could not find employment were drawn to Hitler's message. The Nazis also won the support of disaffected workers by promising good wages; medium and small-scale entrepreneurs who were offered protection from chain stores and trade union wage demands; members of the middle and lower middle classes whose savings had been wiped out in the Depression; farmers who were promised subsidies for their crops; and eventually Germany's leading industrialists, who saw a strong Nazi state as an important buffer against communism and who expected profits under Hitler's proposed rearmament campaign. In short, the Nazis succeeded in winning support from the broadest cross-section of German society who feared the uncertainties of market capitalism as well as the revolutionary agenda of communism.

Could it be said that a "horde of barbarians" had set up their tents in Germany? Some two months after Hitler was named chancellor, the novelist Thomas Mann wrote of a new type of revolution, one "without underlying ideas, against ideas, against everything nobler, better, decent, against freedom, truth and justice." Mann noted that the "common scum" had taken control of the state "accompanied by vast rejoicing on the part of the masses."[6]

What followed this revolution, however, would not improve the lot of the German masses. As a central feature of their dictatorship the Nazis classified Jews as "un-German" and eventually deprived them not only of their property but also civil rights and citizenship. This foreshadowed the state-organized Holocaust leading to the elimination of some six million European Jews. All political parties except the Nazis were outlawed, a secret political police called the Gestapo (*Geheime Staatspolizei*) suppressed all ideas and behaviors contrary to the Fuhrer's and arrested or killed all who were considered threats to the state. Churches, both Protestant and Catholic, were brought under control of the regime and schools and institutions of higher learning indoctrinated the next generation of Nazi citizens. All facets of the media were coordinated to propound Nazi racial doctrines. Full employment was assured through extensive public works projects (the *autobahn*, the world's first superhighway was one result) and, most importantly, a vast rearmament program was put in place to build the massive military apparatus Hitler needed to achieve the Reich of a thousand years. Now, with his political competitors vanquished, and the German masses roaring their approval in Goebbels's giant, torch-light demonstrations, Hitler could proudly proclaim "Today Germany, tomorrow the world."[7]

Varieties of Fascism

The German strain of fascism differed from the Italian brand in a few crucial dimensions. First, the Nazis were racists, whereas Mussolini's followers were not initially anti-Semitic and attacked Jews only after their alliance with Germany. Second, whereas Mussolini's fascism was statist and drew on the legacy of the Roman Empire for nationalist inspiration, the Germans lacked a similar utopian model and focused instead on the "people," a mythical notion that the Germans were a superior "Aryan" race. The historian Karl Dietrich Bracher has pointed out that unlike the statist doctrine of Italian fascism, the governing principle of Nazism was a "Völkish" ideology based on an organic community of the people that produced a superior culture distinguished from that associated with the mechanically created societies of the West.[8]

Finally, Nazism and Italian fascism, unlike Marxism, were not grounded on any consistent philosophy or theory but rather drew on a conglomeration of different anti-liberal and irrational sentiments and ideas that were designed to legitimize a variety of radical political initiatives. Yet, in one crucial way the Nazis, as opposed to their Italian ideological cousins, managed to establish a broader and more compelling justification for wielding power. A careful analysis of Nazi speeches and propaganda films (such as Leni Riefenstahl's *Triumph of the Will*) shows a remarkable and all-important unifying ideological linkage between Bolshevism (Soviet Communism) and Jews that seemed to many Germans a persuasive justification for Hitler's foreign policy. In his Nuremberg Rally speeches Nazi propaganda minister Joseph Goebbels weaved together a seamless conspiratorial connection between Moscow and Jews to destroy Western civilization. Bolshevism, he asserted, was the weapon by which Jews, a "rootless and nomadic international clique of conspirators," aimed to eliminate Christian culture.[9] The Nazi mission was to defend this civilization from complete annihilation, thereby serving the salvation, not destruction, of Europe and the West as a whole. Hitler in his Nuremberg Party Rally speech of 1936 said, "We all know that Bolshevism's goal is to exterminate the existing blood and organically rooted peoples' leadership and to replace it with Jewish elements alien to the Aryan peoples."[10] The German Foreign Office in January 1939 asserted that the United States was the "headquarters of world Jewry,"[11] and that Franklin Delano Roosevelt himself was the handmaiden of Jewish advisers. The Soviet Union, Britain and the United States worked to achieve the Jewish agenda, which was all but invisible to those without the insight of Nazi ideology—this was the conspiracy that served as the driving force of modern history.

An Analysis of the Creed

Fascism and its most virulent German variety were spawned by the collapse of the bourgeois cultural order triggered by the Great War. There are several possible explanations for the Fascist phenomenon. On one level, we can see it as a response to the inherent problems of modernity, a concrete historical illustration of what can occur when social change—either bad or good—takes place so quickly that individuals are no longer able to make meaningful connections between their sense of self and the institutions that previously had provided linkages to a broader social matrix. This resulted in what the French sociologist Émile Durkheim called *anomie*, a feeling of rootlessness caused by the collapse of normative values. The process appears to have occurred in many countries after the trauma of world war and the subsequent economic crisis culminating in the Great Depression.

Those countries where the move to modernization had been difficult, where the values of a liberal democratic order had not had the sufficient time to establish historical roots, were prime candidates for a Fascist experience. Fascist-style movements found their greatest audiences in Spain, Portugal, Italy, Germany, and various eastern European countries. None of these states had a large middle class to serve as a buffer between the higher and lower social orders, and they also lacked the bourgeois cultural confidence needed to stanch fascist-type appeals; nor had these countries reached any popular consensus on political values and institutional structures. It is significant that the United States, Canada, Great Britain, and the other Commonwealth countries as well as nearly all the nations of Western Europe were spared the triumphs of this scourge.

Certainly, one of fascism's singular appeals was to rescue the isolated, atomized individual alienated by the rapidity of social change brought by what Ferdinand Tönnies called *gesellschaft* ("modern corporation") and to reintegrate him once again into a traditional *gemeinschaft* ("community"). Anxiety about the collapse of communal solidarity had intensified in Europe as early as the late nineteenth century when industrial conflict, urbanization, and rising immigration rattled the traditional sense of community. Jarring transformations brought about by these accelerating changes had captured the attention of European sociologists such as Georg Simmel, Émile Durkheim, Tönnies, and others, who noted in their work the disruptions of traditional social relationships brought about by what today we recognize as the advancement of modernization. This collective sense of social dislocation had been exacerbated by World War I. In the midst of the consequent social, psychological, and economic chaos many were prepared—much as the seventeenth-century philosopher Thomas Hobbes had predicted—to sacrifice individual freedom for the security that comes from the immersion of self into a larger authoritarian social collectivity that in the twentieth century became known as **totalitarianism.** This was one answer to Durkheim's *anomie*, the purposeless drift of people without social ties. It has been said that the Nazis offered a "false *gemeinschaft*" as an antidote to the insecurities of modernity—a dynamic in which the "I" becomes the "We."

Yet can we simply associate fascism as the rejection of modernity? Mussolini, for example, was a great admirer of the Italian "Futurists," a cult that celebrated the attributes of modernity in the symbol of its movement: a racing automobile signalizing the liberating virtues of action in a rapid leap into the future. The "Futurist Manifesto" dismissed the cultural legacies of the past preserved in museums and libraries, while praising the revitalizing values of speed and violence. One of the founders of the Futurist movement, the artist Filippo Tommaso Marinetti, was a fan of Mussolini's emphasis on action and violence and a Fascist himself. Hitler, for his part, may have borrowed Tönnies's term for the "People's Community" (*Volksgemeinschaft*) he hoped to create (Tönnies was a supporter of the Nazis), but on another level, he sought an alternative modernity, a technically advanced and militarily powerful society in which "modernity's strains and divisions would be smothered" by the party's totalitarian powers of integration and control.[12] In this respect technology would be used to manage the stresses of modernization but in the context of a traditional yet authoritarian *Völks* community. Even the Nazi's barbarous war against the Jews was based on modern so-called "**eugenic science**," a willingness to weed out the weak and racially impure that rejected moral values in the quest of an aesthetic of the perfect human specimen, notwithstanding the contradictions of Aryan physical and mental superiority represented by Himmler, Goebbels, and other members of Hitler's "gutter elite."

Some historians have asserted that the Nazi version of fascism can best be understood as the natural culmination of German history, which from the days of Martin Luther revealed a tendency to seek protection from the vagaries of modernity by submitting to the powerful, either like the secular princes who protected Protestants from Rome at the time of Luther's apostasy, or to submit completely to an all-powerful God, which Luther preferred to the popes. Subsequent German history was shaped by its people's submission to strong political and religious authorities, who never gave democracy a chance to deepen its roots either in German politics or in the popular psyche. Germany had been forged into a modern state by the "Iron Chancellor" Prince Otto von Bismarck and his Prussian Junkers, a military aristocracy who scorned liberals and devoted their lives to serve as military leaders for an authoritarian and paternalistic monarchy. This was supposedly a military tradition that Hitler and the Nazis manipulated to establish their empire.

The problem with this explanation, however, is that Hitler and his National Socialists got most of their support from Bavaria, the Catholic part of Germany that always resisted the lead of the northern Prussian Protestants who represented the military elites. Moreover, the German army officer class was suspicious of Hitler from the beginning and only after much struggle submitted to Nazi leadership. Even the claim that Nazi anti-Semitism was a unique product of Germany's hatred of Jews must be challenged by the fact that other countries in eastern Europe traditionally were even more anti-Semitic than the Germans, and many willingly collaborated in assisting the Nazis in their so-called "final solution."

An equally incomplete explanation for fascism comes from Marxist historians. They have emphasized the centrality of economic factors and class struggle as forces for bringing successes to Mussolini and Hitler. In their view, the varieties of fascism represented the last desperate stage of the bourgeois elite's struggle to maintain their wealth and privileges against the claims of working-class revolution. They suggest that in a moment of great crises wealthy industrialists, bankers and landowners threw their support to Mussolini or a Hitler to prevent the collapse of capitalism. Both dictators certainly initiated short-term policies and programs that benefited these groups and thereby staved off a communist takeover. Yet it is clear in the long run that both dictators used the elites to advance their own megalomaniacal agendas. Indeed, from the outset Mussolini and Hitler generated popular support by attacking bourgeois capitalist values. In the long run neither dictator was beholden to bourgeois economic or cultural interests, and they systematically eliminated market mechanisms in favor of a command economy that was geared not for capitalist profits but for military success. Finally, their respective irrational foreign policy decisions only served to destroy the wealth and class values of such elites.

In the final analysis, we might well argue that fascism was a product of modernization. But we can perhaps best understand the complexities of the fascist historical moment not as a *reaction against* modernization but rather as a *consequence* of modernization. Fascism's relationship to modernity was complex and ambivalent, but it does reveal to us how certain forms of political movements and ideologies can engineer anti-modernizing sentiments into channels that maximize the powers of party and state. It should also be kept in mind that Italian fascism and National Socialism in Germany required not merely the complicity of ordinary people but also the acquiescence or assistance of traditional elites. These men had a distaste for the crudities of Fascist militants, but they believed that allowing the vulgarians into the governing arena would serve to tame the beasts. They were wrong.

Notes

1 Michael Mann, *Fascists* (Cambridge University Press, 2004), 359. Of course, this emphasis on the élan of youth was also a central feature of the pre-World War I Futurists, a group of young artists and intellectuals who attacked the bourgeois establishment as decadent, supine, and lacking in energy. Not surprisingly, its leading spokesman Filippo Tommaso Marienetti was an early supporter of Mussolini.

2 Benito Mussolini, "The Doctrine of Fascism." In *The Social and Political Doctrines of Contemporary Europe*, ed. Michael Oakeshott (Cambridge University Press, 1939), 178–179.

3 From a speech delivered by Mussolini in 1925. Quoted in Mark C. Henrie, December 23, 2010, *First Principles: ISI Web Journal.* José Antonio Primo de Rivara, a Spanish accolade of Mussolini, expressed the statist creed this way: "Ours will be a totalitarian state in the service of the fatherland's integrity." Quoted in Roger Griffen with Matthew Feldman, eds., *Fascism: Critical Concepts in Political Science* (London: Routledge, 2004), 121.

4 The German writer Norman Ohler has written an astonishing but serious piece of scholarship that has become a best-selling book now translated into English with the title *Blitzed: Drugs in Nazi Germany* (London: Penguin, 2016), that shows

that Hitler, the central leaders of the Third Reich, and even the Wehrmacht's soldiers were given regular dozes of cocaine, heroin, morphine and the newly developed German drug of methamphetamines (aka crystal meth—the central feature of the TV series "Breaking Bad") as a confidence bolster and performance enhancer. Ultimately, the issuance of drugs was regarded as an effective weapon for energizing Nazi political and military objectives. Hitler himself, scholarship has now revealed, was a drug addict, the effects of which seriously compromised his leadership.

5 Excerpts from *Hitler's Table Talk*, 107, as cited in Alan Bullock, *Hitler: A Study in Tyranny*, revised edition (New York: Penguin, 1962), 83.
6 Quoted in Robert O. Paxton, *The Anatomy of Fascism* (New York: Knopf, 2004), 7.
7 Cited by David Welch, *Hitler: Profile of a Dictator* (New York: Routledge, 2001), 64.
8 Karl Dietrich Bracher, *The German Dictatorship: The Origins, Structure, and Effects of National Socialism*, (New York: Praeger, 1971), 24. Bracher makes a distinction here between community (traditional, organic, and superior) and society (modern and mechanically constructed), a demarcation drawn by the pro-Nazi Ferdinand Tönnies in his *Gemeinschaft and Gesellschaft*, 1887. The Nazis proposed to construct a new " *Völksgemeinschaft,* " a cell of superior culture within the confines of a modern and decadent *gesellschaft.*
9 "Goebbels Claims Jews Will Destroy Culture," *Holocaust Encyclopedia*, last accessed August 3, 2017, www.ushmm.org/wlc/en/media_fi.php?ModuleId= 10007986&MediaId=192.
10 The reiteration of this Judeo-Marxist conspiracy to poison the world as the core of Nazi foreign policy to defend the West is developed by Jeffrey Herf, *The Jewish Enemy: Nazi Propaganda during World War II and the Holocaust* (Cambridge, MA: Harvard University Press, 2006).
11 Quoted in Herf, 246.
12 See Henry A. Turner, Jr., *Reappraisals of Fascism* (New York: Viewpoint, 1975).

Suggested Readings

Arendt, Hannah. *The Origins of Totalitarianism*. New York: World, 1964.
Bracher, Karl Dietrich. *The German Dictatorship: The Origins, Structure, and Effects of National Socialism*. New York: Praeger, 1971.
Bullock, Alan. *Hitler: A Study in Tyranny*. New York: Penguin, 1962.
Cassels, Alan. *Fascist Italy*. New York: Thomas Crowell, 1968.
Evans, Richard J. *The Third Reich in Power: 1933–1939*. London: Penguin Press, 2005.
Fest, Joachim. *Hitler*. New York: Harcourt, Brace, Jovanovich, 1974.
Gay, Peter. *Weimar Culture: The Outsider as Insider*. New York: Harper & Row. 1968.
Goldberg, Jonathan. *Liberal Fascism: The Secret History of the American Left from Mussolini to the Politics of Meaning*. New York: Doubleday, 2009.
Herf, Jeffrey. *Reactionary Modernism: Technology, Culture and Politics in Weimar and the Third Reich*. New York: Cambridge University Press, 1984.
Herf, Jeffrey. *The Jewish Enemy: Nazi Propaganda during World War II and the Holocaust*. Cambridge, MA: Harvard University Press, 2006.
Kirkpatrick, Ivone. *Mussolini: A Study in Power*. New York: Hawthorn Books, 1964.
Mann, Michael. *Fascists*. New York: Cambridge University Press, 2004.
Mussolini, Benito. *Fascism: Doctrine and Institutions*. Rome: Ardeta, 1935.
Nolte, Ernst. *Three Faces of Fascism*. New York: New American Library, 1969.

Ohler, Norman. *Blitzed: Drugs in Nazi Germany.* London: Penguin, 2016.

Orlow, Dietrich. *A History of Modern Germany: 1871 to the Present.* Englewood Cliffs, NJ: Prentice Hall, 1987.

Paxton, Robert. *The Anatomy of Fascism.* New York: Knopf, 2004.

Payne, Stanley. *A History of Fascism: 1914–1945.* Madison: University of Wisconsin Press, 1995.

Smith, Denis Mack. *Mussolini.* New York: Knopf, 1982.

Turner, Henry, ed. *Reappraisals of Fascism.* New York: New Viewpoint, 1975.

20 Total War

World War II

Michael G. Kort

Key Terms

anti-Semitism, appeasement, "area" bombing, Axis, *Blitzkrieg*, genocide, isolationist, SS, strategic bombing, superpowers, total war, unconditional surrender

The coming to power of Adolf Hitler and the Nazi Party in Germany was the crucial link in a chain of events that ultimately led to World War II. To be sure, during the 1930s there were undemocratic regimes both in Asia and Europe whose aggressive designs threatened international peace. In East Asia, even before Hitler came to power and began destabilizing Europe, Japan had seized the huge Chinese territory of Manchuria and turned it into a puppet state. In southern Europe, Fascist Italy under Benito Mussolini moved to expand its colonial possessions in Africa and to act on its territorial ambitions elsewhere in the Mediterranean region. Yet only Germany among the world's growing assortment of fascistic and authoritarian countries had the military and economic potential to challenge the international order established after World War I. Hitler's rise to power in 1933 added a key catalyst to that mix: the will and ruthlessness to undertake aggression.

Between 1933 and 1939 the world's most powerful democracies, still traumatized by the carnage of World War I and desperate to remain at peace, ignored or tried to wish away Hitler's growing threat. These sentiments were dominant not only in Europe, which had suffered the most during World War I, but also in the United States, where **isolationist** public opinion deeply opposed American entanglement in European crises and possibly another war. The deep mistrust Europe's democratic leaders held for the Soviet Union, a totalitarian regime officially committed to promoting Communist revolutions worldwide, further stymied efforts to stand up to Nazi Germany. The result was the most total and destructive war in human history.

Hitler's Worldview

Hitler initially masked the threat Nazi Germany posed to other countries by claiming that his major foreign policy goal was to undo what he claimed were injustices imposed on Germany by the Treaty of Versailles. Although during the 1920s the World War I peace settlement had been substantially revised in Germany's favor, some of those claims were not considered entirely unjustified abroad. This certainly was true in Great Britain, where by the 1930s some prominent politicians were arguing that the post-World War I peace settlement had treated Germany too harshly; some even believed that certain remaining restrictions on Germany, such as limits on its armaments and the demilitarization of its western region called the Rhineland, were no longer sustainable or worth defending. This unwillingness to stem the growth of German power was reinforced by the notion that a strong Germany would prevent Soviet expansion; it would serve as a "bulwark against Bolshevism," as the saying went at the time.

But in fact, Hitler had far more radical and far-reaching goals than righting any alleged wrongs of the post-World War I settlement. He based his objectives on Nazi racial ideology, which asserted that the German people were inherently superior to everyone else and destined to rule as the world's "master race." According to Nazi doctrine, Germans were hemmed in by their current borders and needed additional room to live—*Lebensraum* in German—in order to prosper and, indeed, to survive. This view mandated Germany's territorial expansion, into both areas populated by ethnic German minorities and those populated by other peoples, such as the Slavs of Poland and the Soviet Union, whose "inferiority" justified their expulsion or enslavement. To achieve a stronger Germany, Hitler planned a series of conquests, initially against Germany's immediate neighbors, later against the Soviet Union, and finally against the United States. As historian Gerhard L. Weinberg has noted, Hitler planned "to bring about a total demographic and racial reordering of the globe."[1]

The worst fate by far of any people awaited Europe's Jews, and indeed Jews anywhere in the world who fell into Nazi hands. An extraordinarily fanatical and violent **anti-Semitism** was at the core of Hitler's world view. To him, Jews were even worse than the subhuman Slavs or any other group. In Hitler's twisted, hate-filled mind, Jews were evil incarnate, and as such were the main and mortal enemy of the Aryan Germans. Hitler was convinced that Germany would never be safe as long as the Jewish people had any influence in the world, and as early as 1920 he openly called for their complete extermination. Unlike with Slavs or even the despised Gypsies, there was no room for any Jews at all in the new order that Hitler promised to bring about. This in turn explains why Hitler launched his "war against the Jews," as historian Lucy Dawidowicz has aptly called it, immediately upon coming to power, and well before he plunged Europe into World War II.[2]

That assault began with a campaign to drive all Jews from Germany: it expanded quickly from harassment, boycotts, street violence, and far-reaching discrimination to depriving Jews of German citizenship and seizing their businesses and property. Once war came—having announced in January 1939 during a speech to the German parliament that war would bring "the annihilation of the Jewish race in Europe"—Hitler turned this assault against the Jews into a systematic campaign to round up and murder every Jewish man, woman, and child living in the expanding area under Nazi control.[3]

Appeasement and the Road to War

The road from the Nazi rise to power in Germany to the outbreak of World War II was paved by a policy known as **appeasement**: a series of concessions by Europe's democratic powers that, in the hope of avoiding another major war, allowed Hitler to do and take what he wanted. In 1933 Hitler pulled Germany out of the League of Nations. Emboldened by British and French indecision, he then announced a program of rearmament, including the building of an air force, in direct violation of the Treaty of Versailles. Once again Britain and France failed to react. In 1935, when Italy invaded and conquered the African country of Ethiopia, neither country, nor the League of Nations, offered anything but verbal criticism, a weak reaction that did nothing but anger Mussolini and push him closer to Hitler. Their continued failure to act further encouraged Hitler, who in 1936 again violated the Treaty of Versailles by placing military forces in the Rhineland.

That same year a civil war broke out in Spain, when fascist forces led by General Francisco Franco rebelled against the recently elected republican government, which was led by a leftist coalition. While Britain and France, where public opinion was deeply divided on the issue, declined to intervene in Spain, Germany and Italy provided substantial aid to Franco. The Soviet Union gave limited aid to the republican side, but Soviet intervention did as much harm as good because of Stalin's efforts to strengthen local Communists. The result, after almost three years of fighting, was a fascist victory and a serious defeat for democracy—not only in Spain but in Europe as a whole.

By then, British and French appeasement had enabled Hitler to assert control over two other European countries, Austria and Czechoslovakia. The Nazis were popular in German-speaking Austria, where Hitler had been born and raised and which had close cultural and historical ties to Germany. The Austrians were divided on whether they wanted to become part of Germany, but Hitler did not allow them to decide the matter for themselves. In early 1938, after threatening invasion, and having again intimidated Britain and France, he occupied Austria and annexed it to Germany.

The most notorious act of British and French appeasement involved Czechoslovakia, by the late 1930s central Europe's only remaining democracy. Established after the dismantling of the Austro-Hungarian Empire in 1918, Czechoslovakia was home to a number of distinct ethnic groups, including a significant German population along its borders with Germany and Austria in a territory known as the Sudetenland. The Sudetenland's mountainous topography made it vital to Czechoslovakia's ability to defend itself from potential German aggression. After seizing Austria, Hitler demanded that Czechoslovakia cede this area to Germany. However, Czechoslovakia had mutual defense agreements with France and the Soviet Union, as well as a modern army well positioned to defend its territory, and its leaders were willing to stand up to the Hitler if they had international support.

That support was not forthcoming. Neither Britain, which had just begun a rearmament program, nor France was prepared for war. Instead, British Prime

Minister Neville Chamberlain tried to appease Hitler to avoid hostilities. In September, he and French leader Édouard Daladier met with Hitler and Mussolini in the southern German city of Munich, without the presence of statesmen from either the Soviet Union or Czechoslovakia itself. Chamberlain and Daladier caved in to Hitler, agreeing that Germany should have the Sudetenland. Deserted by Europe's strongest democracies, Czechoslovakia had to accept the Munich Agreement. When Chamberlain returned to London, he announced to cheering crowds that he had secured "peace for our time."[4] Another British politician, Winston Churchill, saw it differently. Having noted that Britain and France had faced a choice between war and dishonor, Churchill grimly and presciently observed, "They chose dishonor; they will have war."[5]

At Munich Hitler had promised to respect the sovereignty of what remained of Czechoslovakia, while Britain and France in turn guaranteed that country's truncated boundaries. In early 1939, those assurances crumbled into dust as Germany seized the western section of the country and set up a puppet state on what remained. Next Hitler made a series of demands that threatened the territorial integrity of Poland. These demands finally convinced Europe's leading appeasers that Hitler's objectives were far more extensive than they had believed and that he could not be bought off by further concessions. Britain and France both announced that they would go to war to protect Poland from Germany.

As war clouds gathered during the spring and summer of 1939, Britain and France attempted to surround Germany, as they had done during World War I, by negotiating an alliance with the Soviet Union. That effort was undermined from the start by mutual suspicions between democratic and capitalist London and Paris on the one hand and totalitarian and communist Moscow on the other. Stalin, meanwhile, had his own plans. He desperately wanted to buy time for the Soviet Union to prepare for war; in addition, he believed that conflict between the democracies and Nazi Germany would weaken both sides and facilitate future communist expansion into central and Western Europe. So, while the Soviet Union negotiated with Britain and France, it simultaneously secretly negotiated with Germany. Ideology aside, Hitler and Stalin, totalitarian dictators both, were more comfortable dealing with each other than with democratic leaders. Statesmen in London and Paris, however, never seriously considered the possibility that Nazi Germany and the Soviet Union, sworn ideological archenemies, could work together, which may explain why the British and French negotiated with the Soviets with a marked lack of urgency.

Thus, the Western democracies were stunned when in late August of 1939 Berlin and Moscow announced they had signed a nonaggression treaty. The Nazi-Soviet Pact included a secret protocol in which the two sides divided Poland and other spoils elsewhere in eastern Europe. Hitler could now do as he pleased, free from the potential military nightmare of simultaneously having to fight Britain and France in the west and Soviet Russia in the east. In fact, for the next two years the Soviet Union in effect functioned as a German ally, supplying Hitler with a wide range of supplies vital to the Nazi war machine.

Fewer than ten days after the signing of the Nazi-Soviet nonaggression pact, and less than a generation since the end of last great conflict that had brought such ruin to the continent, Europe was again at war.

Blitzkrieg, the Battle of Britain, Barbarossa, and Pearl Harbor, 1939–1941

World War II began when Nazi Germany invaded Poland on September 1, 1939. Britain and France declared war on Germany two days later. In assaulting Poland, Germany unveiled its concept of *Blitzkrieg*, or lightening war, in which rapidly moving ground forces, supported by advanced mobile weaponry, could overrun, surround, and annihilate slower moving opponents. Both tanks and aircraft, the key weapons in *Blitzkrieg*, had been used in World War I, and all of the major powers had developed far more advanced models during the interwar period. But the way the Germans used them in their slashing war of rapid movement was new and devastating. Poland was defeated within a month and disappeared from the map of Europe: its western half in German hands; its eastern half, in accordance with the Nazi-Soviet pact, occupied by Soviet troops and under Moscow's control.

The winter of 1939–1940 is known as the "Phony War," as there was little serious fighting after the seizure of Poland. Britain and France awaited Germany's next move, the former protected by the English Channel and the latter hunkered down behind a series of supposedly impregnable fortifications along its German border known as the Maginot Line. Meanwhile, the Soviet Union invaded neighboring Finland to seize strategic border territory. Although ultimately victorious, Stalin's army performed poorly, leaving Britain and France skeptical about Soviet military preparedness and prowess. The Soviets also forcibly annexed Lithuania, Latvia, and Estonia, three small countries on the shore of the Baltic Sea that in 1918 had taken advantage of the collapse of the Russian empire to establish their independence. The Germans resumed offensive operations in the spring of 1940, occupying Denmark and Norway against limited opposition.

Blitzkrieg returned with suddenness and a vengeance in May, when German armored forces used speed, surprise, and overwhelming firepower to outflank French and British units in Holland, Belgium, and then France. The French army crumbled, while the British retreated to the French port of Dunkirk on the English Channel coast. In ten days, as the Germans pounded at Dunkirk's defensive perimeter, the British conducted a desperate evacuation of their remaining soldiers and a smaller number of French troops. Though the "Miracle of Dunkirk" significantly boosted Britain's morale and ability to continue the war, it could not negate the stunning victory the Germans had achieved. France surrendered a few weeks later, allowing Germany to occupy the northern part of the country, including Paris, while a puppet regime under World War I hero Marshall Henri Pétain was set up in the southern French town of Vichy. The record of collaboration with the Germans over the next four years, both by the Vichy regime and authorities in occupied France, forms one of the darkest pages in France's history.

The defeat of France left Britain standing alone. However, Winston Churchill, the critic of the Munich Agreement, had become prime minister, and the British rallied behind his fierce determination never to surrender, dashing Hitler's hopes that Britain would make peace. That meant Germany would have to invade Britain, but to cross the English Channel the Germans needed control of the air. The stage was set for the Battle of Britain, the first genuine air war in history and, as such, the beginning of a new era in warfare. This time it was the British who made the best use of modern weapons, specifically newly developed single-wing fighter aircraft, most notably the Spitfire, and radar, a system of using radio waves to detect incoming aircraft from afar. The battle began in August with attacks on British air force bases; later the Germans bombed London and other cities in an effort to break British civilian morale. But German aircraft losses were so severe that by mid-September Hitler cancelled his invasion plans, by which time British bombers were hitting German bases along the French and Belgian coasts. The bombing of British cities, and thus the Battle of Britain itself, continued into the spring of 1941.

By then Britain was being bolstered by American aid. Because of isolationist sentiment, the United States was still officially neutral in the war. This remained the case even though President Franklin Roosevelt was convinced that Britain could not defeat Germany and that Nazi Germany represented a mortal threat to the United States. Although his options were limited, Roosevelt did what he could to prepare Americans for the struggle ahead. As early as 1938 he began a massive rearmament program, and in 1940 the first American peacetime military draft increased the size of the army to one million men. Roosevelt also used what authority he had to funnel aid to Britain, culminating in the 1941 Lend-Lease program under which the United States provided military supplies and equipment to Britain without demanding payment.

Meanwhile, on June 22, 1941, the course and nature of World War II changed in a flash when Hitler broke his non-aggression pact with Stalin and attacked the Soviet Union. In launching Operation Barbarossa, Germany sent more than three million troops, 2,500 tanks, and 2,700 aircraft against the Soviet Union. The Soviet Union's military force was even larger than Germany's, but its officer corps had been ravaged by Stalin's purges of the 1930s, and its units facing the Germans were unprepared for war because Stalin refused to listen to intelligence reports of an imminent German attack. The Soviets suffered appalling initial losses, but their country's vast expanses and reserves enabled them to absorb these defeats without collapsing. As summer turned to fall and then into an early and bitterly cold Russian winter, the German advance stalled. German troops reached the outskirts of both Leningrad and Moscow, but failed to take either city. What followed during the next four years on the so-called Eastern Front was a titanic fight to the death, unequaled in scale and savagery in the history of warfare, between the world's two great totalitarian powers.[6]

As the German advance ground to a halt on the frozen Russian plains, events in the tropical Pacific Ocean changed World War II in yet another fundamental way. In 1937 Japan had launched an all-out invasion of China. The goal was to reduce China to the status of a dependency as part of an overall strategy of making

Japan the dominant power in East Asia. By September 1940, Japan had garnered support for its ambitions through a pact with Germany and Italy that created an alliance known as the **Axis**. By then, the United States was applying economic pressure on Japan to force Tokyo to withdraw from China, which culminated in mid-1941 with an oil embargo. The military officers who controlled the Japanese government correctly recognized the United States as the main obstacle to their plans, and they knew they could not win a long war against the United States because of America's enormous industrial power. They therefore decided to try to destroy the US Pacific fleet, based at Pearl Harbor in Hawaii, in the hope that a crippling defeat in the Pacific and concerns about Germany would induce Washington to accept Japan's East Asian ambitions.

The attack on Pearl Harbor, carried out on December 7, 1941, achieved complete surprise and did great damage to the US fleet. However, the key US warships—its aircraft carriers—were at sea at the time and escaped destruction. On December 8, the United States declared war on Japan. Three days later, fulfilling Germany's treaty obligations to Japan, Hitler declared war on the United States. The last of the world's major powers was now fully committed to World War II, a colossal struggle that would be fought on more than half a dozen major fronts, on four continents, and on three of the world's oceans.[7]

The Grand Alliance, 1942–1944

The events of December 1941 gave birth to a partnership between the United States, Great Britain, and the Soviet Union that Churchill dubbed the "Grand Alliance." In fact, it was strange rather than grand, a tenuous union between two capitalist democracies on the one hand and a totalitarian communist regime on the other, held together only by the threat posed by Nazi Germany. In addition, the United States and Britain were at war with both Germany and Japan while the Soviet Union was at war only with Germany, having signed a non-aggression pact with Japan in 1941. However, from the start Roosevelt and Churchill agreed that most resources would be devoted to defeating Germany, whose industrial and technological strength made it by far a greater menace than Japan. By signing a document drafted by the United States called the "Declaration of the United Nations," several dozen lesser powers in effect became junior members of the Grand Alliance.

The Grand Alliance looked formidable on paper, especially in light of America's unmatched industrial power. But in late 1941, despite having begun rearmament, the United States was unprepared for all-out war and both Britain and the Soviet Union had been severely weakened by their initial defeats. As a result, during the spring of 1942 German forces were able to push deeper into the Soviet Union in several areas, including in the south where they approached the Soviet oil fields south of the Caucasus Mountains near the Caspian Sea. In North Africa, a German army advanced eastward toward the Suez Canal, a key lifeline for the British. Another vital but tenuous British lifeline, formed by supply ships from the United States crossing the Atlantic, was under deadly attack from German submarines. In Asia and the Pacific, the Japanese overran the Philippines; seized Burma,

Malaya, and Singapore; occupied Indochina; and swept southward through the Netherlands East Indies and the Solomon Islands, putting themselves in position to threaten Australia. By mid-1942 there was a very real danger that the Axis powers would win the war.

Then the tide of battle began to turn, with the first major allied victories coming in the Pacific. In May 1942, American and Japanese naval forces clashed northeast of Australia in the Battle of the Coral Sea. The battle was notable for two reasons. Although militarily a draw, it ended the Japanese advance toward Australia. Of equal significance, Coral Sea ushered in a new era in naval warfare: the age of the aircraft carrier. For the first time in history the opposing warships never saw each other; all the fighting was done by airplanes flying from aircraft carriers. In June came the far more decisive Battle of Midway, where four Japanese aircraft carriers dueled with three American carriers near tiny Midway Island, the site of a US military base. Critically, the Americans had broken the Japanese naval codes and therefore learned of Tokyo's plan to attack Midway. They were ready when the Japanese arrived. In a short, fierce battle on June 4, American carrier-based dive bombers sank all four Japanese carriers, while only one American carrier was lost. The Americans had struck a crippling blow: although the Japanese navy remained a formidable force, the losses it suffered at Midway ended its ability to take the offensive against growing US forces in the Pacific.

Another major Allied victory, this time on the hot desert sands of North Africa, followed in October when the British defeated the Germans less than 100 miles west of the Suez Canal at the Battle of El Alamein. Most important of all, on the frozen Russian steppe, the Soviet Red Army crushed the Germans in the Battle of Stalingrad, fought over control of a strategically important city on the Volga River. After German forces reached the city in August 1942, the Soviet defenders turned the battle into a debilitating house-to-house, room-to-room war of attrition before launching a counterattack in November that encircled and trapped the invaders. The frigid Russian winter also closed in on the Germans with temperatures as low as minus 30 degrees. When the end came in February 1943, about 90,000 German soldiers surrendered, all that remained from a force that had once numbered more than 330,000. For the first time in the war, a German army had not only been defeated but entirely destroyed. It was a crucial turning point: after Stalingrad, with rare exceptions—most notably the greatest tank clash in history in July 1943 at the Battle of Kursk—German forces on the Eastern Front were in retreat.

From the day the United States entered the war, the military objective essential to ultimate victory was to invade France. This would enable American, British, and other allied troops to attack Germany from the west, thereby creating a "second front" in addition to the Eastern Front where German and Soviet forces were engaged. However, it proved impossible to mount such a complex and risky assault during 1942 and 1943. After defeating the German and Italian forces in North Africa, the Allies landed in Italy in 1943. But Allied troops advanced slowly up the mountainous Italian peninsula—they did not take Rome until June 1944— while Germany itself was protected from attack via Italy by the Alps.

Until the Allies landed in France in June 1944, the only way to strike directly at Germany from the west was by air. The weapon used was the newly developed long-range bomber, an aircraft based on cutting-edge technology and powered by four engines, that was refined further as more advanced models appeared during the war. The idea behind what was called **strategic bombing** was to cripple Germany's (and Japan's) ability to make war by destroying its industrial infrastructure. The problem with implementing this idea in practice was that the technology did not yet exist to enable bombers—flying at high altitude and under attack from anti-aircraft fire and enemy fighters—to hit specific industrial targets such as factories, a tactic known as "precision" bombing. Early Allied bombing missions often missed their targets by miles, suffering heavy losses in the process. As a result, both the American and British air forces often resorted to what was called **"area" bombing,** that is, attacking entire cities, which meant, inevitably, civilian casualties. Some observers, both then and now, have been critical of that policy, especially as it was carried out in 1945 during the last months of the war. However, as military historian Robin Neillands has stressed, the "alternative was not to attack at all but to leave the enemy's homeland an intact arsenal of aggression."[8]

As it turned out, strategic bombing forced the Germans to devote considerable quantities of weapons and troops to air defense. These otherwise could have been deployed against Allied soldiers on the battlefield, which in turn would have increased Allied casualties and lengthened the war. Such difficult choices were an unavoidable consequence of **total war**, where the destruction of civilian industrial areas became inseparable from the destruction of the enemy's military forces.

Total War

Total war is a conflict in which the entire population and resources of the countries involved are committed to a conflict in which both sides are determined to win a complete victory. As a result, the line between civilian and soldier is largely eliminated and civilians become legitimate military targets. This contrasts with limited wars, in which armies and navies clash without specifically targeting civilian populations. In limited wars, and most wars have been limited, the goal of the combatants is to achieve military victories that force their adversaries to make certain concessions, but that do not result in their destruction. Historians do not always agree about which wars have been total wars. Some argue that total wars have been fought since ancient times while others maintain that it was impossible to wage total war until the technological advances of the twentieth century.

Examples of pre-twentieth-century wars that are considered total wars are the Peloponnesian War between Athens and Sparta, which lasted for three decades (431 to 404 BCE); the wars waged by the Mongols in the thirteenth century, in which huge and ruthless Mongol armies wiped out entire populations; and the Taiping Rebellion in China in the nineteenth century, which claimed between twenty and thirty million lives. Nor is there a better statement describing what total war demands of a people than the decree of France's National Convention of August 23, 1793, when the newly established French Republic was threatened by a coalition of European powers:

> From this moment until that in which the enemy shall have been driven from the soil of the Republic, all Frenchmen are in permanent requisition for the service of the armies. The young men shall go to battle; the married men shall forge arms and transport provisions; the women shall make tents and clothing and shall serve in the hospitals; the children shall turn old linen into lint; the aged shall betake themselves to the public places in order to arouse the courage of the warriors and preach the hatred of kings and the unity of the Republic.[1]

Even if one considers these and other pre-twentieth century conflicts as total wars, there is no doubt that the most total wars in history were fought during the twentieth century. These include World War I and, most of all, World War II. By the time World War II was fought, scientific and technological advances permitted the mobilization of populations and national economies as never before. At the same time, these advances, especially in terms of air power, permitted attacks on civilian populations, especially those hundreds of miles from the front lines, as never before. On the home fronts, women were mobilized by the millions for civilian production as men were drafted into the military. Rationing was extended to most goods and services. New organizations were developed to bring military and civilian personnel together to make many of the war's most important decisions. On the various military fronts, modern science and technology were employed not only to develop fearsome new weapons but also for tasks such as weather forecasting before key battles. In the end, the total war known as World War II brought the world into the atomic age. In doing so, it created forces of destruction so enormous that it is inconceivable that human civilization can survive another world, or total, war. As the great physicist Albert Einstein, whose work made the development of atomic energy possible, put it, "I am not certain with what weapons World War III will be carried out, but they will fight World War IV with sticks and stones."[2] Such remains the potential legacy of total war.

Notes

1 Paul Halsall, ed., *Internet History Sourcebook Project*, Fordham University. Available online: http://sourcebooks.fordham.edu/mod/1793levee.asp, accessed January 25, 2017.
2 Albert Einstein, "Albert Einstein – Zitate," www.quotez.net/german/albert_einstein.htm, accessed June 27, 2017.

In the end, the ability to wage total war rested on the industrial strength and capacity of the combatants, and it was not long before all the major powers had organized their economies for the war effort. It is here that the industrial power of the United States, which far exceeded that of any other country, was decisive. The United States had the world's largest and most modern industrial plant when the war began, and the gap separating it from the others grew as the war continued. During the course of the conflict the United States produced more than 300,000 aircraft of all kinds, including newly developed fighter planes and high-tech, long range bombers that pulverized German and Japanese cities. Its shipyards produced 88,000 landing craft, 215 submarines, 147 aircraft carriers—including massive, fast-moving vessels that could carry up to 90 aircraft—and almost a thousand other warships. The United States also produced thousands of tanks, artillery, rifles, and other equipment for its armed forces and those of its allies. American Lend-Lease supplies, extended to the Soviet Union in the summer of 1941, included thousands of trucks, jeeps, field telephones, locomotives, railway cars, and aircraft, to say nothing of millions of boots and belts; these were crucial to the Red Army's mobility and ability to sustain its offensives from 1942 to 1945. The Soviet Union made enormous sacrifices, produced vast quantities of its own weapons, and ultimately fought and defeated two-thirds of the German army, but without Lend-Lease, as Stalin himself admitted to his closest aides, the Soviets would have been forced out of the war.

The Holocaust

During World War II, Japan's military forces committed mass murder and other war crimes throughout China and elsewhere in Asia. Its army engaged in terror killing and rape, deployed biological and chemical weapons against Chinese troops and civilians, and treated captives and prisoners of war with great brutality. Japanese scientists and doctors at the notorious Unit 731 biological warfare facility in Manchuria did hideous experiments on prisoners, fully as dreadful as what the Nazis did in their concentration and death camps. Japanese authorities throughout Asia carried out policies that caused widespread starvation. All of this, and more, was done under direction from Tokyo.[9]

Nazi Germany treated conquered peoples, especially in Poland and the Soviet Union, with horrible cruelty and committed mass murder on a staggering scale. For example, immediately after occupying its share of Poland, the Germans murdered thousands of Polish intellectuals, clergy, and other members of the elite in order to deprive the country of its leadership. More than three million Soviet prisoners of war, almost 60 percent of those taken captive, died from maltreatment at German hands. But the Germans reached further to yet another and even more insidious realm of evil. Driven by the fanatically virulent Nazi version of anti-Semitism, Germany during World War II attempted to wipe out the entire Jewish people, for no other reason than that they were Jews. All Jewish men, women, and children, no matter where they lived and how much effort it required to round them up, were targeted for extermination. The entire military and civilian institutional infrastructure of the German state was enlisted in the effort, and industrial scale methods using the most modern technology available were developed to facilitate the killing process. This effort continued throughout the war, notwithstanding that it used scarce resources and personnel that could have helped the increasingly desperate war effort against the Allies.

Historian Lucy Dawidowicz has made a crucial point about the Nazi systematic murder of Jews during World War II:

> The deaths of the 6 million European Jews were not a byproduct of the war. The Jews did not die as a consequence of the indiscriminate reach of bombs or gunfire or of the unselective fallout of deadly weapons. Nor were they the victims of the cruel and brutal expedience that actuated the Nazis to kill the Soviet prisoners of war and the Polish elite. Those murders were intended as a means to practical ends: they were meant to protect and to consolidate the position of the Germans as the undisputed masters over Europe. The murder of the Jews and the destruction of Jewish communal existence were, in contrast, *ends in themselves*, [italics added] ultimate goals to which the National Socialist state had dedicated itself.

Even against the horrific background of what Germany did to conquered people across the length and breadth of Europe, the Holocaust, Hitler's war against the Jews, therefore stands out as something qualitatively distinct. It was and remains a **genocidal** crime unique in human history.[10]

Only about 600,000 Jews lived in Germany in 1933, and many of them had emigrated by 1939. Then the invasion of Poland brought more than two million Polish Jews under Nazi control. The Nazis uprooted these Jews from their homes and forced them into ghettos, most of which were in Polish cities that already had large Jewish populations. The most famous of these ghettos, in effect huge prisons surrounded by high walls and fences, was in Warsaw, Poland's capital. Conditions in these severely overcrowded ghettos were terrible and quickly grew worse as deportees arrived from other parts of Poland and elsewhere in Europe. There was not enough food, fuel, or other necessities of life. The few Jews who had jobs worked as slave laborers for the Nazi war machine. People began to die immediately, especially the elderly, infirm, and young children, with the death toll quickly reaching the hundreds of thousands.

The process of outright extermination of Jews began with the invasion of the Soviet Union in June 1941. Specially recruited and trained units called *Einsatzgruppen* spearheaded the killing in the Soviet Union, relying primarily on machine guns to massacre their victims. The *Einsatzgruppen* were assisted by other German military and police units and often by local collaborators. During 1941 alone the Nazis murdered 500,000 Jews on Soviet soil. By the end of the war the *Einsatzgruppen* and other mobile killing units operating in the Soviet Union had murdered at least 1.5 million Jews.

At some point during late 1940 or early 1941 Hitler made the decision to systematically murder all the Jews, although his actual order has never been found and almost certainly was given verbally. On July 31, 1941, Hermann Goering, Hitler's closest aide, ordered the **SS**, the elite Nazi organization that controlled Germany's secret police (the Gestapo) and its system of concentration camps, to submit "an overall plan of the preliminary organizational, practical, and financial measures for the execution of the intended final solution (*Endlosing*) of the Jewish question."[11] Construction of extermination camps began that summer, and on January 20, 1942, the SS convened a meeting known as the Wannsee Conference for representatives from key institutions of the Nazi German state to coordinate the extermination of European Jewry.

It was in the extermination camps—Chelmno, Treblinka, Sobibor, Majdanek, Belzec, and Auschwitz, the largest, a factory of death capable of killing 12,000 people in a single day—that modern science and technology were enlisted in the service of genocide. The victims arrived by train packed so densely in cattle cars that many had died en route. They came from the ghettos of Poland and, often having been rounded up with the aid of modern IBM punch-card technology, from all over Europe. Most were immediately murdered in specially designed gas chambers disguised as showers using a recently developed vermicide called Zyklon-B. Their bodies were then reduced to ashes in massive crematoria, again specially designed. Aside from being faster than the machine guns of the *Einsatzgruppen*, this industrial system of murder had the important advantage of not being face-to-face, a situation that had caused severe morale and psychological problems among *Einsatzgruppen* personnel. By 1945, the Nazis had murdered a total of six million Jews, two-thirds of the entire Jewish pre-war population of Europe.

One of the most disturbing questions about the Holocaust is why the United States and Britain, despite having detailed information about what was happening no later than 1942, did virtually nothing to stop the slaughter. There certainly were possibilities such as allowing additional Jewish refugees entry into their countries or other areas they controlled, and/or bombing the rail lines to Auschwitz. Part of the answer is the widespread persistence of anti-Semitism, including in high places where policy was made, the most notable examples being the British Foreign Office and the US State Department. Ultimately, however, as historian Robert S. Wistrich has noted, saving Jews from the Nazis was "marginal" to Roosevelt and Churchill, the leaders in the position to do the most, when balanced against the "larger global and military and diplomatic strategy" involved in winning the war itself.[12]

Left on their own and confronted by overwhelming German power and often by indifference and hostility from non-German populations among whom they lived, the Jews of Europe resisted as best they could. Many of those who managed to avoid capture fought in resistance movements from the cities of France to the forests of the Soviet Union. The first armed urban uprising against the Nazis by anyone in occupied Europe was carried out by poorly armed Jews in the Warsaw Ghetto during April and May of 1943. They held out against the mighty German army for almost a month. There also were revolts in other ghettos and in several of the death camps, including Auschwitz, although none of these actions could stop the German death machine.

Once the extermination camps were in operation, the Holocaust was carried out with cold bureaucratic and industrial efficiency. It employed the resources and expertise of the most important branches of the modern, totalitarian German state. In that regard, the Holocaust was a function of modernity, as it could not have been implemented without modern technology and institutional organization. At the same time, the motives were strictly primitive. The political leaders who set in motion the ultra-modern Nazi death machine and the bureaucrats who ran it were driven by a pre-modern bigotry—anti-Semitism—with deep roots in European civilization that stretch back to ancient times. Absent that inherited centuries-old hatred, updated to be sure with racial pseudoscience during the nineteenth century and given unprecedented virulence by Hitler and other Nazis in the twentieth, there would not have been a Holocaust. Made technically possible by modernity, its ultimate cause was an old and deeply entrenched cultural demon that modern Western humanistic and liberal values dating from the Renaissance and Enlightenment could not overcome. In short, the Holocaust was modern only in its implementation; its roots lay in pre-modern inhumanity.

Endgame and Reckoning: June 1944–August 1945

On June 6, 1944, ever since known as D-Day, a huge armada crossed the English Channel and American, British, and other Allied forces landed on five beaches along the Normandy coast of France. As with so many World War II operations that set new standards, the Normandy invasion was the largest and most complex amphibious military operation in history. Overcoming strong German resistance, Allied troops slowly pushed inland, and the vise on Nazi Germany began to close. By the spring of 1944, Soviet forces, bolstered by huge quantities of Lend-Lease equipment and supplies, were advancing rapidly westward, and in some places on southern portions of the Eastern Front had driven beyond the Soviet Union's 1939 borders. The Allies suffered some setbacks, most seriously in the Battle of the Bulge, which from mid-December 1944 to late January 1945 became the largest and costliest battle in the history of the US Army. But while painful, these setbacks were temporary. By the end of January 1945, American, British, and other Allied forces had reached, and in some places even inched across, Germany's western border, while in the east the Soviet Red Army had expelled the Germans from most of central Europe and had even overrun part of eastern Germany.

Hitler's last hope to turn the tide of battle rested on a group of new ultra-modern weapons. They included the ME-262, the world's first operational jet fighter, and the jet-powered V-1, a pilotless aircraft packed with explosives, which was used to bomb London and other targets. Most futuristic of all was the V-2 rocket, a supersonic weapon years ahead of its time. These and other weapons were impressive demonstrations of German technological skills and, frighteningly, how far ahead of the Allies the Germans were in certain areas. Fortunately, they reached combat much too late to change the course of the war. Their main impact at the time was to cause a race between the United States and the Soviet Union to get their hands on the advanced German technology and the scientists and engineers who had produced it. As weapons that would affect the balance of power between nations, they belonged to the postwar era.

Meanwhile, by early 1945 the time had arrived to plan for the postwar peace. This effort took place during February 1945 at a conference between Roosevelt, Churchill, and Stalin at Yalta, a resort along the Soviet Union's Black Sea coast. Important agreements were reached at Yalta regarding the occupation of Germany. However, the Soviet Union's clear intent to set up a Communist-controlled puppet regime in Poland and concerns about how Moscow would deal with the other countries occupied by the Red Army caused serious divisions between Roosevelt and Churchill on the one hand and Stalin on the other. The fear in Washington and London was that the Soviet Union, having helped prevent Germany from dominating Europe, was now poised to do the very same thing. In retrospect, it is evident that rather than establishing the basis for a genuine postwar peace, the Yalta Conference set the stage for the Cold War. The subsequent Potsdam Conference, which took place from mid-July to early August, after Germany had surrendered, only deepened the divisions between the two sides, especially as the Soviet Union tightened its grip on Poland and other countries in eastern Europe.

Their disagreements about what would happen after the war notwithstanding, between February and April the Allies carried the war into German territory. On April 25, American and Soviet units met near the center of the country at the Elbe River. By then Soviet forces had reached Berlin, where Hitler committed suicide on April 30 as Stalin's troops completed their conquest of the city after a bloody house-to-house struggle that cost hundreds of thousands of casualties. On May 8, Germany finally surrendered, ending the war in Europe.

Attention now shifted to the Pacific and Japan. By the spring of 1945, the United States had driven Japan back from its conquests in the Pacific, although Japanese forces were still entrenched in China, Indochina, and the Netherlands East Indies, among other places. Since late 1944, once the United States had taken and built airfields on the Marianas Islands, its huge new B-29 bombers—streamlined, high-tech wonders with technological features found on no other aircraft—had been pounding Japan. Yet despite terrible damage to its cities and casualties to its civilians, Japan showed no signs of surrendering.

Meanwhile, as the fighting approached Japan island-by-island, American casualties mounted. Japanese garrisons one after another refused to surrender and fought to the last man. In the battle for Iwo Jima, a five-week struggle during February-March 1945 that had been expected to take four days, the United States suffered almost 27,000 casualties, including more than 6,800 dead, to take an island eight miles square. The Japanese garrison of 22,000 fought until it was virtually wiped out; only a few hundred soldiers, most of them wounded, survived. The pattern was the same on Okinawa in April, where Japanese suicide kamikaze pilots crashing their planes into warships offshore turned that battle into the costliest in the history of the US Navy.

The next battle on the agenda was the invasion of the Japanese home islands. No one knew what the final cost of defeating Japan would be, but estimates of 500,000 or more total American casualties were not unusual. With access to information from broken Japanese military and diplomatic codes, American leaders knew that Japan's government, controlled by military hardliners, was unwilling to surrender on terms satisfactory to the United States and its allies. Allied policy was to demand **unconditional surrender**—that there be no conditions attached to Japan's capitulation—as had already been imposed on Nazi Germany. Unconditional surrender was considered vital because the Allies were determined to occupy Germany and Japan, punish war criminals, and impose reforms that would prevent those countries from causing another war. The Japanese wanted to negotiate an end to the war that would let them retain their authoritarian and militaristic form of government and part of their empire. Meanwhile, as the decrypted enemy cables told Washington, Japan was preparing its defenses for the initial American invasion at the precise points where US forces were slated to land. By the summer of 1945, those defenses already were much stronger than US military intelligence had predicted just a few months earlier.

It is against this background that the use of the atomic bomb against Japan must be understood.[13]

The urgent, top-secret project to develop an atomic bomb, known as the Manhattan Project, had been initiated in 1942 because of fears that Germany was trying to build such a bomb. Those fears were based on dramatic progress in atomic physics during the 1930s, in particular the success by German scientists in creating atomic fission. Between 1942 and 1945 Manhattan Project scientists further pioneered a whole range of scientific and engineering areas; almost everything involved in the project was technologically groundbreaking. On July 16, 1945, at a remote desert site in New Mexico, the designers of the bomb successfully tested a device they called the "gadget," which exploded with the incredible force of 18,000 tons of TNT. World War II had brought the world into the atomic age.

The atomic bomb had been developed for use against Germany, but the war in Europe had ended before Manhattan Project scientists and engineers had completed their work. By the time an atomic bomb was ready, only Japan was still fighting, and even though its cities and industrial infrastructure had already been devastated by aerial bombing, its government steadfastly refused to surrender. Harry S. Truman, who had become president upon Roosevelt's death in April 1945, led a war-weary country, and like his predecessor saw the bomb as a potentially necessary means with which to end the war. On July 26, the United States, Great Britain, and China issued the Potsdam Declaration, demanding that Japan surrender or face "prompt and utter destruction," though it offered some concessions not offered to the Germans.[14] However, despite the urging of its foreign minister to at least consider it, the Japanese government rejected the Potsdam Declaration outright. This made the employment of atomic bombs inevitable.

In this historical context, the sole purpose of these bombs is clear: they were used to force Japan to surrender and thereby end the war as soon as possible. On August 6, a B-29 dropped an atomic bomb on Hiroshima, virtually destroying the city in a matter of seconds. When no response came from Tokyo after three

Image 20.1 Atomic cloud over Hiroshima, Japan, 1945

Image courtesy of the National Archives and Records Administration, USA

days, Nagasaki was bombed, with similar results. Meanwhile, on August 8 the Soviet Union honored the pledge it made at Yalta by declaring war on Japan. Despite all of this, with key ministers determined to fight to the bitter end, Japan's government remained deadlocked about whether to surrender. This caused Emperor Hirohito to take the unprecedented step of personally ordering the government to sue for peace. Japan offered to surrender on August 10, although on terms unacceptable to the Allies. After several days of negotiations, Japan accepted Allied terms based on the Potsdam Declaration and surrendered on August 14. The formal ceremony ending World War II took place on September 2, 1945.

Costs and Results

World War II led to the destruction of German Nazism and Japanese militarist authoritarianism, but at a staggering cost. The war's death toll, military and civilian, probably approached 60 million, including the six million Jews murdered in the Holocaust. An estimated 27 million people died in the Soviet Union alone, although some of those losses must be attributed to the callous and wasteful way Stalin's regime fought the war. From the Atlantic deep eastward far into the Soviet Union much of Europe was a wasteland, its cities strewn with rubble and millions of refugees on the move. In Asia, vast swaths of destruction stretched across China, the Philippines, and Japan itself. Of all the world's industrial powers, only the United States, despite having suffered 400,000 deaths between 1941 and 1945, emerged from the war largely undamaged and with the resources to begin a new era of prosperity.

The war ended the European era of dominance in international affairs. Defeated Germany was occupied by the United States, Britain, the Soviet Union, and France and no longer existed as an independent nation. Britain and France, albeit on the winning side, were exhausted, so much so that their colonial empires, along with those of other European states, soon would begin to crumble. Even more disturbing, the threat posed to Europe by one totalitarian power, Nazi Germany, had been defeated only to be replaced by the threat posed by another, the Soviet Union. The expansion of Soviet power into central Europe and the strength of local Communist forces in countries such as France and Italy raised the specter of Soviet domination of the continent. The only apparent counter to that threat was a non-European power, the United States. With Japan defeated and under American occupation, the United States also was the only counter to the expansion of Soviet influence in the Far East.

With the decline of Europe, the United States and the Soviet Union emerged as the world's dominant powers. As they built up their nuclear arsenals in the first postwar decade—the Soviet Union, having successfully spied on the Manhattan Project, exploded its first atomic bomb in 1949—they would be dubbed **superpowers**. Their global rivalry, in effect a struggle between democratic capitalism and totalitarian communism, would be known as the Cold War. The United States and the Soviet Union managed to avoid a catastrophic nuclear war with each other. But for more than four decades they and the rest of the world lived through a difficult time, a tense nuclear standoff punctuated by a series of crises and nonnuclear conflicts in which the superpowers sparred with each other indirectly. That "hard and bitter peace," as John F. Kennedy called it, was yet another painful legacy of World War II.[15]

Notes

1 Gerhard L. Weinberg, *Visions of Victory: The Hopes of Eight World War II Leaders* (New York: Cambridge University Press, 2005), 18. Weinberg is also the author of the monumental *A World at Arms: A Global History of World War II* (Cambridge: Cambridge University Press, 1994), the standard history of that war. A second edition of that book was published in 2005.

2 See Lucy S. Dawidowicz, *The War Against the Jews, 1933–1945* (New York: Holt, Rinehart, and Winston, 1975).

3 Quoted in Leni Yahil, *The Holocaust: The Fate of European Jewry* (New York: Oxford University Press, 1987), 115.

4 http://news.bbc.co.uk/onthisday/hi/dates/stories/september/30/newsid_3115000/3115476.stm, accessed June 27, 2017. The website is BBC: On This Day.

5 Quoted in Roland N. Stromberg, *Europe in the Twentieth Century*, 4th ed. (Upper Saddle River, NJ: Prentice Hall, 1997), 236.

6 See, for example, Richard Overy, *Russia's War: A History of the Soviet War Effort, 1941–1945* (New York: Penguin, 1997) and David M. Glantz and Jonathan House, *When Titans Clashed: How the Red Army Stopped Hitler* (Lawrence: University Press of Kansas, 1995).

7 The standard work on the Pacific War remains Ronald H. Spector, *The Eagle Against the Sun: The American War with Japan* (New York: Free Press, 1985). A recent outstanding work that covers the last year of that war, from grand strategy to the experiences of ordinary soldiers, sailors, and airmen who actually fought it, is Max Hastings, *Retribution: The Battle for Japan, 1944–45* (New York: Knopf, 2008).

8 Robin Neillands, *The Bomber War: The Allied Offensive Against Germany* (Woodstock and New York: Overlook Press, 2001), 389. See also Max Hastings, *Armageddon: The Battle for Germany, 1944–1945* (New York: Vintage, 2005), 289–337, especially 306–09. Hastings writes that until 1945 "there seems little difficulty in justifying the bomber offensive militarily and morally, as a matter of both desirability and necessity." Hastings is less certain with regard to 1945, but also observes, "We should recognize . . . that it is far easier to pass such judgments amid the relative tranquility of the twenty-first century that it seemed in 1945, when Hitler's nations was still doing its utmost to kill American and British people, together with millions of Nazi captives, by every means within its power."

9 See Werner Gruhl, *Imperial Japan's World War Two, 1931–1945*, (New Brunswick: Transaction Publishers, 2007) for an overview of how Japan fought the war.

10 Lucy S. Dawidowicz, *The Holocaust and the Historians* (Cambridge: Harvard University Press, 1981), 13.

11 Quoted in Yahil, *The Holocaust*, 255.

12 Robert S. Wistrich, *Hitler and the Holocaust* (New York: Modern Library, 2001), 196. This is the best short overview of the Holocaust and some of the key debates surrounding it.

13 The definitive work on the atomic bombing of Japan is Richard B. Frank, *Downfall: The End of the Japanese Imperial Empire* (New York: Random House, 1999). See also Robert James Maddox, *Weapons for Victory* (Columbia and London: University of Missouri Press, 1995), Edward J. Drea, *MacArthur's Ultra: Codebreaking and the War Against Japan, 1942–1945* (Lawrence: University Press of Kansas, 1992), D. M. Giangreco, *Hell to Pay: Operation DOWNFALL and the Invasion of Japan, 1945–1947* (Annapolis: Naval Institute Press, 2009), and Michal Kort, *The Columbia Guide to Hiroshima and the Bomb* (New York:

Columbia University Press, 2007). These works, and others, demonstrate that there is no basis for the charge made by some historians and commentators that the dropping of the bomb was motivated even in part by an intent to intimidate the Soviet Union with regard to postwar matters.

14 "The Potsdam Declaration," July 26, 1945, in Michael Kort, *The Columbia Guide to Hiroshima and the Bomb* (New York: Columbia: University Press, 2007), 226–27.

15 "Inauguration Speech of President John F. Kennedy, January 20, 1961." Available online. www.jfklibrary.org/Historical+Resources/Archives/Reference+Desk/Speeches/JFK/003POF03Inaugural01201961.htm, accessed May 29, 2010

Suggested Readings

Davidowicz, Lucy S. *The Holocaust and the Historians*. Cambridge: Harvard University Press, 1981.

———. *The War Against the Jews, 1933–1945*. New York: Holt, Rinehart, and Winston, 1975.

Drea, Edward J. *MacArthur's Ultra: Codebreaking and the War Against Japan, 1942–1945*. Lawrence: University Press of Kansas, 1992.

Dziewanowski, M. K. *War at Any Price: World War II in Europe*. 2nd ed. Englewood Cliffs, NJ: Prentice Hall, 1991.

Fischer, Klaus P. *Nazi Germany: A New History*. New York: Continuum, 1995.

Frank, Richard B. *Downfall: The End of the Japanese Imperial Empire*. New York: Random House, 1999.

Giangreco, D. M. *Hell to Pay: Operation DOWNFALL and the Invasion of Japan, 1945–1947*. Annapolis: Naval Institute Press, 2009.

Glantz, David M. and Jonathan House, *When Titans Clashed: How the Red Army Stopped Hitler*. Lawrence: University Press of Kansas, 1995.

Gruhl, Werner. *Imperial Japan's World War Two, 1931–1945*. New Brunswick: Transaction Publishers, 2007.

Hastings, Max. *Armageddon: The Battle for Germany, 1944–1945*. New York: Vintage, 2005.

———. *Retribution: The Battle for Japan, 1944–45*. New York: Knopf, 2008.

Kort, Michael. *The Columbia Guide to Hiroshima and the Bomb*. New York: Columbia University Press, 2007.

Lipstadt, Deborah. *Denying the Holocaust: The Growing Assault on Truth and Memory*. New York: Plume, 1993.

Lyons, Michael J. *World War II: A Short History*. 4th ed. Upper Saddle River, NJ: Pearson, 2004.

Maddox, Robert James. *Weapons for Victory*. Columbia and London: University of Missouri Press, 1995.

Neillands, Robin. *The Bomber War: The Allied Offensive Against Germany*. Woodstock and New York: Overlook Press, 2001.

Overy, Richard. *Russia's War: A History of the Soviet War Effort, 1941–1945*. New York: Penguin, 1997.

Spector, Ronald H. *The Eagle Against the Sun: The American War with Japan*. New York: Free Press, 1985.

Stromberg, Roland N. *Europe in the Twentieth Century*, 4th ed. Upper Saddle River, NJ: Prentice Hall, 1997.

Weinberg, Gerhard L. *A World at Arms: A Global History of World War II.* Cambridge: Cambridge University Press, 1994.

———. *Visions of Victory: The Hopes of Eight World War II Leaders.* New York: Cambridge University Press, 2005.

Wistrich, Robert S. *Hitler and the Holocaust.* New York: Modern Library, 2001.

Yahil, Leni. *The Holocaust: The Fate of European Jewry.* New York: Oxford University Press, 1987.

21 The Cold War

Benjamin E. Varat

Key Terms

Berlin Crisis, buffer states, containment, Cuban Missile Crisis, decolonization, détente, hydrogen bomb, International Monetary Fund, Korean War, "mutually assured destruction," proxy wars, sectarian violence, United Nations, World Bank

The Grand Alliance was a marriage of necessity, forced into existence by the threat of Adolf Hitler. The Soviet Union (USSR) had shared an enemy and nothing else with Britain and the United States. The ideological conflict between them was so irreconcilable that even during the darkest days of the war, disagreements and mistrust existed between the ostensible allies. While the combined efforts of these three nations defeated the threat of fascism, their victory left little optimism that the communist and capitalist worlds could work together after the war. In light of this, it is hardly surprising that a dominant feature of the following decades was the tense, ideologically driven struggle known as the Cold War, which affected politics, economic development, and social stability around the globe.

Origins of the Cold War

We can trace the origin of this struggle to the fundamentally incompatible postwar priorities of the United States and Great Britain, on the one hand, and the Soviet Union, on the other. While Churchill and Roosevelt considered German recovery necessary for a larger European recovery, Stalin wanted Germany permanently weakened so that it could never again threaten the Soviet Union. While the democratic powers anticipated postwar freedom for the countries of Eastern Europe, the Soviet leader had no intention of loosening his military control of the areas he was seizing from the Nazis. Stalin planned to keep them as Soviet-dominated "**buffer states**," a line of weak states that would separate the Soviet Union from the bourgeois-capitalist West and serve to protect the Soviet Union from Western aggression. Most fundamentally, the two systems of capitalism and communism contained ideologically opposed visions of what the postwar world should look like. The result was a divided Europe: a western half recovering from the war with the help of American investment and military power, and an eastern half controlled by the closed, dark world of the Soviet Union.

During the last stages of the war, Soviet, British, and American leaders arrived at many general agreements concerning what would happen after the war ended. Yet few of these were specific, and most of the tough decisions were put off until later. When the Nazis finally surrendered in May, 1945, the Red Army held all of Eastern Europe between the Soviet Union and the middle of Germany, while Anglo-American forces controlled most of Western Europe. The eastern part of Germany, which includes the capital of Berlin, was under Soviet occupation, while the western parts and half of Berlin were held by American, British, and French forces.

Neither side was eager to loosen its hold on these territories. The Potsdam Conference in July largely confirmed this division of Europe, including the partition of Germany, when Churchill and new American President Harry Truman grudgingly agreed to some of Stalin's demands. Needing to give a positive public spin on the conference, Anglo-American representatives played up Stalin's statements about free elections, while no one discussed the potential long-term significance of having two massive armies each occupying half of a devastated Europe. Thus, the foundations of the Cold War were established even before Japan surrendered.

Soviet-American difficulties did not yet, however, dim the optimism felt by many that a better world could be rebuilt on the ashes of the old one. Several new organizations appeared at the end of World War II that seemed capable of creating this new world: the **United Nations** (UN), **the International Monetary Fund** (IMF), and the **World Bank**. Even as the victorious powers met in Potsdam, delegates from across the globe gathered in San Francisco to put the finishing touches on the UN Charter and launch the replacement for the defunct and ineffective League of Nations. Delegates hoped that this new world government would act as a forum in which grievances and disagreements could be aired and equitable compromises constructed, so that diplomacy rather than war would rule human affairs. The charter embraced the principles of cooperation in international law, international security, economic development, social progress, human rights, and the achievement of world peace.[1] The UN's General Assembly, where most debate took place, had representatives from all recognized sovereign states, while much of the organization's decision-making capability lay in a smaller Security Council.

Besides the hopes pinned to the UN, many world leaders also believed two new economic institutions, the IMF and World Bank, would assist in preventing war in the future by ensuring economic stability and cooperation on a global scale. Economists from dozens of nations had met in Bretton Woods, New Hampshire in 1944 and laid the foundations for these organizations with the Bretton Woods Agreements that contained guidelines concerning international trade and currency valuations. The intention was to facilitate trade and avoid the sorts of monetary chaos that had weakened democracies, prolonged the Great Depression and contributed to the rise of fascism. The IMF and World Bank would provide

The United Nations

The United Nations is an intergovernmental international organization created by treaty on October 24, 1945 for the purpose of promoting permanent international peace. Conceived of during World War II as the successor to the failed League of Nations, the UN consists of five separate bodies, two of which, the General Assembly and the Security Council, handle issues related to international conflict. The General Assembly, consisting of 193 countries, is the primary body for discussing international disputes. Although the General Assembly can pass resolutions, they are non-binding. Binding decision-making authority resides in the fifteen-member Security Council. Of these fifteen, ten are rotating, chosen on a regional basis for two-year terms. The remaining five—the United States, Russia, China, Great Britain, and France—are permanent members, each of whom possesses an absolute veto over any resolution up for vote in the Security Council. The other three bodies handle economic, judicial, and information-gathering responsibilities, while a number of other agencies within the UN deal with more specialized concerns such as health, agriculture, and education. UN member countries frequently contribute military troops for humanitarian activities, including peacekeeping in regions prone to violence and political instability.

financial assistance, through credit and debt restructuring, to struggling economies in order to promote overall global economic development, which they hoped would encourage peace and stability throughout the world.

These earnest initiatives toward international cooperation enjoyed uneven success in the postwar era. The IMF and World Bank helped strengthen and develop the global economy, but only the non-communist portion, as the Soviet Union and its Eastern European satellites refused to join either body. The UN experienced a similarly mixed outcome. On the one hand, it has provided a frame-work for international cooperation on issues of health, education, and economic development that has undoubtedly saved and enriched the lives of millions, especially children in the developing world. On the other hand, the power of individual Security Council members, which included the United States and the Soviet Union, to veto the General Assembly's initiatives eviscerated the UN's ability to influence, much less settle, contentious issues connected to the Cold War. Unfortunately, most important world issues of the postwar era were central to this struggle.

The essentials of the Cold War slowly came into focus in the remainder of 1945 and early 1946 as Soviet-American relations deteriorated further. Stalin continued to consolidate his hold over Eastern Europe through intimidation and violence. Occasionally he allowed elections and then nullified the results when local communist parties received little support; some promised elections never took place at all. In other places, such as in Iran, Greece, and Turkey, provocative Soviet actions increased diplomatic tension. Mutual mistrust dominated the relationship between the former allies, and from that point on, virtually every move each side made was regarded as suspicious by the other side.[2]

Containment

Stalin shocked the world in early February 1946 when he addressed the Soviet people to tell them that he expected another war: a massive conflict between the communists and capitalists that would be started by the United States and its allies. In March, Churchill gave the Western response, the strongly-worded Iron Curtain Speech in which he explicitly spoke of a Soviet-enforced division of Europe. Churchill's pronouncement brought into high relief the serious disagreements that were evolving into the Cold War. Though it was clear that there was a fundamental clash of interests, Stalin puzzled the leaders of the Western democracies. What were his goals? Did he intend to act aggressively, like a Hitler, or would he work more subtly, behind the scenes, to undermine the capitalist democracies? The most important question, after Stalin's February speech, was whether he wanted World War III.

Worried that defeating Hitler had simply opened the door to Stalin's conquest of Europe, Truman sought a concrete strategy to deal with the apparent communist threat. To do so, Truman turned to George Kennan, a long-time American diplomat and historian specializing in Russia. Kennan linked Stalin's apparent paranoia and his takeover of Eastern Europe to a combination of the historical Russian concern with protection from invasion and his belief in an inevitable final battle between the forces of capitalism and communism, which the latter would win. By interpreting Soviet behavior through this lens of defensiveness and a long-term certainty of victory over the capitalist world, Kennan argued that the Cold War would not turn hot. Instead, it would be a battle fought through propaganda, the ability of each economic system to provide for people, and the strength of each superpower's allies. To win the Cold War, Kennan suggested a policy of **containment**, a grand strategy designed to prevent the geographic, political, and ideological expansion of an enemy. Kennan called on the United States to build alliances with countries along the periphery of the Soviet sphere through the provision of American economic aid and political support. This assistance would strengthen these countries, prevent the growth of communism within them, and demonstrate to the world the superiority of democracy and capitalism; Soviet attempts to expand their ideological reach would fail. Kennan was confident that containment would send the Soviet Union into the "dustbin of history" and bring the Cold War to a peaceful, successful end.[3]

Truman accepted Kennan's containment concept, which remained the foundation of American Cold War policy until the conflict itself ended in 1989. As the world's only relatively intact capitalist industrial power, the United States had the means to provide enormous economic and political support to the war-devastated European countries west of the Iron Curtain. The most important

American initiative in this direction was the 1947 Marshall Plan, which supplied billions of reconstruction dollars to the democratic governments of Western Europe. These commitments demonstrated that the United States would not return to isolationism, as it had done so disastrously after World War I, but intended to protect and support Western Europe during its time of rebuilding.

The Marshall Plan proved a remarkable success, allowing the shattered economies of Western Europe to rebuild their manufacturing capacities and put their people back to work. By the time the program ended in 1952, most of Western Europe had begun an economic expansion that would last nearly thirty years. Not only did such aid stimulate global economic growth and development, but, as Kennan had foreseen, it also undermined support for communist parties in these resurgent European democracies, which dashed Stalin's hopes of expanding communist influence in Western Europe. The Marshall Plan represented a major triumph for American foreign policy by not only revitalizing the global economy, but also strengthening democracy, which at the outset of World War II had seemed in danger of extinction, worldwide.[4]

Divided Germany, which included a divided Berlin, provided a stark example of the fundamental differences between postwar capitalist and communist societies.[5] While Marshall Plan money stimulated rapid rebuilding and recovery in the three western zones, Stalin pillaged and impoverished the Soviet-controlled eastern zone. The Soviet dictator, who feared the return of a strong Germany, provoked a confrontation in mid-1948 known as the **Berlin Crisis**, when he cut off road access to Berlin in violation of the Yalta agreements. When France, Britain, and the United States refused to abandon the free citizens in the western part of Berlin and flew in supplies for them, Stalin backed down. Shortly thereafter, the Western powers formed the nation of West Germany, which turned into a thriving democracy with a powerful industrial base. Meanwhile, in the East, the German Democratic Republic became a Soviet-dominated police state that offered its citizens neither freedom nor prosperity.

Polarization

Despite these early successes of containment, Kennan's emphasis on economic and political support for American allies soon proved too passive for American policymakers and public opinion, which became increasingly fearful of communist hordes tearing across the globe in an orgy of slaughter and destruction. These fears and the overheated rhetoric that stoked them soon changed containment into a military-centered doctrine premised on providing military assistance and even American troops to countries seemingly threatened by communist takeover. The first hints of this change came in April 1949 at the end of the Berlin crisis, with the creation of the North Atlantic Treaty Organization (NATO), a military alliance binding together the United States, Canada, and Western Europe. NATO served as the template for a series of additional American-led security alliances that eventually spanned the globe from Latin America to the Middle East to Asia. A few years later, the Soviets constructed their own alliance, the Warsaw Pact, which essentially placed the armies of Eastern Europe directly under Soviet Red Army control and left Europe divided between two powerful military coalitions.

By 1950, other developments strengthened the sense of a world barreling toward World War III: the USSR developed nuclear warheads of their own, Mao Zedong's Communists seized control of China, and the **Korean War** erupted between a communist supported North and a UN-supported South. In the last case, President Truman committed hundreds of thousands of American troops to a conflict that dragged on for three years to an inconclusive end. Meanwhile, Senator Joseph McCarthy led a highly public and destructive "witch hunt" for communist spies and traitors within the American government. Stalin's death in 1953 allowed for a truce in the Korean conflict and removed a volatile element from the tense international situation, but did little to lessen the mutual mistrust between the two "superpowers."[6]

By the mid-1950s, containment had evolved into a rigid set of policies based on the threat of military force instead of the promise of economic aid and political freedom. American leaders, preoccupied with stopping the spread of global communism, began to actively promote and arm anticommunist governments throughout the world. Simultaneously, the new Soviet leader, Nikita Khrushchev, put together a global Soviet-led network to battle what he called "capitalist imperialism," sending military advisers, weapons, and money to sympathetic political movements around the world. The post-World War II world provided many areas of fertile ground for this ideologically driven conflict between the superpowers, nowhere more so than in the many newly independent nations that were emerging from decades of colonial rule.

Decolonization

Before and during World War II, nationalist movements of various sorts had emerged in many colonial territories to demand freedom from their European masters. The postwar situation provided nationalists with opportunities to make national self-determination a reality, as the exhausted nations of Europe generally lacked both the resources and the will to successfully hold onto their colonies. But over the next three decades, **decolonization**, the process through which the dependent territories freed themselves from imperial control, did not unfold as anyone had foreseen.[7]

Decolonization dramatically changed societies across the developing world. Self-rule meant that political control passed from the imperial powers into indigenous (native) hands. After decades of being exploited and living as second-class citizens, the peoples of the least developed parts of the world believed that they could determine their own future, one full of peace and prosperity. A boundless optimism arose, born in the belief that the national unity forged through combating and then defeating imperialism would remain intact and rocket these new countries into the modern, industrial world.

With some exceptions, however, this optimism proved terribly misplaced. Regardless of whether decolonization occurred relatively peacefully, as with the

British withdrawal from India, or after a brutal war, such as those that forced the French out of Vietnam and Algeria, in almost all cases the exit of the imperial nation left a power vacuum that various ill-prepared local groups tried to fill. Rather than a smooth and gentle passage into the modern world, many of these new states experienced destructive combinations of foreign domination, political corruption, ethnic hatred, and superpower interference. These factors combined to work against development and often stalled significant progress for years in these new nations. Much of the social change of the Cold War period, therefore, was not due to the modernization process, but resulted from authoritarian governments, political violence, and civil wars, all of which forced people to adapt to a world far different from the old colonial structure. Colonialism in some sense was over, but in its place arose a set of problems that would haunt much of the less-developed world even after the end of the Cold War.

Africa, in particular, suffered acutely from the decolonization process. Throughout much of the continent, the phenomenon of neocolonialism arose, whereby the former colonial power continued to exert economic control over its old territorial dependency. Europeans saw little reason to change the unequal economic relationships of colonialism, since they still needed the mineral and agricultural resources of the less developed world to fuel their own industries, as had been the case since the Industrial Revolution in the 1800s. Although European governments and corporations often provided substantial money and technical assistance to former colonies, much of it went into modernizing the process of extracting natural resources rather than redistributing land, mechanizing farming, or developing an industrial base. Foreign aid often came as loans from the former colonial powers, organizations such as the IMF and World Bank, or other industrialized nations. Much of this money went into the military, badly planned development projects, or corrupt politicians, which frequently led to crippling debt that led to even more economic dependency. The net result was that many former colonies continued to act as suppliers of cheap natural resources for the industrialized countries while remaining dependent on them for economic assistance.

Besides the serious problems caused by neocolonialism, many of these new nations, again especially in Africa, had borders that rarely conformed to neat ethnic divisions and often lacked even the beginning of a civil society. New leaders in Africa, therefore, faced a daunting development task and most proved unable to establish the political, economic, and social institutions that could accomplish it. When governments failed to meet even the basic needs of their ethnically diverse, poverty-stricken populations, struggles for power ensued. Since few of these nations possessed legal and political outlets for protest, power struggles often became violent and divided the country along ethnic, linguistic, and religious fault lines. Frequently military dictatorships were the only successful means of restoring order, but such governments were usually more interested in stealing for themselves development aid and profits from the export of natural resources, instead of building modern, economically independent societies.

This brutal mix of economic dependency, incompetent and corrupt leadership, and the lack of any stable civil society, left these countries highly vulnerable to outside interference, which arrived almost everywhere in the form of the Cold

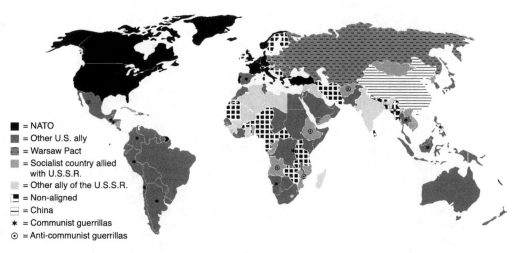

= NATO
= Other U.S. ally
= Warsaw Pact
= Socialist country allied
  with U.S.S.R.
= Other ally of the U.S.S.R.
= Non-aligned
= China
★ = Communist guerrillas
⊙ = Anti-communist guerrillas

Map 21.1 Proxy wars, 1945–1989

War. Soviet and American efforts to gain as many allies as possible frequently reduced many of these nations into little more than pawns in the superpower struggle. Wars of decolonization morphed into **proxy wars**, as the superpowers avoided all-out war between them by choosing sides in the colonial conflict. In proxy wars, each superpower provided economic and military support to its ally, but never engaged the other superpower directly. Where such a conflict resulted in a communist victory, this exacerbated the myriad development problems further. Countries as diverse as Cambodia, Angola, and Nicaragua tried to follow the Soviet or Chinese communist models of industrialization, ignoring how disastrous both had been. This outcome frequently disrupted whatever economic development already existed and set back the industrialization process by decades. American-backed anti-communist groups in many of these countries added further chaos. In sum, the Cold War greatly exacerbated the problems underdeveloped countries already faced from their colonial legacy.

Some glimmers of hope existed, notably in Asia and Latin America, where countries had a somewhat longer experience with self-rule and ethnic divisions were less intense, but substantial progress eluded much of the developing world during the Cold War. When this conflict ended forty-five years after World War II, many of these least developed countries had advanced little since they had thrown off colonial control decades earlier.

Deterrence and Détente

By the 1960s, the Iron Curtain marked a stark divide between the communist and capitalist halves of Europe, and the Berlin Wall that physically separated the former German capital had become a potent symbol of the global ideological struggle. While "proxy wars" continued to rage outside of Europe, the two coalitions stared

Image 21.1 "Checkpoint Charlie," at the border of East and West Berlin, 1960s
© Universal Art Archive / Alamy

at each other in Europe across barbed wire. Despite the obvious mutual hostility and ideological incompatibility, one intriguing element of the Cold War was the fact that the Soviets and Americans never directly took up arms against each other. Despite Stalin's grim warning in 1946, World War III never happened.

The unlikely "peace" of the Cold War came largely from an even more unlikely source: the nuclear bomb. Hiroshima and Nagasaki had illuminated the awesome and horrifying power of atomic weapons. Once the Cold War began, a nuclear arms race ensued, resulting by the early 1950s in American and Soviet scientists developing the **hydrogen bomb**, a weapon at least 500 times more powerful than the atomic bombs of 1945. Unlike the single fission reaction of the atomic bomb, the hydrogen bomb goes through two internal stages—a fission reaction leading to a fusion reaction and then a final fission reaction—before detonation. Although the nuclear arms race drained Soviet and American coffers and sometimes panicked their populations, superpower possession of nuclear weapons led, somewhat ironically, to a certain stability in the Cold War. This was largely due to the shocking simplicity of the nuclear equation: the destruction of Washington would ensure the destruction of Moscow, and vice versa. No rational leader would contemplate such a tradeoff. In this way, peace was guaranteed by deterrence, the certainty that any use of nuclear weapons would lead to an annihilating counterstrike. The Soviets and Americans specifically built "second strike capability," nuclear weapons designed to survive an initial attack that could then be launched against the attacker's cities. "Victory" in a nuclear war would be impossible, or at least so costly as to be pointless. This situation of nuclear stalemate became codified in the 1960s under the moniker **"mutually assured destruction,"** which had the so-appropriate acronym, MAD.[8]

Fear of a nuclear holocaust did not, however, prevent one side or the other from making serious miscalculations. The two superpowers came perilously close to nuclear war in the **Cuban Missile Crisis** of October 1962. Nikita Khrushchev rashly precipitated the crisis by secretly putting nuclear weapons in communist Cuba in an attempt to establish a relatively even Soviet-American nuclear balance, which at that time decisively favored the United States. President John Kennedy, upon learning of the missiles, publicly proclaimed that the United States would not allow them to stay in Cuba, and would take them out by force if necessary. For several tense days, the world held its collective breath in expectation of a nuclear exchange that might dwarf the damage caused by World War II. Khrushchev, however, finally recognized the folly of his actions and, fearful that nuclear war was imminent, agreed to remove the missiles. The Cold War remained cold.[9]

Hot wars did occur during the Cold War although, as mentioned above, never with the direct military involvement of both superpowers. In two cases, Vietnam and Afghanistan, conflicts in developing nations compelled the United States and Soviet Union, respectively, to directly deploy substantial numbers of their own troops. In each case, this intervention resulted in a long war that was costly and unpopular, and disastrous for both the superpowers and the nations where the fighting took place.[10]

By the time the United States sent troops into Vietnam in 1965, the Vietnamese already had experienced decades of French colonial rule, a brutal Japanese occupation during World War II, and an extensive war of independence against France that ended in 1954. That year, superpower maneuvering split Vietnam into a communist North and an American-backed South. This division precipitated a decade of civil war before American President Lyndon Johnson decided that containing communism required a massive military commitment to South Vietnam. Eight years of US military involvement accomplished little beyond further destruction of Vietnam and the death of millions of Vietnamese and thousands of American soldiers. Although President Richard Nixon claimed a victory for democracy when he withdrew the last American troops in 1973, North Vietnam conquered the South and reunified Vietnam under communist rule in 1975. To the surprise of some, North Vietnam's victory meant little in the Cold War; the "fall" of South Vietnam, along with Laos and Cambodia, to communism resulted in more terrible years for all three countries, but communism spread no further.

America's full-blown intervention in Vietnam, however, had caused serious social and political instability at home while giving the Soviet Union the time to close the substantial "missile gap" that had led to Khrushchev's dangerous gamble in the Cuban Missile Crisis. By the late 1960s, at a tremendous cost, the Soviet Union achieved approximate nuclear parity with the United States. The mutual recognition that the arms race could not continue led to successes at the negotiating table and ushered in a period of reduced tensions, known as the **détente** era of the Cold War.

Détente proved temporary, lasting a little more than a decade from late 1968 until December 1979. At that point, the Soviets, who had apparently learned nothing from the US misadventure in Southeast Asia, jumped into their own quagmire when they sent one hundred thousand Red Army troops into Afghanistan. This mountainous nation, which bordered several central Asian Soviet Republics, had experienced many difficulties over the previous century, including interference by Britain and Russia before World War I and a series of civil wars thereafter. Despite a few years of stability after World War II, a stagnant economy and ethnic divisions slowly undermined societal cohesion until a full-fledged civil war finally broke out in 1978 when a Soviet-backed Marxist party took power. When the Afghan communist regime appeared on the verge of being overthrown in late 1979, the Soviet leader, Leonid Brezhnev, sent Soviet troops in to prevent it. The Soviets fought changing coalitions of guerrilla armies in a region where the difficult terrain nullified the Red Army's advantages in military power. Meanwhile, covert American aid supported Afghan rebels, many of whom were Islamic fundamentalists who abhorred the official atheism of communism. The 1980 election in the United States of Ronald Reagan, a hardcore anticommunist, expanded US involvement in the Afghan resistance movement and other proxy conflicts around the globe, leading to ever-greater defense spending by both superpowers.

Vietnam and Afghanistan highlighted a basic Cold War dilemma the superpowers faced, the dilemma articulated by Kennan at the dawn of the conflict: How did one win a Cold War? With no actual fighting between the two main combatants, the struggle had to play out in the hearts and minds of the world population. Prestige mattered more than numbers of tanks, and propaganda was as powerful as nuclear weapons. As the Cold War stretched across the globe, the United States and the Soviet Union found themselves entangled in and often dramatically complicating local problems that had little to do with superpower security, communism, or democracy.

Gorbachev and the End of the Cold War

Ultimately, these foreign entanglements proved far more costly to the Soviet Union than the United States. By the early 1980s, the Soviet economy was stagnant, barely able to provide even the basic necessities for its people. Yet despite the massive economic and social problems facing the USSR by 1985, Mikhail Gorbachev, who took power that year as General Secretary of the Communist Party of the Soviet Union, perceived them as solvable. The fifty-four year old Gorbachev, much younger and more vigorous than his predecessors, attacked them with energy. He spent his first four years in power trying to make the Soviet Union a more open, prosperous society through internal reforms, reduction of Cold War tensions, and ending the occupation of Afghanistan. It was a noble, well-meant effort. It also destroyed the Soviet Union.[11]

Gorbachev's reforms at home, most notably his willingness to allow a more open society, undermined communist power in Eastern Europe, where most citizens loathed Soviet domination of their countries. Gorbachev's decision to countenance criticism and change in the Soviet Union raised a fundamental question: If the Soviet people could question their government, why couldn't the Czechs or Hungarians or East Germans do the same?

Protests against communist rule began in Eastern Europe late in 1988. By early 1989, Gorbachev made it known to the communist leadership of Eastern Europe that he would not intervene in their internal affairs, in contrast to the iron hand frequently used by earlier Soviet leaders. Without the Red Army to back them, communists quickly lost control of the situation in Poland and Hungary, resulting in open borders and free elections in each state. The demands for freedom spread to the other Warsaw Pact nations over the course of 1989, even into East Germany, where in November celebrating throngs dismantled the ultimate symbol of the Cold War, the Berlin Wall. Eastern European governments recognized the futility of clamping down on public demands for political freedoms. One by one, they liberalized their political systems, allowing for the creation of multiparty states with free elections. These developments, in turn, encouraged the various non-Russian peoples of the Soviet Union to demand states of their own, unchained from Moscow's control. The Union of Soviet Socialist Republics soon crumbled into a collection of separate states and by the end of 1991 it had ceased to exist.

Gorbachev's actions ensured that the Cold War ended peacefully. He deserves tremendous praise for this outcome, but ultimately, he failed in his own task: to make the Soviet Union work better. His reforms at home became increasingly frantic and incoherent as both the extent of the problems and the Soviet people's hatred of the regime became clear. This peaceful outcome to the Cold War with the implosion of the Soviet Union neatly mirrored Kennan's original hopes for containment, although the costs, especially human ones, turned out to be far greater than he had ever anticipated. Nonetheless, the demise of the Soviet Union and the end of the Cold War seemed to complete a chapter in history, one that had created a great deal of misery, but undoubtedly could have resulted in so much more.

By the early 1990s, many observers hoped that the end of this communist-capitalist ideological struggle might usher in a new era of global peace. Such optimism, however, was not entirely warranted. **Sectarian violence**, a form of conflict generally based in religious or ideological divisions within a single community or nation, already present during the Cold War, emerged with ever greater ferocity from the Middle East to the former Yugoslavia to central Africa. Meanwhile, the pace of modernization, for so long stunted in much of the least developed parts of the world, began to quicken, though at an uneven rate, further contributing to international and domestic tensions. As the new millennium dawned, it became clear that few societies could effectively escape involvement in global issues, and that the fates of the diverse populations around the world were becoming linked ever more tightly together.

Notes

1 "Charter of the United Nations," *United Nations Website*, www.un.org/en/documents/charter/intro.shtml, accessed September 10, 2010.
2 For an excellent introduction to the Cold War see William Keylor, *The Twentieth Century World and Beyond: An International History Since 1900*, 6th ed. (Oxford: Oxford University Press, 2011). Also see John Lewis Gaddis, *We Now Know: Rethinking Cold War History* (Oxford: Oxford University Press, 1997), 1–25.
3 The best source for understanding containment is John Lewis Gaddis, *Strategies of Containment: A Critical Appraisal of Postwar American National Security Policy* (New York: Oxford University Press, 1982), 25–53.
4 The starting point for understanding the Marshall Plan is Michael Hogan, *The Marshall Plan: America, Britain, and the Reconstruction of Europe, 1947–1952* (Cambridge: Cambridge University Press, 1987).
5 Henry Ashby Turner, Jr., *Germany from Partition to Reunification* (New Haven: Yale University Press, 1992), 22–32; Tony Judt, *Postwar: A History of Europe Since 1945* (New York: Penguin Press, 2005), 45–51.
6 Jones, *Crucible of Power*, 253–81.
7 On decolonization as a process, see John Springhal, *Decolonization Since 1945: The Collapse of European Overseas Empires* (London: Palgrave MacMillan, 2001). For a keen understanding of how the Cold War impacted the post-colonial world see Odd Arne Westad, *The Global Cold War* (Cambridge: Cambridge University Press, 2007). Also see: Hal Brands, *Latin America's Cold War* (Cambridge, Massachusetts: Harvard University Press, 2010).
8 Robert L. O'Connell, *Of Arms and Men: A History of War, Weapons, and Aggression* (New York: Oxford University Press, 1989), 296–303.
9 Aleksandr Fursenko and Timothy Naftali, *Khrushchev's Cold War: The Inside Story of an American Adversary* (New York: W. W. Norton, 2006), 465–92.
10 Stanley Karnow's comprehensive examination of the Vietnam War is the standard general history of the conflict: Stanley Karnow, *Vietnam: A History*, 2nd ed. (New York, New York: Penguin Books, 1997). For the war in Afghanistan see Vladislav M. Zubok, *A Failed Empire: The Soviet Union in the Cold War from Stalin to Gorbachev* (Chapel Hill: University of North Carolina Press, 2009).
11 Zubok provides a thorough analysis of Gorbachev's hopes and failures. Zubok, *A Failed Empire*, 265–335.

Suggested Readings

Applebaum, Anne. *Iron Curtain: The Crushing of Eastern Europe, 1944–1956*. New York: Doubleday, Random House, Inc., 2012.

Brands, Hal. *Latin America's Cold War*. Cambridge, Massachusetts: Harvard University Press, 2010.

Conquest, Robert. *Reflections on a Ravaged Century*. New York: W. W. Norton., 2000.

Dinan, Desmond. *Europe Recast: History of European Union*. Boulder: Lynne Rienner Publishers, 2004.

Fursenko, Aleksandr and Timothy Naftali. *Khrushchev's Cold War: The Inside Story of an American Adversary*. New York: W. W. Norton & Company, 2006.

Gaddis, John Lewis. *Strategies of Containment: A Critical Appraisal of Postwar American National Security Policy*. New York: Oxford University Press, 1982.

———. *We Now Know: Rethinking Cold War History*. Oxford: Oxford University Press, 1997.

Haynes, James Earl and Harvey Klehr. *Venona: Decoding Soviet Espionage in America.* New Haven: Yale University Press, 1999.

Hogan, Michael. *The Marshall Plan: America, Britain, and the Reconstruction of Europe, 1947–1952.* Cambridge: Cambridge University Press, 1987.

Hook, Steven W. and John Spanier. *American Foreign Policy Since World War II.* 20th ed. Thousand Oaks, California: CQ Press, Sage Publications, Inc., 2016.

Jacobs, Seth. *Cold War Mandarin: Ngo Dinh Diem and the Origins of America's War in Vietnam, 1950–1963.* New York: Rowman & Littlefield Publishers, Inc., 2006.

———. *The Universe Unraveling: American Foreign Policy in Cold War Laos.* Ithaca, New York: Cornell University Press, 2012.

Jones, Howard. *Crucible of Power: A History of American Foreign Relations from 1897.* 2nd ed. Lanham, MD: Rowman & Littlefield, 2008.

Judt, Tony. *Postwar: A History of Europe Since 1945.* New York: The Penguin Press, 2005.

Karnow, Stanley. *Vietnam: A History.* 2nd ed. New York: Penguin Books, 1997.

Kempe, Frederick. *Berlin 1961: Kennedy, Khrushchev, and the Most Dangerous Place on Earth.* New York: G. P. Putnam's Sons, 2011.

Keylor, William. *The Twentieth Century World and Beyond: An International History Since 1900.* 6th ed. Oxford: Oxford University Press, 2011.

Kinzer, Stephen. *The Brothers: John Foster Dulles, Allen Dulles, And Their Secret World War.* New York: Times Books, Henry Holt and Company, LLC, 2013.

Kort, Michael. *The Soviet Colossus: History and Aftermath.* 7th ed. Armonk, NY: M. E. Sharpe, 2010.

Lowe, Keith. *Savage Continent: Europe in the Aftermath of World War II.* New York: St. Martin's Press, 2012.

Merriman, John. *A History of Modern Europe: From the French Revolution to the Present*, Vol. 2. 3rd ed. New York: W. W. Norton, 2010.

O'Connell, Robert L. *Of Arms and Men: A History of War, Weapons, and Aggression.* New York: Oxford University Press, 1989.

Springhal, John. *Decolonization Since 1945: The Collapse of European Overseas Empires.* London: Palgrave MacMillan, 2001.

Turner, Henry Ashby. *Germany from Partition to Reunification.* New Haven: Yale University Press, 1992.

Westad, Odd Arne. *The Global Cold War.* Cambridge: Cambridge University Press, 2007.

Zubok, Vladislav M. *A Failed Empire: The Soviet Union in the Cold War from Stalin to Gorbachev.* Chapel Hill: University of North Carolina Press, 2009.

22 Globalization and Social Change

John McGrath

Key Terms

division of labor, global market volatility, globalization, neoimperialism, terrorism, transnational corporations

During the late twentieth century and the end of the Cold War, the term **"globalization"** began to appear frequently in connection with all sorts of issues and developments. By the 1990s, observers were noting that world societies were becoming linked in so many different ways that it seemed as if the world was shrinking: diffusion and acculturation were taking place so regularly and rapidly that national borders had less and less relevance to the events taking place within them. Even before the end of the century, it was clear that the era of globalization had arrived.

In one sense, globalization represents the logical culmination of processes that began deep in the historical record, when separate societies first began to interact, resulting in both direct and indirect exchanges of goods and ideas. Obviously, some societies engaged in cross-cultural exchange more than others, but even 500 years ago, all but the most isolated societies in the world were being significantly affected by some other society in one way or another. This often took place gradually, but sometimes it happened with an awesome suddenness and force that transformed or even destroyed existing societies.

The modernization of Western society contributed in a major way to this process. Though Western Europeans were not the first to engage in trans-oceanic trade, the trade links and colonial systems that they began to create in the sixteenth century formed and maintained lasting connections among many previously isolated societies, and this intensified over the course of the Early Modern Period. The Industrial Revolution enabled European nation-states to develop formal empires, as growing industrial economies created both a demand for far-flung resources and the technological means to communicate, travel, and conquer. By the late nineteenth and early twentieth centuries, energized by political competition and nationalist ideologies, European nations were absorbing some of the remotest corners of the world into dependent parts of their colonial networks. Even after the Second World War, this process of international interconnection continued, despite the independence of many former colonies. The Cold War collision between capitalism and communism only encouraged the two superpowers to expand their "spheres of influence" over other nations throughout the world, through what has sometimes been called **neoimperialism**, a domination of their political and economic systems without formally absorbing them. Meanwhile, further advances in transportation and communication continued to permit more frequent contact among different world societies.

While the rate of diffusion and acculturation unquestionably accelerated throughout the course of the last century, it did not amount to what most would call "globalization" until late in the twentieth century. Only then did certain key developments transform the ongoing process of internationalization into something qualitatively, not just quantitatively, different. Globalization has become both a process and a consequence of social change, on an international scale, that has gained in momentum over time. And while we can clearly see globalization as a product of modernization, globalization has also become the chief means by which modernization is now taking place around the world.

Globalization as Economic Change

It is difficult to come up with a precise definition of what globalization is, because it has become a thorough process of systemic change that affects all aspects of societies. Many who study it focus on the economic aspects, while others look at how globalization affects politics, social organization, and culture.[1] Most observers would point to the primacy of economic forces, broadly defined, as being the essential motors of the process, and examining these helps both to define globalization and to understand its dynamics. What we can consider to be globalization, as a distinct phenomenon, is the result of significant changes in the international economy that first became pronounced around the end of the Cold War era. By then—the decade of the 1990s—it displayed certain prominent, mutually reinforcing characteristics, all of which have been made possible by modernization.

The first, and perhaps most obvious, is an increased volume of trade, as economic, technological, and political developments have all allowed and encouraged international commerce to grow exponentially. Since 1950, as world economic output has tripled, international trade has expanded by a factor of twenty-seven. More societies have become active participants, and they are exchanging a widening spectrum of goods and services.[2]

One important reason for this expansion of trade is the tremendous advances in transportation and communication that have linked different parts of the world ever more closely, and this constitutes another defining element of globalization. In today's world, physical distances have less and less relevance, as labor and raw materials can travel the globe in a day, while information and capital can be transmitted within seconds. As opposed to earlier eras, the movement of goods, people, capital, and ideas is both faster and less expensive, and this has an enormous impact on the way that different societies relate to one another.

Such logistical advances have both contributed to and been enabled by a third characteristic, which is greatly expanded capital investment. Due largely to the research and development of specialized technology demanded in today's economy, the proportion of fixed costs to variable costs has steadily increased. This means that initial startup costs require access to large amounts of capital, a point made over a century ago by Marx, who regarded it as inevitable in an investment-driven economic system. When only larger businesses that can operate with an economy of scale can compete in today's global marketplace, this presents a "barrier to entry" that interferes with the ability of producers to enter and leave the marketplace freely. A growing proportion of fixed costs leads unavoidably to the domination of the largest business enterprises, and less true business competition.

Economy of Scale

The principle of economy of scale states that the larger an economic enterprise is, the more efficient it can be in terms of the proportion of outputs (production) compared to inputs (cost). There are a number of reasons for this. The most important is that in many economic enterprises, especially in the modern era, there may be significant costs incurred in setting up production in the first place. These are the "fixed costs" such as investing in the land, buildings, and technology whose costs do not vary no matter how much or how little production takes place after they are paid for. Other costs, such as labor and materials, vary according to how much is produced, and hence are known as "variable costs." The higher the proportion of one-time fixed costs to variable costs, the more incentive an enterprise has to increase its output, since each additional item produced only increases variable costs.

A simple example demonstrates this principle. If a factory and machinery cost a million dollars, and each product produced requires an hour of labor at $10 per hour and material costing $10 per item, the first item produced will cost $1,000,020. However, all subsequent items will only cost an additional $20. To produce 1,000 items, the total cost will be $1,020,000, at an average cost of $1,020 per item—far less than the cost of the first item.

Given this reality, such a producer has a clear incentive to produce as many items as possible in order to benefit from an economy of scale. As the European capitalist economy developed, economy of scale became an important reason for its expansion. The large state-supported businesses of the mercantilist age—in manufacturing, trade, and finance—relied increasingly upon fixed "startup" costs, and operated most efficiently (that is, with the least cost per item produced) when maximizing production, often becoming monopolies. Later, the factories that emerged during the Industrial Revolution also benefited from economies of scale.

Other factors, such as labor specialization, the ability to purchase material in large quantities, and the ability to have more influence with government authorities, also contribute to an economy of scale.

This in turn has contributed to another defining element of globalization: the emergence of **transnational corporations**. Also referred to as "multinational corporations," such entities are able to conduct their planning and production processes in many separate nations, while their scale of operations makes transportation costs relatively minor as a proportion of cost. Thus, the physical location of their business activities can be adjusted according to the most favorable current conditions, such as access to natural resources, labor availability, tax rates, or access to transportation. Even their financial operations are conducted internationally, as the capital upon which their operations depend can and often must move quickly back and forth across national boundaries. While the largest of such companies have revenues and expenditures that exceed those of many independent nations, at the same time, they operate largely independently of national allegiances.

What these factors add up to is the last major characteristic of globalization. In the last two decades we have seen, for the first time, a true internationalization of economic *production*, as distinct from the international *distribution* that had defined international trade for thousands of years. This means that separate elements of the production process can be carried out in many different places, and a **global division of labor** has emerged that is based on the principle of comparative advantage. While this increases overall efficiency, it also makes the nations of the world economically dependent upon each other. The age of globalization means that even highly developed nations with abundant natural and human resources, such as the United States, no longer enjoy true economic self-sufficiency.

The global economy takes the advantages demonstrated by Adam Smith's pin factory to an entirely new level. In the pin factory, a division of labor enables an exponential increase in output by dividing the stages of the pin-making process among individual workers, each responsible for only a single operation. Yet even with this advantageous division of labor, Smith's pin-makers all performed their tasks under the same roof.[3] In contrast, global production, with the costs of transport and communication steadily declining as elements of cost, now takes place in multiple locations often thousands of miles apart.

For example, the manufacture of a single automobile often takes place in literally dozens of nations. The various parts of a car—headlights, carburetors, tires, dashboards, GPS systems, and many other components of the finished product—may be produced in a number of separate countries, using parts and materials that themselves have been imported from other nations. While the final "assembly" of the automobile may occur in a single factory, it has become common for even this stage of production to take place in a different nation than the one in which the corporate headquarters is located. In this way, literally dozens of different nations can take part in the manufacture of a single automobile. Admittedly, many other economic activities—agriculture, insurance, or education, for instance—may not be as complicated as manufacturing is in terms of benefiting from different tasks being performed in many different places. Yet even these economic sectors are becoming dominated by large transnational corporations, and increasingly rely upon new technologies, greater economies of scale, and global divisions of labor.

Of course, the forces of change unleashed by globalization have had an impact that goes far beyond just the economic realm. Globalization has affected and continues to affect politics, culture, social organization, and even the natural landscape. Any process this powerful is bound to provoke controversy, and globalization has attracted both critics and defenders who represent a wide variety of perspectives. Let us now turn our attention to the ways in which globalization contributes to social change.

Growth and Inequality

Perhaps the most evident impact of globalization has been economic, and the economic results have provided globalization advocates with their most persuasive evidence that globalization has been, on the whole, a force of positive change. It is a fairly undeniable fact that in the last three decades, overall economic growth worldwide has increased, and most economists would agree that the globalization of the economy is the major reason for this.[4] For the reasons outlined above, the global economy has made it possible to produce more goods and services for less cost. The direct result has been greater overall productivity, that is, economic growth, and this economic growth has translated into a higher average standard of living around the world over the last twenty years. Economic data also support the conclusion that even many less-developed countries have increased their average wealth during this time period.[5]

The cause and effect comes right out of Adam Smith and classical economic theory: given an opportunity for profit, people and businesses will compete in the marketplace, and competition fosters innovation and higher productivity. This stimulates both demand and investment, which in the long run, leads to higher employment and higher wages. While some groups may do better than others, the resulting creation of wealth ultimately benefits all sectors of the economy. If economic growth is the goal, and if globalization results in economic growth, then it is logical that globalization should be promoted and that restraints on the process are counterproductive. It is a compelling argument, made all the more persuasive by the dismal economic performances of the societies that have participated least in the global economy in the last two decades, such as Cuba, Myanmar, and North Korea.

Yet other economists criticize the way that globalization has contributed to wealth creation. Some point out that statistics about economic growth can be deceptive, because they measure long-term averages and fail to acknowledge the uneven and inconsistent distribution of benefits.[6] Critics of globalization have pointed out that that in the last two decades increases in wealth have been concentrated among certain groups: specifically, the most developed nations, and, in societies at all levels of development, the social groups who are already the most well-off. The wealthiest fifth of the world's nations—mostly located in Western Europe, North America, and East Asia—have vastly increased their relative wealth compared to the rest over the last fifty years. In contrast, average standards of living have stagnated or declined in the poorest quarter of the world's countries. Meanwhile, within all nations, modernized or not, the last two decades have seen a growing concentration of wealth and power in the hands of fewer people, whose often-remarkable gains significantly distort the overall averages. It is argued that the era of globalization has actually made most people throughout the world either no better off or worse off in terms of wealth and income.

In other words, while overall and even average wealth has increased, so has economic inequality, and this inequality operates on two levels. First, critics argue, the gap between the most developed societies and the still-developing nations has grown in recent years. In particular, the poorest nations, including most nations in sub-Saharan Africa, have seen their economic fortunes decline in both real and relative terms. Second, it has been noted that the wealth differential between well-off groups and poor groups within individual societies, both developed and less developed, has also widened.[7] Both sorts of inequality have historically been destabilizing social factors, as observers from Marx and Durkheim right up to the present have pointed out, especially when combined with some of the less-quantifiable consequences discussed below.

Power and Authority in an Era of Globalization

While even firm economic statistics can be open to interpretation, other effects of globalization are difficult if not impossible to describe with objective data. One area where this is especially true is in the political realm: one of globalization's most important impacts has been on the way power and authority work in the modern world, especially in developing societies.

In the modern world, it has become an accepted dictum that a nation that wishes to raise the standard of living of its citizens needs to attract capital investment to create jobs and infrastructure. In the developing parts of the world, almost by definition, this means that development is reliant upon foreign investment. Most sources of foreign investment are in the private sector, such as transnational corporations, or are guided from international entities such as the World Bank or the International Monetary Fund that rely on private investment. To invest in a developing nation, the potential source of investment must believe that there is a reasonable prospect of profit, and in practice, what this means is that national governments are under pressure to create a "positive investment climate" where profit seems more likely. Yet, obviously, investment capital is not infinite, which means that the governments of developing nations must compete to attract it.

Most often, the creation of such an investment climate has pressured national governments into changing and restricting their roles in their national economies. Certain related conditions that contribute to the "liberalization" or "restructuring" of national economies are typically required to attract foreign investment.[8] These include such elements as deregulation, lower corporate taxes, and less protection of domestic industries, and together they amount to the reduction of the role of government in the economy. Increasingly, the International Monetary

Fund and the World Bank insist on such restructuring for client states to qualify for debt relief and the procurement of loans.[9] Moreover, if a given government refuses to conform to such requirements, it is likely that some other nation, one even more desperate for investment capital, will conform to them, and will thus be a better candidate for investment. What this often means is that if the government of a particular nation does not liberalize enough, that nation will get little investment capital, and find it difficult or impossible to create or sustain economic growth.

While these conditions are usually justified on the basis of economic efficiency, they undermine national sovereignty by restricting the role of government in national affairs. Less government power does not automatically translate into more productivity and efficiency. In fact, classical liberal economic theory notes that the efficient operation of a free market system works best when there is a balance of power between private and public interests, because economic competition needs a legal and infrastructural framework within which it can take place lawfully and openly. Early proponents of market economies, such as Smith and John Stuart Mill, explained that governments, acting on behalf of the public interest, must play the role of "referee" to ensure an orderly and stable "playing field." One evident effect of globalization is that this balance is upset, because the demands of investment capital, in the view of some critics, hold governments "hostage" to the demands of large transnational businesses and the international organizations that represent their interests. This has meant that governments in the era of globalization have had to accept a smaller role and less authority in economic matters. At the same time, international businesses, through mergers and acquisitions, have become larger and fewer, which has diminished the amount of true competition in the marketplace, as Marx had foreseen.

Of course, one may argue that larger economic enterprises are more efficient, and that globalization has not undermined competition enough to allow monopolistic behavior; some in fact contend that a freer flow of investment stimulates competition. Yet even if this is so, a highly problematic structural problem remains. This has to do with incentives: while national governments exist for the explicit purpose of protecting the public welfare, private businesses do not. In fact, the primary—some might argue the only—responsibility of a private business is to its stockholders, by expanding market share and providing a return on investment. Corporate directors, if they have to choose between profitability and public interest, have a clear and obvious choice.

It is largely for this reason that much contemporary criticism of globalization focuses on the way that private gains are frequently achieved by businesses in direct opposition to the public interest.[10] In particular, market incentives can do little to solve major social crises like famines, epidemics, or rampant inflation, or to deal with long-term problems such as environmental damage or the exhaustion of natural resources. Conforming to the requirements of capital investment often erodes governments' ability to carry out their primary responsibility of "protective security," which can have ominous results throughout the society in question. As one recent critic noted,

Some of the fundamental responsibilities of the state in a market economy—responsibilities first recognized, described, and discussed by Adam Smith over two hundred years ago—are not now being discharged by anyone. At the heart of the international political economy, there is a vacuum . . . the diffusion of authority away from national governments has left a yawning hole of non-authority, ungovernance it might be called.[11]

Economic Volatility

Government's definition of the "public interest" can be problematic. One critical lesson of the twentieth century is certainly that expanded government power is not always benign. The careers of such leaders as Stalin, Hitler, and Pol Pot demonstrate how dictators and warlords can employ the fruits of modernization—technological, military, and bureaucratic—to oppress, persecute, enslave, and even kill their own citizens. Yet it is a logical fallacy to conclude that less government power automatically increases individual liberties. Increasingly, globalization has shown a distinct tendency to put people at the mercy of different types of power, ones that are not only beyond their control, but even beyond their understanding. As public power declines, the net result is not always more freedom for the individual.

Over a century ago, observers like Durkheim, Marx, and Weber warned of the vulnerability of societies to the effects of powerful economic forces that come with a modern capitalist economy.[12] One reason is that when investors rapidly move their capital from one investment to another it can result in dramatic swings both in economic sectors and throughout the economy as a whole. This phenomenon is known as **market volatility**. Especially at the higher levels of finance, markets tend to rise and fall according to perceived future values that may or may not have any grounding in economic reality. In the age of the World Wide Web, when financial transactions can take place automatically and instantaneously, the prices of such investments as stocks, bonds, and national currencies are determined by the behavior of the "electronic herd," instead of reflecting whatever objective material value they may have originally represented.[13]

Because of this, one of the most serious consequences of globalization is that nations, industries, regions, and even individuals lose control over their economic destinies. As buying and selling takes place in international financial markets, the flows of capital that fuel the modern economy affect interest rates, prices, employment rates, and the value of money, which have direct impacts on the livelihoods of citizens. Quite literally, decisions that are made in corporate boardrooms or in stock exchanges halfway around the world can have more real impact on the lives of individuals than anything their national or local governments can do. Globalization has meant that this new sort of power has reduced the abilities of most people to control their own welfare.[14] The result has been that the global era of "economic freedom" hardly resembles what classical liberals had in mind when they promoted the virtues of independence and self-reliance.

Today, the problem of volatility is a critical issue in developing nations. The rapidly shifting flows of capital upon which today's global economy depends seldom allow for the type of steady and reliable investment that is necessary for long-term economic development. This is even true when investment is managed by international organizations. For instance, one former World Bank official notes that the policies of this organization actually discourage investment and increase the tax burdens on the middle class and working classes. They also lead to high interest rates and do little to encourage job creation, even though two of the most serious economic problems in developing nations are the scarcity of capital and high unemployment rates.[15]

The Asian Financial Crisis of 1997 demonstrates the sorts of havoc that economic volatility can create in widely different parts of the world.[16] While the 1980s and early 1990s had seen steady and occasionally spectacular economic growth in Southeast Asia, worries about the financial stability of certain governments had emerged in financial markets. In July of 1997, actions taken by the government of Thailand caused international investors to suddenly lose confidence in the value of that country's currency, and in just a few days, the Thai *baht* lost more than 80 percent of its value on international markets. As a result, Thailand's government was essentially bankrupted, and a spillover affect in neighboring economies encouraged private and public investors alike to quickly "dump" their investments in Asian governments and stock markets. The result was a financial collapse that within weeks paralyzed the economies of not just Thailand but Indonesia and South Korea, while severely affecting the Philippines, Malaysia, Hong Kong, and other East Asian nations. Over the course of the summer, financial panic contributed to a variety of economic ills in the region that ranged from massive unemployment, to corporate bankruptcies, to roaring inflation, to rioting in the streets, and even to the collapse of the Indonesian government. It also affected many private firms and national governments throughout the world that had significant financial involvements in the countries directly affected.

In retrospect, the primary cause of this crisis was financial overspeculation by investors seeking to profit from fluctuations in world financial markets. When confidence suddenly evaporated, the "electronic herd" panicked, as investors all over the world scrambled madly pull their money out of areas perceived as risky. These financial decisions, made by executives and government officials, victimized literally millions of people who had no influence whatsoever over this chain reaction of investment and disinvestment; these included business owners, individual investors, workers, farmers, consumers, and, perhaps especially, the desperately poor in the nations affected. Almost all of these groups were harmed for no reason that had anything to do with their own actions or choices. Vulnerable to huge, incomprehensible market forces over which they had no control whatsoever, people suffered unemployment, poverty, hunger, homelessness, and even violent death because of the volatility of the global marketplace.

Despite the purported benefits of such economic freedom, globalization and the economic dependency it promotes undermines peoples' abilities to control their lives. For many, the determinants of their success in life are not hard work or wise choices or being good citizens. Instead, sweeping economic forces resulting from business decisions made in New York, Shanghai, and London have become the factors most responsible for whether many people today, and their children, will enjoy a promising future—or, in some cases, whether they will enjoy any sort of future at all. Weber, Marx, and Durkheim were only among the first to explain the social destruction that results when individuals lose control over their own destinies.

Those of us living in more fortunate situations may think, as our ancestors have done, that while life is often unfair, the misfortunes of others don't really affect our own lives. However, in a global world in which the world's societies are ever more interconnected in all sorts of ways, the misfortunes of others are becoming less distant, and more relevant to our own welfare, every day.

Urbanization and the Environment

Recent demographic trends reveal another troubling element that is intimately connected with globalization: as the world population has grown over the last century from about one billion in 1900 to close to eight billion today, most of the growth has taken place in the developing world.[17] The reasons for this are clear and logical. Since the Industrial Revolution, wealthier and more developed societies have lowered their birth rates, and this has meant that even while average lifespans have increased, population levels have been largely steady. In contrast, in most developing parts of the globe, modernization has brought advances in health care and food production, without a corresponding decline in birthrates. Hence, the demographic balance between developed and less-developed nations has shifted in both real and relative terms. The implications of this are enormous: should this trend continue, in another fifty years, about 10 percent of the world's

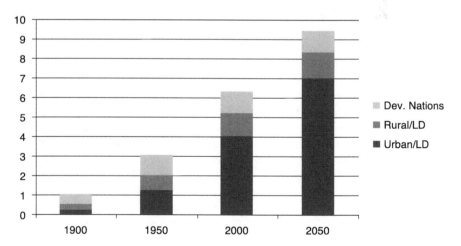

Figure 22.1 World population growth

population will control as much as 80 percent of the world's total economic output, while accounting for more than 90 percent of the consumption of the world's resources.[18]

While this projection is unsettling in and of itself, it is compounded by another key demographic feature of the modern age, which is steadily growing urbanization. Undoubtedly globalization has contributed to this trend by creating far more jobs in cities than in the countryside.[19] One reason why this is a problem is that urban growth in the developing world contributes to environmental change and degradation, which is perhaps the most serious threat affecting the world today. The continued growth of cities contributes to global warming, ozone depletion, the disruption of hydrologic processes threatening water supplies, erosion, the loss of biodiversity, and a shrinking supply of key resources such as clean water and fossil fuels.[20] Since the Industrial Revolution, half the world's wetlands have been destroyed and two-thirds of the world's farmlands have been designated as either "somewhat degraded" or "strongly degraded."[21]

Solutions to such problems are difficult in the global era. As noted above, globalization has made national governments, especially those in the developing world, less able to prevent or repair such damage, because the need for capital investment discourages governments from enacting more stringent environmental restrictions. Meanwhile, it is difficult to expect the private enterprises that are both directly and indirectly contributing to such environmental damage to help in more than a symbolic way. For corporations whose responsibility is to shareholders, the need to operate profitably is a higher priority than long-term environmental interests. The latter is irrelevant to input and production decisions, except as scarcity affects costs; at most, corporations may adopt more environmentally friendly policies to enhance their corporate image for marketing purposes. In the words of one observer, "In modernity, nature has come to be considered as a 'resource' to be used instrumentally to fulfill human desires."[22]

Governments of developing countries, even when they do intervene in the public interest, often find that their choices are quite difficult. A good example of the dilemma faced can be seen in the case of the Brazilian Amazon, where hundreds of acres of environmentally critical rainforest are cleared every day. It is largely a misperception that large transnational corporations are responsible for this; instead, these practices are mostly being carried out by common Brazilians who are trying to make a living in the region by clearing areas where they can establish farms and ranches. If their government prevents them from doing this, as some environmental groups insist, such people will remain in Brazil's overcrowded cities, where there is already significant unemployment.[23]

In the era of globalization, it is the people living in the developing world who are paying most of the environmental price tag for the global economy. In exchange for jobs and tax revenues, they get toxic chemicals in their air and water, have less good farmland to grow food, and a shortage of needed natural resources for their own people. While affluent nations can often afford the added costs that come with environment protection and recovery, poorer nations usually cannot. It is in places like Indonesia, India, Brazil, and China, where swelling urban populations are putting unsustainable pressure on nature, that the environmental costs of globalization become brutally clear.

Globalization and Cultural Backlash

As a complex and far-reaching process, globalization can affect every aspect of a society. In many cases, it forces change on people whose societies have been functioning successfully for many generations, by disrupting traditional types of authority, ways of doing business, and patterns of social interaction. Some societies are able to absorb the social change it puts into motion better than others, while within a given society, some groups usually benefit more than others.[24]

What this means is that today most people experience a different kind of poverty than the poor of a century ago. While their more rural ancestors were isolated, traditional, uneducated, and more concerned with local issues, the vast majority of today's poor are living in cities where traditional cultures have been disrupted by rapid social change. One commonality that globalization brings is an emphasis on money transactions. In the global world of economic dependency and specialization, nearly everybody needs money in order meet basic needs such as food, clothing, and housing, yet money economies are more compatible with some cultures than others, and can disrupt kinship, social, and political relationships. In fact, some have argued that globalization is driven by the immense power of modern media to manipulate tastes and preferences, consciously forcing a consumer-oriented culture upon traditional world societies.[25]

In 1944, in the midst of the most destructive war in human history, the economist Karl Polanyi linked the rise of European militarism and totalitarianism to the uncertainties of the global free market economy that had emerged out of the Industrial Revolution.[26] In Polanyi's view, both the First World War and the economic chaos that followed were consequences of rapid modernization that made many political states helpless to protect the interests of their citizens, while tearing apart the social fabric that held communities together. By the 1930s, socialism and fascism appeared to many as reasonable solutions to the collapse of civil society. Sociologically, these phenomena represented a backlash against rapid social change and modernization, and legitimately or not, opportunistic leaders gained popular support by demonizing "free market" economic policies. While Lenin and Stalin denounced worldwide capitalist exploitation, the Nazis promised to create a "*volksgemeinschaft*" that would give alienated Germans a sense of belonging and purpose.

The trends of the more recent age of globalization offer a frightening parallel. An increasing proportion of the world's population can be found in overcrowded urban areas that feature damaged ecosystems and few opportunities to earn the money necessary to maintain a reasonable standard of living. Poverty, of course, is nothing new, but today's poverty takes place in a far more combustible environment. While in past ages the world's poor tended to be rural and ignorant, this is no longer the case. Today's poor not only share urban space with the wealthy, but they have access to all sorts of media, from television to billboards to the Internet, that make them keenly aware of their own disadvantages. The bombardment of images of "the good life" made possible by global consumerism forces them to compare their situations to that of wealthier neighbors and wealthier societies elsewhere, and wonder, "why do they have what we can't have?" A seemingly inescapable result of the modernization of the world is that today's poor are far more conscious of global inequality than ever before, and it should surprise no one that resentment and anger are reaching new levels as well.

One may well ask whether globalization is really the cause of these people's helplessness and misery, as well as whether the Western world, especially the United States, should be held accountable for it. Persuasive cases can be made either way, because globalization is obviously a complicated process. But whether blame is justified isn't really the issue; instead what does matter is that a growing number of people, primarily outside the Western world, increasingly *believe* that globalization is responsible. The actual accuracy of this belief is far less relevant than the potential consequences of the belief.

This is why it may be helpful to view **terrorism** (see Chapter 23) not as an element in and of itself, but as a symptom of a larger phenomenon. In many respects, terrorism is an expression of growing frustration and resentment against the huge, incomprehensible global forces that have come to dominate so many people's lives. Charismatic leaders, positioning themselves as defenders of traditional values, offer the helpless and dispossessed the opportunity to defend themselves and their cultures against outside enemies.

Perhaps the attacks on September 11, 2001 may attain a deeper significance to future historians. Thus far in the twenty-first century, only certain groups, such as al-Qaeda and ISIS, have had both the means and the ideology to justify violence in the name of what they see as "self-defense," and have been able to carry out terrorist attacks effectively. It may be just a matter of time before other frustrated societies start to take the same path.

"Gift from the West" or "Western Curse"?

As the Nobel Prize-winning economist Amartya Sen points out, there is currently a tendency to see globalization as one of two extremes, either as a "gift from the West to the world" or else as a "Western curse."[27] Those who agree with the first view naturally conclude that globalization should continue without restraint, while those who agree with the second idea work to prevent or reverse it.

Neither viewpoint is especially helpful. The conclusion that globalization is an unalloyed blessing leads to a denial of its role in the problems that face world civilization today. This clearly undermines our ability to understand and solve such problems. The second view is equally shortsighted, since it encourages a backlash that can create even more problems, such as quasi-fascist states or terrorism.[28] Instead, what is needed is an understanding of how globalization works, so that we can take advantage of the opportunities it presents while being aware of the challenges it creates. In all likelihood, as modernization proceeds in the coming decades, the world's communities will become even more interdependent, and we will need to deal with this continuing process in a constructive and thoughtful way.

Notes

1 For a spectrum of definitions, see Manfred B. Steger, *Globalization: A Very Short Introduction* (London: Oxford University Press, 2009), 13.
2 World Trade Organization, December 4, 2007, www.wto.org/english/news_e/, accessed August 10, 2010.
3 Adam Smith, *An Inquiry into the Nature and Causes of the Wealth of Nations*, Book 1, Chapter 1 (New York: Modern Library, 1937), 3–12.
4 The connection between globalization and increased economic growth has been noted by many, including Thomas Friedman, *The World is Flat: A Brief History of the Twenty-First Century*, (New York: Farrar, Straus & Giroux, 2007); and Martin Wolf, *Why Globalization Works* (New Haven: Yale University Press, 2004).
5 Wolf, *Why Globalization Works*, 140–44.
6 Steger, *Globalization*, 106–11; Amartya Sen, "How to Judge Globalism," *The American Prospect* 13:1 (January 2002), 19–24.
7 In addition to the sources cited in note 6, see Joseph Stiglitz, "Globalism's Discontents," eds. Lechner and Boli, *The Globalization Reader*, 3rd ed., 210–12; Robert Hunter Wade, "Is Globalization Reducing Poverty and Inequality?" *World Development* 32, no. 4 (2004), 567–89.
8 International Forum on Globalization website. "A Better World is Possible!" (2002) www.ifg.org/alt_eng.pdf, accessed August 10, 2010; Kenichi Ohmae, *The End of the Nation State and the Rise of Regional Economies* (New York: Free Press, 1995), 11–16.
9 Some of the problems created by such conditions are discussed in Stiglitz, "Globalism's Discontents," 208–15; Sen, "How to Judge Globalism," 19–24; Steger, *Globalization*, 54–7.
10 Amartya Sen, *Development as Freedom* (New York: Anchor Books, 1999), 123–29, 183–88.
11 Susan Strange, *The Retreat of the State* (Cambridge: Cambridge University Press, 1996), 14; Dani Rodrik, *The Globalization Paradox: Democracy and the Future of the World Economy*. (New York: Norton, 2011).
12 Marx, *Capital*, 1887, vol. I, section one, ch. 25; vol. III, part one, ch. 6; Marx, *Wage Labour and Capital*, "Effect of Capitalist Competition on the Capitalist Class, the Middle Class and the Working Class" (1847), www.marxists.org/archive/marx/works/, accessed August 10, 2010; Weber, "The Antagonism of the Economy and Political Domains to Ethical Action," Ch. 18, *Max Weber, Readings and Commentary on Modernity*, Stephen Kalberg, ed. (Oxford: Wiley, 2005), 251–54; the concept is an essential foundation of Durkheim's *Division of Labor* and *Suicide*.
13 The term "electronic herd" was coined by Thomas Friedman in *The Lexus and the Olive Tree* (New York: Anchor, 2000).
14 Steger, *Globalization*, 101–6; Stiglitz, "Globalism's Discontents," 211–12.
15 Stiglitz, "Globalism's Discontents," 210–12.
16 On the 1997 Asian financial crisis, see Paul Blustein, *The Chastening: Inside the Crisis that Rocked the Global Financial System and Humbled the IMF* (New York: Public Affairs, 2001).
17 Jeffrey D. Sachs, *Common Wealth: Economics for a Crowded Planet* (New York: Penguin, 2008), 26–46; United Nations, *World Urbanization Prospects: The 2003 Revision* (New York: United Nations, 2004), 1–35.

18   www.un.org/esa/population/publications/wup2003/WUP2003Report.pdf, accessed August 10, 2010.
19   Sachs, *Common Wealth*, 25–8.
20   Peter Marcotullio and Gordon McGranahan, "Scaling the Urban Environmental Challenge," in *Scaling Urban Environmental Challenges,* eds. Peter Marcotullio and Gordon McGranahan (New York: International Institute for Environment and Development and United Nations University/Institute for Advanced Studies, 2007) 1–17; Barbara Boyle Torrey, "Urbanization: An Environmental Force to Be Reckoned With," Population Reference Bureau website. April, 2004. www.prb.org/Articles/2004/, accessed August 10, 2010.
21   Steger, *Globalization*, 87; Sachs, *Common Wealth*, 39–41.
22   Steger, *Globalization*, 84.
23   Margulis, Sergio. *Causes of Deforestation of the Brazilian Amazon*. (Washington, DC: World Bank, 2004); Imazon: Amazon Institute of People and the Environment website www.imazon.org.br, accessed August 10, 2010.
24   Sen, *Development as Freedom*, 240–42.
25   Leslie Sklair, *Globalism: Capitalism and its Alternatives*, 3rd ed. (London: Oxford University Press, 2002), 62–9; Steger, *Globalization*, 70–80.
26   Karl Polanyi, *The Great Transformation: The Political and Economic Origins of Our Time* (New York: Beacon Press, 1944). His argument has been elaborated and expanded by more recent observers, including Susan Strange, *The Retreat of the State*
27   Sen, "How to Judge Globalism," 1.
28   Ibid., 1.

Suggested Readings

Baldwin, Richard. *The Great Convergence*. Cambridge: Harvard University Press, 2016.

Blustein, Paul. *The Chastening: Inside the Crisis that Rocked the Global Financial System and Humbled the IMF*. New York: Public Affairs, 2001.

Friedman, Thomas. *The Lexus and the Olive Tree*. New York: Anchor, 2000.

Lechner, Frank J., and John Boli, *The Globalization Reader*. 5th ed., New York: Wiley-Blackwell, 2015.

Polanyi, Karl. *The Great Transformation: The Political and Economic Origins of Our Time*. New York: Beacon Press, 1944.

Ritzer, George, and Paul Dean. *Globalization: A Basic Text*. 2nd ed. New York: Wiley Blackwell, 2014.

Rodrik, Dani. *The Globalization Paradox: Democracy and the Future of the World Economy*. New York: Norton, 2011.

Sachs, Jeffrey D. *Common Wealth: Economics for a Crowded Planet*. New York: Penguin, 2008.

Sen, Amartya. *Development as Freedom*. New York: Anchor Books, 1999.

Sklair, Leslie. *Globalism: Capitalism and its Alternatives*. 3rd ed. London: Oxford University Press, 2002.

Steger, Manfred B. *Globalization: A Very Short Introduction*. 3rd ed. London: Oxford University Press, 2013.

Strange, Susan. *The Retreat of the State*. Cambridge: Cambridge University Press, 1996.

Wolf, Martin. *Why Globalization Works*. New Haven: Yale University Press, 2004.

23 Terror and Terrorism

John McGrath

Key Terms

asymmetrical warfare, Islamism, "propaganda of the deed," suicide bombings, terrorism

Since 2001, America and many of its allies have been waging a "War on Terror" that has proven exceptionally difficult to either win or withdraw from. In large part, this is because of the challenge of strictly defining the enemy; after all, what exactly does "War on Terror" actually mean?

In modern English, the term "terror" is often used as a synonym for "fear." But while fear is a normal aspect of human life, terror is not: every day, millions of people fear missing a bus, or public speaking, or that their favorite sports team might lose, but few of them, if any, view those possibilities with genuine terror. The sort of terror that liberal democracies have been waging war against has been created by individuals and groups that we call "terrorists," who engage in activities that we call "**terrorism**." While modernization has enabled many of us to live in a far more materially comfortable world than our ancestors did, it has also, arguably, played a major role in injecting an element of terror into our daily lives.

Definition and Foundation

If terrorism in fact poses an existential threat to world societies, as some argue, we need to make the effort to understand it. But the very definition is controversial; like "democracy" or "tyranny," terrorism has been proven to be a term that is difficult to define. It has frequently been stated that "one man's 'terrorist' is another's 'freedom fighter,'" depending upon the perspective; almost no one calls him or herself a terrorist. Complicating things further, political authorities, the media, the public, and academic experts often disagree about the aptness of the term in any given case.[1] With few exceptions, people apply the term to others for the purpose of demonizing or delegitimizing their actions.[2] As well, many so-called terrorist groups have blurred the boundaries among political movements, guerilla warfare, rebellion, cults, and criminal behavior. Max Weber would have had a difficult time coming up with an "ideal type" of "terrorism" or "terrorist."

Weber defined the political state as the possessor of a monopoly on the legitimate use of violence.[3] Terrorism challenges this monopoly; while, historically, terrorist movements have had varying goals, they have inevitably sought to bring about change by attacking the established system of authority by employing violent means. In the words of one historian, terrorism is "a conscious, deliberate strategic use of violence against a specific target to affect the political process."[4]

What makes it different from war? One useful brief definition is "the use of violence by the armed against the unarmed," contrasting it to conditions of war where, presumably, the targets of violence are opposing military forces instead of unarmed civilians.[5] This implies the conditions that, first, terrorism does not take place within a context of formally declared war, and secondly, that even if such actions did occur during war, they would violate the (frequently) accepted norm of warfare that prohibits intentional attacks on noncombatants.[6]

A more comprehensive explanation that represents a rough consensus in the academic community begins with:

> Terrorism reflects on the one hand, a doctrine about the presumed effectiveness of a special form or tactic of fear-generating, coercive political violence and, on the other hand, to a conspiratorial practice of calculated, direct violent action without legal or moral restraints, targeting mainly civilians and noncombatants, performed for its propagandistic and psychological effects on various audiences and conflict parties.[7]

Actions and groups that fit these definitions have appeared regularly in recorded history, in many different societies, under many different conditions. Actions that we might regard today as having been "terrorism," though not referred to as such at the time, go back at least two thousand years.

The French Revolution, which created so many other new social and political concepts and principles, was the incubator that first brought the term "terror" (*"la terreur"*) to prominence. In this case, the French Republican government used *la terreur* as a means of securing its own legitimacy. In the unforgettable words of the Jacobin leader Maximilien Robespierre, "the springs of popular government in revolution are at once virtue and terror: virtue without which terror is fatal; terror, without which virtue is powerless."[8]

Robespierre and the Jacobins viewed "terror" as an unfortunately necessary means toward a positive end: a "Republic of Virtue" based upon social and economic equality. The Reign of Terror, which featured tens of thousands of executions, many of them carried out publicly, was designed to intimidate the French people, or terrorize them, into obedience not just of action but of thought as well.[9] Edmund Burke's remark that "thousands of these Hellhounds called terrorists are let loose on the people" is among the first published use of that term in English.[10]

In revolutionary France, it was political authority—no matter how tenuous its claim to legitimacy—that employed terrorism as an expression of state policy. Since then, other governments, especially in the twentieth century, have also employed terror as an instrument of social control. This has included the governments controlled by Hitler, Stalin, Pol Pot, and the Taliban. Perhaps unsurprisingly, some of them labeled their victims "terrorists," as a way of justifying their actions. Thus, it is probably better to make a distinction between that sort of state-sponsored "terror" and the terrorism that emerged in the nineteenth century, even though the use of terror as a means of control, made possible by advances in communications, transportation, and weaponry, continues to be a feature of the modern world.

Early Terrorism and the "Propaganda of the Deed"

There are at least a couple of ways in which historians look at the history of terrorism and how it has changed. Commonly scholars distinguish among types of terrorism according to its goal.[11] Though the borders are often blurry, terrorist goals have been most commonly categorized as either primarily revolutionary, nationalistic, or religious. Many historical terrorist organizations have had elements of more than one, such as the Palestine Liberation Organization (PLO) and the Irish Republican Army (IRA), both of which might be described as nationalist organizations that contain a significant religious component. Other historians make a distinction on the basis of era, noting that at different points, terrorism has shifted according to three or more somewhat distinct eras, each primarily characterized by one of these types. One scholar sees four successive historical "waves" of terrorism—revolutionary, nationalist, leftist, and religious— positing that in the present day we are moving into a fifth, technological age of terrorism.[12]

Most would agree that modern terrorism, as applied to non-state organizations using violence to achieve change, began in the late nineteenth century with Russian groups attacking the tsarist government. An important factor in this case was the invention of dynamite, which enabled terrorists, for the first time, to strike hard and fast against political authority, somewhat "evening the odds" in terms of weaponry.[13] In Russia, both anarchist and socialist groups—which often over-lapped to some degree—at first demonstrated their hostility to the tsar through assassinations of government officials. Tsar Alexander II was one of the earliest victims, in 1881, falling to a bomb thrown by a member of an anarchist terrorist organization known as "The People's Will." Before the turn of the twentieth century, terrorist groups elsewhere used similar tactics for similar ends, including the assassinations of the president of the French Republic in 1894 and American President William McKinley in 1901.

Such early terrorists claimed that the purpose of their actions could be understood by the phrase **"propaganda of the deed."** In an era when anarchists appealed largely to workers and peasants, many of whom were illiterate or did not read often, they felt that a dramatic act of violence could grab public attention and publicize the conflict between the revolutionaries and the tsarist government.[14] The act itself served as a statement of anger and resistance, intended to increase public awareness and encourage others to use violence as well. The desired result was a violent response from the political authorities, which they hoped would set off an escalating spiral of violence that would culminate in a revolutionary uprising.[15] One early anarchist strategist argued that a single act of terrorism could "in a few days, make more propaganda than thousands of pamphlets."[16]

Since this early date, the concept of "propaganda of the deed" has remained an influential part of modern terrorism. Episodes of sudden dramatic violence—such as the September 11 attacks by al-Qaeda—raise the public profile of such organizations, framing their struggle as **asymmetrical warfare** between a large and tyrannical "establishment" and a smaller group with far fewer weapons at their disposal. Seldom calling themselves terrorists, the latter have typically regarded themselves as victims of oppression—economic, ethnic, or religious—who lack legitimate means to defend their interests. In the modern era, according to one scholar, "The forces of nationalism and technological development produced enormous bureaucratic states with more power than ever before . . . terrorism emerged as the ultimate act of individual protest against not just the state, but the modern condition."[17]

As it happened, Alexander II's assassination did provoke the desired vicious response from his son and successor, Alexander III, though its thoroughness actually undermined the ability of different groups to engage in terrorism. But it did have a significant impact: during the reign of the next tsar, the ill-fated Nicholas II, terrorist action expanded greatly. In 1905–1907, in connection with the Revolution of 1905 that featured the "Bloody Sunday" massacre and the catastrophic Russo-Japanese War, terrorism increased dramatically. It has been estimated that between 1905 and 1917, more than 17,000 people, primarily officials of some sort, were assassinated in Russia.[18] Most of these assassinations were carried out by terrorist groups loosely affiliated as "Social Revolutionaries," an umbrella term that included a variety of anarchists, populists, and socialists. Arguably, the seizure of power by the Bolsheviks—rivals of the Social Revolutionaries—was the rare instance of a terrorist group overthrowing an existing government.

The nineteenth century also witnessed the emergence of terrorist movements whose goals were nationalistic instead of revolutionary. The predecessor of the Irish Republican Army appeared in the 1880s, as did various ethnic nationalist groups in eastern Europe struggling against the foreign domination of the Ottoman and Austrian empires. In some sense, the assassination of Archduke Franz Ferdinand in 1914, the event that sparked the First World War, was "the culminating act of the first age of terrorism."[19] The Archduke's killers belonged to a recently formed Serbian nationalist organization that wanted to join parts of Bosnia, where a significant population of Serbs lived, to the newly independent neighboring kingdom of Serbia. The Black Hand, a splinter group of the nationalist Young Bosnia Movement, had a complicated relationship with the Serbian government, which supported it for at least a while.[20] So this instance of terrorism, like many to come, had significant ties to foreign sovereign governments.

The post-WWI world, with its political and economic difficulties, saw a decline in terrorist activities directed at governments. However, this era also saw the growth of state-directed terror from above, especially in Europe with the emergence of fascist governments.[21] During World War II, various resistance groups, including fascists and communists, employed terrorism to contest the domination of foreign armies, especially those of Germany and Japan. The end of the war saw an increase in nationalistic terrorism, including nationalist anti-imperialist movements against European domination.[22]

Three of the most significant of these were in Palestine, Vietnam, and Algeria. In the first case, both the Palestine Liberation Organization (PLO) and Jewish Zionists employed terrorism in Palestine soon after the war, both against each other and against British authority.[23] In Vietnam, a communist-supported guerrilla movement, which had fought against Japan during the war, contested the return of French colonial rule after the Japanese were expelled. Employing violent purges of Vietnamese who had collaborated with the French, as well as military campaigns, they forced the French out of their colony of Indochina, and during the 1950s, wound up with control of North Vietnam, while the United States got involved as the defender of the southern part of the country where anticommunist Vietnamese claimed power.[24] Terrorism on both sides played a major role in the Algerian War of Independence against France in the late 1950s, representing probably the bloodiest anticolonial conflict aside from Vietnam.[25] The independence of many other former European colonies in Africa and Asia during the 1950s and 1960s was frequently assisted by the emergence of terrorist groups, such as the Mau Mau in Kenya and communist-backed terrorists attacking British rule in Malaya. Cuban revolutionaries led by Fidel Castro and Che Guevara managed to overthrow the American-backed Bautista regime, and with aid from the Soviet Union, established the first communist state in the Americas by 1960. This in turn encouraged other Soviet-backed terrorist movements in other parts of Latin America, some of which have continued into the twenty-first century.[26]

By the 1960s, terrorism reached industrialized capitalist nations, especially leftist groups operating in Italy and Germany. Italy had more than 12,000 terrorist acts between 1969 and 1980, many of them carried out by the avowedly Marxist Red Brigades, while in Germany, the Red Army Faction, or Bader-Meinhof Gang, carried out bombings, assassinations, kidnappings, and bank robberies.[27] Also in Germany, during the 1972 Munich Olympics, the Palestinian Black September group carried out one of the most dramatic and internationally visible terrorist acts yet, when they murdered eleven Israeli Olympic athletes. In the United States, both the Weather Underground and Symbionese Liberation Army pursued terrorist tactics to publicize their struggle as "freedom fighters" against the forces of global capitalism.

In many of these cases, in both developed and less-developed nations, terrorist groups operated under similar justifications. They intended the "propaganda of their deeds" to win them international publicity and sympathy. In this view, terrorism was necessary for small "peoples' organizations" to be able to fight back against the ambitions of larger, more powerful nations.[28] As the spokesman of one group put it, "a pipe bomb left in a crowded marketplace was a 'poor man's airforce,' no more morally reprehensible than aerial bombing," such as American airstrikes against North Vietnam.[29]

"Just War" Theory

The concept of "Just War" in the Western tradition is a venerable one, stretching back to the Middle Ages, when European intellectuals first grappled with the moral dilemmas presented by warfare. The Catholic theologian Thomas Aquinas (1225–1274) was the first major figure to try to draw an ethical distinction between wars that were morally permissible and those that were not. He posited that any armed conflict must meet certain conditions if it was to be considered "just," and if it did not meet them all, it was morally indefensible. Since Aquinas's time, philosophers and scholars have debated and elaborated on his conditions.

Although some observers over the centuries have judged that certain of these conditions should be eliminated or modified, the following elements of "Just War" theory enjoy a general consensus. If a war is to be considered "just," it must:

1. be conducted for a morally acceptable cause, such as self-defense
2. be sanctioned by legitimate authority
3. be fought for righteous motives
4. be employed only as a last resort, after all means to avoid it have failed
5. have an intended result that accomplishes more good than the negative consequences of such a war
6. have a reasonable chance of success

Along with these stipulations concerning the morality of engaging in warfare, "Just War" theory is also concerned with the ways in which combatants must conduct themselves, that is, "rules of warfare" that protect the innocent and discourage unnecessary suffering.

Much of the terrorism that has occurred in the recent past has come under attack from proponents of "Just War." In particular, terrorist attacks on unarmed civilians, even if the perpetrators argue that the overall purpose of the attacks is morally justified, have received widespread international condemnation.

Religious Terrorism

In the last part of the twentieth century, to the surprise of many observers, religion rather suddenly emerged as the dominant and most publicized source of terrorism.[30] Religious terrorism was not a new phenomenon; in fact, some would argue that it dates back more than 2,000 years, and has included Hindus, Christians, Jews, and even Buddhists, but they seldom referred to themselves as terrorists.[31] Since the nineteenth century, terrorism has mostly had secular motives, even though religion sometimes was a factor in conflicts among different groups.

By the 1980s, many people assumed that continued modernization would result in continued secularization.

The year 1979 saw both the Iranian Revolution and the Soviet invasion of Afghanistan, raising a sense of consciousness among many Muslims around the world. By the end of the next decade, the dissolution of the Soviet Union left many former Soviet Republics with unhappy religious and ethnic factions struggling for power. These developments shifted the nature of terrorism relatively quickly. According to one expert, of eleven identifiable international terrorist organizations in 1968, none were religious, but by 1995, sixteen out of forty-nine terrorist groups were primarily religious in purpose.[32] Since then, religious terrorism as a proportion of overall global terror has increased steadily, especially among followers of Islam. In 2011, about two thirds of worldwide terrorist attacks were carried out by Muslim extremist groups.[33]

The roots of ideologies that provide the foundation of fundamentalist Islamic movements, often referred to as **"Islamism,"** extend at least to the early twentieth century, with the emergence of such groups as Palestine Liberation Organization (PLO) and the Muslim Brotherhood in Egypt. Such entities, though they carried out terrorist acts, were not purely terrorist in nature, since they were also involved in education, social services, and occasionally politics. As far as the Western world was concerned, Hezbollah, a Muslim organization backed by Iran, was the first major Islamic terrorist group, emerging in Lebanon during the chaotic civil strife that was taking place there in the early 1980s. Hezbollah-directed **"suicide bombings,"** where a single person, often a teenager, blew themselves up along with their targets. Such attacks killed hundreds of civilians and foreign military personnel and caused international shock and revulsion. Other smaller fundamentalist organizations appeared, playing roles in conflicts in the Middle East and in other heavily Islamic regions, spreading their operations to many nations, and sometimes even attacking each other, notably over the schism between Sunni and Shia Islam.[34]

It was also during the 1980s that al-Qaeda appeared. Osama bin Laden, a wealthy Saudi Arabian of Yemeni background, created this organization to recruit Muslims as *mujahadeen*, or "holy warriors," against Soviet forces in Afghanistan. Bin Laden portrayed himself as defender of traditional culture against the invasion of godless communism. With some covert aid from the United States, al-Qaeda formed a working partnership with the Taliban, the fundamentalist Afghan organization that hoped to seize power. Al-Qaeda's focus changed during the first Gulf War in 1991, when American-led coalition forces used Saudi Arabia as a staging area for the invasion of Iraq. This enraged bin Laden, who believed that this military presence polluted the Islamic holy land, and the United States became the new enemy.

In following years, al-Qaeda operated as a loose organization that utilized new technology such as cell phones and the Internet to plan and coordinate attacks against a variety of American targets, including embassies and military forces. Bin Laden, fond of making various pronouncements claiming responsibility for these attacks, earned his place on the FBI's "Ten Most Wanted" list in 1999.

The World Trade Center and Pentagon bombings in 2001 represented the culmination of many years of planning, much of it conducted through the Internet among widely scattered members of the group.

ISIS, sometimes considered a "splinter group" from al-Qaeda, is now seen as the greatest terrorist threat to Western nations.[35] Whether through suicide attacks in major cities including Paris and Brussels, or graphic internet videos showing them beheading bound prisoners, they have declared themselves warriors fighting a crusade against non-believers. Like Osama bin Laden, they are fundamentalist Sunni Muslims, but their goal is quite different from most of their predecessors. Their mission is the creation of an "Islamic Caliphate," based on literal interpretations of Koranic and other holy writings that are more than a thousand years old, in order to prepare the way for a final apocalyptic battle between good and evil.[36] ISIS, even more so than al-Qaeda, disdains political or social change, and is concerned instead with carrying out the will of Allah as defenders of the faith.

Islam, when it first appeared in the seventh century CE, was a religion adopted and spread by groups of conquering warriors, in an era of considerable disorder in the Middle East. The content of the Koran reflects the violence of the age. Unlike most of the world's leading Islamic scholars, Sunni terrorists insist upon literal interpretations of the Koran and other sacred writings, such as that "*jihad*" ("struggle") requires not just a striving to be a good Muslim, but a violent holy war against unbelievers.[37] Their goal is not terror, or forcing their enemies to make concessions, but instead to destroy their enemies, even at the cost of their own lives. It is important to understand that the vast majority of Muslim religious leaders, as well as the vast majority of Muslims in the world, consider the views of ISIS and other Muslim terrorist groups to fall well outside the mainstream of Islamic belief. Blaming the religion of Islam for fundamentalist Islamic terrorism makes about as much sense as blaming all Christians for bombings of abortion clinics.[38]

Terrorism in Modern America

Yet much of the religious terrorism that so terrifies the United States today has not been the direct work of such visible entities. A high proportion of such terrorist actions have been carried out by Muslims without formal ties to ISIS or other groups. Since 2001, more than half of the individuals who have committed terrorist acts in the United States in the name of Islam were either born in the United States or have been naturalized US citizens.[39] For instance, Omar Mateen, who carried out the 2016 Orlando nightclub massacres, was a native-born American of Afghan descent. Syed Rizwan Farook, who slaughtered civilians at a social service center in San Bernardino, California in December 2015, was American-born, though his wife, Tashfeen Malik, was born in Pakistan and had lived much of her life in Saudi Arabia. Boston Marathon bombers Tamerlan and Dzhokhar Tsarnaev were born in a Muslim-dominated region of today's Russia, though both had lived most of their lives in the United States. None of these were, as far as can be determined, formal members of any foreign or international terrorist groups. Yet all had significant Internet contact with fundamentalist Muslim groups and they proclaimed religious intentions after the fact.

In addition to these sorts of violence, one of the most significant varieties of contemporary terrorist actions in the United States is from white supremacist groups that frequently display some historical continuity to the Ku Klux Klan and neo-Nazi organizations.[40] Timothy McVeigh's bombing of the Oklahoma City courthouse in 1995, which killed 168 people, was the most-deadly terrorist act in American history until September of 2001. Dylann Roof's massacre of African-American churchgoers in 2015—almost unique in its cold-bloodedness—was motivated at least in part by Internet contacts with hate groups. Other home-bred American terrorists included Unabomber Ted Kaczynski and terrorists attacking clinics that provide abortions. Like the attacks by Muslim-American citizens mentioned above, most of these individuals planned and carried out their missions either completely alone or as parts of very small groups.[41] The dozens of school shootings that have occurred in the last two decades, such as those at Sandy Hook Elementary in Newtown, Connecticut, might not be strictly defined as terrorist acts, though their success in spreading terror has been undeniable. Such "lone wolf" terrorists, whether white supremacist, Muslim or otherwise, remain a potent threat both in the United States and elsewhere.[42]

Predicting Terrorism

The study of terrorism as a social phenomenon is still in its early stages. It is as yet difficult to make useful generalizations about what circumstances provoke it, or what sorts of individuals are likely to engage in it. Scholarly study of terrorism in the 1970s and 1980s focused to a great degree upon what forms a "terrorist personality," with the goal of making it more possible to identify and detect such perpetrators before they are able to act, but success in this has proved elusive.[43] For one thing, it is methodologically difficult to arrive at firm conclusions about what sorts of individuals are most likely to engage in terrorism, since terrorists by their very nature are difficult to locate and perhaps even more difficult to convince to cooperate with psychologists wanting to analyze them.

But what evidence there is seems to suggest that the large majority of terrorists do not have "abnormal personalities"—in fact, the characteristics most evident among those who are able to work successfully in clandestine organizations are loyalty and organizational skills. Not only that, terrorist involvement is hard to predict on the basis of such objective personal characteristics as ethnicity, social class, or education. In other words, most terrorists are not crazy, and many of them are unusually capable.[44]

Instead, as Philip Zimbardo and others have argued, if we want to understand the phenomenon of terrorist violence, we are better off looking at situational factors, especially group dynamics within organizations.[45] In many ways, the motives that underlie terrorism are normal human responses to particular situations. Terrorists have desires to fulfill the expectations of reference groups and authority figures, aided by ideologies that bestow admirable roles upon them. Necessarily, they develop the ability to think of their victims in abstract terms, that is, to use the term employed by Robert J. Lifton in his study of Auschwitz doctors, "psychic numbing." But how these factors work in in any given case are difficult to generalize about. The situational factors that mold the actions of terrorists depend upon the nature of organizations that have great variety in terms of size, locations, structure of command, and decision-making processes.[46]

Terrorism and Democracy

The phenomenon of terrorism raises important questions about the value systems of modern democracies. Democratic societies are in a particular dilemma, since the individual rights and freedoms that are so central to such societies make it easier for terrorist groups to operate, compared to more authoritarian states. To what extent are liberal democracies willing to undermine such rights and freedoms to seek out terrorists before they act? Should they focus on preventing terrorism? Destroying it? Discouraging it by ruthless retribution?

Since 2002, Guantanamo Bay has been used as a military prison by the US government to hold the terrorists judged as the most dangerous threats to American public safety. Attempts to close it have met with both political and public opposition. Detaining prisoners there without formal charges, or the chance to make their case in a court of law, has been justified by the claim that these individuals are "enemy combatants," not criminals; meanwhile, many prisoners have been subject to torture as a means of interrogation. But many see the continued operation of Guantanamo as fundamentally incompatible with America's founding principles. Guantanamo stands as a prime example of how those who like to portray themselves as "tough on terrorism" have advocated, and sometimes employed, nondemocratic means of fighting it. Since 2001, this has included government intimidation, violating citizens' privacies, and restricting constitutional rights.[47]

As discussed in Chapter Twenty-Two, globalization shows few signs of slowing down. Conflict, oppression, and a lack of opportunity in many parts of the world continue to encourage a flow of migrants to the West, especially the growing number of refugees, many of them victims of terror who are fleeing violence in their home countries. The response by many in the West, as evidenced by the Brexit vote in Britain in 2016 and the election of Donald Trump in the United States, has been to reduce or even eliminate the admission of such people, in the belief that creating "firmer borders" will help solve the problem of terrorism. However, as a means of fighting terror, this is probably counterproductive. When Western governments seal their borders from the rest of the world, it provides a useful marketing tool for ISIS and others, allowing them to claim that people in the Western world consider Islam to be their enemy.

In closing, it is worth considering that the chance of any American, or for that matter, anyone in the world, becoming a victim of terrorism is quite remote. The unexpectedness and viciousness of many recent terrorist acts has rightfully generated headlines, but they have also created a situation that unscrupulous leaders can take advantage of, by sowing the seeds of suspicion and xenophobia. The real level of danger created by terrorists to most Americans and Western Europeans is, if not insignificant, at least extremely unlikely. This is not to minimize the horror and destructiveness of this phenomenon, but it is useful to compare the incidence of terrorism to that of other threats to our livelihoods, and here the verifiable statistics are informative. According to the United States Center for Disease Control, between 2004 and 2013, Americans were well more than a hundred times more likely to die from gun violence at the hands of another American than they were likely to be victims of terrorism. Death from cancer, for Americans today, is about 30,000 times more likely than being killed in a terrorist attack.[48] These statistics are worth thinking about if we want to consider undermining our most valuable principles in response to terrorist acts. If we do that, the terrorists will have accomplished their goal.

Notes

1 John Horgan, *The Psychology of Terrorism* (Abingdon: Routledge, 2014), 840–880, 24–25.
2 Ibid., 557–67; Charles Townshend, *Terrorism: A Very Short Introduction*, Kindle ed. (New York: Oxford University Press, 2002), 237–55.
3 "The Antagonism of the Economy and Political Domains to Ethical Action," in *Max Weber: Readings and Commentary on Modernity*, ed. Stephen Kalberg (Oxford: Wiley, 2005), 254.
4 Horgan, *Psychology of Terrorism*, 28.
5 Alex Schmid, cited in Horgan, *Psychology of Terrorism*, 886.
6 Lewis Vaughn, *Doing Ethics*, 3rd ed. (New York: WW Norton, 2013), 599.
7 Schmid, A. "The Revised Academic Consensus Definition of Terrorism," *Perspectives on Terrorism* 6, no. 2 (May 2012), available at: http://terrorismanalysts.com/pt/index.php/pot/article/view/schmid-terrorism-definition, accessed: February 16, 2017.
8 "Justification for the Use of Terror," trans. Paul Halsall, in *Robespierre: On the Moral and Political Principles of Domestic Policy*, Internet Modern History Sourcebook, online, Fordham University (1997), http://sourcebooks.fordham.edu/mod/robespierre-terror.asp. accessed February 16, 2017.
9 Randall D. Law, *Terrorism: A History*. 2nd ed. (Cambridge: Polity Press, 2016). 61–3; Bruce Hoffman, *Inside Terrorism*. 2nd ed. (New York: Columbia University Press, 2006), 3–4.
10 Cited by Hoffman, *Inside Terrorism*, 4.
11 Townshend, *Terrorism: A Very Short Introduction*, 477; Hoffman, *Inside Terrorism*
12 David C. Rapoport, "The Four Waves of Modern Terrorism," *Attacking Terrorism*, eds. Audrey Kurth Cronin and James M. Ludes (Washington, DC: Georgetown University Press, 2004), 46–73.
13 Ibid., 46–8; Law, *Terrorism: A History*, 81.
14 Law, *Terrorism: A History*, 83–4.
15 Ibid., 83; Townshend, *Terrorism: A Very Short Introduction*, 900–32.
16 Peter Kropotkin, quoted by Townshend, *Terrorism: A Very Short Introduction*, 921.
17 Law, *Terrorism: A History*, 106.

18 Ibid., 86.
19 Townshend, *Terrorism: A Very Short Introduction*, 985.
20 Hoffman, *Inside Terrorism*, 11–14.
21 Law, *Terrorism: A History*, 152–53; Hoffman, *Inside Terrorism*, 14–16.
22 Townshend, *Terrorism: A Very Short Introduction*, 1215–1397.
23 Law, *Terrorism: A History*, 174–5; Townshend, *Terrorism: A Very Short Introduction*, 87–89.
24 Townshend, *Terrorism: A Very Short Introduction*, 61–2, 985–1005.
25 Law, *Terrorism: A History*, 193–206.
26 Townsend, *Terrorism: A Very Short Introduction*, 1015–68.
27 Townshend, *Terrorism: A Very Short Introduction*, 1098.
28 Hoffman, *Inside Terrorism*, 17.
29 Ibid., 26.
30 Townshend, *Terrorism: A Very Short Introduction*, 1447–91.
31 Law, *Terrorism: A History*, 31–45; Hoffman *Inside Terrorism*, 82–3.
32 Hoffman *Inside Terrorism*, 4–85.
33 United States National Counterterrorist Center, *2011 Report on Terrorism*, https://fas.org/irp/threat/nctc2011.pdf; Townshend, *Terrorism: A Very Short Introduction*, 1447–695; Law, *Terrorism: A History*, 272.
34 Law, *Terrorism: A History*, 272–85; Townshend, *Terrorism: A Very Short Introduction*, 1458–80; 1580–90.
35 On the origins and nature of ISIS, the highly readable and informative work *ISIS: The State of Terror*, by Jessica Stern and J. M. Berger (New York: Ecco/Harper Collins, 2015) is especially recommended.
36 Graeme Wood, "What ISIS Really Wants," *The Atlantic* (March 2015), 2–27; Stern and Berger, 233–56.
37 Townshend, *Terrorism: A Very Short Introduction*, 1542
38 Townshend, *Terrorism: A Very Short Introduction*, 1635–91; Stern and Berger, 241–44.
39 Sergio Peçanha and K. K. Rebecca Lai "The Origins of Jihadist-Inspired Attackers in the U.S.," *New York Times* (December 8, 2015).
40 Law, *Terrorism: A History*, 305–14.
41 Law, *Terrorism: A History*, 305–20.
42 Jeffrey D. Simon, *Lone Wolf Terrorism: Understanding the Growing Threat.* (Amherst, NY: Prometheus Books, 2016) 199–260.
43 Horgan, *Psychology of Terrorism*, 1–5.
44 Horgan, *Psychology of Terrorism*, 47–72.
45 Philip Zimbardo, *The Lucifer Effect: Understanding How Good People Turn Evil* (New York: Rider, 2007), 3–19; 288–93.
46 Horgan, *Psychology of Terrorism*, 84–7.
47 Law, *Terrorism: A History*, 326, 341.
48 Reported by CNN, December 30, 2015.

Suggested Readings

Hoffman, Bruce. *Inside Terrorism*. 2nd ed. New York: Columbia University Press, 2006.

Horgan, John. *The Psychology of Terrorism*. 2nd ed. Kindle ed. Abingdon: Routledge, 2014.

Kalberg, Stephen, ed. *Max Weber: Readings and Commentary on Modernity*. Oxford: Wiley, 2005.

Law, Randall D. *Terrorism: A History*. 2nd ed. Cambridge: Polity Press, 2016.

Rapoport, David. "The Four Waves of Modern Terrorism." In *Attacking Terrorism*. Edited by Audrey Kurth Cronin and James M. Ludes. Washington, DC: Georgetown University Press, 2004.

Stern, Jessica and J. M. Berger. *ISIS: The State of Terror*. New York: Ecco/Harper Collins, 2015.

Townshend, Charles. *Terrorism: A Very Short Introduction*. Kindle ed. New York: Oxford University Press, 2002.

Vaughn, Lewis. *Doing Ethics*. 3rd ed. New York: WW Norton, 2013.

Zimbardo, Philip. *The Lucifer Effect: Understanding How Good People Turn Evil*. New York: Rider, 2007.

Index

The number of the page on which a key term is defined is given in **bold type**.